GERMANY UNDER THE SALIAN AND HOHENSTAUFEN EMPERORS

KARL HAMPE

GERMANY UNDER THE SALIAN AND HOHENSTAUFEN EMPERORS

Translated with an Introduction
by RALPH BENNETT

OXFORD · BASIL BLACKWELL
1973

ISBN 0 631 14180 4
Library of Congress Catalog Card No. 71-185304

Translated from the twelfth German edition of *Deutsche Kaisergeschichte in der Zeit der Salier und Staufer* by Karl Hampe, edited by Friedrich Baethgen, and published by Quelle & Meyer, Heidelberg, in 1968.

PRINTED IN GREAT BRITAIN
BY A. T. BROOME AND SON, 18 ST. CLEMENT'S, OXFORD
AND BOUND BY THE KEMP HALL BINDERY, OXFORD

CONTENTS

		PAGE
Preface		vii
Abbreviations		x
Introduction		1
1.	Conrad II (1024–1039)	33
2.	Henry III (1039–1056)	47
3.	The Empire during the minority of Henry IV (1056–1065)	60
4.	Henry IV and Gregory VII before the conflict (1065–1075)	68
5.	The conflict between Henry IV and Gregory VII (1075–1085)	80
6.	The conflict continues: to the death of Henry IV (1086–1106)	94
7.	Henry V and the end of the Investiture Contest (1106–1125)	108
8.	Lothar of Supplinburg (1125–1137)	123
9.	Conrad III (1138–1152)	138
10.	The first years of Frederick I (1152–1157)	153
11.	Imperial policy under the influence of Rainald of Dassel (1157–1167)	166
12.	From the death of Rainald to the end of the schism (1168–1177)	188
13.	Barbarossa's last great successes (1178–1190) ...	198
14.	Henry VI (1190–1197)	220
15.	Innocent III and the German succession (1198–1216)	233

Contents

16. The rise of Frederick II, to the Peace of Ceprano
    (1216-1230)   251

17. Frederick II at the height of his power (1230–1239)   268

18. The final struggle between Empire and Papacy (1239–
    1250)   287

    Index   307

MAP

Between pages 306 and 307

PREFACE

To translate a work of historical scholarship sixty years after it was published may at first seem strange: knowledge has increased meanwhile, and fashions in writing history have changed. But Karl Hampe's *Deutsche Kaisergeschichte in der Zeit der Salier und Staufer* still retains in Germany the position it won for itself in 1909 as the most reliable and most readable account of two great centuries of German history. Its lasting influence is attested by the fact that some general attitudes and even several turns of phrase which evidently derive from it are still traceable in the 1970 edition of the standard German handbook of medieval history, which still refers to it as an authority.[1] The book has thus lived up to the high expectations which showed through the author's modesty when in the first sentence of his preface he hoped that it would 'not only instruct but also stimulate, not be merely studied but also read for pleasure'.

Deutsche Kaisergeschichte has been through twelve editions, two of them since 1963.[2] Along with *Das Hochmittelalter* (1932) and critical editions of sources (mainly the work of his earlier years) it is its author's chief surviving monument. Hampe himself saw it in this light, and was preparing a definitive edition of it during the last months of his life. He had only reached the beginning of Frederick Barbarossa's reign when he died; his former pupil Friedrich Baethgen[3] took over the awkward task of completing the revision without obscuring the author's personality. The seventh edition of 1937, which Baethgen produced, took account of new evidence and fresh views down to that time. A few further alterations were made for the eighth edition (1943), but all subsequent editions are merely reprints.

Karl Hampe (1869–1936) was born in Bremen and graduated at Berlin University. In 1902 he was appointed to a chair at Heidelberg, where he remained for the next thirty-one years. He resigned in 1933, when Nazi pressure on the universities

---

[1] B. Gebhardt: *Handbuch der deutschen Geschichte* (9th ed. 1970) vol. i.

[2] This and the next paragraph are based on an autobiographical sketch Hampe wrote in 1923. It was published in *SBHAW phil.-hist. Klasse*, 1969.

[3] Later professor at Munich University and president of the Monumenta Germaniae Historica.

threatened, as he wrote at the time, to make a historian 'abandon the search for objective truth and judge with conscious bias in accordance with the needs and passions of today. . . . To my mind, he thus becomes a traitor to his lofty calling'. Ten years earlier, he had written that interpretation must always be based upon a critical examination of the facts, thereby linking himself with the tradition of the great nineteenth century German historians, many of whom he had known as a young man. But exposition delighted him most of all, and once the foundation was secure he wanted opinion to be expressed in lively fashion. History should not be dull: 'It has usually seemed more stimulating to make my own attitude clear', he wrote in the preface to the first edition of the *Kaisergeschichte*, on the subject of historical controversies, 'rather than simply to give a colourless account of the conflict of opinion'.

The *Kaisergeschichte* was commissioned as one volume in a series; since other volumes were to deal with the Saxon emperors and with economic history, for instance, Hampe's terms of reference restricted him more narrowly to political history than he would have wished (he often planned to lengthen the period covered by his book and widen its scope, but never found the time to do so). The restriction is apparent, but the subtlety and effectiveness of the work lies in the way in which other things are woven into the political narrative, enriching it without interrupting its flow and movement, their own significance at the same time enhanced through being seen in the context of contemporary events rather than isolated from them by separate treatment. This applies even to the descriptions of the monarchs' physique and personality with which Hampe begins so many chapters: past events stir into fresh life when presented as the acts of men with recognisable features. Political narrative divided according to the reigns of kings is now an unfashionable way of writing history, but in the hands of so fine a master of the style as Karl Hampe its clarity and flow provide the best possible introduction to medieval German history.

I have translated from the twelfth edition of 1968, omitting all footnotes but adding references to standard English translations of sources where this seemed appropriate.

It would be as presumptuous as it would be impossible to 'modernise' a text which has become a classic by commenting extensively on it in the light of what has been written during the last thirty years. In the belief that it may be useful, however, I have tried in my Introduction to indicate some lines of thought and inquiry which have been prominent lately and a few of the books which have proposed them.[1] My selection has been deliberately severe and necessarily personal; full and up-to-date information can be found in the 1970 edition of Gebhardt's *Handbuch der deutschen Geschichte*.

My thanks are due to Professor Roland Hampe, Professor Friedrich Baethgen and Messrs. Quelle and Meyer for permission to make this translation and for help in preparing it. Mr. Nicholas Boyle kindly allowed me to show him such passages in the German text as I found difficult to render into suitable English. I am extremely grateful to him for saving me from a number of mistakes and infelicities; but he did not read the whole translation, and any errors that remain are my own. Mr. Henry Schollick's lively prompting has been mingled with great patience, and he has watched over the book at all stages with his customary skill; to him too I am deeply indebted.

Professor Philip Grierson of Gonville and Caius College, Cambridge, kindly supplied the photograph of the *augustale* for the jacket from his extensive collection of coins.

[1] To avoid multiplying footnotes I have often made only one—as it were, sample—reference to a book where more were really appropriate. I have also taken it for granted that G. Barraclough: *Origins of Modern Germany* (1946) and *Medieval Germany* (2 vols., 1938) will be familiar to readers of this book.

RALPH BENNETT

Magdalene College
Cambridge
April 1972

B

ABBREVIATIONS

ASP	Archivio Storico Pugliese
CHJ	Cambridge Historical Journal
Emerton	E. Emerton: *The Correspondence of Gregory VII*
Gesta Friderici	Otto of Freising and Rahewin: *Gesta Friderici* (trans. C. C. Mierow as *The Deeds of Frederick Barbarossa*)
MGH	Monumenta Germaniae Historica
MHP	Monumenta Historiae Pontificiae
MÖIG	Mitteilungen des oesterreichischen Instituts für Geschichtsforschung
Mommsen and Morrison	T. E. Mommsen and K. F. Morrison: *Imperial Lives and Letters of the Eleventh Century*
NHJ	Neue Heidelberger Jahrbücher
Pullan	B. S. Pullan: *Sources for the History of Medieval Europe*
RHM	Römische Historische Mitteilungen
RSC	Rivista di storia della Chiesa in Italia
SBHAW, SBÖAW	Sitzungsberichte der Heidelberger (oesterreichischen) Akademie der Wissenchaften
Schroeder	H. J. Schroeder: *Disciplinary Decrees of the General Councils*
Tierney	B. Tierney: *The Crisis of Church and State*
TRHS	Transactions of the Royal Historical Society
VFKA	Vorträge und Forschungen herausgegeben vom Konstanzer Arbeitskreis
ZRG	Zeitschrift fur Rechtsgeschichte

INTRODUCTION

BY RALPH BENNETT

Because the reigns of the three Ottos in the tenth century, and that of Henry III in the middle of the eleventh, were so much more striking and dramatic than the forty years that separated them, the latter often pass relatively unremarked in English accounts of German and imperial history. Yet although these years saw no single event the significance of which bears comparison with Otto I's defeat of the Magyars[1] and his assumption of the imperial crown, nor with Henry III's Synod of Sutri and the introduction of reform to Rome through German power, the reigns of Henry II and Conrad II were still very much more than merely an intervening period. The abruptness with which Hampe begins his book scarcely makes this clear; and although Henry II counts as the last of the Saxon kings because he was Otto III's cousin, and Conrad II as the first of what was later called the Salian[2] dynasty, the two reigns have much in common.

If Otto the Great had, as it turned out, linked the fortunes of medieval Germany inseparably with those of Italy and if, after experimenting unsuccessfully with alternatives, he had based his government principally on the institutions and personnel of the Church, Otto III's grander if somewhat impractical schemes had been in their way just as decisive for the future of both kingdoms. Less difference than formerly is now seen between the outlook of the two rulers: Rome exercised a powerful attraction upon both. Henry II shared the religious viewpoint of Otto III; and although Conrad II can fairly be represented as a more secular ruler, controlling the Church from the outside instead of experiencing its life almost from within like his predecessor, yet he maintained the connection with the reforming movement which Henry had begun and it was under him that the title *imperium Romanum* was first regularly used to describe the lands over which he ruled.

The elections of 911 and 919 had already shown that in spite of the violence and uncertainty of the times and a constant

---

[1] K. Leyser: 'The Battle on the Lech, 955', in *History* 50 (1965) 1–25.

[2] It was so called because as a Franconian count Conrad came from what was by then the only German part of the original Frankish homeland, and because this was later regarded as equivalent to his being a Salian Frank.

tendency towards autonomy on the part of the dukes there was a certain will towards some form of political union among the leading inhabitants of the eastern Frankish territories. The election of Conrad II marks a further stage in this process. Till now, the concept of kingship had been almost inseparable from the person of the king; Wipo's account of Conrad's election and reign was intended, recent work has emphasised, to stress the continuity of something less entirely personal; though of course not calculated to convey any idea of the impersonal state of later times, the words Wipo puts into Conrad's mouth ('The kingdom goes on though the king is dead, just as the ship remains afloat though the helmsman may be drowned'[1]) mark an advance on the past.[2]

The occupation of Burgundy in 1032[3]—which meant that the Empire now included three kingdoms—lent added ceremonial significance to the Emperor's position; but because it gave the German ruler control over the western passes of the Alps it also increased the effectiveness with which he could deploy his power. When Conrad intervened in Italy in support of the lesser feudal class of *valvassores* against the powerful archbishop Aribert of Milan[4] he was in some degree reversing previous imperial dependence upon prelates for the maintenance of his political authority. A similarity can be seen between this action and Conrad's new policy of using secular officials in Germany,[5] probably the topic upon which later research has most importantly changed the balance of Hampe's account of the next two hundred years. So long as the bishops acted in a supervisory capacity over the local nobles, they were convenient instruments of royal government; but when a relaxation of royal control enabled them to assume authority on their own account, the next active king was bound to replace or counterbalance them if he wished to retain more than the mere semblance of power. Henry III's good intentions are unquestionable: his adoption of the Cluniac-Burgundian idea of the *treuga Dei* and his conversion of it from a consequence of weak central government into a positive instrument of royal policy and a counterweight to the magnates' claimed right of resistance to the

[1] Mommsen and Morrison 73; cf. Hampe 42.
[2] H. Beumann: 'Das Imperium und die Regna bei Wipo', *Aus Geschichte und Landeskunde, Festschrift für Franz Steinbeck* (1960) 11–30.
[3] Hampe 40.
[4] H. E. J. Cowdrey: 'Archbishop Aribert II of Milan', *History* 51 (1966) 1–15.
[5] Hampe 38–9 and see below, p. 7.

crown; his renunciation of simony; his sponsorship of the ecclesi-astical reform movement and his introduction of it to Rome. Whether his good intentions and high ideals strengthened or weakened the monarchy is an often debated but probably quite insoluble question. Neither he nor anyone else could foresee that there would soon come a time when royalism (as it was then understood) and Church reform would be held incompatible, although the thoughts of a few reformers were already moving in that direction; the principal reason is that the contradiction between the two only became apparent after a series of events in Rome which did not take place until Henry was dead.[1] Religious emotion could be no lasting source of strength to the monarchy,[2] however, because its chief appeal was soon felt in potentially hostile quarters: in Rome, where the thought of independence from the German ruler had long been latent and now, as a result of Henry III's and Leo IX's actions, took a universalist instead of a merely urban form; and among a growing number of the German nobles, in whose interests it of course was to prevent the development of a strong monarchy. But a natural concomitant of Henry's religious feeling was his renewed emphasis upon the bishops as the pillars of monarchical power, and his gifts of lands and jurisdiction to them (as well as to the *ministeriales*) were already beginning, before the end of his reign, to cause complaints that he was an 'unjust' ruler simply because he was strong. Conrad II had already been called a tyrant by the nobles, who made a significant reservation when they elected Henry III's son king in 1053—they would only accept him *si rector justus futurus esset*.

Even more than some famous battles, the confrontation of Henry IV and Gregory VII at Canossa has always seemed a ready-made historical drama—particularly since Erdmann[3] emphasised Gregory's bellicosity: Henry's baffled fury is plain enough in the words of his 'Come down, come down . . .' letter of deposition—and even now most accounts present it as a turning-point in history.[4] But neither the scene outside the castle gates nor the

---

[1] G. Tellenbach: *Church, State and Christian Society* (Eng. trans. 1940) 108–112.

[2] Hampe 48-9.

[3] C. Erdmann: *Die Entstehung des Kreuzzugsgedankens* (1935).

[4] *Canossa als Wende* (ed. H. Kampf (1963)), which reprints (in German translation) essays by French, German and Italian historians originally published between 1927 and 1952, still expresses this in its title—'Canossa as a turning-point'.

settlement within them (the exact nature of which is uncertain) reflected at all fully the issues which divided the two men at that moment: still less does Henry's penitent demeanour symbolise total victory for the pope. Hampe's nicely-balanced account gives full weight to the political advantage over the German opposition with which Henry returned to Germany;[1] and ever since Southern forcibly expressed[2] the truth that the Investiture Contest ended without giving the Church a secure or decisive hold over episcopal elections Canossa has been less used in English as a symbol of ecclesiastical success.

The significance of the occasion was well summarised by Karl Morrison a few years ago in an article[3] which refused to see Canossa as the 'testing-ground of new hierocratic theories', laid renewed emphasis on Gregory's concern with morals rather than politics and saw each of Gregory's depositions of Henry as the outcome of challenges by Henry to the moral prestige of the papacy. But in one important sense the limelight had already been shifted away from the events of a single day and diffused (as it should be) over fifty years of recurrent conflict by the pace and scope of Hampe's narrative—his method shows its virtues to great advantage here.

The queen-regent Agnes's inability to control the great nobles with sufficient firmness during her son's minority gave its chance to the movement towards Church 'reform' (a word with many shades of meaning, even more abused by modern historians who fail to define it than by the eleventh-century propagandists for whom it was a moral bulldozer to clear every obstacle from their path). The movement drew most of its inspiration from Cluny, a monastic source in many respects seemingly ill-suited to be the origin of political Hildebrandinism. Cluniac monasticism nevertheless appealed directly to a Gregory whose moral positions were the base upon which his political conclusions were erected, and Cluny's own practical advantage lay with an extension of papal power: the latest study[4] has challenged Tellenbach's argument

[1] Hampe 82-6.
[2] R. W. Southern: *The Making of the Middle Ages* (1953). His remark that after 1122 the system was 'as practical men knew, capable of being manipulated to give much the same results as had been obtained in a simpler and cruder age' (p. 134) has often been quoted.
[3] K. F. Morrison: 'Canossa, a revision', *Traditio* 18 (1962) 121–148.
[4] H. E. J. Cowdrey: *The Cluniacs and the Gregorian Reform* (1970); cf. Tellenbach 50–56, 82–85, 166, 186–192.

and re-emphasised the 'papalist' side of the Cluniac movement. The late 1050's, which saw the German government weakening and Cluniac influence spreading, saw also the first victories of the reformers in Rome[1] and the rise of a spontaneous lay anti-clerical reform movement in Milan.[2] The papacy promptly allied with this movement, although by so doing it contradicted the principle that the priest was superior to the layman and could therefore judge him but not be judged by him—the principle upon which under Hildebrand's direction it was to insist elsewhere. Milan was a danger-point, because (against a background of intensifying class conflict, the result of economic change) the career of the colourful archbishop Aribert (1018–1045) had already shown, long before Henry IV's minority, that the emperor could be balked by the power of an Italian prelate who was theoretically his instrument, and that the imperial Church system was not always as secure as Sutri suggested.[3] The coup d'etat of Kaiserswerth gave the reformers a foothold in German government circles and set Alexander II securely on the papal throne. But it also made the young Henry despise and distrust the magnates, and it was thus partly responsible for his later hostile attitude towards the Saxon and south German opposition and for the violence which marked his progress from a peak of success in 1075 to the disillusionment of Tribur-Oppenheim and the sudden decision to risk a winter journey over the Alps in order to prevent the junction of his Italian and German enemies. Another peak of success when he occupied Rome in 1084 was followed by the impotence and decline of his last years. This ebb and flow of Henry's fortunes in a succession of events the motive force behind which was as often German as Italian provides an indispensable background to what otherwise easily seems a conflict which became unaccountably suspended between the death of Hildebrand and the Concordat of Worms.

What was, to Hampe, only one important part of this background has during the last twenty-five years become the most prominent feature of the whole Investiture period in Germany—

[1] Hampe 60–64, Tellenbach 108–112.
[2] H. E. J. Cowdrey: 'The Papacy, the Patarenes and the Church of Milan', TRHS 18 (1968) 25–48.
[3] Above, p. 2. The Saxon-Salian Church system, the stability of which was here first threatened, is described by L. Santifaller: 'Zur Geschichte des ottonisch-salischen Reichskirchensystems', *SBÖAW phil. -hist. Klasse* 229 (1954) 1–154.

if indeed not of all German medieval history—as some German historians have ceased to concentrate upon the Empire[1] and upon the rightness or wrongness of papal claims and imperial intervention in Italy and have found instead profitable new lines of inquiry into the extent of royal resources and the policies by which the kings tried to enlarge them. These policies derived in part from natural acquisitiveness and the kings' desire to see their descendants well provided for, but also from a combination of several other factors. Most of the land (and thus the wealth) of Germany was monopolised by a few hundred inter-related and influential families; the royal family of the moment naturally acted like one of them. The imperial Church system had been Otto the Great's last resort, not his first choice, and was always a fragile instrument of royal authority. The five duchies were difficult to control and were ruled by dukes who were partly feudal persons, partly still retained the character of royal officials which they had had in Carolingian times, and partly embodied reminiscences (in law, for instance) of ancient tribal exclusiveness.[2]

It was to counteract these solvents of their authority that early in the eleventh century the German monarchs turned to the *ministeriales*. The *ministeriales* were an unfree feudal class, peculiar to Germany, who did no homage and held no fiefs but were bound to their lords by such strict ties of obedience that when the crown used them on a large scale the effects were comparable to those which resulted from contemporary French and English kings' use of civil servants, in spite of the very real differences between the conditions which prevailed in Germany and in the two western monarchies.[3] The German kings used them to administer their estates,[4] to garrison their castles, to

[1] The 'idea of Empire' and its historical effects is discussed by R. Folz: *The Concept of Empire* (1953, Eng. trans. 1969) and W. Ullmann: 'Reflections on the medieval Empire', TRHS 14 (1964) 89–108.

[2] W. Kienast: *Der Herzogstitel in Frankreich und Deutschland* (1968) and K. Leyser: 'The German aristocracy in the early Middle Ages', *Past and Present* 41 (1968) 25–53 deal with the nobles, the duchies and the related problems. In its concern to rescue the nobles from particularist obloquy, J. B. Gillingham: *The Kingdom of Germany in the High Middle Ages* (Hist. Ass. pamphlet, 1971) does not give the crown enough credit and seems to regard the collapse of the monarchy as beyond argument inevitable.

[3] Like the French *baillis* (at least until they began extending their activities in the thirteenth century), and unlike the English sheriffs, the *Reichsministeriales* had jurisdiction only over royal (and the royal family's private) property, not over subdivisions of the whole realm.

[4] Under the Salians very little distinction was drawn between Salian family estates and royal estates held by the Salian kings *ex officio*. The end of the dynasty and Lothar's unusual position forced a distinction in 1125, but it was often lost sight of later on under Barbarossa and Frederick II.

provide manpower for their armies and to secure money for their treasury. The work of Karl Bosl and Carlrichard Brühl[1] in particular has revised older beliefs. At an earlier date and to a far greater extent than was previously held, German kings were trying to build up their resources in these ways. To grasp this is to add new depth—indeed, very nearly an altogether new dimension —to the history of medieval Germany and give it an existence more distinct from the old question of Empire versus papacy than ever before.[2] Hampe more than once[3] debates whether Henry IV was a reformer or a reactionary; the new approach suggests that the debate is somewhat beside the point in these terms—to Bosl, Henry was a revolutionary, but in the skill and persistence with which he pursued his territorial policy—and that the establishment (or otherwise) of a stable monarchy depended as much upon events inside Germany as upon Italian distractions.

Bosl has shown that Conrad II made great use of *ministeriales* in both Germany and Italy at the same time as he was favouring the lower feudal classes against the Lombard bishops, and that Henry III followed suit. Henry was thus not merely the penitent of Constance or the theocrat of Sutri; he showed how useful a more secular system could be when he founded Nuremberg castle as a base for operations against Bohemia.

So long as he was still a minor, Henry IV was unable to prevent large-scale alienation of royal property. It was his ruthless (but, as Hampe says, also too hasty) attempts to recover the old Liudolfinger estates in the Harz (they had remained with the crown at the change of dynasty in 1024 but had since been lost again) which brought violent reaction from the nobles, who had good reason to fear that the integrity and independence of their lands were endangered by Henry's castle-building in Saxony and by the wealth he might derive from the silver mines of Goslar.[4] It was because Sighard of Burghausen later tried to limit their power that

[1] K. Bosl: *Die Reichsministerialität der Salier und Staufer* (1950–1); C. Brühl: *Fodrum, Gistum, Servitium Regis* (1968).
[2] This is not a totally new development, of course—e.g. Barraclough's chapter on 'The Hohenstaufen State' in *Medieval Germany* (1938) i. 113–137, which insists that the fate of Germany (and hence of the medieval Empire) depended on the rise and fall of the Hohenstaufen principality.
[3] For instance, pp. 69 and 101.
[4] The *ministeriales* sometimes exceeded their instructions and committed atrocities. Some of the complaints against them—and thus against Henry's policy—were no doubt justified.

the *ministeriales* rose against him,[1] but the nobles were able to exploit the incident to set Henry V up against the too authoritarian Henry IV—only to find the son adopting his father's policy.

All this means that as early as the second quarter of the eleventh century the German monarchy was feeling its way towards what it is not too much to call a new system of government, secular in character and based directly on the available sources of wealth—it relied prominently upon the towns[2] as well as upon *ministeriales* in castle garrison and estate management, for instance—and thus intrinsically more reliable than the ecclesiastical system it was evidently intended to replace as the mainstay of monarchy. This impression is heightened by another leading feature of Salian rule —the promotion of the 'peace movement' and the use of it to justify the unusual action of legislating for the whole realm.

Under the influence of Cluny, local movements directed at ensuring peace and order had begun in the kingdom of Burgundy, mainly because central authority, the natural guarantor of peace, was virtually absent there. The movement flourished in France for the same reasons.[3] It was no doubt a sign of society's desire for greater security now that the Norse and Magyar invasions were over, and it was nourished by the same emotions as those which were soon to make crusading popular. In 1085 Henry IV set himself at the head of this till now spontaneous movement,[4] and thereby enhanced the prestige of the crown by allying it with a new and potent force as well as providing himself with another means of reducing the magnates' ancient privileges—when they used their right of resistance[5] they disturbed the peace of the realm—and of encouraging a degree of social levelling consistent with the *constitutio de feudis* and his friendship with the towns. The first imperial Landpeace of 1103 was also the first act of general legislation by a German ruler since Carolingian times.[6] Its

---

[1] Hampe 103.
[2] On the rise of the towns, see F. Rörig: *The Medieval Town* (1967) 48–51 and *Cambridge Economic History* iii (1963) 3–41.
[3] H. Hoffmann: *Gottesfriede und Treuga Dei* (1964) traces the history of the peace movement in Burgundy and eastern France, whence it spread to Germany.
[4] Hampe 94, 101. J. Gernhuber: *Die Landfriedensbewegung in Deutschland bis zum Mainzer Landfrieden von* 1235 (1952).
[5] F. Kern: *Kingship and Law in the Middle Ages* (Eng. trans. 1939).
[6] Gernhuber 81, confirming Hampe 101. The account in *Vita Heinrici* (Mommsen and Morrison 120–1) shows that the Landpeace was issued with the consent of the nobles, stresses the benefits it conferred on the poorer classes and makes the resentment of some of the nobility the origin of Henry V's rebellion.

effectiveness as a sign of central power was shown when it contributed to the reaction after the Sighard incident next year.[1]

Nearly seventy-five years of disturbance (1056–1125) ended by
increasing the ancient dualism of crown and nobles in the German
constitution, and this meant that the allodial right of the latter to
much of their land now constantly escaped from royal control.
But Gregory VII was not the only villain of the piece, nor had a
royal policy been lacking. The excommunication of Henry actually
pointed towards the secularisation of the monarchy, but the
nobility reaped the benefit when their right to elect the king and
impose conditions on him was strengthened. It is less often
noticed that this applied even more to the spiritual than to the
secular nobles; they became imperial vassals in 1122, and it had
been the fear that they would lose all the advantages of landed
wealth which had made them oppose Paschal II so bitterly. They
now used their own *ministeriales* to develop material resources
sufficient to enable them to act almost as independent rulers.

Thus the Investiture Contest gravely weakened the monarchy,
although the Concordat of Worms deprived it of nothing essential.[2]
Indeed, to deny royalty its old sacerdotal function was almost
inevitably to make its newer and more essentially secular attributes
stand out in sharper relief.[3] Twelfth-century kings claimed that
it was their particular duty to enforce peace and maintain justice,
and proceeded to engage the necessary staff and issue the appropriate instructions. The Roman curia raised no objection, for
these were the proper activities of the *rex justus*, the standard by
which the reformers had measured Henry IV and found him
wanting; but by remaining silent the curia allowed the king a new
monopoly and thus permitted the growth of a secular royalism
which was later to prove more powerfully hostile than ever Saxon

[1] This, and what has been said above (pp. 7-8) suggests that the quarrel
between father and son was not so merely personal as Hampe implies.
[2] R. L. Benson: *The Bishop-elect* (1968) 228–250, 303–315: the concordat
was only an armistice, but the canon lawyers regarded it as a defeat which would
perpetuate the Church's slavery to the crown, even if in slightly altered form. The
effect of the concordat on the Church is sometimes overlooked. Bishops used
the 'freedom' which it gave them not so much to achieve the spiritual ends
which the reformers had in mind as to concentrate on enlarging their secular
(feudal) rights and to dispose of ecclesiastical benefices to their agents and
supporters. The dilemma in which this placed conscientious churchmen is
illustrated by the career of Gerhoh of Reichersberg (1093–1169); see P. Classen:
Gerhoh von Reichersberg (1960).
[3] This point is well made by J. R. Strayer: *On the medieval origins of the
modern state* (1970) 23–4. Cf. below, p. 15.

and early Salian theocracy had been. In Germany the Salians had begun policies which the Staufen were to take up later with more success, and from this point of view the thirty years between Worms and Barbarossa's accession were not so much a disastrous break with royalist tradition as a pause during which the continuity of royal policy can still be discerned: for instance, Henry V issued three Landpeaces during his last few years; Lothar did the same in 1125 and 1135, Conrad III in 1147, and Henry IV's initiative of 1103 is thus linked with Barbarossa's larger-scale legislation of 1152 and 1158.

Two great disadvantages were that Germany had acquired neither a capital (the peace legislation could only be enforced by constant royal journeyings and a court which never settled for long in one place)[1] nor a true central administration.[2] To point out that Barbarossa succeeded to a territorial policy which both Lothar III and Conrad III had maintained is, of course, not to pretend that Lothar was anything but the prisoner of the circumstances which had put him on the throne; but in spite of the painting which Innocent II commissioned for the Lateran,[3] Lothar is not now regarded as abjectly subservient to the papacy and a betrayer of German interests.[4] The painting has something in common with Hadrian IV's *beneficium* letter twenty years later: more an effort to create a precedent for the acceptance of a papal superiority which was in fact still disputed than an attempt to reproduce accurately the relationship of the two powers as it was generally understood at the time.

Continuity was not the most characteristic feature of the first half of the twelfth century, however. There is a very real sense in

[1] Compare France, where the nobles' practical autonomy prevented large-scale royal journeying and forced the kings to reside at Paris or Orleans for long periods at a time. When, under Philip Augustus, the habitual place of residence became also the seat of government, the monarchy reaped a double advantage.

[2] Hampe (p. 119) speculates on Otto of Freising's report that Henry V considered adopting central taxation on Anglo-Norman lines from his father-in-law Henry I of England. The death of both Henries without male heirs ended the close contact of the two countries, both of which faced civil war in the 1140's. Both recovered soon after 1150, but the English alliance was soon with the Welfs, and thus against German royalism. Cf. K. Leyser: 'England and the Empire in the early 12th century', TRHS 10 (1960) 61–84.

[3] Hampe 132. The fresco is known only from a sixteenth century copy, reproduced in an article by G. Ladner in *Rivista di archaeologia cristiana* 2 (1935) 265–292 and as Plate 1 in M. Maccarrone: *Papato e impero dalla elezione di Federico I alla morte di Adriano* IV (1959).

[4] F. J. Schmale: 'Lothar III und Friedrich I als Könige und Kaiser', *VFKA* 12 (1968) 33–52.

which the development of both Empire and papacy was checked during these years, and it is of course essential to note that now for the first time the Roman curia became the foundation upon which the pope's power rested and the armoury where skilful legal minds forged weapons of argument for use against German kings.[1] A rise in population—itself perhaps due to the end of the invasions —had been accompanied by greater prosperity both in the countryside and in the towns, the great novelty of the age. Only a tiny handful of men were concerned with the things of the mind, but the hundred years between (say) cardinal Humbert's book against the simoniacs and bishop Otto of Freising's *Chronicle* saw this minority grow enormously.[2] Far larger numbers of people became urgently concerned with religion during the same period; and although the Hildebrandine political Church capitalised on their concern, emotion was its chief expression. The new monastic orders drew thousands of recruits, the first two crusades generated vast and almost uncontrollable enthusiasm (as well as giving Rome a useful new weapon against the Germans: it was Urban II who brought Henry IV down), and outside the Church heresy began to spread alarmingly. Both Lothar and Conrad were too preoccupied with German problems to play much part in Italy. The Normans[3] preoccupied the popes in the same way, but so long as St Bernard (1090–1153) lived an ascetic rejection of material things diverted some of Rome's attention away from high politics, and popes intervened in German affairs as little as Emperors in Italian. Perhaps Arnold of Brescia's republicanism and the failure of the second crusade broke the spell: secularism was certainly the dominant note after the mid-century.[4] Because of the great strides which had recently been made in law and logic and in the machinery of civil and ecclesiastical government, by then both sides were more intellectually sophisticated and more

[1] G. Barraclough: *The Medieval Papacy* (1968) 95–101, R. W. Southern: *Western Society and the Church in the Middle Ages* (1970) 100–133, W. Ullmann: *Short History of the Papacy* (1972) 179–182. Barraclough greatly exaggerates, however, when he writes (p. 90) that 'Gregory's stormy pontificate appears almost as a distraction, if not a deviation' and that Gregory 'led the Church into a blind alley', and when he implies that the Bernardine 'reaction' was more than a transient phenomenon.
[2] P. Wolff: *The Awakening of Europe* (1968) 197–295, C. N. L. Brooke: *The Twelfth Century Renaissance* (1971) 53–74, 155–183, V. H. H. Green: *Medieval Civilisation in Western Europe* (1971) 266–7.
[3] J. J. Norwich: *The Normans in the South* (1967) 189–331 and *The Kingdom in the Sun* (1970) 3–167, D. Mack Smith: *Medieval Sicily* (1968) 13–35, D. C. Douglas, *The Norman Achievement* (1969).   [4] Hampe 147, 161.

determined than before. After 1150 each displayed a more resolute will and a greater power to act, a more sustained relentlessness than in the eleventh century—with the result that the material stakes were higher and the conflict more prolonged and more violent. This new aggressive temper was first apparent in the personalities of the two men who came to power within a few months of St Bernard's death: Frederick Barbarossa and Hadrian IV.

The German royal succession had been broken in 1125 by the lay and ecclesiastical nobles' exercise of their electoral rights. It was restored twenty-seven years later[1] when the magnates chose Frederick Barbarossa in preference to his infant nephew, thus confirming Conrad III's death-bed decision. The succession of the Hohenstaufen was a victory for legitimism, since they were the blood-heirs of the Salian house (and therefore also the inheritors of its private possessions); and in Barbarossa more conspicuously than in any other member of the family there was shown the wisdom of the choice Henry IV had made in 1079 when he picked out Friedrich von Büren from among the second-rank nobles of the upper Rhine valley, made him his lieutenant and married him to his daughter. The chief royal estates were already located on both sides of the river between Basel and Mainz; here, in the heartland of the old Empire, von Büren built castles and held them in the royal interest, and here—perhaps more even than round Goslar, and certainly against less furious opposition—a new style of territorial policy struck roots deep enough to ensure that this part of the country still contained many royalist strongholds as late as 1250 in spite of the serious break in continuity caused by the civil wars at the beginning of the thirteenth century. Thus the Staufen inherited the traditions of Salian royalism and improved upon them. But on the other hand Barbarossa was also the choice of the nobility among whom (as a member of the royal family indeed, but one unlikely to ascend the throne) he had been brought up; and he was expected, because he was related to the Welfs, to heal the growing breach between the two factions and bring peace to Germany.[2] The complex origins of his rule go some way

---

[1] The 1137 election had scarcely done so: Conrad III was the choice of a minority only, and Lothar's heir, Henry the Proud, was ruled out by the nobles because he was too powerful and by the Church because he had recently upheld imperial interests in Italy.

[2] This hope was expressed in Otto of Freising's metaphor of the cornerstone, which Hampe uses on p. 156.

towards resolving the disputed question of Barbarossa's motives and policy, particularly when it is realised that they—together, no doubt, with his evidently strong personal inclination towards justice and the preservation of rights—impelled him to a 'forward' policy just at the moment when the papacy under Hadrian IV was itself ready to take the political initiative once more.[1]

Within five years of his accession, Barbarossa had committed himself to courses of action which can be described as appeasement in Germany and aggression in Italy. Yet the aptness of both descriptions is called in question by the extreme difficulty of determining the origin and purpose of each course of action. Munz's recent attempt[2] to trace both to a common source—the 'Great Design' of establishing a territorial base astride the Alps in Swabia, Burgundy and Lombardy—is symptomatic of this difficulty: persuasive as the theory is (whether in this form or in the simpler form in which it has often been advanced) there is no contemporary evidence for the existence of such a concept and only presumptive grounds even for supposing a deliberate and logical connection between Barbarossa's actions in Germany and Italy.

Except in a very broad sense, Barbarossa's motives remain conjectural: they have to be inferred from his actions, yet his actions are hard to interpret.[3] In at least four ways, however, they seem to have proceeded from the novel characteristics of the age:

(1) A rise in population combined with social change in Germany since the Investiture Contest called for corresponding changes in the institution of monarchy. Barbarossa may have realised this and acted upon his realisation. He undoubtedly

---

[1] Adrian IV's conception of the pope's authority—particularly his authority over the Emperor—is forcibly expressed by W. Ullmann in CHJ 11 (1955) 233–252. There is a much slighter essay by R. W. Southern: *Medieval Humanism* (1970) 234–252. For interpretations of Adrian's intentions over the 1157 Besançon incident, see W. Ullmann: 'Cardinal Roland and Besançon' in MHP 18 (1954) 107–125, M. Pacaut: *Alexandre III* (1956) and M. Maccarrone: *Papato e impero.* Pacaut points out the practical, even opportunist, element in Alexander's actions, discusses at length the sources (mainly canon law) and nature of his political ideas, and shows that Alexander was prepared to allow a qualified independence to the Empire, the pope's intervention occurring only in exceptional circumstances.

[2] P. Munz: *Frederick Barbarossa* (1969) 103 sq. M. Pacaut: *Frederick Barbarossa* (1967, Eng. trans. 1969) is a much slighter work.

[3] The risk of over-refined interpretation is correspondingly great. Perhaps 'what really happened' was in this case only 'the play of the contingent and the unforeseen': cf. G. Barraclough: *History in a Changing World* (1955) 93, who suggests that Barbarossa 'reacted to events by a series of expedients'.

modernised the kingship, but he did not wholly transform it. Staufen aims were at bottom the same as Salian: to incorporate the nobility (lay and ecclesiastical alike) into the structure of monarchical government and to draw strength from the protection they gave to the new social and economic forces. Hampe's disparagement of the notion of a specifically Hohenstaufen 'idea of Empire' still stands, although less would now be made of the extent to which Barbarossa's reinvigoration of traditional ideas was marked by claims to universal dominion.[1]

(2) Legal learning and legal terminology were taking a firm hold on both lay and ecclesiastical society about 1150, and the practice of the German chancery was becoming more standardised.[2] In these circumstances it was natural for Frederick to formulate his claims at Roncaglia and Besançon in more precise legal terms than his predecessors had used. Neither his appeal to Roman Law nor Rainald's militancy led him to adopt rigid and inflexible attitudes, however: his adaptability and readiness to compromise have lately been given particular emphasis.[3]

(3) To modernise kingship and to define it in legal language was in itself equivalent to an essay in political theory. The Besançon incident and the display of majesty at Roncaglia a year later gave further impetus in the same direction. In reaction against an apparent assertion of the pope's feudal lordship, Barbarossa proclaimed that his power was derived directly from God—i.e. that coronation by the pope was not the constitutive source of imperial authority but only the ceremonial recognition of it.[4] This flatly contradicted the *translatio imperii*—where the papacy stood on secure historical ground—and amounted almost to a declaration of ideological war. Some of its force was drawn from Roman Law, whose newly fashionable professors Barbarossa patronised (more because they were conversant with the facts he

[1] H. E. Mayer: 'Staufische Weltherrschaft' in *Festschrift Karl Pivec* (1966) 265–278; cf Hampe 154. But compare also Folz: *Concept of Empire* 108–114. See also below, pp. 15-16, 21, 25.

[2] R. M. Herkenrath: 'Rainald von Dassel als Verfasser und Schreiber von Kaiserurkunden', *MÖIG* 72 (1964) 34–62.

[3] P. Rassow: *Honor imperii* (2nd ed. 1961) also shows that the plan to revive the territorial integrity of the Empire dates back to the 1153 treaty of Constance. —The evidence for flexibility is scanty between Roncaglia and Legnano, however, and these twenty years seem marked by persistence in a policy of force which was totally unacceptable to the Lombards and repeatedly proved itself unworkable; cf. Barraclough: *Origins* 182–186.

[4] The contrary papal viewpoint and some of its consequences are described in W. Ullmann: 'Reflections on the medieval Empire'; TRHS 14 (1964) 89–108.

wished to establish, however, than because of their scholarly
knowledge of Justinian's text), but neither the rights the lawyers
defined for him at Roncaglia nor the word *regalia* itself (which
was an offspring of the Investiture Contest) came from that source.[1]
The classical idea of the ruler as legislator also played its part, but
Barbarossa laid more weight upon another concept derived from
it—the ruler's duty to protect the welfare of his people and to
represent public power acting for the common good: *ut regni
utilitas incorrupta permaneat*.[2] By destroying the old sacramental
monarchy, the Investiture Contest had left European kings with
only scanty ideological garments, however well they might
exploit the rights guaranteed to them by the Concordat of Worms
and its equivalents. Royalty needed new and more secular dress,
and in the exchanges after Besançon Frederick Barbarossa began
to supply it. This did not mean that Divine Right withered away
—old and new coexisted happily for many centuries yet—but that
secular authority was derived directly from God and credited with
a divine sanction (as when Barbarossa added *sacrum* to *imperium*,
for instance), and that the European king was in future rather the
image of Justice than the image of Christ.[3] Because no fully
satisfactory logical or historical basis can be found for it in terms
of the medieval Empire, the idea of 'secular Romanism' has sometimes been held up to ridicule. But this is to overlook its most
important aspects. The use of Roman legal language did not
represent a dangerous shift away from the monarch's German
foundations,[4] and for three principal reasons: First, because for

[1] H. Appelt: 'Friedrich Barbarossa und das römische Recht', RHM 5
(1961–2) 18–34.
[2] Gaines Post: *Studies in Medieval Legal Thought* (1964) 359, 380, E.
Kantorowicz: *The King's Two Bodies* (1957) 95–6. The quotation is from the
Roncaglia decree, Pullan 183. In an age familiar with feudal nobles' exercise
of their right to settle private quarrels by force of arms, the first requirement of
the 'common good' was law and order, i.e. peace; cf. Gernhuber: *Landfriedensbewegung* 80, who stresses the Hohenstaufen idea of *Herrschaft* and writes that
Barbarossa sought internal peace 'through the Empire as a modern state'.
[3] Kantorowicz: *Two Bodies* 140–3. Kantorowicz quotes with approval a
remark of Maitland's (Pollock and Maitland: *History of English Law* i. 208n)
which goes even farther: an English royal lawyer like Bracton, quoting *justitiam
colimus et sacra jura ministramus* from the Digest, 'feels that he is a priest of the
law, a priest for ever after the order of Ulpian'.
[4] Cf Ullmann: *Short History* 186–200. The logical impossibility of finding a
secure foundation for the independence of secular authority by means of a
dualistic political theory is well contrasted with the secular rulers' (particularly
the emperors') overriding need to do so in M. J. Wilks: *The Problem of Sovereignty in the later Middle Ages* (1963) 70–78.

C

the next hundred years it was accompanied (albeit intermittently) by a marked increase in the economic resources and the
administrative capacity of the German crown; secondly, because
Barbarossa and his advisers believed that he was entitled to imperial
rights even before coronation in Rome and made no clear distinction between *regnum* and *imperium*; and thirdly, because by a
deliberate shift of emphasis election by the princes (instead of
coronation by the pope) was made the foundation of imperial
authority. The second of these represented an outlook which
went back to Conrad III's use of the title *imperator*, and the third
reached a climax in the Speyer declaration of 1199 which credited
the German electoral process with the ability to endow the chosen
king with imperial attributes.[1] His experience of Sicilian-Norman
absolutism, together with some admixture of Aristotle, enabled
Frederick II to give secular political thought a further twist a
generation later, but the development had been continuous ever
since Besançon and Roncaglia.[2] Its consistent theme was dualism,
the separate but equal origin of secular authority, and it was
largely the product of the papacy's hostility to every sign of
imperial independence and self-determination. In this sense the
Hohenstaufen unquestionably made a novel contribution to the
imperial idea and professed a 'theory of the state' which was valid
for the purposes for which it was devised and only transient and
unsuccessful inasmuch as its originators' fall from power in the
years after 1250 brought about the collapse of the state to which it
applied.

That (4) the fiscal and economic motive of gaining a share in
Italy's prosperity underlay Barbarossa's attempt to reestablish
undoubted but ill-defined and lately neglected imperial rights in
Lombardy is beyond question,[3] and so is the communes' reluctant
alliance to resist it. But all efforts to quantify either the wealth of
Italy or the revenues which the Staufen actually raised there have

---

[1] Pullan 193. Cf R. Folz: 'La chancellerie de FB et la canonisation de
Charlemagne', *Moyen-Age* 76 (1964) 13–31, showing that Rainald's intention
over the canonisation of Charlemagne in 1165 was to assert the indissoluble
union of *regnum* and *imperium*. On the whole theme of 'the efforts devoted by
the Hohenstaufen to assuring the independence of the Empire as an institution',
see Folz: *Concept of Empire* 98–108. The account in C. C. Bayley: *The formation
of the German College of Electors* (1949) 106–114 is useful.

[2] H. Wierusowski: *Vom imperium zum nationalen Königtum* (1933) 151–3.
Cf Wilks: *Problem of sovereignty* 78 and see also below, pp. 21, 25.

[3] 'Imperialism tainted by economic motives' (Barraclough: *History in a
Changing World* 87).

failed for lack of adequate evidence.[1] Brühl's thorough examination only enabled him to write of Barbarossa's 'very considerable' Italian income and to offer some confirmation of Otto of Freising's well-known estimate. More significantly, perhaps, it has failed to reveal the uses to which the money was put: some of it no doubt paid the salaries of the *podestàs* in the royalist towns and of the officials who administered the demesne lands in Lombardy and Piedmont, and some was probably spent on mercenary troops: but there is no sign of a systematic diversion of Italian revenue to German purposes,[2] and any idea that Barbarossa harboured the thought of using Italian resources to enforce his authority in Germany must be discarded along with now antiquated arguments about whether it was wrong for him to desert Germany's alleged 'national interests' in the pursuit of imperial ends.[3] On the contrary: what requires emphasis is the complementary nature of policies aimed at enlarging the extent of royal authority throughout the whole Empire in terms of both law and economics and at improving its cohesion in Germany by a novel application of familiar feudal principles. It is tempting to speculate how far the two nevertheless ultimately collided with each other and to ask whether the harmful repercussions of Italian action upon the government of Germany should have been recognised before 1175-6; but no conclusion is likely.[4]

[1] The two classical articles on this subject are both by G. Deibel: 'Die italienischen Einkünfte Friedrichs I', NHJ (1932) 20–58 and 'Die finanzielle Bedeutung Reichsitaliens für die staufischen Herrscher des 12 Jhdts', ZRG German. Abt. 54 (1934) 134–177. H. Appelt: 'Friedrich Barbarossa und die ital. Kommunen', MÖIG 72 (1964) 311–325 emphasises the skilful diplomacy which enabled Barbarossa to secure wider recognition of imperial rights than ever before and to hand over a far better position in this respect in 1190 than he had inherited forty years earlier. The immediately following references in the text are to Brühl: *Fodrum* 745–9 and 759–61.—The background of Italian economic prosperity is sketched in Rörig: *Medieval Town* 54–7, G. Luzzatto: *Economic History of Italy* (1961) 66–85 and in C. Cipolla (ed): *Fontana Economic History of Europe* (1971) i. 284–299.

[2] Although Italian revenue was far greater than anything which Germany could yield. Henry the Lion complained, for example, that 5,000 marks was beyond his means, but single Italian cities more than once paid five-figure sums to Barbarossa (Deibel, NHJ (1932) 54).

[3] National sentiment of a kind was plainly becoming evident—in Walther von der Vogelweide's writings, for instance—during Barbarossa's later years, but the patrons of the new poetry and the builders of the first Gothic cathedrals were the same princes who were to ruin the *Reich*. It was not until the sixteenth century that the collective concept 'Germany' displaced that of a number of territories under separate lords.

[4] 'Who would dare to say exactly where the limit of justified intervention lay —the boundary beyond which danger began?' (E. Maschke, in L. Just: *Handbuch der deutschen Geschichte* (1956) I. iv. 47.

In order to incorporate the German nobles more fully into the structure of government[1] and to gain their acquiescence in his own direction of policy, Barbarossa had first to get rid of the now out-dated concept of the tribal duchy. For this purpose he used feudalism not only to settle his relations with Henry the Lion but also to create new-style dukedoms in Austria, the Rhine Palatinate and elsewhere. Under the influence of Mitteis,[2] this use of feudalism was seen as a major constitutional experiment. Its advantages and its limitations were both thrown into sharp relief when—after the Chiavenna interview had demonstrated that co-operation with Henry was no longer possible, after successful negotiations with Alexander III had suggested that a change in German demesne policy was the necessary concomitant of a shift in Italian and ecclesiastical policy, and after Legnano had driven both lessons home—it was used to bring about the fall of Henry the Lion. This reversal of Barbarossa's previous practice of supporting Henry against his vassals' complaints of his oppression did not, however, mark a stage in the drawing together of crown and rear-vassal like that which was already beginning to make the fortunes of the French and English kings, but the opposite: although they were the liegemen of the Emperor, the new-style imperial princes effectively cut off the crown from the lower feudal classes (and even, later on, from the *Reichsministeriales*, to whom the process of feudal systematisation gave an inferior rank in the *Heerschild*). The latest investigation[3] of Henry the Lion's eclipse tends to reinforce Hampe's conclusion that it did not finally decide the balance of power in Germany, and is at particular pains to deny that 1180 saw the establishment of a legal principle (*Leihezwang*) under which the Emperor was bound to regrant vacant fiefs within a year and a day. Werner Goez insists on the point that Barbarossa regranted Henry's fiefs before the campaign which enforced the court's decision to confiscate them, and suggests that two convergent pressures explain his action: he needed the nobles' contingents for the campaign, while they feared that unless he were committed to the contrary in advance, he might push his

---

[1] It is essential to bear in mind that this purpose underlay both the 'imperial' and the 'German' aspects of Barbarossa's restoration of strong government: cf. election by the princes as the source of his authority, above p. 16.

[2] H. Mitteis: *Lehnrecht und Staatsgewalt* (1931), *Der Staat des hohen Mittelalters* (3rd ed. 1948).

[3] W. Goez: *Der Leihezwang* (1962) 235–7, 250–254. Cf Hampe 203–6.

already very successful territorial policy one stage further by annexing Henry's lands. Goez shrewdly remarks that it was not a feudal ruler's legal right to demand this or that service from his vassals which determined his political success or failure, but the terms on which he could secure it; and he lays more weight on the persistence of allodial land quite outside the feudal framework than on particular forms of feudal law when he seeks to explain why centralisation failed in Germany. By reducing to fragments what Mitteis called the 'latent Welfic kingdom' of Henry the Lion in eastern Germany, the affair of 1180 made Barbarossa suddenly by far the most powerful man in the Empire, and it thus laid the political foundations for the unassailable position which he held during the next ten years; but it is easy to exaggerate both its significance as a legal precedent and its longer-term consequences.

There is in any case good ground for supposing that any intention to feudalise the German constitution took second place in Barbarossa's mind after a plan to consolidate and extend throughout the Empire (but with some deliberate emphasis on eastern Germany) the lands directly administered by royal officials. By the end of his reign much progress had been registered in Germany; in Italy only the competition between imperial and papal claims to the Matildine lands and the dispute over the Emperor's right to quarter troops round Rome still remained unsettled. The marriage of Henry and Constance lent added importance to this piece of unfinished business; Constance's succession in 1189 transformed it into a vital interest in controlling the central Italian lines of communication between Empire and kingdom.[1] Rome can thus be more than figuratively regarded as Henry VI's centre of political gravity: the suppression of Sicilian revolts and the further extension of territorial power in Germany were essential at the extremities, but the plan to assimilate the Norman custom of heredity to the imperial succession was bound to be his chief preoccupation—for nothing else could guarantee

[1] See D. Waley: *The Papal State in the Thirteenth Century* (1961) 17–30 for imperial occupation of the papal state, and 33–44 for Innocent III's 'recuperations'. P. Partner: *The Lands of St. Peter* (1972) 211–228 gives many examples of German soldiers on Roman territory under Barbarossa and Henry VI. Partner follows Waley in dating the foundation of the papal state from Otto IV's Neuss guarantee of 1201, which abandoned Staufen claims to occupy central Italy and accepted Innocent's 'recuperations', and later (253) shows how German military superiority in this area disappeared for ever during the 1240's.

that the same head would in future always wear both crowns and thus preserve the connection between the two realms.[1]

By offering them similar inheritance rights in their own lands, Henry persuaded all but a minority of the princes to surrender in exchange the control over the imperial succession which the Investiture period had confirmed to them. Fearing encirclement and the obliteration of all the claims to world dominion made by his predecessors during the last hundred and fifty years, Celestine III refused the tempting financial bait which Henry held out. When German opposition at once revived, the plan quickly collapsed. It nevertheless deserves more attention than it often receives; for it was simply because the succession still depended upon the electors' whim that, once the Hohenstaufen had disappeared, later Emperors—who could never be quite sure that even their sons would follow them on the throne—were bound to prefer family advantage to anything resembling the 'common good' of the state as a whole and to define the latter in the narrow terms of the former. Strictly, therefore, it was the collapse of the plan to link Sicily and Germany in a hereditary Empire, rather than Henry's premature death, which deserves to be called 'the greatest of the catastrophes which overtook medieval Germany'.[2] On the other hand, it threatened Rome's independence even more than anything Barbarossa had done, and if carried into effect might have been an equal catastrophe for the papacy: thus the irreconcilable nature of the conflict between the two institutions is plain in the 1190's, and Innocent III's 'recuperations' of 1198 and his reasoning in the *Deliberatio* can be seen as necessary defensive measures.

Concentration on Italy did not lead Henry to neglect Germany, however. His father had steadily extended his estates eastwards and south-eastwards from the old base in the upper Rhineland so that he controlled trade-routes to the Danube valley (with its outlets in the Levant) through Nuremberg and Regensburg, for example, while *ministeriales* in Egerland and Vogtland[3] were already exercising functions almost identical with those of the French

[1] This preoccupation with central Italy was foreshadowed, for instance, by Henry's appointment of the great *ministerialis* Markward of Anweiler as margrave of Ancona and duke of the Romagna, and by the withdrawal of his own brother Philip from an ecclesiastical career in 1193 to become duke of Tuscany and administrator of the Matildine lands.

[2] Hampe 230.

[3] See map at page 308.

baillis several years before the latter are first mentioned.[1] Henry
VI's most notable contributions to this policy were further north
in Thuringia and Meissen, where he also contravened the so-called
'principle' of *Leihezwang* in order to annex feudal fiefs to the
crown and administer them by salaried officials, thereby extending
his direct rule as far east as the Elbe.

The Meissen experiment was ruined by the civil war which
broke out soon after Henry's death, and it is thus a symbol both
of Henry's pursuit of the same German objectives as his father
and of the severe interruption which Staufen territorial policy
underwent during the next twenty years. Had the *Reichsministeriales* been a full-blown state bureaucracy entitled (after the English
fashion) to carry royal authority into feudal fiefs and allodial
lands, or had their history as French-style demesne officials been
more continuous and less contested, they might perhaps have
provided the stability required to see the Empire through a decade
of nominal rule by a minor. But they were not the former, and
they lacked the continuity of the latter, closely though they
resembled each. However, it was their pressure, rather than the
transparent self-interest of the archbishop of Cologne in crowning
a Welf candidate who only had minority support, which persuaded
Philip of Swabia to abandon his moral scruples and let himself be
elected in 1199. Their hand may also be suspected in the drafting
of the 'in imperaturam' declaration of Speyer in which the majority
meeting of Staufen lay and ecclesiastical supporters announced
their action to the new pope, and in the Halle protest of 1201: for
it is tempting to see these documents as the calculated successors
to the embryonic political theory of secular divine right contained
in Barbarossa's pronouncements after the Besançon incident.[2]
Their successive transfers of allegiance—first to Otto IV after
Philip's death, later to Frederick II—threw their cause into even
more disarray than that into which Innocent III might easily have
plunged the Church by his two-fold change from Welf to Hohenstaufen and back again; and by the time of Bouvines French

---

[1] Since Munz (*Frederick Barbarossa* 356) asserts that one reason why
Barbarossa did not annex Henry the Lion's lands in 1180 was that he had too
few *ministeriales* to administer them, it is worth pointing out that Bosl (*Reichsministerialität* 167) expressly states—in a passage to which Munz refers without
comment!—that Barbarossa disposed of enough manpower to pursue a demesne
policy like that of the Capetians. Philip of Swabia claimed that he did not know
how many *ministeriales* he had, so numerous were they (Bosl 618).

[2] See above, p. 16.

money and papal support were necessary to rescue Frederick II
in the nick of time and to ensure that the German succession was
once more determined by outside interests.

Seventeen years before his triumph at the Fourth Lateran
Council partly obscured his relative failure to take full advantage
of the magnificent opportunity to put the Vicariate of Christ into
practice by showing that the pope could 'build and plant' as well
as 'root out and destroy',[1] Innocent's 'recuperations' had confirmed
the lesson of Alexander III's pontificate: namely, that control of
central Italy was so vital to both sides that bitter conflict for it was
not likely to be restrained by legal or moral scruples—Innocent
'recovered' twice as much as his predecessors had even claimed,
for instance. Derogation of him as 'too political' is properly
countered by pointing to his recognition that under the prevailing
conditions of social and religious ferment poor preachers stood the
best chance of converting heretics, to the negotiations by which he
reconciled several dissenting groups to Catholicism, and to his
concern with the reform of the Benedictine Order as well as to his
encouragement of St Francis and to the Lateran Council's
reforming decrees.[2] This restores a balance and demonstrates
that spiritual motives underlay his actions as much as they did
Gregory VII's. But it was perhaps not in this but in another way
that he came nearest to averting the war to the death between
Empire and papacy which distracted the next generation and
inaugurated the long decline of both: his negotiations with Philip
of Swabia in 1207–8 seem to have offered some prospect (the
marriage of Philip's daughter and Innocent's nephew, who was to
receive Tuscany, Spoleto and Ancona as fiefs of the Empire) of
settling the territorial dispute by a compromise which might have
been both flexible enough and stable enough to stand up to the
strains of Frederick II's reign. Any such prospect disappeared
when Philip was murdered and Innocent thus enabled to withdraw from a forced and no doubt unwelcome compromise and to
return, in his dealings with Philip's two successors, to an attitude
more closely resembling the intransigence of the *Deliberatio*.

[1] Cf. Southern: *Western Society and the Church* 144–5, Ullmann: *Short
History* 210–213, 221–226. J. A. Watt: *The Theory of Papal Monarchy in the
Thirteenth Century* (1965) sets out the attitude of Innocent III and the canon
lawyers to the papacy's right over secular monarchies.
[2] M. Maccarone: 'Riforma e sviluppo della vita religiosa con Innocenzo III',
RSC 16 (1962) 27–72. On Innocent's pontificate in general, A. Fliche-V.
Martin: *Histoire de l'église* 10 (1950) 11–43.

In the Golden Bull of Eger of 1213, Frederick renounced central Italy and accepted Otto IV's dismantling[1] of the rights over episcopal elections which the Emperors had held since the Concordat of Worms, and his last promise to Innocent in 1216 was to give up Sicily as soon as he became Emperor; thus in order to obtain the crown he was obliged to surrender the oldest and the newest sources of its power—control over the German Church and easy access to the wealth of Sicily. The renunciation of the ancient royal rights over the German Church turned out to be permanent, although the promise to leave Sicily was soon broken; but neither of these things could be foreseen with any confidence in 1216. It would have been equally impossible to predict whether or not Frederick could halt the dissolution of the Hohenstaufen 'state'—the third of the chief sources of royal power—which had been going on for nearly twenty years. These uncertainties were the great defects of Innocent's solution of 'the affair of the Empire', for there was no way in which the papacy could enforce the undertakings Frederick had given, formally binding though they were. Since they were also sure to seem unduly onerous before many years had passed, Frederick could be expected to evade them. In short: the circumstances in which Frederick succeeded to the throne were such as to magnify the likelihood of future conflict and to multiply its grounds, while denying the papacy effective sanctions upon his conduct.

The extent of Frederick's resources was still to be discovered, but his strategy became plain directly Innocent's death gave him a little freedom of action. The immediate despatch of his five-year-old son Henry to Germany, and Henry's election as king in 1220, broke his promise to separate Germany and Sicily—for now Henry would unite them again when he eventually inherited the Norman kingdom from his father—and the high price paid for the election (the confirmation to the ecclesiastical princes of the royal sovereign rights they were already exercising) showed how great an importance Frederick attached to the exchange of kingdoms and how deliberate was his intention to secure a political and financial base in the far south as a first step. Hampe[2] described this as a calculated decision and enumerated several convincing reasons for it.

---

[1] At Neuss in 1201 and at Speyer in 1209.
[2] Hampe 253. His opinion was uncommon when he wrote, but is now widely accepted.

Others[1] have since revived the old charge that Frederick wrongly and unnecessarily deserted Germany. To credit Frederick with founding his whole policy upon an emotional preference for the Sicilian climate and countryside—deep-rooted though this preference evidently was—is plainly absurd. The more serious arguments advanced in support of this view are equally unconvincing, however, for they overlook the difficulty of reconciling it with the critical and rationalist outlook which is so characteristic both of Frederick's political propaganda and of his actions—as Klingelhöfer says,[2] we cannot call Frederick 'the first modern man to sit upon a throne' (Burckhardt's phrase is still in regular use) if we are at the same time to believe that he threw away without a moment's thought all the royal rights which he had inherited in Germany—and they fail to distinguish between a total disregard of Germany and a purely tactical decision to postpone dealing with it until Sicily and central Italy were firmly under control. It was self-evidently best to begin where he would meet least resistance to the restoration of absolute royal authority, and this meant starting in Sicily and moving northwards; and it is possible—contrary to what is often asserted—to show that Frederick devoted considerable and increasing attention to Germany and that it formed an integral part of his plan for the Empire.

Kantorowicz' exaggerated emphasis upon the classical and Roman aspects of his rule[3] has tended to obscure, for English readers at least, the truth that Frederick was thoroughly committed to the religious traditions of the medieval Empire which he inherited from his predecessors, and that (for instance) his acceptance of the Church's heresy laws[4] was more than just a necessary

[1] Notably E. Kantorowicz: *Frederick II* (Eng. trans. 1931) and Barraclough: *Origins* 219 ('A Sicilian on the German throne'), 221 ('Germany sank under him to the level of a subordinate province'), 224 ('He left Germany to the princes'), etc. This point of view has been demolished in an essay (first published in 1955) by E. Klingelhöfer: 'Die Reichsgesetze von 1220, 1231–2 und 1235' in G. Wolf (ed.): *Stupor Mundi* (1966) 396–419.

[2] *Stupor Mundi* 417.

[3] Folz: *Concept of Empire* 112–3 shows greater moderation, but unfortunately continues 'In his eyes the role of Germany, whose feudal disintegration he hastened by his own actions, was simply the reservoir of forces, a place where the Emperor could draw on means to carry out his policies'; see below, pp. 28–9.

[4] By a curious reversal of their ultimate roles, Frederick II agreed to follow up the clergy's sentence of excommunication with the imperial sentence of outlawry in the same decade as that in which Louis IX refused to do the same in France; but as Louis' dilemma at Lyons twenty years later and the similarity between some of their pronouncements about clerical 'interference' also show, France and the Empire were at a much more closely similar stage of development during the first half of the thirteenth century than is always recognised.

piece of tactics at the beginning of his reign: he repeatedly asserted his orthodoxy, admitted that the pope held both Swords[1] and made frequent attempts to come to terms with him,[2] devoted much of his propaganda[3] to polemic about evangelical poverty, and never set up an anti-pope. There has been general agreement with de Stefano's contention that Frederick's policy was 'semplicemente imperiale'—that is to say, neither narrowly German nor exclusively Italian, but intended to embrace all, from feudal princes to urban communes, in a single comprehensive purpose—and that it prominently included a conception of himself as protector of the Church;[4] while a study of Frederick's chancery has confirmed the half-spiritual, half-secular nature of his ideal of an *ecclesia imperialis*.[5] A king who protects religion is a king whose power comes direct from God, however, according to the dualistic theory of the origin of temporal authority to which Barbarossa had given currency, and Frederick II did not neglect its secular aspects.[6] As the maker of law, the Emperor was above it, and he called upon other secular rulers to show solidarity with him in resisting a clerical threat directed equally against them all,[7] although for the moment he alone might be the principal sufferer. Aristotelian influence is traceable in the Sicilian laws, where temporal power is attributed to 'necessity' as well as to Providence,[8] but it did not play the leading part in the political ideas of a man

[1] Wierusowski: *Vom imperium . . .* 166.

[2] Sometimes with temporary success, and of course sometimes with an obvious political motive—for instance, while he was suppressing Henry (VII)'s rebellion. Carlyle (see next note) enumerates these frequent occasions.

[3] O. Vehse: *Die amtliche Propaganda in der Staatskunst Kaiser Friedrichs II* (1929) 176–184. Vehse analyses and lists the propaganda items; a small selection of them is printed by H. M. Schaller: *Politische Propaganda Kaiser Friedrichs II und seiner Gegner* (1965). R. W. and A. J. Carlyle: *History of Medieval Political Theory in the West* v (1928) 235–317 comments extensively on the propaganda and prints many extracts from it.

[4] A. de Stefano: *L'idea imperiale di Federico II* (1952) 113, 195–202 .

[5] H. M. Schaller: 'Die Kanzlei Friedrichs II' (1958) in *Stupor Mundi* 550–553.

[6] W. Ullmann: 'Some reflections on the opposition of Frederick II to the papacy', ASP 13 (1960) 1–26 illustrates it and denounces Hohenstaufen dualism as 'merely a postulate based on a fictitious and chimeric abstraction', comparing it unfavourably with the hierarchical viewpoint of the papacy; only on the last two pages does he grudgingly admit the possibility of some genuine grounds for Frederick's position.—Hampe's frequent assertion that Frederick stood for 'a politically hopeless cause' which was bound to fail (251, 267–8, 290) has something of the same flavour but consorts rather ill with his views on the prospects of the monarchy.

[7] By contrast with Barbarossa, however, he claimed no superiority over them.

[8] Pullan 221.

who seems to have accepted the Augustinian *remedium peccati* and
to have regarded the state as divine in origin as well as natural in
its consequential activity, the human instrument of man's liberation from sin.[1] It has indeed been suggested that it was only the
unrelenting hostility of the Church which gradually forced
Frederick's thoughts out of the traditional Christian mould and
made him a forerunner of the 'natural state' ideas which became
prominent in the second half of the century.[2]

For more than a hundred years the Lombard towns had been
independent and self-governing; their autonomy was comparable
to the autonomy which Frederick claimed for the Empire. Yet he
mistook the moral force of the citizens' convictions as completely
as he underestimated their material strength, regarded them (it
has been said)[3] as 'political heretics' because they closed the Alpine
passes to his armies and reconstructed the Lombard League, and
conducted his campaigns against them with the fervour of a
crusade. Hampe drew an unfavourable contrast between the
rigidity of his demand for unconditional surrender after
Cortenuova and Barbarossa's flexibility after Legnano;[4] the
incompatibility of urban self-government with the monarchical
omnipotence and administrative uniformity which were Frederick's political ideals has since been stressed.[5] Save where (as in
Sicily) they bowed to his will, the towns had no part in Frederick's
bureaucratic system because theirs was necessarily the spirit of
contradiction.[6] The 'modernity' which they shared with him

[1] de Stefano: *L'idea imperiale* 15–21.
[2] Vehse: *Die amtliche Propaganda* 160, 188.
[3] de Stefano: *L'idea imperiale* 113.
[4] Hampe 284, 288. Italian towns nevertheless paid large sums into Frederick
II's treasury (Brühl: *Fodrum* 649–650).
[5] de Stefano: *L'idea imperiale* 104–121, E. Sestan in *Atti del convegno
internazionale di studi Federiciani 1950* 473–480 (=*Stupor Mundi* 331–341).—
Although Frederick flattered the Romans after Cortenuova and spoke of the
city as 'the seat of our Roman Empire' (the letter is printed in Folz: *Concept of
Empire* 203–4) he did not behave any the less authoritatively towards them than
towards the Lombards: four years earlier, for instance, imperial troops had
helped to suppress a Roman rebellion against the pope.
[6] Yet they had never shrunk from admitting the dictatorial authority of a
(self-chosen) *podestà* within their walls, and their democracy soon yielded to the
signorie which proliferated after 1250. If they resisted Frederick's Caesarism, it
was to Caesarism (though in fragmented rather than monolithic form) to which
they speedily fell victim.—A letter of July 1238 from the citizens of Bologna to
Brescia (then under siege by Frederick) illustrates the related point that they
did not cooperate easily: it speaks of defending 'the incomparable treasure of
liberty' against 'the evil persecutor of God and man', but ends by lamenting
that they are too far away to help (Schaller: *Politische Propaganda* 21). Bologna
is about a hundred miles from Brescia.

makes it proper to see his insistence on total submission as an opportunity missed, however, and his intransigence was suitably repaid by the obstinate resistance on their part which was the unwelcome focus of his attention in the 1240's. There is a curious parallel here between Frederick and Innocent IV. Both misunderstood the rising social forces of their time and mistakenly adopted too legalistic an approach towards them: Frederick rightly saw the need for secular sovereignty, but used it to crush all initiative out of his Italian subjects; Innocent's actions were completely justified by the Petrine commission upon which he based them, but he failed to realise that Christendom could not now be satisfied with this alone and that it was increasingly inclined to require unequivocally moral conduct as an additional justification. Nemesis was not long delayed: Even the Sicilians showed no loyalty to Frederick at the end, and only twenty-five years later the Second Council of Lyons recognised that Europe was disillusioned with the Church.

Frederick's hatred of communal independence in Lombardy was not matched by a similar dislike of the German cities, although much has been written to this effect; and here again Hampe's judgement has been borne out by later opinion.[1] It would be too much to claim for Frederick a general policy of favour to the German towns, but on the other hand the idea that he delivered them over as victims to the princes' greed must be abandoned. His long-term object was to restore effective government everywhere, and this involved cooperation with a variety of interests in order to draw each into his plan and eventually subject them all to his will. The treaty with the ecclesiastical princes in 1220 was no surrender, but an agreement which secured its object—tranquillity in Germany—at the price not of extending princely jurisdiction or of alienating more royal rights but simply of confirming existing practice. The same is true of the *Statutum* of 1231–2. The princes had recently been of service to Frederick and might be so again (they negotiated the treaty of Ceprano and they mediated on several subsequent occasions during the next ten years), and to oppose them before Lombardy was pacified would double his anxieties.[2] The restrictions on the towns upon

---

[1] Hampe 277.
[2] As late as 1245 his letter of protest against his deposition by Innocent IV declared, after the fashion of Barbarossa's 1157 proclamation, that he owed his 'status' and the imperial crown to them (MGH. Const. ii. 365; cf Wilks:

which they insisted show how serious a threat the princes felt the towns to be; but the *Statutum* was the consequence of Henry (VII)'s hasty and ill-considered attempt to keep the princes down, not of his father's deliberate policy. Frederick was compelled to accept it (though he secured some modifications in the monarchy's favour) in order to restore peace in Germany; but his action three years later, when at Mainz he legislated upon the very matters which in 1232 he had apparently declared to be no longer the crown's concern, suggests that he would not voluntarily have sought it.[1] The most recent appraisal of the 1241 tax-list[2] is not alone in emphasising that the two pieces of evidence complement each other in illustrating the strength of the German towns and the extent of Frederick's favour to them at least where he had the power to show it—on the royal and private demesne, to which alone the 1241 tax-list refers. But the wealth which even the towns on ecclesiastical territory could put at the crown's disposal is suggested by the gift of 3250 marks to Conrad IV by the citizens of Worms,[3] who had been forced in 1231 even to destroy their newly-built town-hall and who do not appear on the 1241 list at all.

Like the affair of 1180, the agreements of 1220 and 1231–2 did not so much mark a new departure in themselves as reinforce a long-standing tendency in the German constitution which only became irreversible after 1250;[4] until then, everything hung in the balance. That Frederick did not intend the debilitation of German royal power appears most plainly in the Landpeace of Mainz[5] and in his attitude towards the Hohenstaufen 'state'.

It was Mitteis who first argued that Frederick aimed at monarchical centralisation in Germany, using the Landpeace as the main evidence for his contention. His most extreme formulations[6]

Theory of Sovereignty 199), and in spite of his difficulties in Italy it was not until even later that Innocent IV managed to recruit an opposition party among the princes (Bayley: *College of Electors* 7–22).

[1] Klingelhöfer, in *Stupor Mundi* 408–411.

[2] G. Kirchner: 'Die Steuerliste von 1241', ZRG German. Abt. 70 (1953) 64–104.

[3] Kirchner 104.   [4] Cf Hampe 277.

[5] The brilliance of the court at Mainz in 1235, at which the Landpeace was promulgated, was as striking a manifestation of the Emperor's prestige as the ceremonial at Barbarossa's court at Mainz in 1184.

[6] *Staat des hohen Mittelalters* (3rd ed. 1948) 410: Frederick regarded the 1231–2 concessions as 'only temporary . . . to silence the princes' opposition for the moment . . . he hoped to regain the lost ground later, when he had carried out his reform plans in Italy', and believed that by permitting the consolidation of princely territories he was preparing the way for their return to the Reich as administrative areas after the fashion of 'concentric concentration' in France.

have not found favour, but a recent study[1] has confirmed his chief conclusions and has stated the reclamation of royal rights and the subordination of all territorial jurisdiction to the crown as Frederick's object. Some provisions of 1220 and 1231-2 were now silently dropped (the unlimited jurisdiction of the ecclesiastical princes and the severest restrictions on the towns, for example) and royal rights over tolls and safe-conduct were reasserted, but above all the Emperor now appeared once more in person as legislator over his German subjects, not (as Frederick may hitherto have seemed) the timid and absentee maker of treaties with them. Moreover, the institution of the *justitiarius curiae* clearly suggests an intention to import absolutist Sicilian methods into Germany and to make imperial justice supreme—although in practice Apulian officials would probably have caused more friction in Germany even than Barbarossa's *Reichsminister-iales* had caused in Lombardy and might, if successful, have converted Germany into a subordinate part of a non-German whole.[2]

It is tempting to suppose that the necessity of confronting Henry taught Frederick that the monarchy's immediate prospects in Germany were better than he had believed[3] after so long an absence from the country (although presumably he would have preferred to crush the Lombards' resistance before exploring them—i.e., that Cortenuova should precede Mainz, not *vice versa*) but it is more probable that the difference between father and son had never been so great as their enmity in 1231-4 suggests. Another possible speculation[4] is that Frederick's interest in Germany was still not lively enough even five years later for him to appreciate the Mongol threat correctly—he did not realise that catastrophe and annihilation threatened not only the Empire but the whole continent—and that it was a psychological blunder to allow himself to be pinned down in Italy by the outbreak of the

[1] H. Angermeier: *Königtum und Landfriede im deutschen Spätmittelalter* (1966) 1-33. Cf also Sestan in *Atti del convegno* 333-338 (=*Stupor Mundi* 474-478).

[2] Cf Hampe 306.

[3] The direct descent of the 1235 Landpeace from Henry (VII)'s text of 1234 may lend some colour to the suggestion. The two are compared in Gernhuber: *Landfriedensbewegung* 191.

[4] Georgina Masson: *Frederick II of Hohenstaufen* (1957) 314-5, 338. This book gives the most generally useful account of Frederick in English.

final struggle with the papacy and thus appear to desert the Germans.[1]

There is nevertheless sufficient evidence to suggest that in spite of being obliged to concentrate his main attention on fighting the pope and his urban allies Frederick made some serious attempt during his last years to put into operation a scheme of government embracing all his territories. The vicariates-general in Italy, the work of this period, were never wholly secure, but they represent an administrative plan which (as the orders instituting them show) concentrated on maintaining law and order and on protecting the security of long-distance road communication.[2] The area they covered extended right up to the Alps, where the acquisition of the Zähringen estates in the Bern-Zürich area in 1218, the purchase of neighbouring lands with the income from German taxation[3] and the annexation of Austria gave Frederick almost complete control over the frontier between Germany and Italy and over the passes which were vital to his lines of communication. The double act of annexation by which Austria and Styria were added to the royal demesne in contravention of *Leihezwang* is proof enough of deliberate intent, while the administration of both by *Reichsministeriales* with terms of reference identical with those of the Apulians who ruled the Italian vicariates meant that—in theory at least—an absolutist royal system was operating on both sides of the Brenner before Frederick died.[4] Bosl calls this system 'part

[1] Kirchner: *Steuerliste* 76 speculates rather similarly on the great future which the Hohenstaufen 'state' would have had but for the distraction of its head by the conflict with the pope after 1239.

[2] Several essays in the *Atti del convegno* show Frederick's concern with castle-building and roads in Italy. The documents establishing the vicariates-general are in MGH Const. ii. 299–301 (Romagna 1239), 301–2 (all Italy 1239), 306–7 (Tuscany 1240), 372–4 (Tuscany and Emilia 1246), 379–380 (Lombardy above Pavia 1248), 381–2 (Lombardy above the river Lambro 1249), 377–8 (Styria 1248). The terms of reference given to the vicar or legate are nearly identical in all the texts, and particular emphasis is placed by each on peace and the security of roads. Cf. Waley: *Papal State* 145 for the necessity to secure communications through central Italy and Frederick's consequent invasion of the papal state.

[3] Bosl: *Reichsministerialität* 150–163, Kirchner: *Steuerliste* 94; cf. Hampe 282.

[4] Frederick secured control over the Inn valley and the northern approaches to the Brenner through the count of Tyrol and a group of former Welf *ministeriales*, one of whom he appointed in 1235 to administer the bishopric of Trent, which covered the southern approaches to the pass (Bosl 464–7). The friendship of duke Otto II of Bavaria was a further protection for this route from Italy into Germany and through Styria to Austria. Frederick also used the Pontebbe route via Aquileia and Villach (Brühl: *Fodrum* 586) and further west attached particular importance to the St Gotthard 'as if he wanted to make central Switzerland and southern Germany into a strong-point of his rule' (Bosl 626).

of a comprehensive reshaping of the state, designed to check the disintegration of Germany into separate territories'.[1] The foundation of towns in Alsace and Frederick's frequent visits to its administrative capital, Hagenau, show that he was equally concerned for the security of the more traditionally royal western end of the Alpine frontier.[2] In Germany proper, most of the extensive former royal estates had been resumed by 1230, although the tendency of the *ministeriales* to become feudalised sometimes made control over them a little insecure.

Thus the Hohenstaufen 'state' was thriving right up to the end; the men who served it and the economic power they wielded were capable of providing the motive power for a more effective and a more unified imperial government than had yet existed, and thus of realising Frederick's purpose. There is striking evidence that since about 1235 Frederick had devoted as much attention to his German as to his Italian lands, and perhaps even some indication that his handling of the princes, the chief obstacle to his schemes in Germany, was better and more successful than his handling of the towns in Italy. It may therefore be that (symbolically at least) he could more profitably have spent the year 1248 in his new imperial city of Vienna than at the siege of Parma—that is to say, in consolidating his recent authority in eastern Germany, the future source of power, rather than in pursuing ancient Italian quarrels.

Confronted with the task of ruling territories so historically and geographically diverse as to be almost ungovernable as a single whole, and of doing so in conditions immensely more difficult than those which had faced his grandfather, Frederick had correctly identified—in Sicily and Germany at any rate—the elements in the situation which were most favourable to the monarchy and had devised a suitable strategy for exploiting them: the benefits conferred by the Melfi settlement might have held the Sicilians' loyalty had not the exigencies of a war which was not of his

[1] Bosl 479, 600.
[2] Brühl: *Fodrum* 141–2 and map 7. Frederick II paid 24 visits to Hagenau during his reign; among other places in Germany which he visited frequently were Speyer (17), Nuremberg (15) and Augsburg (10). A comparison of these figures with his 18 visits to Capua, 20 to Cremona and 35 to Foggia, for instance, gives a rather different picture of the proportionate distribution of his attention from that of the often-repeated charge that he spent only nine years in Germany during his whole reign, most of them at the beginning. Masson: *Frederick II* also draws attention to the importance he attached to Alsace.

D

choosing driven him to excessive fiscal pressure, while in Germany his combination of mildness with the firm assertion of crown rights had kept the princes proof against all but Innocent IV's last and most powerful seductions, and his 'state' had gone on from strength to strength. There is ample confirmation for what seems to have been Hampe's opinion—that the prospects of the imperial and German monarchy were still bright in 1250.[1] If both suffered eclipse soon afterwards, the principal reason may be not the impossibility of victory in a fight to a finish with the papacy because he could neither forge sharp enough ideological weapons to defeat the hierarchy nor dominate central Italy with his armies (as Hampe and others have said), but his failure to recognise that reason of state and a fundamental similarity between his interests and those of the Lombard cities (the other 'modern'phenomenon of the age) bade him cease exhausting himself in fruitless conflict with them and seek instead to enlist their support in a common secular cause: for—as the Concordat of Worms had once shown, and as years of collusion between Avignon popes and European kings were soon to demonstrate beyond doubt—the secular power could always disregard ecclesiastical censure and manipulate events to its own advantage if it were well armed, supported by the opinion of its most influential subjects and prepared to be supple in its political conduct.

NOTE—Two important books have been published since the above was written.

Boyd H. Hill: *Medieval Monarchy in Action* prints royal and imperial documents 919–1075 and analyses them in a long introduction.

T. C. van Cleve: *The Emperor Frederick II of Hohenstaufen* explicitly bases many of his judgements on Hampe's opinions and confirms several of the views expressed above (for instance, pp. 100–105, 237–242, 381–386).

[1] Hampe 275-283, 299-300, 305.

1

CONRAD II (1024–1039)

When the Ottonian House came to an end with the death of Henry II, there was no feeling that the Empire would collapse although no arrangements for the succession had been made. Electoral right, which had never been extinguished and which had become still more prominent in 1002, now came into its own, but the blood-right of the ruling house was so deeply ingrained in Germanic law that the only two serious candidates were descended through it in the female line; both were great-grandchildren of duke Conrad the Red of Lorraine and of a daughter of Otto the Great, both were called Conrad and both were recommended by being members of the Frankish tribe. The duchy of Carinthia had been lost to this family under Henry II, and in the struggle over it the elder Conrad had been for a long time under the imperial ban. Through the early death of his father, his share of the family lands on the upper Rhine and in Franconia had been less than that of his younger cousin (who called himself the duke of Worms) in spite of the fact that he was the senior, and he was now counted merely as a simple nobleman. The nobility of the right bank of the Rhine, under the leadership of Aribo of Mainz and with the support of the dowager Empress, took his side, while archbishop Pilgrim of Cologne and a Lotharingian minority supported the younger Conrad. Both personal motives and the contrast between Aribo's conservative attitude in ecclesiastical politics and the enthusiasm of the Lotharingians for reform seem to have determined party allegiance.

Inaccurate views about the election, which took place on a plain between Mainz and Worms, have become widespread through Uhland's poetical version of the account given by Wipo, an eye-witness; for there is more rhetorical ornament than real understanding in Uhland's version.[1] It was not a matter of a popular decision between the two candidates on grounds of their

---

[1] Johann Ludwig Uhland (1787–1862), romantic poet and politician. The passage referred to occurs in Act II of his play *Ernst, Herzog von Schwaben*, published in 1818.

suitability, but a question of gaining the west German minority for the elder Conrad; west Germany was important because of the possibility that Lorraine would turn to France. At all events, an understanding with the defeated candidate was soon reached. The archbishop of Cologne brought it about by crowning Queen Gisela, after the stubborn Aribo had refused to do so because she had married within the prohibited canonical degrees. When the Saxons also accepted a member of another tribe as king, in return for the confirmation of their ancient rights, Conrad had been recognised by practically the whole of Germany; a little later the Lorrainers also withdrew their opposition.

Conrad was at that time a fully-grown, bearded man of about thirty-four years of age. Family characteristics, the experiences of his youth and personal disposition had worked so uniformly in the same direction that in his person there came to the throne perhaps the most decisive and determined ruler of the whole German Middle Ages. Far more than the Ottos and most of the Staufen, the Salians tended towards harsh and ruthless action. As an orphan Conrad had bitterly learned in his early years how the rights of a minor could be set aside by relatives and by the Emperor. Bishop Burchard of Worms, well-known for his collection of canons and for his description of the law of his court, had undertaken his education; his position as an unimportant lord, not even in possession of comital rights, did not call for literary training, but he gained a correspondingly deeper understanding of the situation of the lower classes. He had grown up as a full-blooded layman with an ever ready sword-hand and clear good sense, little touched by the world of ideas but always with both feet on the ground of present reality, and it was not long before he found himself at home in all the duties of a German king.

The confident words, full of a sense of his office, which he spoke on the way to his coronation to the nobles who tried to prevent him from listening to the complaints of a peasant, a widow and an orphan, were a programme of government in themselves: justice for all without delay and without respect of persons. So he became the promoter of peace, the protector of the weak, the unyielding defender of the law, who took offence at the sale of the serfs of the bishopric of Verden 'as if they were senseless cattle' and roared at the robber count Thasselgard 'Is this the lion that has devoured the flock of Italy? By the Holy Cross of the Lord, this lion shall eat my bread no longer' and hanged him like a common criminal. Sharply worded and picturesque sayings and easily-applied symbols, often not without the grim humour so beloved of the old German law, were well calculated to make him popular. It made a great impression in the army, for instance, when he ordered the people of Ravenna to fill with coins the leather boot of a nameless soldier whose leg they had cut off during their revolt, and to put it by his bed. He was paid perhaps the greatest compliment a German ruler could receive when men compared him with Charlemagne and coined the saying 'Charlemagne's sword hangs at Conrad's saddle'.

But he claimed the right which he protected in others with equal force for himself and for his kingdom, asserted it ruthlessly against all resistance and imposed it with overwhelming force when real danger threatened his position as ruler. The veil which the ecclesiastical account would otherwise have drawn over the real events is violently torn aside by a description of the Reichstag of Bamberg in 1035 which has been accidently preserved in a letter in the Lorsch collection. Conrad wished to depose Adalbero of Carinthia (an old enemy of his house whom he accused of treason) from his duchy as a false vassal, but his long-prepared plan to do so by a decision of the princes came up against unexpected opposition from his son and co-king Henry. Anger so overcame Conrad that he fell senseless to the ground. When he came to himself he was not too proud to prostrate himself before his own son; having thus touched Henry's heart, he dismissed the bishop of Freising (who had incited Henry to oppose his father) with a torrent of abuse and got his own way after all.

This impetuous and violent defence of the law sometimes took on more absolutist forms, as it did later under Barbarossa, but in each case it benefited the state. Conrad's prudent and decisive nature qualified him as statesman and general as much as it did as judge. His power of quick and effective decision is shown in incidents like his springing straight from sleep to arms during the rebellion in Ravenna, or by the occasion when under still greater pressure in Parma he suddenly ordered the city to be set on fire so as to give the alarm to his troops encamped outside. He was constantly on the move—when necessary, in burning haste; he appeared at all corners of his widespread empire, always throwing the weight of his personality into the scales on the side of order.

Conrad was more conservative in domestic politics than Giesebrecht thought. He followed Ottonian practice in securing the succession for his son by having him elected and crowned as early as 1028. The firm relations with the German Church which his predecessor had recently strengthened were the most reliable foundation of power for Conrad too. But in the entirely realistic way which was characteristic of him, and which caused the Burgundian reformers to accuse him of lack of faith, he was cool in his attitude towards the Church and lacked all mystical feeling, so that the priestly aura of royalty diminished. His episcopal appointments took more account of politics than of ecclesiastical and cultural needs; on occasion he took harsh measures against intractable prelates. Imperial lands were less frequently granted to churches, and it was family interest which led him to make two important foundations: the great monastery at Limburg on the Haardt, and the magnificently planned and richly-endowed cathedral of Speyer which was to be the burial church of his family. In order to provide fiefs for temporal magnates he arbitrarily interfered with ecclesiastical property more often than his predecessor had done, and even decided important ecclesiastical matters by the mere expression of his own will; he showed little understanding of the inner life of the Church and made no particular effort to direct it.

In monastic politics Conrad seemed at first to go some way towards meeting the wishes of the reformers. His trusted supporter, abbot Poppo of Stablo and Malmedy, not only reformed twelve Lotharingian monasteries but was also able to introduce reform for the first time into four royal abbeys in other parts of the Empire. This marked the beginning of the Romanisation of German monastic life, although it met serious opposition from the monks. But the Emperor needed the Lotharingian reformers for the security of his designs upon Burgundy and other western territories, and any favour he showed towards them was rather the reward for political services than the consequence of any personal conviction. As soon as the spheres of the imperial Church and of Cluny came into contact for the first time on Burgundian soil and the impossibility of combining imperial control of the Church with monastic independence became apparent, serious tension replaced a friendly relationship. Conrad's violent interference (which even on one occasion drove reform from a monastery into which it had already been introduced) and his simoniacal practices were bound to cause increasing offence to the Cluniacs. Conrad can scarcely have perceived the inevitability of future conflict between the high ecclesiastical ideal and the necessities of the temporal power enshrined in the old customary law, but sure instinct guided him to strengthen the lay as well as the ecclesiastical structure of his kingdom.

The most characteristic feature of his attitude towards the realities of temporal power in the Empire was his recognition of the heritability of fiefs in the male line. He himself had bitter memories of the way in which the rights of his family to the duchy of Carinthia had been thrust aside, and as king he preserved the inheritance rights of the dukes. He did not want to destroy their power altogether and replace it by direct imperial rule. Had this been the case, he would scarcely have given Carinthia to his cousin, the younger Conrad, after the fall of Adalbero in 1036, nor would he have strengthened Lorraine by uniting its two halves in order to put down anarchy and set up a firm authority on the frontier in 1033. His grant of Bavaria (vacant owing to the childless death of the Lützelburger duke) to his son Henry in 1027, which secured a duchy for his family for the first time, was entirely in the spirit of the law and of Ottonian policy. When the Swabian line of the Babenberg house came unexpectedly to an end with the deaths in 1038 of the emperor's two stepsons by the first marriage of his wife Gisela, Henry III became their heir because he was Gisela's son, and his well-founded claims secured him the succession to Carinthia soon after his father's death in 1039. This great extension of the power of the imperial house over the whole of south Germany derived therefore directly from the law and not from a deliberate policy of opposition to the lay princes, who therefore came to realise how strongly the Emperor upheld the law and were in return prepared to accept his strong emphasis on their official position.

In consequence of the narrowing experiences of his early life, however, Conrad felt himself most drawn to the counts and the lesser feudality: for instance he did honour to one of his friends, the son of a count, who had died in Rome, by having him buried next to the Emperor Otto II. By applying the principle of the heritability of fiefs to their lands, where it had hitherto not been recognised, Conrad gained extremely valuable support from these vassals upon whom the military strength of the kingdom depended.

This was soon of practical importance during the repeated risings (1025–1030) of his stepson Ernst II of Swabia. The family quarrel was of no serious significance. A later and fantastically embellished story confused Ernst with Liudolf, the son of Otto the Great, but Ernst lacked the political gifts with which Liudolf must be credited even when later nationalist exaggerations have been discounted. By his inability to prefer the public good to his private interests Ernst rather recalls Johann Parricida,[1] whom he also resembles for his self-will, obstinacy and excitability, although his actions were not so wicked. The conflict between his private claims to Burgundy and the governmental policy of the Emperor no doubt provided a motive for this immature youth, who was never won over by Conrad's frequent magnanimity towards him. His fate only became tragic and deserving of sympathy when he refused his ducal obligation to carry out the sentence of outlawry against his friend Werner von Kyburg for persistent rebellion, and preferred instead to maintain his friendship at the cost of their common ruin (1030). Even after his repeated breaches of faith the Emperor saw in him only the rebel against authority, and on hearing of his early and childless death said bitterly 'Mad dogs seldom have pups'. If these risings never developed into a serious threat to Germany, in spite of their foreign connections and the early participation of the younger duke Conrad, this was not least because the Swabian counts and lords refused to follow their feudal superior, the duke, in arms against the Emperor because they felt the Emperor to be the chief protector of their own rights.

Conrad's careful policy in this affair brought new strength to the monarchy, but this was not the only occasion on which his actions revealed, faintly but perceptibly, the lineaments of the future. Under him the policy of favouring the development of the towns, so characteristic of the later Salians, saw a notable beginning in the encouragement of merchants and the grant of market and coinage rights. It was perhaps the example of his teacher, bishop Burchard of Worms, which had early made him aware of the importance of the ministerial class. Although we only know that he made an admirable choice of court officials soon after his coronation, he is not likely to have overlooked the rest of the

[1] Murderer of the Emperor Albert I in 1308.

ministeriales[1]—the less so because he was in urgent need of them for the administration of the growing imperial demesne, which he turned into a considerable source of power for the German monarchy by means of reclamations and new acquisitions in all the duchies.

The authority which he had established at home soon had its effects abroad. On the foundations solidly established by his predecessor, Conrad raised the Empire once more to a position of high regard among neighbouring peoples. In east and west he thought it his duty to secure peace by calculated compromise. A strip of territory between the Danube, the Fischa and the Leitha was ceded to Stephen of Hungary, with whom he had quarrelled over the Bavarian succession and frontier problems, in a treaty drawn up in 1031 after an unsuccessful campaign by his son Henry. He formed a close friendship with the powerful ruler of the north, Canute the Great (who had added Norway and Scotland to his Danish and English territories and had extended his influence along the south coast of the Baltic) by marrying his son to Canute's daughter Gunhild and by restricting German territorial claims to the Eider frontier—although in prevailing conditions this was more a surrender in principle than the abandonment of lands that were actually occupied. Had he been able to foresee that this, the only great power in the west apart from Germany, would begin to break up soon after Canute's early death in 1035, he would perhaps have been less accommodating. However, he needed to protect his northern flank against Poland, and peaceful relations were to be of great importance for the progress of German missions and trade in this area.

Conrad had more striking successes in both east and west. Luck was with him in Poland. Like his predecessor, he would have been powerless against the conquering genius of Boleslav the Great. But with Boleslav's death and the quarrels of his sons the loosely-knit Polish state collapsed, and the Emperor was able to take advantage of the disturbance to regain both Lausitzes and the old frontier in 1031, and even to make Poland feudally dependent on the Empire in 1033. Authority was also gradually established over Bohemia, and in fierce battles the Liutizi were again reduced from alliance to subjection and the payment of tribute.

---

[1]An unfree class, peculiar to Germany, whose obligation was to serve their lord as administrators rather than as warriors or peasants.

The losses of recent years were thus made good in the east. In the west new territory was gained and the character of the whole empire thereby changed. After a century of independent existence, the kingdom of Burgundy came to an end in 1032 with the childless death of Rudolf III. Here again it was a matter of chance that the eventuality for which Henry II had long ago prepared the way by a treaty now at last came about. But it depended very much on the energy and statesmanship of Conrad whether, even after Rudolf's assent to the treaty, he would be able to enforce his own interpretation of it and inherit all his predecessor's claims both against candidates with better rights in private law and against the Burgundian nobles' boast of their electoral privileges. One of the claimants, Ernst of Swabia, was already dead at the crucial time, however, and the other, count Odo of Champagne, had to abandon his resistance in 1034 in face of the military superiority of the Emperor, who also kept him in check by allying with the king of France in his rear. Conrad then had himself elected and crowned king by his Burgundian supporters; later he was able to secure the same for his son Henry III.

What significance for the imperial authority had the acquisition of a third kingdom? It brought a real extension of power only in those areas in which Rudolf's weak kingship had meant anything, that is to say, in the at any rate partly German lands of what is now French Switzerland; and here it was entirely advantageous from the economic as well as from the national angle. Politically, suzerainty over the more southerly, half-independent lands westwards as far as the mouth of the Rhone and eastwards as far as Nice was also valuable enough, little as they had in common with Germany from the national point of view. For it brought to a halt the French attempts at expansion which earlier on had aimed in a southerly direction—just as they did later, after the end of imperial control in Burgundy in the thirteenth century—and thus, reinforced by the occupation of the western Alpine passes, it promoted the security of the Empire's Italian possessions. The union under one crown of three great kingdoms in the middle of Europe henceforth provided a broader foundation for the Empire's leadership in the west. Finally, the political union with the centres from which the Church reform party exercised its influence was of great importance from the cultural point of view and undoubtedly increased that influence in the Empire—although, of course, this cut both ways.

His misunderstanding of the dangers which henceforth threatened the German government from this direction was the one weak point of Conrad's policy. He was so conscious of his almost limitless power over the Church that he underestimated the strength of ideas. On the one hand, he heedlessly allowed matters to take their own course and did not oppose the further advance of the reformers in the Empire, but on the other he countenanced a scandalous state of affairs in Rome which was in violent contrast with the respect in which the Empire itself was held.

The secularised papacy of the Tusculan house had at least been represented in Benedict VIII by a statesman of ability, but it sank back on his death in 1024 into insignificance and corruption. While he was still lay ruler of Rome, his brother John XIX had bought both the papacy and his own ordination, and would have sold the papal primacy and the right to the title of 'universal bishop' to the Greek patriarch if he had not been prevented by the opposition of the reformers. 'If the brook is warm at its source', wrote William of Dijon, 'it stinks however far it flows'. The low esteem in which the papacy was held in Germany at that time is sufficiently shown by the fact that bishop Warmann of Constance burned, in open synod, a bull of John XIX to which he objected, yet remained unpunished. From such a papacy Conrad II need fear neither interference with his ecclesiastical policy in Germany nor hindrance to his Italian plans.

It was soon necessary to take Italy into account in order to strengthen his rule. For the Lombard magnates, who had wanted to make the change of monarch an excuse for freeing themselves from Germany, had found a ready-made candidate for the Italian crown in a son of duke William V of Aquitaine. Their enterprise became threatening when they also allied with other powerful French nobles. Conrad, however, managed to break up the alliance. The pretender's efforts in upper Italy came to nothing against the firm attitude of the episcopal and imperial party under the leadership of Leo of Vercelli (d. 1026). In order to make peace more secure, however, Conrad made an expedition to Rome in 1026–7.

To begin with, Conrad followed the traditions of Henry II's policy in Italy, as he had done in Germany. By having himself crowned (without a separate Italian royal election) with the Lombard crown by archbishop Aribert of Milan, he emphasised

the point that the change of monarch had not extinguished
imperial rights for an instant, just as he did when he said to the
people of Pavia, who had revolted and destroyed the royal palace:
'The kingdom goes on though the king is dead, just as the ship
remains afloat though the helmsman may be drowned'. By a
carefully calculated mixture of severity and mildness, he managed
to secure peace in Italy without any great difficulty. He was
crowned emperor in Rome in 1027 by John XIX in the presence
of Canute the Great and the king of Burgundy. He issued his
own regulations for the government of Rome, dominated the
Lateran synod although he had summoned it jointly with the pope,
and arranged the subordination of the patriarchate of Grado to
that of Aquileia because this was to the imperial advantage. He
never visited Rome again, but the docile submission of the papacy
even in the most important ecclesiastical affairs—the counts of
Tusculum being allowed their independence only in trivial
matters—was to continue after John's death, under his young and
frivolous nephew Benedict IX (1032–1046). It suited the
Emperor to be able to treat the pope like one of his officials if he
needed to use his name in the settlement of Lombard affairs, for
class conflicts there gave him a good deal of trouble.

It was no longer possible to re-establish the old and already
crumbling central government of the royal house of Pavia, although
one of its officials wrote the *Instituta regalia* with this object in
mind. Italy could only be ruled by lesser authorities with their
combination of ecclesiastical and temporal outlook. To begin
with, Conrad used the appointment of German bishops almost
more than his predecessor had done as the chief link between the
two kingdoms, but he met opposition from Aribert, the ambitious
archbishop of Milan, who would have liked to make his ecclesiastical province into a closely-knit state dependent on himself
alone.

The Italian towns' development had outstripped that of the
German towns at this time. The growth of their economic power
had raised the standing and the incomes of the urban bishops,
who had been entrusted with the exercise of the royal rights of
peace-keeping and trade-regulation, and who usually had comital
rights as well. Whereas in other places there had already been
occasional risings against the bishops by citizens discontented
with episcopal control and aiming at self-government (similar

risings began in Germany half a century later), Milan was a special case because there a lay representative of the emperor held the position of count. Archbishop and citizens united against him.

Here, as in Germany, Conrad sought for a counterbalance in the power of the lay nobility. All round Milan he took care to conciliate the great margravial families and to bind them more tightly to Germany by marriage alliances: for instance, the margraves of Turin (who had already been closely connected with the Salians), the margraves of Tuscany-Canossa (whom he brought into fateful contact with the Lotharingian dukes) and the Otbertines of Este, who, through marriage with a Welf princess were to fall heirs to the Welfs of Alemannia and Bavaria when the male line died out in 1055, and were to found the junior Welfic line.

Alongside these great lay nobles, another class soon appeared in both Germany and Italy as supporters of the monarchy: the numerous knightly tenants of the second grade, the *valvassores* as they were here called, to distinguish them from the superior nobility and vassals of the first rank who possessed counties or comital rights, the *capitanei*. The archbishop of Milan came into violent conflict with them in 1035, when he arbitrarily annexed their fiefs (which were not yet generally recognised as heritable) in order to maintain and extend his ecclesiastical principality. The whole of Lombardy was soon split into hostile camps. On one side was Aribert with his bishops and a part of the higher lay nobility, on the other—drawn together by the similarity of their status—the *valvassores*, who in the long run faced a choice between sinking in the social scale or managing to achieve a higher status. It was the first great class war of medieval history. Out of it grew the rising of the *valvassores* and their expulsion from Milan in 1035; and since the same legal uncertainty threatened the other members of their class, the struggle soon spread over the whole of Lombardy. When the *valvassores* were victorious in battle, first the bishops and then their conquerors turned for mediation to the Emperor, who announced his decision to make a second expedition to Rome with the haughty words 'If Italy hungers for law, I will satisfy it'.

The fundamental principles he had already applied in Germany favoured the *valvassores* of Lombardy. Conrad demanded the removal of the disabilities under which they suffered and summoned Aribert to judgement at Pavia in 1037. When Aribert insolently refused to surrender any of the Church's possessions and the court held his disobedience to be high treason, Conrad threw him into prison. Aribert, however, escaped to Milan in a monk's habit; in the city (now besieged by Conrad) he received the full support of the citizens, who made common cause with him against the authority of the emperor and the counts.

Before the emperor raised the siege at the onset of the summer heat, he issued his famous feudal law, the *Constitutio de feudis*,[1] which guaranteed to the *valvassores* the inheritance of fiefs in the male line, gave them the protection of the popular courts against arbitrary deprivation, and offered them the right of appeal to the emperor or his legates as a final security. This step meant a break with the episcopal policy followed by his predecessors, but it ensured enthusiastic support for the emperor from all the *valvassores*; the majority of the higher lay nobility were in any case on his side.

Conrad's other measures show that he was aware of his un-challenged supremacy. It was an altogether unprecedented action, flying in the face of every contemporary ecclesiastical conception, to declare the obstinate archbishop deposed and to name his successor without enlisting the co-operation of the pope and a synod. A group of bishops under Aribert's leadership, annoyed both by this and by the *Constitutio de feudis*, now formed a conspiracy with the object of destroying German authority, allied with Conrad's enemy Odo of Champagne and put him up as pretender to the throne. This was in complete contrast with the situation at the beginning of Conrad's reign, when the lay nobility had threatened his Italian position in a similar way but the bishops had saved him. Conrad now took measures of a terrifying severity: he had three bishops condemned by the judgement of the lay nobles and sent into banishment across the Alps, and he got the complaisant pope to excommunicate Aribert in 1038; an invasion of Lorraine by Odo was repulsed by the forces of the whole duchy and ended with Odo's death.

Further steps against Milan, which still sheltered the arch-bishop, were put off because the affairs of south Italy, which had only been of minor concern during the first expedition to Rome, now made speedy intervention desirable. Conrad's aim here was not to extend his territory. He entered instead into friendly

[1] Pullan 128–9.

relations with the Greek empire, which was feeling some renewal of its ageing powers and might even have been dangerous to Italy if it had not been diverted by conflict with the Arabs of Sicily. A peaceful delimitation of spheres of influence in southern Italy was therefore possible if Conrad confined himself to the western part. Here the main need was to tame the insubordinate prince of Capua and to set up a united force under German control for the defence of the frontier. This was achieved when Conrad enfeoffed Waimar of Salerno, the strongest of the smaller rulers, with Capua and when Waimar went on to conquer Amalfi, Sorrento and Gaeta as well. Conrad separated the county of Aversa from Naples and assigned it in 1038 as a fief of Waimar to Rainulf, one of the leaders of the wild Norman soldiery who for the last twenty years had repeatedly intervened in the south Italian strife and now for the first time gained a territory for themselves. Conrad could not foresee that within the space of a generation there would grow from this seed the powerful Norman state which was to support a hostile papacy against his grandson.

From southern Italy Conrad would have moved to a new attack on Milan if the heat of summer had not caused an epidemic in his army from which many died, among them his son's Danish wife and his own stepson Hermann of Swabia. This forced Conrad to hand over the execution of the sentence against the archbishop of Milan to trustworthy Italian nobles and to beat a hasty retreat to Germany. But he too was suffering from a fatal illness: he died of convulsions in the following spring, still under fifty. He left to his son a power more extensive than anyone had wielded since the days of Otto the Great. There is no reason to suppose that if he had lived longer he would not have managed to crush the opposition of Milan within a short time. It was otherwise, however, with the problems of ecclesiastical politics which he had created by his forceful action against Aribert. Little though Aribert was to the liking of the reforming party, the ruthlessness with which the emperor had ignored both Church law and religious sentiment had shown up in a harsh light the impossibility of reconciling Conrad's style of ruling with the clerical ideal of independence, and it was well known that father and son were not of the same mind about this. Although Conrad's small understanding of the inner life of the Church and the cold, unprincipled and entirely secular way in which he treated its ideals and claims was certainly the weakest point in his whole policy, it must on the other hand be emphasised that these problems were scarcely capable of solution under existing conditions if a strong imperial authority was to be maintained. It was quickly to become clear under Conrad's immediate successor that the alternative policy—to build on Henry II's foundations and to set a more priestly kingship at the head of the reforming movement—could not lead to a satisfactory solution either.

2

HENRY III (1039–1056)

The Empire continued at first to progress under the new ruler, who was barely twenty-one but had been introduced to politics and war at an early age. His first years brought useful successes in the east. The plans of Bretislav, the king of Bohemia, for a national Church and an enlarged Czech realm were overthrown, and his feudal subordination confirmed in 1041, while Henry also intervened later in the internal quarrels of the west Slav kingdom in order to bring about peace within it. In Hungary he not only recovered the recently lost territories and made the Leitha once more the imperial frontier, but attacked its again untrustworthy ruler, defeated him in battle in 1044 and replaced him by King Peter, who accepted feudal dependence and promised tribute. This extension of power, backed by the Bavarian and Frankish colonisation which he encouraged in Austria, Styria and Carinthia, together with the unlimited authority over the papacy which he exercised during the following years, make Henry III's reign seem the high point of the medieval Empire. It is difficult, however, to decide whether Henry was the equal of his father or superior to him, because of the silence of contemporary sources and the contradictory opinions of modern historians. To some he appears the mightiest German ruler since Charlemagne, for others he is the man who ruined the German kingdom. When both modern research and the ideals of his own time are taken into account, however, the verdict seems to be in Henry's favour.

Physically, Henry was the image of his father, but in temperament he was entirely different. Conrad's outlook had been rough and entirely secular, but Henry had been carefully educated by bishops who had taught him to love books, music and architecture and had awakened in him a sensitive response to clerical culture and Christian ethics. His earnest and serious nature always acted from a sense of duty. The grandeur of his quasi-priestly office exalted him and yet at the same time weighed him down. He bent every effort to his task, and yet was never satisfied. Because he

E

was driven on by a sense of duty himself, he demanded the same of everyone else, and trusted less to the persuasion of force and self-interest than to the attraction of a moral ideal.

His efforts for peace in his early years are the clearest signs of this attitude. In the chaos of western Europe, it was the Church that first sought to put a stop to private war by peace agreements. The Truce of God, which it first proclaimed in 1040 and which spread northwards and eastwards from southern France, forbade fighting on the great feasts and from Wednesday night to Monday morning under penalty of ecclesiastical censure. Henry felt the royal duty of preserving the peace as a personal obligation and embraced it fervently; half measures were not good enough for him. He wanted to put the heavenly ideal into earthly practice, and sought to lead the masses to his own high conceptions by setting them a good example. During the Synod of Constance in 1043 he made a moving admonition to peace from the pulpit, but first he forgave his own enemies. At the great ceremony of thanksgiving and penance after the victory over the Hungarians in 1044 he was the first to throw himself on his knees in the hair-shirt of a penitent before the fragments of the True Cross, and later issued another general pardon. Behaviour like this by him was not unusual; it made a deep impression and encouraged emulation. But these emotions were too transient to be a lasting source of strength, and private war was again rife in Germany in Henry's later years.

His efforts for peace are, however, very characteristic both of Henry's personality and of his policy. Shortly before his death he offered to risk his life in personal combat with the king of France to settle the quarrel over Lorraine, and throughout his reign the uprightness of his behaviour and his conscientious pursuit of high ideals attracted much attention. His feeling for justice gave him strength and confidence; he was never false to his own nature. But in the last resort did Christian ethics correspond with the demands of successful statesmanship? Henry tried to bring the two together; his was a nature on the grand scale, satisfied with nothing but the best. He resembled Otto the Great in many respects, but lacked Otto's buoyancy, determination and vigour. His sober earnestness, single-minded obstinacy and unsmiling reserve prevented his people from loving him. His second wife, Agnes of Poitou, the daughter of William V of Aquitaine, pushed him further in the direction he had already chosen by strengthening his connexions with the Cluniac reform in Burgundy. He lost popularity at their marriage-feast in 1043, however, when he drove away the wandering players, the usual mouthpieces of popular opinion; and when he became depressed by frequent illness in later years, there were more and more complaints about his unapproachability and his failure to preserve customary rights.

With such a disposition, Henry's attitude towards the Church reform movement was bound to be completely different from that of his father. Discrepancies between the claims of canon law and the actual state of affairs, which Conrad had condoned and even exploited, were intolerable to his almost clerically-oriented conscience. Only in purity could the Church fulfil its lofty task as the handmaid of the state. Here too Henry gave a personal lead, maintaining close contact with the leaders of the Burgundian and Lotharingian reform movement and continuing the work of Henry II on a larger scale. By deliberately renouncing simony he gave up a considerable portion of his revenue. In contrast with his father's policy, he brought to an end the struggle with Aribert of Milan, who had been uncanonically deposed, and again recognised him as archbishop. This was not in any sense intended as a renunciation of his sovereign rights over the bishops and the imperial abbots, however. On the contrary, it was precisely his right to appoint them, on grounds of spiritual suitability as well as political usefulness, and to give them the ring, the symbol of their marriage with the Church, as well as the pastoral staff, which offered him the surest means of putting the reformers' plans into effect; similarly, he made the fullest use of his right to summon and preside over synods and to take decisions over a wide range of ecclesiastical affairs.

Naturally, he could not foresee that his whole attitude would soon be attacked as contradicting clerical freedom and the hierarchical order of the world. Yet there came to his ears from time to time expressions of reforming opinion which showed the desire for a sharp division between ecclesiastical and secular authority clearly enough. 'We owe the pope obedience, and you fealty; we have to account to you for temporal things and to him for spiritual things', said bishop Wazo of Liège in 1046, disputing the king's right to depose an Italian archbishop by the decision of a German synod, and expressly reserving this right to the pope.

A haughty answer of the same bishop on another occasion showed how well aware he was of hierarchical ideas: 'There is a great difference between priestly orders and those which a king receives: ours are life-giving, while yours bring death. And by as much as life is greater than death, by so much are our orders exalted above yours'. In the same year the newly-elected archbishop Halinard of Lyons refused, as a monk, to do fealty to the king. Was it then desirable to give such monks an official position in the realm? It was the great error of Henry's life to believe that he could transform the Church in accordance with the views of the reformers and yet keep his old authority over it. This was also apparent in his relations with the papacy.

Confused party struggles in Rome since the end of 1044 had again shown Europe that the dependence of the papacy upon the nobles could not be reconciled with the progress of reform. The young and immoral Tusculan pope Benedict IX was driven out by the Crescentii. He returned, however, and forced the anti-pope Sylvester III to retire to his bishopric of Sabina. But the uncertainty of his position soon led Benedict to make over the papacy for a consideration to his godfather, who had capital behind him through his relationship with a converted Jew, the head of the Pierleoni family. The new pope, who took the name of Gregory VI, was pious and of blameless reputation; he was supported by the reforming party, who overlooked the disguised simony in order to gain control. Since Gregory was generally recognised and would have gained full acceptance if he had had the support of the German king, there were not really three popes, as it is sometimes said. But Henry made his first expedition to Rome in 1046, and held a reform synod at Pavia with the object of freeing the curia from party strife. For this purpose he needed a pope to whom no exception could be taken; and so, as soon as he had sized up the situation in Rome, he decided to disregard Gregory although he had already met him at Piacenza. He invited Gregory and Sylvester to the synod of Sutri (20 December 1046), and deposed them both. Gregory, whose support in Rome made him dangerous, went in exile to Cologne; in his company travelled one of his relations, a chaplain from southern Tuscany called Hildebrand, who thus appears in history for the first time. Three days later a synod in Rome also deposed Benedict in order to dispose of the last remaining claim, and then at Henry's request raised bishop Suidger of Bamberg to the papal throne as Clement II. Henry received the imperial crown at Clement's hands. When the Romans also bestowed the patriciate upon Henry, they mingled in this title memories of the dignity the popes had once conferred on the Carolingians with the office which the counts of Tusculum had inherited from the former rulers of Rome when they replaced them in 1012. The decisive voice at papal elections which he thus gained was the vital thing from Henry's point of view, for it excluded the influence of the nobles and made it possible for him to appoint members of the German imperial Church to the papacy. The merely practical and often indirect control over the papacy which recent rulers had exercised was now replaced by a full authority like that of the Ottos. Just as in the days of Otto the Great, the papacy stood only to gain in moral tone and universal significance by being taken out of party strife in Rome and put under the imperial wing. The reformers placed all their hopes in Henry, and as long as he lived none of them thought of challenging him. But a new hierarchical spirit, strong and self-assured, immediately grew up on the soil of Rome itself.

The short pontificates of the first two German popes whom Henry appointed are noteworthy only for the spread of German influence everywhere in Rome and particularly in the papal chancery. After them, with Leo IX (1048–54), began the papacy's great leap forward; alternatively, it might be said that Leo—of course in amicable cooperation with his cousin the Emperor—prepared the springboard for this leap.

Bishop Bruno of Toul came of a family of Alsatian counts. He was of striking appearance and of a kindly and winning nature, with a gift of gripping oratory, boundless energy and immense drive. He brought from his bishopric to Rome a great enthusiasm for reform of the Lotharingian type. Although the subsequent canonical election by clergy and people which he made a condition of his acceptance of the papacy was perhaps little more than the customary acclamation, the fact that he demanded it betrayed not only consideration for the Romans but also a tendency towards independence. It was consistent with this that henceforth the dating of papal documents by the regnal years of the emperor disappeared for good.

The universality of the papacy depended upon its self-sufficiency. Leo reshaped the college of cardinals, to fit it for the greater tasks he had in mind for it. Until now it had been a purely spiritual body, whose functions were limited to supporting the pope in the fulfilment of his liturgical obligations; but now it began to play the part of a senate in the government of the Roman Church. The circle from which it was recruited was enlarged correspondingly: the clergy of Rome and the bishops of the Patrimony were now for the first time joined by outstanding foreigners, particularly from Burgundy and Lorraine, reformers who had not been exposed to the influence of the Roman nobles and were well-informed about conditions north of the Alps. The great figures of the struggle that was to follow now appear among the advisers of the pope—men like Frederick, the brother of duke Godfrey of Upper Lorraine, Humbert of Moyenmoutier, the great publicist, the restlessly ambitious Hugh Candidus and (though at first only in the modest office of subdeacon) the monk Hildebrand, who had by now returned from Germany to Italy.

With the lively support of the emperor, Leo and his helpers now began a reforming activity which, although it was only mild at first, continued the work of Henry II's later years and aimed at putting into force the decrees against simony and the marriage of the priesthood and at securing a general purification of Church life. It is in the same light that we should regard the decree of the Council of Reims in 1049 which forbade the assumption of ecclesiastical office without canonical election; this was designed primarily as a measure against simoniacs from outside the diocese, although of course formal election could at any time be given real substance as well. Most important of all was the universalist character which Leo regained for the papacy. In the short years of his pontificate he crossed the Alps six times; everywhere he assembled the clergy around him in synods or at the great feasts of the Church. He was constantly on the move, intervening repeatedly in church affairs in the spirit of the pseudo-Isidorian decretals—which now for the first time found widespread acceptance—and drawing tighter his control over the metropolitans. The French and German bishops, accustomed to considerable independence, regarded him with misgiving; but monks and people welcomed him with jubilation wherever he went. Everywhere he accumulated invaluable prestige for the papacy, and laid the foundations for a really active and widespread ecclesiastical government.

A measure of the independent spirit in which this universalist policy was pursued is provided by Leo's attempt to extend the revived Roman primacy to the east as well, an attempt which through the clumsiness of Humbert—whose writings at this time exalt the new apostolic Rome over the pagan and sinful city of the past—succeeded only in widening the breach with the Byzantine Church. Leo's self-confidence and his drive for independence appear also in his efforts, along with the 'two arms of the Church' —the western Emperor and the Greek Basileus—to combat the turbulent Normans in the south and to secure a sphere of influence for the papacy there. Frequent references to the Donation of Constantine are a characteristic of these efforts. Under the leadership of the princes of Salerno, the Normans had spread out from the county of Aversa by conquering Apulia; the days of Byzantium in the south of Italy were numbered. Henry III had paid little attention to this confused situation during his stay in Rome, though he had given the Normans imperial confirmation of their newly-won territories. It was at this time that Robert Guiscard began the occupation of Calabria.

The progressive destruction of Byzantine power in the south of Italy was in itself welcome enough to the pope, for the Roman Church would thereby regain provinces lost to it since the Iconoclastic Controversy. But Leo sought to extend political and ecclesiastical influence together, and this the Normans violently resisted. Conflict flared up over Benevento, which did homage to the pope in 1051 to protect itself from the Normans. Leo seized the opportunity eagerly, without sufficiently considering imperial claims to sovereignty over the city. But when the papal army fled from the field of battle, Leo was forced to seek help from Henry by going to Germany. The results of their meeting were remarkable. Henry showed himself ready to promote Leo's territorial ambitions. In return for concessions on Leo's part in Germany, in particular his renunciation of the valuable papal rights of ownership over Fulda and Bamberg, Henry transferred Benevento to the pope (though reserving imperial sovereignty) and assembled an army to protect it. Although the drawbacks of Leo's independence had already been apparent in a charter which reduced the patriarchal rights of German Aquileia in favour of Venetian Grado, Henry seems to have discounted the idea that the curia could ever be hostile to the empire. The German bishops, led by Gebhard of

Eichstätt, strongly opposed the use of German resources for
outside purposes, however, and this decided Henry to recall most
of his troops.

But Leo felt that his alliance with the Byzantines of south Italy
made him strong enough to take the offensive alone; the result was
his total defeat at Cività in 1053. The pope himself fell into the
hands of the Normans and was forced to give up his territorial
plans. He was released when he became seriously ill, but died
soon afterwards in Rome (1054). The first attempt to set up papal
dominion over south Italy had collapsed, but it nevertheless
settled the direction of future policy. The Norman proposal—
made before the battle but refused by Leo because he thought
himself strong enough to do so—pointed the way forward: they
offered to hold all their conquered lands as a papal fief and to pay
tribute for them.

The curia was plainly still dependent on the strength and
goodwill of the emperor, however, and could not follow an
independent policy. Henry's participation in the choice of a
successor to Leo was essential, for instance, and the movement for
papal independence suffered a setback when Henry appointed the
leader of the German opposition to Leo's Norman policy,
Gebhard of Eichstätt (who was related to the royal house), as
Victor II (1055–7) and sought through him to keep Church
reform within the bounds dictated by state interest. Far more
than his predecessor, Victor retained his former character as
Henry's supporter and a loyal bishop of the empire. He secured
from Henry a comprehensive restoration of lost possessions of St.
Peter in the Romagna which had formerly belonged to the exarchate, but this imperial confirmation of his specifically Roman
position meant that he turned his back on southern Italy; while the
offices of duke of Spoleto and margrave of Fermo, which Henry
conferred on him, were intended to counterbalance the new threat
presented by the recent alliance of Tuscany and Lorraine.

Henry had the reins in his hands at last. He still held the
imperial Church in strict dependence upon himself. The right of
appointment which the patriciate gave him enabled Henry to
make his influence over the papacy felt on several occasions
within a short period of time. Scarcely any danger threatened
from this direction while he lived. Yet he had raised the papacy to
a position of power which, although at the time it never equalled

his own, was bound to overtop his successor's if the latter was a child.

The rest of his domestic policy also turns upon his relations with the Church. Gifts to the Church were increasing again after the pause in Conrad's reign, and the royal estates were correspondingly diminished; this was not all loss, however, for further resources made the bishops' power greater and in particular increased the capacity of those on the eastern frontier to resist an invasion. The bishops remained the chief support of the government and provided the greater part of its administration, and Henry placed the greatest emphasis on their political usefulness as well as on their suitability as clergy. Scarcely anyone conceived at this time that their dual position could ever be denounced by the reformers as uncanonical. The other forms of administration which Conrad's more secular nature had preferred were pushed into the background. The rise of the *ministeriales* and the growth of the west German towns continued, but without much encouragement from above; and Henry did not show as much care for the extension of the immediate royal estates as his father had done. Having renounced simoniacal gifts from the clergy, he was compelled to demand similar payments from secular officials and from vassals when they took up their positions, and was consequently accused of extortion. Because he was so friendly to the Church, he was little to the liking of the lay nobility whom Conrad had tried to unite on both sides of the Alps, and the discontent of the nobles made itself felt in all parts of the Empire. At first Henry's power was overwhelming, but the multiplicity of his obligations prevented him from keeping a constant watch on the duchies of Bavaria, Swabia and Carinthia, all of which had been directly subject to him at the beginning of his reign. To keep the unruly local nobles in check, he bestowed these duchies as early as the 1040's on men from other tribes—since he had as yet no sons to whom he could give them—but not all of them proved worthy of his trust. The growing discontent was at its greatest in Saxony and Lorraine, the two duchies which had the strongest sense of independence from the Empire. The danger from Saxony lay in the future, but in Lorraine it was of immediate significance.

Henry had specially close connexions with Saxony, where the Ottonian family possessions had become undisputed imperial property. Goslar, whose prosperity was growing because of its silver mines, was one of his favourite resorts, and there he built a magnificent palace and richly endowed his new cathedral of St. Simon and St. Jude, setting up in it a training school for the clerical administrators of the empire. The growth of the emperor's power on Saxon soil filled the duke and the Saxon nobility with misgiving, but further disagreements arose between Henry and the new archbishop of Bremen, Adalbert, who was appointed in 1043.

There is hardly a personality of the time who comes so completely to life today as Adalbert, thanks to Adam of Bremen's vivid description of him. Adalbert was the handsome, gifted son of a Thuringian count, born to authority and endowed with a bold and soaring spirit, utterly devoted to the high calling he had chosen and yet full of restless ambition and a proud and sensitive vanity, deeply imaginative and at the same time capable of enjoying worldly pleasures to the full. He endowed the cathedral of Bremen with his own rich inheritance of two thousand peasant holdings, and refused Henry's offer of the papacy in 1046 because he preferred his own archbishopric. He spent a lifetime in the service of the church of Hamburg-Bremen, always seeking to extend its spiritual and temporal influence by means which included cunning, violence and even the forging of documents, so that his tireless energy eventually over-strained his resources and some of his plans came to nothing.

The history of German relations with the northern lands is closely bound up with the imposing figure of Adalbert. He promoted the existing missionary efforts on a wide scale and with the greatest energy. His first great success was won in the neighbouring Wendish kingdom, which was ruled by the converted Abotrite prince Gottschalk: the bishoprics of Mecklenburg and Ratzeburg, which were founded there about 1060, were put under the metropolitan jurisdiction of Bremen, and from them missionaries penetrated still deeper into Wendish territory.

In the northern kingdoms too, particularly in Denmark, great opportunities were presented to the archbishop of Bremen by the collapse of Canute's empire, and Adalbert succeeded in giving the Danish Church its permanent organisation. But a growing national solidarity demanded ecclesiastical independence as well. In order to combine this irresistible pressure with Bremen's rights, Adalbert planned to establish a patriarchate over the territorial churches of the north, as a result of which Bremen would have had authority even over archbishops. In order to justify a rise in his status in accordance with the prescriptions of the Pseudo-Isidorian canons, Adalbert increased the number of his suffragans to twelve, a figure higher than his real needs. His plan was only partly successful in Rome, however. The pope applauded his direction of the missions and his organising ability, gave him the support he needed and the titles of legate and even of papal vicar; but to go beyond merely personal honours and set up a permanent intermediary between Rome and the northern churches would have been quite contrary to the whole absolutist trend of papal policy, and so Adalbert's schemes remained unfulfilled.

This scarcely checked Adalbert's wide and growing influence, however. Missionaries from Bremen travelled all over Scandinavia and penetrated as far as Finland, the Orkneys, Iceland and Greenland, and German trade naturally followed them.

So productive an activity abroad required a firm foundation at home. Adalbert did not confine himself to extending Church property in the dioceses of his province and keeping control of it entirely in his own hand, but sought also to bring as many as possible of the counties of northern Germany under his control, so as to obtain a quasi-ducal position like that which the bishop of Würzburg later obtained on a smaller scale. This was of course contrary to the interests of the secular nobility of Saxony, particularly to those of the Billung family, and their discontent naturally turned against Henry as well because of the specially favoured position which Adalbert held at the imperial court. As early as 1047 an attempt was made on Henry's life while he was visiting Adalbert at Lesum—by a brother of the duke of Saxony. The misgiving of which this was a sign grew steadily from this time onwards, but did not as yet lead to open rebellion.

On the other hand, Henry had to contend almost all through his reign with the opposition of Godfrey the Bearded of Upper Lorraine, to whom in 1044 he had refused possession of Lower Lorraine, which Godfrey's father Gozelo I had held. Two opposing views of the dukes' position were in conflict here: their rights of inheritance and their character as imperial officials. It is difficult to decide where to lay the blame—on Conrad II for uniting the two halves of the duchy (an action which stood him in

good stead against French claims to it), or on Henry III for
dividing up so large and threatening a frontier power and thereby
making a deadly enemy of its powerful and unscrupulous duke.
The frontier position of Lorraine was all the more awkward for
Henry because the war with Hungary, which broke out again in
1046, turned his attention in the opposite direction. Flanders,
which he had never subjected, gave Lorraine help openly, while
the French king Henry I gave it in secret. Henry had no fleet, and
he even tried to make up for his lack of one by employing Danish
and English ships in 1049. The combination of all these factors
made the continual risings in Lorraine extremely inconvenient
for Henry. Instead of crushing his irreconcilable enemy, he several
times accepted his submission, leaving him with Upper Lorraine
(or, later on, at any rate his private estates there), only to be
disillusioned once more by Godfrey's renewed hostility.

The marriage of Godfrey with Beatrix, the widow of Boniface
of Canossa, margrave of Tuscany, in 1054 was particularly
threatening for the Empire, since besides the estates she inherited
in Lorraine, Beatrix held the large properties and fiefs of the
house of Canossa and had secured the imperial offices of her first
husband; thus Beatrix wielded great influence in central and
northern Italy. This marriage threatened the dependence of the
papacy on the Empire and forced Henry to make his second
expedition to Rome in 1055. He took firm and not unsuccessful
action to hem Beatrix's power in by surrounding it. He gained the
support of the north Italian towns against the house of Canossa by
giving them grants of freedom and promoting their trade, and
Beatrix and her daughter Matilda fell into his hands. Godfrey
himself, however, had hastened back to Germany, where in
alliance with the south German opposition he raised a new
rebellion which spelt serious danger for Henry.

Dukes Conrad of Bavaria and Welf III of Carinthia, whom
Henry had himself appointed, had proved themselves unreliable.
It was perhaps the close links of the Emperor with the Bavarian
bishops which drove Conrad into rebellion in 1052; he was
deposed, replaced in turn by the two sons whom Agnes had borne
to Henry, and fled to Hungary, where the feudal suzerainty of the
Empire had only recently been asserted. Henry's vassal, Peter III,
had been overthrown as long ago as 1046 by an anti-German
rising, and under his successor Andrew the old frontier war began
again in 1050. Terms of peace satisfactory to the Empire seemed

possible in 1053; but the duke of Bavaria succeeded in renewing the war, in the course of which all German influence over Hungary was lost.

By ruthlessly exploiting the dynastic interest of the Salians in subjecting the duchies, duke Conrad set on foot a widespread plot during Henry's expedition to Rome in 1055; its object was to depose and murder Henry and set up Conrad in his place. The unexpected death of Conrad and Welf, the two chief conspirators, had brought this scheme to nothing by the time Henry returned from Italy, however, and Godfrey too had to submit. The available sources do not make it clear whether Henry pardoned Godfrey and released Beatrix and Matilda from prison during his lifetime, or whether this only occurred afterwards, perhaps in consequence of orders given by Henry as he lay dying; but it was certainly consistent with his magnanimous nature to carry Christian forgiveness well beyond the bounds of prudent statesmanship. He himself could rightly feel that he was capable of dealing with all opposition, although there had lately been critics who took an unfavourable view of his recent actions. It was too early to speak of a real weakening of his power, although under the surface there were growing all the forces which were, in combination, to bring disaster to his successor: the hostility of the lay nobility of Saxony and south Germany, the alliance of Lorraine and Tuscany, the papacy's struggle for independence, and the Normans of south Italy.

The real tragedy lay in the fact that the last years of a ruler who had peace more at heart than most others were disturbed by war and widespread discontent. Perhaps the task of bringing Church and state, kingdom and tribes, prelates and lay princes to agreement at a time when the reform movement had already gained momentum was beyond the power of a single individual. Henry was not yet forty when he died at his palace of Bodfeld in the Harz, and he was full of anxiety about the succession of the six-year-old son whom the princes had already elected and crowned king in 1053–4. It was due to Victor II, who happened to arrive at Bodfeld while Henry was dying and made himself the boy's guardian, that those princes who were present renewed their allegiance and thus secured the succession. Henry once again forgave all his enemies and begged their forgiveness before he died on 5 October 1056. Germany stood at a turning-point in her history.

3

THE EMPIRE DURING THE
MINORITY OF HENRY IV (1056-1065)

Victor II himself died soon afterwards, in 1057, so that Henry III's widow Agnes found herself facing, without advice, a task well beyond her powers. Agnes was a devout but weak and uncertain woman, lacking in political judgement and inclined to follow her own whims, and her feeble rule paved the way for future trouble. The men to whom she gave the dukedoms of south Germany were soon to show themselves extremely dangerous opponents of the crown: the Burgundian Rudolf of Rheinfelden, to whom she gave Swabia, the Saxon Otto of Nordheim, who received Bavaria, and the Swabian Berthold[1] whom she appointed to Carinthia. Loss of power at home and failure abroad recalled the bad days of Otto III's minority, but the great measure of independence which the papacy gained for itself in the decade after Henry III's death makes any such comparison very much to the disadvantage of his son.

On the death of Victor II, the reform party took the law into their own hands and elected Frederick, the brother of duke Godfrey of Lorraine, as Stephen IX (1057-8). Godfrey, who was at this time extending his central Italian power to include Fermo and Spoleto, was expected to protect the independence of the papacy, even against the Empire if necessary. Stephen's election hinted at the direction in which affairs were moving, but the short duration of his pontificate robbed it of further significance. At the next election the reformers were only able to defend themselves against renewed pressure from the Roman nobility by admitting their dependence on the Empire and securing Agnes's sanction for their candidate. He called himself Nicholas II—a name which, by recalling the great pope of the ninth century, was a programme in itself—and the three years of his pontificate were of the greatest importance for the future of the papacy. They saw consolidation,

---

[1] Berthold's descendants later called themselves after their castle of Zähringen in Breisgau.

preparation for the future, and the definition of the objectives towards which the reformers were aiming; these objectives were symbolised by the double-hooped mitre, indicating a claim to supremacy over the German kingdom and Empire, which Nicholas II seems to have been the first to wear.[1]

Cardinal Humbert of Silva Candida's *Adversus simoniacos*— probably the greatest of the publicistic writings of the whole Investiture period—had been finished during the preceding vacancy, in the summer of 1058; in it the ultimate goal of the clerical reform party was for the first time made unmistakeably clear. Humbert did not only define simony as heresy and declare all ordinations by simoniacs invalid; he also condemned as heresy the conferment by laymen of churches or monasteries or of any property rights in them as well as the investiture of laymen with ecclesiastical possessions or rights. Churches and all their property were thus to be removed entirely from lay control—a complete reversal of prevailing legal conceptions and the establishment, in their place, of a divinely-ordained hierarchical order. It was proclaimed that secular prostitution of the virgin purity of the Church had begun with the Ottos, and the investiture of clergy with the ecclesiastical symbols of ring and staff by lay hands was condemned and declared of no effect—still more so if the ceremony was performed by a woman. The only right conceded to the secular power was that of consenting to the election of bishops; all wider claims were rejected. Not reform alone, but the freedom of the Church was now the ultimate objective, and popular revolution was already in mind as a means of securing it. But in view of the way in which the two spheres were inseparably interlinked, the freedom of the Church was bound to lead to its supremacy over earthly powers, because of the ancient imagery which compared the priesthood to the soul and the kingship to the body and gave the former authority over the latter.

Moderate reformers like Peter Damiani—who was summoned from his hermitage of Fonte Avellana in the Romagna to the cardinalate—would not draw conclusions so drastic and so likely to disturb the peace of the world. The more radical group however, took its stand on this clearly defined programme, carried the hesitant pope along with it, and gained the dominant voice in Rome;

---

[1] The symbolism of this new form of papal mitre is explained by Ullmann, *Growth of Papal Government*, 313–4.

among its leaders, apart from Humbert (who died in 1061), an ever more decisive influence was exercised by Hildebrand, who was now promoted from subdeacon to be archdeacon of the Roman Church. His friends called him the 'keen eye' of the pope; an enemy wrote that 'he fed his Nicholas in the Lateran like an ass in its stall'. From now until he became pope himself, Hildebrand was responsible for all the most important decisions of the curia.

The Lateran synod of 1059 at once showed the influence of Humbert's tract by forbidding lay investiture, but it sought above all to preserve the papacy from further interference and to maintain the dominance of the reforming party by new regulations for the election of a pope; and here too Humbert played a decisive part. In future, the cardinal bishops alone were to have the right of proposing a candidate whom the rest of the cardinals could then either accept or reject, while the remainder of the clergy and people of Rome were to retain only a formal right of consent; thus the influence of the Roman nobility on elections was to be excluded once and for all. This, and the legalisation of certain irregularities in Nicholas's election, were the two main objects of the new decree. Besides this, however, the decree represented a unilateral alteration of the imperial rights over papal elections which Henry III had regularly exercised and which had recently been strengthened by his assumption of the office of *patricius*, rights which were here recognised only in an obscure reference to the personal prerogative of Henry IV (and even this was missing from the decree in which the synod's decisions were announced to Christendom).[1] The reformers still sought to avoid an open breach with the imperial government, but they looked round in good time for allies in case conflict should arise sooner or later.

Godfrey of Lorraine's central Italian power at once suggested itself as a natural support. In south Italy, however, a notable change came over papal policy at Hildebrand's instance. Like Leo III, Stephen IX had hoped to strengthen the curia by overthrowing the power of the Normans. The impossibility of doing this was now realised, and the same result was achieved by a friendly understanding with them. Both Norman leaders were recognised as rulers of the lands they had succeeded—partly at

---

[1] The contrasting attitudes of Humbert and Damian are illustrated by extracts from the writings of each in Tierney 36–42. Pullan 131–4 prints a passage from Humbert. The 1059 Election Decree and prohibition of lay investiture are in Tierney 42–4, Pullan 134–5.

the Church's expense—in occupying: Richard of Aversa as prince of Capua, and Robert Guiscard, the ruthless conqueror and crafty diplomat, as duke of Apulia, Calabria and (when he should conquer it) of Sicily as well. In return, the Normans in 1059 promised tribute and armed assistance, and recognised the feudal supremacy of the papacy over all these territories,[1] although such lordship could be justified by no legal title and in fact contradicted well-founded claims on the Empire's part. The Norman sword at once served its purpose against the Roman nobility by securing the pope entry to Rome, and it might at some future time provide protection against the Empire. The curia found useful allies in northern Italy too. In Milan, there had been a change in the social basis of party groupings since the days of Conrad II; then, there had been divisions among the nobles and co-operation between the archbishop and the citizens, but now the lower classes were rising and were hostile to the higher clergy and the whole of the nobility, who were bound together by identity of interests, family relationships and the desire to preserve their privileges. In the last year of Henry III's life this democratic movement had become linked with the movement for Church reform which, worked up by impassioned agitators who exploited social prejudice, had turned against the simony and priestly marriage which were particularly common among the Lombard clergy. This Milanese Pataria was thus the first manifestation of the popular revolution which Humbert was shortly to describe in his *Adversus simoniacos*. Inflammatory speeches which described the masses of married priests as dogs' dung and their churches as cowsheds led to the breaking up of church services and the mobbing of priests, and finally to open revolt. Both parties turned to Rome. Once more it was Hildebrand, who had recognised the value of the Pataria to the papacy as long ago as the time of Stephen IX, who brought about a close alliance between the two, principally through the influence of Damiani. The alliance benefitted the curia at once. Under its pressure the weak archbishop of Milan, Wido, took an oath of obedience to the pope, and by receiving his office a second time from the pope's hands through the symbol of a ring clearly admitted that his earlier simoniacal appointment by the emperor had been invalid. Here again the advancing claims of the reform party clashed with those of the Empire.

[1] Guiscard's oath to Nicholas II is in Tierney 44.

F

The papacy thus disposed of allies in all parts of Italy when the conflict now broke out with unexpected suddenness, for the repeated invasions of imperial rights could not be tolerated even by the weak German government of the time. As early as the pontificate of Nicholas II, diplomatic relations had been broken off and a German synod had condemned the pope and declared his innovations void. His death in 1061 led to open schism. But it was only the reformers who knew what their objectives were and had the strength to achieve them. With Norman help, Hildebrand immediately raised bishop Anselm of Lucca to the papal throne as Alexander II (1061–73); Anselm was a strong supporter of the Pataria, though this had not in fact made the imperial court regard him as an enemy. It was a month before the imperial government let itself be dragged by the Italian opponents of reform, the Roman nobles and the Lombard bishops, into recognising their antipope Cadalus of Parma as Honorius II, and even then it was half unwilling and made no effort to support him. The Empire from which the renewal of the papacy had sprung was now plunged into confusion and forced to change course suddenly. On the side hostile to reform, the party which looked to the past, the struggle was to be led by an Empress-regent who at once took the veil of a nun as a sign of her devotion to clerical ideals. The German bishops might well have been startled by the curia's immediate attempt to reduce them to mere instruments of the papal will by demanding an oath of obedience from the metropolitans and requiring them to come to Rome in person for their *pallia*, but they either remained lukewarm or actually recognised Alexander. Irresolution and precipitancy marked the German government's measures, which were determined only by the influences of the moment; under such conditions victory was not to be expected.

The growing discontent of the ecclesiastical and secular magnates with the regime of favourites at court, his own personal ambition, and above all the conviction that imperial policy had taken a wrong turn by allying with the opponents of reform, led archbishop Anno of Cologne to the coup d'état of Kaiserswerth in 1062; his action was taken with the foreknowledge of Godfrey of Lorraine and of Otto of Nordheim, the duke of Bavaria, and it put both the person of the young king and the conduct of the imperial government into his hands and forced the empress to withdraw from secular affairs and to spend the rest of her days mainly in Rome.

Anno was sole regent for a year. His chief rival was Adalbert of Bremen, proud and masterful like him, and as much concerned for his own and his church's advancement. Anno sought to secure a middle position between crown and curia which was in fact untenable; and because he was narrower and more short-sighted in outlook and less agreeable personally than Adalbert, the latter was able to win for himself a position close to the young king and to dispute Anno's influence by 1063.

The change of government had brought with it a complete change in attitude towards the conflict of Church and state. The new regency did not feel itself in any way bound to the antipope, and from the beginning sought an understanding with Alexander II which would at least preserve some imperial authority if not full imperial rights; while Alexander, like Cadalus, expected the settlement of the schism to follow from some decisive stroke by duke Godfrey. Anno's point of view gained the day against the Lombards' at the synod of Augsburg in 1062, where it was decided not to dispute the election of Alexander II, although it had taken place without imperial participation, but to make recognition of him dependent on an inquiry into the charge of simony which had been brought against him. The charge was soon shown to be groundless, but the continuation of the struggle for Rome between the two popes called for renewed intervention by the German government. At the synod of Mantua in 1064 Anno and the German bishops might well think that they held the decisive voice in the settlement of the schism, but Alexander—who presided over it and took an oath purging himself of the charge of simony, but carefully avoided revealing the treaty with the Normans—was in reality in a commanding position from the outset. The imperial rights in papal elections were tacitly set aside and the reforming papacy emerged from the struggle stronger than ever.

The hopes of its Lombard opponents lived on, however, so long as Cadalus was alive (though excommunicate), and at least able to maintain himself in his bishopric of Parma; and Cadalus did not die until 1071. Henry IV, who in spite of his youth had been declared of age in 1065, might have been able to play a part in the Italian party struggles and might even have secured the imperial crown, had not his planned expedition to Rome been blocked by archbishop Adalbert, who reached the height of his influence after Anno went to Italy in 1064 and would not surrender it again to his rival.

It is as false to suggest (as the Saxon party legend does) that Adalbert gained Henry's favour at this time by pandering to his lowest desires as it is to suppose, with Nitzsch and his followers, that Adalbert planned a great nationalist revival in imperial policy and tried to strengthen the economic resources of the crown. It is true that he gained credit for the successful campaign which temporarily imposed German authority upon Hungary in 1063, that his personal advantage coincided in large measure with that of the crown (which granted him large rights and great possessions in Saxony), and that the grandiose plans for a patriarchate which he was even then engaged in making helped to promote German interests in the northern lands. But in hindering the Roman expedition he acted from purely selfish motives, and his scheme to distribute the wealthiest German abbeys among the German bishops (the chief share falling to himself) would, had it been carried out, have cut the life-line of the imperial government. It was this scheme which led to his fall; for the higher aristocracy, under Anno's leadership, objected to the sole advancement of one of themselves. At the Diet of Tribur in 1066 Henry was compelled to dismiss Adalbert in disgrace; his Saxon enemies at once rose against him and reduced the territory of the archbishopric of Bremen to scarcely a third of its former extent. Finally, a counter-blow by the heathen Slavs of the right bank of the Elbe, the Abotrites and others, did serious damage to both the empire and to Christendom.

There was now another chance for Henry to lead an army into Italy, since the advance of the Norman Richard of Capua in Campania presented a threat that made even the curia desire it for a moment; this time it was Godfrey (duke of Lower Lorraine since 1065) who frustrated it, out of concern for his own influence in Italy. Hildebrand, to whom any imperial intervention was unwelcome, at once restored the earlier relations with the Normans, who now confined themselves to southern conquest and by capturing Palermo in 1072 took what proved to be the decisive step towards the conquest of Sicily.

The schism had finally ended with the death of Cadalus a short time before this. It was the first time that a pope appointed by the Empire had not been victorious. From now on, however, no imperially-appointed pope was ever to succeed. This alone shows the enormous change which had come about in the relations of Empire and papacy. The decade following the death of Henry III, with its history of instability, disintegration and princely self-interest, is one of the most shameful periods in German history. The position of the young king was seriously weakened by it before he could begin to play his own part in government.

HENRY IV AND GREGORY VII BEFORE
THE CONFLICT (1065–1075)

Henry IV and Gregory VII henceforth hold the stage. Each
has been reviled and misunderstood, both by enemies in their own
time and by succeeding ages, but Henry's difficult character has
suffered more, and more lastingly, than the iron figure of the pope.
The hostile sources have preserved a cruel caricature of the
emperor, almost worse than Suetonius' descriptions of the
Caesars; they depict him as a revolting mixture of lust and cruelty,
either a kind of Bluebeard or sunk in unnatural vice, neglecting his
duties as ruler in order to indulge his own evil desires, the breaker
of every law, a second Nebuchadnezzar. In this form his memory
lived on for centuries, until at last Protestant historians of the
Reformation period revealed that some of his contemporaries held
a more favourable opinion of him and inscribed his name on their
banner as one of their forerunners in the fight against the hierarchy.
But they too allowed party prejudice to distort the evidence. It
was only the source-criticism of the nineteenth century which
created the foundation for a really historical judgement, but even
today opinion is not entirely agreed.

Henry was a well-built and attractive man, and of great
physical toughness in spite of frequent illnesses. Even his enemies
praise his shrewdness, his penetrating insight and his persuasive
tongue. He had grown up under the guardianship of clerics, who
had given him a good literary education: he knew Latin, enjoyed
reading and learned discussion, and had a feeling for music and
architecture. Inclinations like these did not reflect his deeper self,
however; he was unaffected by the clerical and moral principles
of his father, and his nature was more akin to that of the thoroughly
secular Conrad. As a young man he reacted violently against the
restraints he had suffered as a child, and with defiant self-will used
his freedom to live a dissolute life. He only gave up his attempts to
secure the annulment of his marriage to Bertha of Turin—to
whom he had been engaged at five and married at fifteen—when

the pope refused it, and this strengthened the rumours about his frivolous conduct and gave rise to slanders the embellishment of which by legend can be followed in the sources.

A childhood full of discouragement, during which he had been exploited and allowed only the semblance of power, had created in Henry a pride in his office so intense that it could easily under-estimate the opposing forces, but it was founded on a strong feeling for the dignity of the Empire, the preservation of the dynasty and the prerogatives of kingship. All his actions were governed by the purpose of defending his rights. Henry pursued this object through a life of constant disturbance punctuated by dreadful blows of fate which allowed no rest to a passionate nature torn between over-confidence and self-doubt. Lacking the gifts of statesman or general and devoid of any real understanding of the irresistibly rising forces of his time, in essence he defended his rights by the means which the predatory nobles of his day were accustomed to use—trickery, deceit, forgery, and all the methods of a crafty diplomacy the sudden twists of which sometimes gained surprising success but were bound in the end to destroy all faith in his honour and trustworthiness. His endurance and tenacity in the thirty-year-long struggle were remarkable, however, as was the constant personal effort which even made him able to bear the severest disappointments for the sake of the end in view, his inexhaustibly combative spirit and the unusual gift of regaining his poise after almost hopeless defeat. In his later years he showed a desire for peace and social adjustment, and right to the end steadfastly refused to surrender the prerogatives of the crown. Even so bitter an enemy as Lampert of Hersfeld praised his royal spirit when he wrote 'he would rather die than give in'.

Henry began as a revolutionary seeking to overthrow the constitution, it is often said, only to end as its last defender, but this neat formula (which originated with Nitzsch) scarcely expresses the whole truth. Both the temperament and the tactics of the young man who rushed 'like a mettlesome charger into battle' were very different from those of the prematurely aged king who was forced back on the defensive, but the object was in each case the same: to preserve and strengthen the royal power and to regain the possessions and the rights which the monarchy had lost during the years of his minority. This policy was reactionary, not revolutionary. But it could not be achieved with the help of the nobility, who had benefited from the events of recent decades. Shortly before his death in 1072, Adalbert of Bremen was the only one among them to gain any prominence at court, and he perhaps suggested Henry's policy of recuperation; apart from him, however, the lesser vassals and the *ministeriales* gained an increasing influence over the king.

An increase in the territorial power of the crown was to be expected principally from the establishment and extension of the royal possessions in Saxony, which had been inherited from the Ottos. From the late sixties it became clear that the object was to extend the royal domain between the Harz and the Thuringian forest and even farther east into the Mark of Meissen, so as to create a firm economic basis for the monarchy and enable it to be independent of the will of the nobility; had it come about, this would have been as important for Germany as the Capetian domain later was for France. The means by which Henry sought to attain this goal closely resemble those of the young Frederick II in Sicily, where the situation was similar. It was a struggle against the recent usurpations, conducted with every legal weapon and in disregard of the special rights of the Saxon tribe which Henry II had recognised and which were now broken down by the royal courts' inquisition procedure, with its presiding judges and its preference for the testimony of witnesses over oath-helpers and trial by battle—a new procedure quite foreign to the Saxons. Castles were built on a large scale, to dominate the local inhabitants, while strong garrisons of south German *ministeriales* ensured the security of territory gained by confiscating the property of outlaws and by laying claim to ownerless land. This policy of territorial expansion seems to have run counter to the interests of the duke of Bavaria, Otto of Nordheim (probably the ablest statesman and strategist in Germany) because his Saxon allods and fiefs bordered the royal domain. A man was found to bring a charge of high treason against Otto, whom Henry had hated since the events of Kaiserswerth and who now stood inconveniently in his way. When Otto, who was plainly innocent, put himself formally in the wrong by refusing trial by battle, Henry quickly and craftily used this to bring about his fall and to force him to submit in 1071 in spite of his stubborn resistance and his alliance with Magnus, the son of duke Ordulf of Saxony. Otto lost his duchy, which was given to his son-in-law Welf IV, the founder of the younger Welf line, which was descended from Azzo II of Este and was related to the elder line only through females. Otto was later pardoned and regained his allods, but his reduced power was no hindrance to Henry's plan for strengthening the royal estates. There is no doubt that the idea of creating for the crown a firm basis in a key position in the heart of Germany between Saxony and Bavaria was as bold as it was sound, but the violent and hasty way in which it was carried out awakened lively resistance. Property and men whom usurpation had made free were now being forced back into a dependent condition, so that their privileges were endangered and slavery seemed to stare every Saxon in the face; even their tribal independence seemed to be in the balance when, on the death of duke Ordulf in 1072, Henry delayed the release of his successor Magnus from the prison into which he had been thrown for his support of Otto of Nordheim. A general discontent, spreading from the aristocracy to the people, led to the great Saxon rising of 1073, and Otto of Nordheim was soon the leader of it.

Henry was surprised in the Harzburg and only escaped with the greatest difficulty. His position became critical when he was deserted by the Thuringians and refused help by the nobility—by the lay nobles because they distrusted his whole policy, and by the prelates because of his increasing financial demands and a renewal of the simony which was so profitable to him—and he was forced for a time to treat with the rebels. He was threatened with a charge similar to that which he had made use of against Otto of Nordheim; this was plainly a plot on the part of his enemies to alienate the south German dukes (whom he was said to have instigated attempts to murder) still further from him. His fortunes took their first turn for the better when he moved towards the Rhine and the citizens of Worms joined him, driving out their anti-royalist bishop and welcoming him within their walls. In Worms and soon afterwards in Cologne—that is to say, in that Rhineland area which was from the economic and cultural point of view the most advanced in the whole of Germany—were to be seen the first signs of a struggle by the new citizen bodies in the towns to free themselves from the rule of their bishops, signs like those which had been evident in Italy for the past half-century or more. The political significance of this by no means widespread popular movement must not be exaggerated; it only benefited imperial

authority in Worms (whose merchants were exempted from taxes
in return for their support), and archbishop Anno cruelly
suppressed the revolt in Cologne. The movement had more
importance for the future than in the present: it indicated the
possibility that a friendly relationship between the monarchy and
the towns, which now became a feature of Henry's reign, might
one day be as important for the German ruling house as for the
Capetians of France. The unexpected help of the urban revolutionary forces gave Henry immediate encouragement, however,
and checked the German episcopate by forcing them closer to the
king. Henry was able to nullify the acts of an assembly of nobles
at Mainz which attempted to assume jurisdiction over the Saxon
affair, and it seemed a judgement of God in his favour when his
accuser shortly went mad and died. He therefore risked a winter
campaign against the Saxons; he won over some of their leaders
with promises and (to the dismay of the south German dukes) got
them to agree to the peace of Gerstungen (1074) which settled the
quarrel temporarily on a compromise basis: crown property was
not to be reduced, but the rebels were to go unpunished, to keep
their old rights and to be allowed to demolish Henry's new
fortresses.

Soon after he had thus divided the German opposition he saw
an opportunity for annulling a compromise so hurtful to his pride.
When the angry Saxon peasants desecrated the church and the
graves of the royal family while they were pulling down the
royal castle of Harzburg, he proclaimed that they had broken the
peace, cleverly whipped up feeling against the Saxons and won
the majority of the nobles over to his side, with the result that
next year (1075) a large royal army (led by duke Rudolf) inflicted a
decisive defeat on them at Homburg on the Unstrut and soon
forced them to unconditional surrender.

Henry had gained his object: the Saxon leaders were in his
power, he could annex still more of their property, and the
reconstruction of the fortresses could start at once. The desired
economic foundation for the monarchy seemed to have been
secured, and the succession was made certain when the nobles
promised to elect Henry's twelve-month-old son Conrad as king.
He planned an expedition to Rome to receive the imperial crown.
But he was denied the undisturbed quiet that was essential if the
new situation was to be consolidated. The loss of crown estates

and the growth of independent authorities were only one aspect of his inheritance; beside them stood threateningly the newly-won independence of the papacy and the growing Church reform movement, to which Henry had not for many years paid sufficient heed. A clash with them was about to come.

As early as the synod of Mantua in 1064 the German bishops, with Anno of Cologne at their head, had flattered themselves that the fate of the papacy lay in their hands. Alexander II, whom they accepted at Mantua, showed them their mistake when he used every available means to destroy the independence of the German Church. Pleased, perhaps, at their humiliation, Henry IV gave the proud archbishops no support against the demands of Rome, but his failure to do so only helped to undermine the power of the monarchy. The curia soon came into conflict with the court over nominations to bishoprics, particularly Milan, and in 1073 excommunicated the royal advisers for their renewed simony (the king himself was for the moment spared). Conflict was in the air, and Rome's language grew steadily more severe. The death of Peter Damian in 1072 had removed the chief representative of the moderate reformers who were friendly towards the empire, and the decisive voice in papal policy had for a long time been that of cardinal Hildebrand whom (according to Damian) Alexander II called his 'God'. It had been the driving force of Hildebrand which had greatly widened the power-base of the reformed papacy in recent years by extending its authority to cover the Normans' new conquests in the south of Italy and taken advantage of the greater freedom of action which the death of duke Godfrey invited to do the same in the centre of the peninsula. Hildebrand's influence had also been behind the French knights who, increasingly inspired by clerical ideals, had helped the Cid Campeador to push forward the Christian frontier against Islam in Spain, while the papal banner under which the Normans had conquered England symbolised the carrying of continental reforming ideas across the Channel and the Romanisation of the upper classes of the Anglo-Saxon kingdom. Insofar as the Roman and German world of the south and west was becoming a clerical, social and cultural unity, there was being prepared the basis on which a reformed and strengthened papacy could declare war on the growing power of the Salian king with the object of freeing the Church from the grasp of the laity. On the day after Alexander

II's death in 1073 Hildebrand was elected pope as Gregory VII in the midst of a tumultuous assembly which demanded his elevation but thereby infringed the procedure laid down in the election decree of 1059.

The true significance of Gregory VII, like that of Henry IV, has only been understood quite recently. His contemporaries often thought him a sinister figure, and for centuries he was regarded as a self-seeking clerical tyrant. It is only in modern times that he has been properly assessed. A fiery spirit dwelt in the body of this short, pale and ugly fifty-year old Tuscan. He was not learned; but the tremendous natural penetration of his mind—and perhaps his inclination to fantasy—had no difficulty in seeing a clear and definite pattern behind the confusion of events. His was no cool and reflective temper; he was possessed by a mystical energy and a sense of his direct relationship with supernatural powers. Above all, he had a masterful will, steeled by the conviction that his cause was that of divine justice, and a demonic temperament which he could turn on those around him 'like a blast of the north wind' and which drew from Peter Damian the description 'Holy Satan'. Hildebrand, the monk of humble origin, felt himself called to free the Church from the fetters which the secular powers had put upon it. Simony and the marriage of priests had to be ended once and for all, the feudal and territorial tendencies in the Church broken down, the bishops turned into humble tools of an absolute papacy by the elimination of provincial synods and metropolitan rights, and the whole Church subjected to an all-pervasive papal will. This meant that the prohibition of lay investiture—hitherto more an ideal objective than a realistic policy—was now to be enforced in practice. The conflict of two systems of law—the deep-rooted customary law of the lay world on the one hand, and divine law on the other—was bound to be violent, for the eleventh century could not distinguish spiritual office from the property conferred by the lay power upon the possessors of it: in German proprietary church law the lord who had provided the endowments had authority over both, but canon law took the view that both had been removed from the temporal sphere by the action of dedicating them to God. Passionate as an Old Testament prophet, Gregory was not afraid of such a conflict, and often quoted the words of Jeremiah: 'Cursed be he that keepeth back his sword from blood'.[1]

---

[1] Jer. xlviii. 10.

If it was to overcome the forces ranged against it, the papal Church needed force itself. In order to secure and maintain its 'freedom' (that is, the God-ordained hierarchical order), it had to be the lord of the world. But this was a dangerous extension of previous reforming claims, for how could it be certain that purity would be preserved if the Church took a hand in political affairs? Would not the world in future be brought into the Church, just as up till now the Church had been brought into the world? At this point, Gregorian thought based itself squarely on Augustinian concepts. The Kingdom of God could only be realised on earth if the pope, the possessor of the apostolic power of binding and loosing which Christ had instituted, formed a bridge between the Here and the Hereafter and had the final right to decide whether the actions of earthly powers were good or evil. Everything else flowed together into this idea, and Gregory was its embodiment. All his thoughts and actions were dictated by it, and he could not understand any contradiction of it. He despised all who sought independence and their own goals, and held that no temporal right or custom could prevail against 'the prerogative of St. Peter'. Secular resistance taught him nothing and did not change him in the least; it simply made him lonely and suspicious. It is easy to understand that for so passionate, idealistic and combative a nature moral values were readily distorted: his opponents were damned, and everything which promoted his own supreme ideal naturally seemed acceptable—though we sometimes judge differently today. The precipitate haste with which Gregory sought legal justification for the Church's claims reversed the natural order of things either deliberately or accidentally, and led to astonishing distortions of the truth: to understand Gregory we must constantly bear in mind the outlook of the medieval clerics who so often turned even to forgery in order to extend the rights of their churches.

Gregory himself was always convinced that he was only restoring the ancient rights of the Church; but although he relied on Augustine and Pseudo-Isidore, he everywhere went beyond these ancient rights through the extremism of his formulations and the structural completeness of his thought. He converted at least one part of these claims into actual practice, and instituted propaganda of so violent and so lasting a character for the rest that it can never be forgotten. Hauck refuses to call him a great statesman because he had no sense of the possible; but Gregory was not content simply to reckon up possibilities—his aim was to be a reformer, a man who changed the entire world. The fact that so all-embracing an ideal could not be put into effect either completely or at once counts no doubt against the realism of the policy, but it can hardly count against the greatness of the man. Gregory threw the whole of his very considerable energy into the pursuit of an ideal, and to call his pontificate 'a series of defeats' is to overlook both the earlier successes of the papacy—for which he was largely responsible—and the fact that the influence of revolutionaries like Gregory does not end with their lives but often gains renewed impetus after their death. Ranke's opinion is more acceptable; he calls Gregory 'perhaps the greatest figure who had yet appeared in the field of ecclesiastical politics'.

Fiercely though Gregory advanced to the attack, his actions still show traces of cool calculation, of the ability to profit from party conflicts within states, and of opportunism—for instance, the completely different ways in which he dealt with England and Germany. The great blows of his policy were struck one after another in deliberate sequence, not wildly or at random: once the freedom of the papacy had been secured, there followed the establishment of the pope's absolute power in the Church; the loosening of the chains which bound prelates and their ecclesiastical property to secular society led to the prohibition of lay investiture and thus to the declaration of war on the lay powers, the Empire in particular; the Investiture Contest itself developed into a struggle for world-dominion when the pope used the well-trodden path of feudalism to move towards supreme authority over the individual states. Besides the case of the Normans in south Italy, Gregory had at first used this sort of claim only against weaker or more distant powers like Aragon, Provence, Croatia-Dalmatia, Hungary[1] and (for a short time) Kievan Russia, although he had made similar demands on the German anti-king, Spain and (in accordance with the Donation of Constantine[2]) the islands of England, Sardinia and Corsica as well. In Denmark, Poland and Bohemia, long-established customary payments or free-will offerings provided a precedent for further demands. Gregory's bellicose and imperious nature sought to reorganise

[1] Cf. Tierney 50–51.
[2] Pullan 8–11.

the papacy as a military power, and envisaged Europe as a unity under clerical leadership. In 1074 he planned a large-scale military expedition to the East, as a defence against the Seljuk advance through Asia Minor towards Constantinople, and one of its objects was to secure the adherence of the Greek Church to Rome. Although the liberation of the Holy Places was not its primary objective, and although it was never carried out, this plan was nevertheless a significant forerunner of the Crusading movement. The sentences which he entered in his Register for 1075 were intended to serve as guide-lines for his own future actions in founding and extending papal primacy. According to them (the Dictatus Papae), princes must kiss the pope's feet and he alone may use imperial insignia, depose emperors and release subjects from their obedience.[1] The more the Empire stressed its derivation from the Romans and disputed the papacy's claim to be the guarantor of European peace, and the tighter became the bonds that bound it to the German Church, the more violent was the conflict between papacy and Empire thus certain to become.

Gregory's and Henry's paths lay parallel at first, and for a time they did not cross. The king was fully engaged with German affairs, and the pope was preoccupied in Italy with the insubordination of Robert Guiscard, the disturbed condition of Rome and the opposition of the anti-reformist Lombard bishops. Further, a very submissive letter of 1073[2] from the young king—who hoped that it would serve to separate the pope from the German opposition —gave Gregory grounds to hope that Henry would give way. He thereupon began serious efforts to enforce priestly celibacy and to prohibit simony in Germany; both, of course, were by now well-established clerical demands. At once he met passive resistance from the German bishops, who foresaw that the bitter opposition of the married clergy would make rapid enforcement impossible, and who were in any case irritated by the pope's repeated invasion of their rights. But Gregory continued to bear heavily on the bishops—who had been deprived of energetic royal support by the disturbed state of Germany—and threatened them with severe penalties. A prominent part in all this was played by the contrast between the plebeian on the papal throne and the episcopal aristocrats, whose predominantly noble birth bound them up far

[1] Pullan 136–7, Tierney 49–50.
[2] Mommsen and Morrison 141–2, Emerton 18–19.

too closely with territorial interests for them to consider themselves passive instruments of the curia. Archbishop Liemar of Bremen wrote of Gregory in a private letter: 'This dangerous man takes it upon himself to order bishops about like servants on his estates; if they do not do everything he wants, they are either summoned to Rome or suspended without trial'. It was this contrast above all which drove the German bishops back on to Henry's side.

The Lenten Synod of 1075 in Rome brought important decisions. Since the properly established authorities of the Church had failed to put the reforms into effect, Gregory sponsored a revolution of the lay masses against the simoniacal and married priests by making strike action against them a matter of obligation. It was a risky step, for it encouraged popular violence and the ill-treatment of priests, and it soon caused the sacraments to be derided in Germany just as they already had been by the Patarini in Milan. It was a step, moreover, which flatly contradicted the whole principle of authority in the Catholic Church. Siegbert of Gembloux has described how it awoke excited discussion of the most serious subjects even among artisans in their workshops and women at their spinning-wheels.

It had even more weighty consequences when the pope forbade the German king to take any part in the appointment of prelates by prohibiting lay investiture at any rate before consecration, and threatened severe penalties for both parties.[1] The whole of German history since Otto the Great shows that such an action was equivalent in fact, if not in intention, to an attempt to strike at the root of imperial power. To deny to the king the nomination of bishops and the abbots of imperial abbeys was to deny him the right to choose the chief officials of the Empire, and by thus destroying his claims to the property of the imperial Church it also directly threatened the resources of the central power. No responsible German ruler could let an action of this kind pass unchallenged. Yet Gregory himself thought at first that he could delay an open breach, and made private advances to Henry for an agreement; he even congratulated him on the victory he had just won over the Saxons.[2] In return Henry took some account of the pope's demands for reform in the matter of simony, with the result

[1] Tierney 51–2.
[2] Emerton 83–5.

that the tension in the German Church was relieved for the time being.

The gulf that separated the two parties was too wide to be bridged by any such merely tactical agreement, however. The overthrow of his German opponents increased Henry's sense of power, and the renewed excommunication of five trusted advisers made him more intransigent towards the pope than ever. Now that his hands were free, he turned once more to Italy, and in direct opposition to the pope appointed and invested an archbishop in strife-ridden Milan, where the curia's allies the Patarini were having the worst of renewed conflicts. In a stern letter written towards the end of 1075 Gregory thereupon warned Henry that further disobedience might bring upon him the fate of Saul, and ordered the messengers who carried it to speak sharply about Henry's moral shortcomings and to threaten him with excommunication and deposition.[1] This was an ultimatum, and it made open conflict inevitable.

[1] Emerton 86–90.

G

5

THE CONFLICT BETWEEN HENRY IV
AND GREGORY VII (1075–1085)

If Gregory perhaps miscalculated when he acted with such
severity that he drove the king and the German bishops together,[1]
Henry did his cause even more harm when at the Synod of Worms
in January 1076 he overestimated the strength of his still uncertain
position and plunged himself precipitately into the threatened
conflict. The blame for this must lie with Henry's failure to grasp
the prevailing ideas of his time and his misreading of opinion in
Rome, with the unrelenting bitterness of the German bishops and
with the grossly slanderous accusations which Cardinal Hugh
Candidus (who had already deserted Gregory and been deposed)
brought against the pope's moral character at the synod by
suggesting that countess Matilda of Tuscany was Gregory's secret
mistress. Instead of branding the pope as the aggressor by defending the customary rights of the crown and calling for a modification
of clerical demands, Henry went at once to extremes by forcibly
denouncing Gregory and declaring that because of his irregular
election he had never been truly pope. Since Gregory had held
his office without dispute for three years, this was bound to make
him seem the innocent victim of unprovoked attack.

Besides the letter in which the German bishops (who were soon
joined by the north Italians) renounced him, Henry also sent
Gregory a manifesto in which he reproached him for his threat
to the monarchy and his ill-treatment of the bishops, cancelled all
Gregory's rights to the papacy by virtue of his own office of
patricius and demanded that he lay down his office. This letter
was then refashioned and broadcast among the German clergy.
Addressed to Hildebrand 'no pope, but false monk', it repeated the
accusations in a form suited to its propaganda purpose, and ended
dramatically with the words 'I, Henry, king by the grace of God,

[1] There was in addition already considerable opposition to him in both
France and Italy.

together with all our bishops, say to you: Come down, Come down!'[1]

When earlier German rulers deposed popes, they held the upper hand because their armies were in Italy. Henry was deluding himself if he thought that with a sheet of parchment and without striking a single blow he could overthrow a papacy which had grown much stronger since those days. Gregory answered the decree of Worms with a powerful counterstroke. In the solemn form of a prayer to St. Peter, the prince of the apostles, he excommunicated Henry at the Lenten Synod of 1076 in Rome, deposed him and absolved his subjects from their oaths of obedience: 'I bind him thus as commissioned by thee, that the nations may know beyond doubt that thou art Peter, that upon thy rock the Son of the Living God has built his Church and that the gates of hell shall not prevail against it.'[2]

In spite of everything in the situation as a whole which helps to explain Gregory's conduct, to expel a German king and Emperor-elect from the Church and depose him from the throne was a startling and absolutely unprecedented action, for it upset the sacramental balance of papacy and Empire. Did it completely reverse the traditional relationship between the two powers? Which of them would be victorious?

The hollowness of Henry's position became apparent very quickly. The external shock reopened the scarcely-healed internal wounds. By crippling the tyrant, the sentence of excommunication strengthened the right of resistance to tyranny permitted by German customary law. Supported by the Lombard bishops, Henry might answer one condemnation with another; he might point to the two swords offered to Christ in St. Luke's Gospel as symbols of the equal authority of pope and emperor;[3] he might feel himself secure enough, after the fateful murder of duke Godfrey of Lower Lorraine and Tuscany (who had been about to lead an Italian expedition), to give his German duchy to his own two-year-old son Conrad; but his affairs did not prosper. A new national council, summoned to decide upon the election of a new pope and an expedition to Rome, failed to assemble. Defections began during the summer in both north and south. The Saxon magnates, who had been entrusted as hostages to the safe-keeping

---

[1] Tierney 59–60, Pullan 138–140, Mommsen and Morrison 145–151.
[2] Tierney 60–61, Pullan 141–2.
[3] Cf. Mommsen and Morrison 16, 152.

of various princes, were allowed to escape; they hastened home
and called their people to arms. Even Otto of Nordheim, whom
Henry had won over by concessions and received into his confidence after the defeat of the Saxons, turned traitor after some
hesitation and put himself at the head of the rebels. The south
German dukes allied with the Saxon opposition, and a meeting
was fixed for Tribur in October to concert measures between
them.

How could a king with a divided and rebellious people at his
back fight a defensive war against an enemy as powerful as the
papacy? Moreover, Gregory wooed some of the bishops back to
obedience by the clever device of a sliding scale of penalties. His
object was still to force Henry to accept his reforming decrees, not
to annihilate him, and his legate to the Tribur meeting was given
instructions accordingly. Henry encamped with his army on the
left bank of the Rhine at Oppenheim. He was in no mood for
concessions until the legate seemed on the point of bringing about
a repetition of the Field of Lies at Colmar in 833 by shaking the
loyalty of some of his supporters and even persuading them to
cross the river to the other camp. He tried to prevent his enemies
from uniting by showing himself ready to treat with both parties,
for this seemed to offer the best chance of softening the blow to his
pride which the humiliation of the kingship by clerical power
represented. He came to an agreement with the legate which took
the wind out of the sails of the radical group among the princes
who wanted to elect a new king at once, and went so far to meet
the pope's demands that his representatives secured a temporary
understanding between him and Gregory. Admittedly, the
conditions were humiliating enough: he was to dismiss the excommunicated advisers, hand over the loyal citizens of Worms to
the mercy of the bishop whom they had driven out, lay down his
authority for a time, and write a letter of apology to the pope in
which he was to admit his faults and promise satisfaction and
obedience. Henry hoped to secure the pope's absolution by this
means, but it is unlikely that he was prepared to do more than
give a promise in very general terms or that he would really have
surrendered lay investiture. Indeed, the last sentence of the
letter he sent to Rome, demanding that the pope also purge himself
of the accusations made against him, was probably added
(quite contrary to the agreement) by the king's still unbroken

pride; and it had the result that the envoys of the German opposition, who had also been sent to Rome, were able to make it out to be a forgery.[1] For his part, Gregory was even less inclined to take Henry's advances at their face value and was readier than ever to accept the German nobles' invitation. Before the Tribur assembly dispersed, the nobles had agreed among themselves to deprive Henry of his crown if he had not secured his release from excommunication within a year, and they had invited the pope to a Reichstag in Augsburg to give judgement in their dispute with him. Gregory immediately accepted the invitation—which of course suited his purpose admirably, for it would give him the chance to play the German parties off against each other—rejected Henry's request to be allowed to come to Rome to seek absolution, and set off exultantly northwards. This at once lost Henry the advantage which he might have gained from the policy of dividing his enemies. They were now bound to draw still closer together in the near future, while his own situation at Speyer (where he spent the next few months in inactivity) was more uncertain than ever. It was at this point that he made the surprising decision to hurry to meet the pope in Italy, and by penance and submission force a quick absolution from Gregory himself; if the worst came to the worst, he could reckon on the support of the Lombard bishops.

With his wife, his two-year-old son and only a small retinue, Henry crossed the Mont Cenis in the depth of winter into Bertha's family domain in the neighbourhood of Turin, and moved on into Lombardy. The German nobles were so astonished by this turn of events that they failed to send Gregory the escort they had promised him, and Gregory had therefore to put off his journey and take refuge in countess Matilda's castle of Canossa. This was a first success for Henry who, however, disappointed his warlike Lombard supporters by appearing before the castle peacefully.

The steep cliffs of Canossa with their cramped and (in those days) impregnable castle rise a hundred and fifty feet above a bare plateau at the point where the Apennines are torn by the gorge of a torrent as they slope towards the level plain of the Po.[2] Henry probably spent three days in the village at their foot, praying and fasting, and in spite of the freezing weather presented

---

[1] Mommsen and Morrison 154–5.
[2] Canossa is 12 miles S.W. of Reggio Emilia.

himself in the dress of a penitent, barefoot and in a hair shirt, to beg admission at the castle gates—actions which hostile chroniclers later exaggerated into three days' and nights' continuous penitence amid snow and ice. Meanwhile negotiations went on through intermediaries like abbot Hugh of Cluny and countess Matilda herself, who was related to the Salian family. It was Matilda who finally overcame the pope's stubbornness and secured Henry's admission to the castle on 28 January 1077, just as he was on the point of departure. Henry came before Gregory in the garb of a penitent, bound himself by the solemn oath of the nobles present[1] to accept either the pope's mediation or his decision of the dispute with the German opposition within a period to be determined later, and undertook not to hinder the pope's journey to Germany or allow his supporters to do so.[2] Gregory then released Henry from excommunication and gave him Communion, although he did not (as Lambert of Hersfeld suggests) turn the Communion into a trial by ordeal. The prohibition of lay investiture seems not to have been discussed on this occasion, but at a second meeting six days later at Bianello, a little to the north of Canossa, the possibility of further negotiations at a council to be held in Mantua was mentioned. On his way to Mantua, Gregory was forced to turn back by the hostility of the Lombard bishops. Henry returned to Germany about Easter, on the news that an anti-king had been elected.

So much for the narrative. What is the significance of Canossa? Earlier writers describe it as a boundless triumph for the pope; more recent accounts call it a political victory for the king. It is essential not to exaggerate the success of either side, and to avoid judging medieval events by modern standards. Penance was not quite so humiliating in eleventh-century eyes as it is today; but on the other hand it would be perverse to represent an act in which strong emotions were involved on both sides as if it were simply a calculated political counter-move. After three days' heart-searching, the priest in Gregory—who could not refuse absolution to the penitent Christian—won the victory: but only after the politician in him felt that he had secured sufficient guarantees.

---

[1] It was held that the king should take no further oath in person after that which he swore at his coronation.

[2] Pullan 143–5, Tierney 62–4, Mommsen and Morrison 156.

He conceded only readmission into the Church, not full reinstatement as king. The question of the Empire must remain unsettled, he wrote to the German nobles directly afterwards. After Canossa, just as much as before it, his object remained to act as a judge between the German parties and to keep continually open the possibility of inclining to one side or the other according to the extent to which each was prepared to make concessions in matters of ecclesiastical politics. The conditions he imposed on Henry were calculated to this end. As late as May, he still intended to cross the Alps to Augsburg, but obstacles kept cropping up, until news of unrest in Rome finally called him back there during the summer. His policy was still dominated by the same purpose during the next few years.

On the other hand, the principal reason why Henry impetuously sought absolution (though not without realising its religious significance) was because excommunication tied his hands and he desperately needed room to manoeuvre. No price was really too great to pay for this, not even the humiliating novelty of accepting the pope as judge over the internal affairs of the Empire. He had no doubt secretly hoped to prevent Gregory's journey through Lombardy, and he used the new freedom of action which absolution gave him with masterly diplomatic skill during the next few years, putting the curia off with empty promises and preventing his opponents from uniting on German soil. By giving him this opportunity, Canossa undeniably brought him a tactical advantage.

But if we look beyond the immediate political situation and consider the way the relationship between Church and state had been changing, and if we compare the Empire's role at Sutri with its role at Canossa, the sharp decline in its power in only a single generation is clear enough: whereas the Emperor had once been the arbiter of Europe, now he bowed to the pope's tribunal; where once popes had been deposed at the command of an Emperor endowed with priestly authority, now the power of their successor —against the orthodoxy of whose faith not a single voice was raised—to excommunicate a king was admitted by the king's own request to be freed from it. Henry's step may have been a well-calculated one in the difficult circumstances, and it may have begun a change for the better in his situation, but it undoubtedly set the seal on the developments of the last few decades which had completely changed the relations of papacy and Empire. Political defeats are not usually recognised until they are manifest in some striking context; the mistakes which led to them are often overlooked. In this sense, as the last link in a chain of errors, Canossa must always be a symbol of the capitulation of secular power before ecclesiastical claims to dominion, exactly as Bismarck proclaimed it to be.

Gregory's behaviour aroused lively misgivings in the German opposition: the raising of the sentence of excommunication deprived them of both a legal basis and of a good propaganda weapon. They could not turn back, but they would have to follow their chosen path without the pope. At Forchheim, the traditional town for Frankish royal elections, they raised the ambitious Swabian noble Rudolf of Rheinfelden, a brother-in-law of Henry, to the throne as anti-king in March 1077. It was the first victory of the unfettered right of election over the principles of inheritance and legitimacy. Gregory held back for the present, and instructed his legates to remain neutral, although their presence at Forchheim nevertheless gave some encouragement to the anti-royalists. But the opposition's victory had only been made possible by the co-operation of the papacy with particularism, and the new-style kingship now had to pay the price which these two powers demanded: to the nobility it surrendered the principle of a hereditary monarchy, and it gave way to the curia by accepting the free election of bishops and royal investiture after consecration. Further, Rudolf declared himself ready to obey the pope in all things, an action which could easily be the first step towards the recognition of Roman overlordship after the Aragonese model of 1068. Even Henry would have been able to live in peace with pope and nobles under such conditions, especially as Gregory would have found the subjection of the legitimate monarch to the curia preferable to any other solution. But a shadow-monarchy of this kind was of course quite unacceptable to Henry, and he still had the upper hand. Open civil war began when he returned to Germany and deposed the three south German dukes.

There would be no point in describing all the vicissitudes of war and diplomacy that followed; only the essentials need emphasis. Saxony remained the main seat of resistance, and the anti-king established himself there. Swabia was hotly disputed and terribly devastated. It was Rudolf's own duchy, but Rudolf soon handed it over to his son Berthold. In Swabia were also located the chief territories of the two other deposed dukes, Welf of Bavaria and the Zähringer Berthold of Carinthia, and there too —in the monasteries of the Black Forest—was the main centre of papal propaganda. Besides St. Blasien, which had been reformed from Fruttuaria (near Turin), the little monastery of Hirsau was a particular source from which the spirit of reformed monasticism spread very widely. At Hirsau the influence of the papal legate, abbot Bernhard of St. Victor, Marseilles, coincided with the wishes of abbot William (1069–91), so that by 1079 Cluniac observances had been introduced—severer disciplinary regulations, emancipation from the proprietary rights of the founder's family, a more democratic constitution and direct sub-ordination to Rome. From that time on, Hirsau rose to be the head of a whole group of similarly inspired houses. The incorpor-ation of lay brothers, who were suitable as itinerant preachers because they were freer to move than the monks, increased the opportunities for agitation.

But the king had considerable estates in the south-west of Germany too, and plenty of supporters there. Henry found a reliable agent in count Frederick of Büren, to whom he gave the duchy of Swabia and betrothed his daughter Agnes in 1079. It was a symbol of the ambition of a new family that Frederick moved his seat from the cramped little castle of Büren, which today scarcely stands higher than the farm-buildings that surround it, to the proud summit of the Hohenstaufen;[1] the Staufen first mount the stage of history in defence of the legitimate royal house against the papacy and particularism. The objective of the rebels in Saxony and Swabia was naturally to join forces. When Henry, whose strongest bases were in the Rhineland and in the south-east, came between them and tried to win back first Swabia and then the royal estates in Eastphalia and Saxony, the heaviest blows fell in the Main and Neckar valleys or further north in Thuringia. But in contemporary conditions of warfare these could not be decisive and it mattered more that the king was able to keep his enemies apart than that he suffered a few reverses in the field, for it ensured his safety during the next few years.

In the sphere of diplomacy, however, he was outstandingly successful. No weaker description will do: for three whole years, using every imaginable kind of delay, deceit and corruption, he

[1] Both are some 20 miles east of Stuttgart.

led so formidable an opponent as Gregory an unholy dance. His task was made easier by the fact that during this entire period the pope seemed almost mesmerised by the single objective of sitting in judgement between the two parties—which would, of course, have been the greatest possible triumph for the papacy—and therefore kept putting off a complete and final breach with Henry even though he allowed his real opinions to become clearer and clearer as time passed; while Henry, for his part, paid lip-service to the idea of papal arbitration and even seemed ready to pave the way for it. Hence the annoyance and complaints of the Saxon opposition (who were much more farsighted in this respect than the pope), hollow peace negotiations that brought no results, quarrels between Rudolf and the Saxons, the growth of the royal party and the increasing confidence of Henry, who in the end was even able secretly to enlist a papal legate into his service and is said to have commissioned his envoy to the Lenten synod of 1080 to demand Rudolf's excommunication by threatening to set up an anti-pope.

Gregory, who had occupied himself with the promotion of reform in several countries, at last realised that it was time to stop this dangerous policy of procrastination. In the form of a prayer to the prince of the apostles, he pronounced the second excommunication and deposition of Henry at the Lenten synod of 1080.[1] His passionate words betray anger at his own defeat. If the supremacy of the Church could not be made clear by a tribunal at which the pope pronounced judgement, at any rate a crushing blow could be delivered at all who opposed the papacy's claims to world dominion. These claims were openly expressed in the deposition, and were more fully explained and justified in the great letter which Gregory wrote to bishop Hermann of Metz in 1081.[2] From the pulpit of St. Peter's on Easter Monday he prophesied that Henry would fall by the first of August, and bade Henry have no more faith in him if the prophecy did not come true, so absolutely confident was he that the apostles would intervene on behalf of their Church. His final estrangement from Henry coincided with his recognition of Rudolf as king of Germany, and he now awaited Rudolf's acceptance of papal vassalage, though he never in fact received it.

Everything depended on whether this second excommunication would be as effective as the first. Repetition was bound to dull its

[1] Tierney 64–6.
[2] Pullan 147–157, Tierney 66–73.

edge, and the masses were naturally disappointed when their hopes of peace were dashed by a new declaration of war in which the pope of course appeared as the aggressor. But the consequences of the other decisions of the Lenten synod had also to be taken into account: the reaction of the lay nobility—the owners of proprietary churches—to the threat of excommunication against any layman who invested a cleric with a church of any kind, and that of the episcopate to the decree which had revealed the full scale of the curia's demands over the appointment of bishops. The pope or the metropolitan was to make the arrangements for every election through a visitor, to give consent to it (in place of the royal consent of former days), and to make the nomination himself through the right of 'devolution' if anything irregular occurred. If we remember that the curia had for some time past already been trying to force the archbishops to surrender their former independence by coming to Rome to receive the pallium directly after their election and by taking an immediate oath of obedience, the reference to the metropolitan as well as the pope is seen to have little significance; the decree means nothing less than that the curia will no longer be content simply with the free canonical election which it had only recently been demanding, but now intends to replace the former royal influence by its own. This in fact remained its programme until the thirteenth century, though it was only put into effect by stages. The objective was already clearly visible, however, and must have startled the German bishops. Faced with the question whether they wished to be princes of the Empire or servants of the pope, the majority chose the first and stood solidly with Henry when conflict broke out once more. Relying on them, Henry took a step which he had not taken in 1075 because they had deserted him then: as soon as nineteen German bishops and archbishops had decided, at a council at Mainz at Whitsun, to depose Gregory and hold a new election, he set up an anti-pope at the synod of Brixen (1080),[1] which included north Italian bishops. The mood and the actions themselves recalled Worms.[2] The ex-cardinal Hugh Candidus, claiming to represent all the Roman cardinals, led the attack this time with even more absurd slanders, ending with the charge that Hildebrand had cleared the way for his own succession by poisoning his four predecessors. Neither side could wage a war to the death

[1] Mommsen and Morrison, 157–60.
[2] Above, pp. 80–81.

without defaming its opponents. Even the former royal chancellor, archbishop Wibert of Ravenna, now the anti-pope (a man of blameless life in whose person the ancient rivalry of Ravenna was joined to the north Italian bishops' hostility to Rome) who had filled his office with uncommon skill and energy for twenty years, was soon branded by Gregory as a criminal. A wide gulf now divided Germans from each other. 'O lamentable condition of the empire,' wrote the Augsburg annalist, 'As we read in a certain comic poet[1] "we are all doubled", so now the popes are doubled, the bishops are doubled, the kings are doubled and the dukes are doubled.'

When Henry returned to Germany and advanced into Thuringia as far as the Elster with a new army, fortune—usually so grudging—smiled on him for once. He suffered another defeat himself, but his adversary Rudolf received his death-wound. Gregory's prophecy was strangely fulfilled when the rebel who had broken his oath of fealty to his king lost his right hand—the hand with which oaths are sworn—and this naturally strengthened the impression of a judgement of God. It was only after a good deal of hesitation that a new anti-king was elected in 1081. Hermann of Salm, the count of Lützelburg, was chosen—'a vile person, to whom they shall not give the honour of the kingdom';[2] the people called him King Garlic. It was the curse of election by the nobles that the best candidate, who might have led their cause to success, was passed over because he was feared. After some weeks of sullen indecision, Otto of Nordheim declared for the new king and brought the Saxons over to him. But Otto died in 1083, and Hermann's authority was no more than a shadow from that time on. Gregory had been displeased at the election and seems not to have made anything like a close alliance with Hermann, although he at once sent him a form of words in which he was to swear obedience and vassalage, as Rudolf had done. Henry was not able to come to any understanding with his German opponents, but they were now so little danger to him that he could leave Germany and turn against his chief enemy, the pope. This time Gregory was to be deposed by force of arms.

Gregory's situation was unenviable. When the new break with Henry came, he tried to ensure himself a strong ally in south

---

[1] Plautus, Amphitryon, l. 786: omnes congeminavimus.
[2] Daniel xi. 21.

Italy, by recognising (although unwillingly) duke Roger Guiscard's arbitrary annexations, even of papal territory, in return for an oath of homage: for his chief fear was that Henry's repeated efforts to secure an alliance with Guiscard might succeed. But his truculent vassal was far too concerned with his own schemes for invading Albania and attacking Byzantium, as well as with domestic troubles, to be either a strong or a reliable support at first. The alliance had the contrary effect, by causing the Greek emperor to join Henry against their common Norman foe—and thus against the pope—and to supply him with money which Henry found very useful for stirring up discontent among the Romans.

In Lombardy, the election of the anti-pope brought an increase in the number of Henry's supporters. Gregory could rely confidently on no one but countess Matilda. She had just (1080) given striking proof of her devotion by endowing the Roman Church with the whole of her enormous private possessions—apart from estates in Lorraine, they lay scattered across Italy from Romagna and the north-east over the Apennines to Lucca, and south as far as Siena and Perugia—retaining only a life-interest for herself. These lands were of course to play an important role in the history of the Empire during the next century. Tireless and sparing no pains, she now organised resistance to Henry; but Henry outlawed her, drove her towards Mantua by an attack on Ravenna, and drew a net round her in Tuscany by a policy of friendliness to the towns. Matilda was forced on to the defensive, and could not hinder Henry's advance on Rome. Gregory's safety depended on the Romans.

Henry invested the city four times during the next few years (1081–4), each time withdrawing his German troops and leaving the siege to the anti-pope and the Italians as soon as the hot weather began. After he had stormed St. Peter's and the Leonine City on the right bank of the Tiber in 1083, he made a last effort to reach an agreement with Gregory, who had taken refuge in Castel Sant' Angelo. A synod consisting of delegates from both sides was to meet in Rome and settle the dispute; it was an unpromising proposal from the start, and it collapsed when Henry began to have misgivings, refused the safe-conduct he had promised, and hindered the prelates' journey to Rome. Gregory held obstinately to his demands: no reconciliation and no imperial

coronation until Henry had done public penance. This was quite
unacceptable to Henry, who felt himself on the point of complete
victory. But now the Romans began to see the obstinate pope as
the destroyer of the peace they longed for, and it was not only
Byzantine gold that increased the number of defections in both
city and curia. No fewer than thirteen cardinals deserted Gregory,
besides other prelates and the standard-bearer of the army. The
Romans called Henry back from a campaign in Apulia at the
beginning of 1084, and opened their gates for his triumphal entry.
At Henry's demand, a synod at St. Peter's deposed and excom-
municated Gregory for high treason and rebellion, and confirmed
Wibert as pope by electing him a second time and enthroning him
as Clement III—all with unmistakeable reference to the Synod of
Sutri, at which another Gregory had had to give way to another
Clement. Henry then had himself and Bertha crowned by
Clement.

He had reached his goal, and his position was not fundamentally
changed when, soon after the coronation, he had to withdraw
northwards in front of the large army which Guiscard had at last
brought to succour Gregory, who was still holding out in Sant'
Angelo. For the dreadful Norman sack of the city, which really
reduced it to ruins for the first time, awakened so furious a hatred
of Gregory among the citizens that it would have been impossible
for him to stay in Rome without Norman protection. The anti-
pope was able to establish himself there for a time, and to receive
recognition from the whole of the Empire, from Hungary, Serbia
and even for a moment from England.

Gregory followed his rescuer south. He died in Salerno on
25 May 1085, broken in body by the strain and the privations of
the last few years. His energy of spirit remained undiminished to
the last, and he renewed the excommunication of Henry and
Wibert. At the end, however, he was oppressed by a sense of
failure. The bitterness of his last words can only be understood by
comparing them with the psalm on which they are based:[1] 'Thou
hast loved righteousness, and hated iniquity: wherefore God, even
thy God, hath anointed thee with the oil of gladness above thy
fellows'. The thought that mistakes of his own might perhaps
have contributed to his defeat did not even occur to Gregory in
his mood of self-justification: 'I have loved righteousness and

[1] Ps. xlv. 8.

hated iniquity . . .' and then the cruel paradox '*therefore* I die in exile'.

More than any of his predecessors, more even than Nicholas I, Gregory VII set the papacy on the road to world dominion. He completed, though he did not begin, the Romanisation of the Catholic Church; that is to say, he detached it from German control and the influence of German legal ideas, made the Mediterranean lands its chief foundation, and carried out a purifying and liberating reform by extending to the whole Church the disciplinary hierarchy of Cluny, culminating in the absolute authority of the pope. By insisting on these ideas with a passion and emphasis which guaranteed their impact for centuries to come, he influenced the course of history so decisively that it is impossible to deny his claim to greatness.

6

THE CONFLICT CONTINUES:
TO THE DEATH OF HENRY IV
(1086–1106)

There seemed for a time to be a real prospect of peace when (after a prolonged vacancy, which may have been due to Norman pressure) abbot Desiderius of Monte Cassino was deservedly raised to the papacy as Victor III in 1086. Desiderius was conciliatory by nature, and for this reason was soon attacked by the high Gregorians. However, he never gained control of the situation, felt himself more abbot than pope, and died next year. The second phase of the conflict began with the election of Urban II in 1088.

Henry's Italian victories at first helped his cause in Germany when he returned there after the imperial coronation, although he could not quite bring the civil war to an end. Few features of these confused years of conflict are of much significance. Henry failed to persuade either the German nobles or the increasingly prosperous episcopal cities to contribute towards the repayment of the money he had borrowed in Italy, but he found support in all quarters when he took up the idea of the Peace of God, which had originated in France. Under Henry III, the German monarchy had felt itself able to dispense with this kind of ecclesiastical support, but increasingly disturbed conditions since then had led his son to give his consent to ordinances after the French model which had been issued in Liège in 1082 and for the province of Cologne in 1083. At Mainz in 1085 Henry proclaimed the Peace of God for the whole empire, an act which not only helped to restore order, but also strengthened his relations with the German Church and gained him general support.

The opposition party began to break up at the same time. A peaceful expedition to Magdeburg in 1085 secured most of the Saxon and Thuringian nobility for Henry in return for the recognition of their rights, and the anti-king fled to Denmark. But an obstinate and (in view of his situation) untimely attempt to resume his earlier demesne policy was the signal for renewed opposition under the leadership of the ambitious margrave Ekbert of Meissen and led to a bitter struggle from which Henry finally emerged victorious. His conciliatory offer to be satisfied if the Gregorian bishops recognised him as Emperor, and not to demand that they accept his anti-pope, combined with the Saxons' war-weariness to bring the civil war to an end in 1088. Ekbert (d. 1090) and Welf held out with a few supporters in east Saxony and Swabia respectively, but Hermann of Salm was killed while besieging a castle in his native Lorraine, to which he had withdrawn.

There were no more anti-kings after Hermann. Henry had secured the throne for his family by the coronation of his son Conrad, and he was now accepted almost everywhere. The imperial cause was not defended by military and diplomatic means alone, however: first-rate publicists fought for it with spiritual arguments, and at any rate in Germany they had the better of the Gregorians. They still heaped text upon text, and used symbol and sophistry in place of logical proof, but the need to make independent decisions when sources conflicted shook belief in authority and sharpened critical judgment. Many of these writings show the intellectually liberating effect of the tremendous conflict.

The exultation that Henry may have felt towards the end of the 1080's was more justified than it had been after his great victory over the Saxons in 1075. His tireless energy and astonishing skill had triumphed over the most adverse circumstances. If from these heights he was later to plunge even lower than before, this was not due to blind fate alone but to the dangerous enemy who had lately ascended the papal throne.

Urban II (1088–99) was a highly cultured man from the north of France who had been prior of Cluny before Gregory raised him to the cardinalate as bishop of Ostia. As pope, his ecclesiastical objectives were the same as his predecessor's, but his tactics were markedly different. He was unquestionably Gregory's inferior in originality and emotional force, but he surpassed him in everything that ensures political success. Urban, the spirited and versatile aristocrat, had none of the uncouthness of Hildebrand the peasant's son, and none of his violence. He was unwavering in his pursuit of the ultimate objective and less fastidious than Gregory in his choice of means, adapting himself more skilfully to the

H

circumstances of the moment and combining clarity of thought with dogged persistence to attain his ends step by step. His first task was to raise the papacy out of the impotence of its exile among the Normans and to regain general respect for it. More firmly than even Gregory, he set it in the framework of the Mediterranean world which was at that moment advancing its frontiers against Islam in Spain, Sicily, Sardinia and Corsica: and he drew his principal support from the rising tide of monasticism, which helped him to hold the episcopate in check. He proved himself everywhere the efficient organiser of the churches which were being refounded under the Roman obedience, and was able at last to realise Gregory's eastern plans on a grand scale.

Great obstacles stood in the way of an improvement in the papacy's fortunes. Even Rome itself (to which the papal name he chose referred) was not recovered from the Wibertines for a year. Henry might perhaps at first have been prepared to compromise by abandoning the anti-pope—although this would have nullified his Italian successes and called the consecration of his most loyal episcopal supporters in question—but he could not bring himself to it: personal factors had come to play too lively a role in party allegiance during the years of conflict. There could be no doubt that in the long run the balance of ecclesiastical advantage was bound to be on Urban's side. In Germany the ranks of the Wibertine bishops began to thin as soon as Urban threw them a lifeline by recognising their schismatic consecrations in 1095. Henry was prepared to put up with this, as he had been earlier in Saxony, provided they remained politically loyal. But if his position north of the Alps could not be seriously threatened at first, he lost almost all his power in Italy during the last decade of the century.

In order to renew and strengthen his links with the German nobility, which had been much neglected of late, and to put new life into their opposition, Urban had in 1089 arranged an alliance like that which had brought Henry III to Italy. It was an unnatural and purely political marriage between duke Welf's seventeen-year-old son (also named Welf) and Matilda of Tuscany, who was now forty-three. For one side its only object was the birth of an heir, for the other it had no lasting prospect and was regarded as yet another sacrifice to the Church; but its immediate effect was to present Henry with the threat of an almost solid

block of hostile territory between south Germany and Tuscany—
a threat which he had to remove at all costs. So in 1090 a bitter
new struggle broke out in Italy. Henry was at first victorious: he
captured the enemy's base at Mantua and occupied their territory
as far south as the Apennines, forced the south Germans to sue for
peace and saw Matilda hard pressed by her own vassals. But his
progress came to a halt with the failure of an attack on Canossa at
the end of 1092, and this can only be explained in the light of a
counterstroke which his enemies had meanwhile prepared in the
bosom of his own family.

In their dire need, the papal party had not hestitated to
encourage treason among those nearest to Henry. Their first
success was to bring about the desertion of his young son Conrad
in the spring of 1093. Conrad was open to clerical pressure, and at
Matilda's inducement he abandoned his father and allowed himself
to be crowned king of the Lombards in Milan. Under the shelter
of his name northern Italy, hitherto the strongest base of Henry's
power and the indispensable bridge between Germany and the
south, was to be separated from the Empire. His partisans in fact
managed to suborn most of the imperial troops and to revive the
Pataria, thus breaking the back of the Milanese Church. A
Lombard league between Milan, Cremona, Lodi and Piacenza in
close alliance with Welf and Matilda cut Henry's last Alpine links
with Germany and prevented him from receiving reinforcements.
Conrad soon drew closer to the pope; he held Urban's stirrup
when he met him at Cremona in 1095 and took an oath which, if
it was not quite that of a vassal, nevertheless made his subordination to the curia plain. Urban took advantage of the occasion to
move a step beyond Gregory's position by forbidding the clergy
to take feudal oaths to laymen, held out prospects of the imperial
crown to Conrad and tried to strengthen his position by marrying
him to a daughter of the powerful count Roger I of Sicily and
Calabria. Urban seemed, with little trouble and by the back door,
to have reached the goal which Gregory had so long vainly striven
to attain—the reduction of the Salian house to dependence upon
the See of Peter.

Further strife in Henry's family followed in 1094. His second
wife Praxedis or Eupraxia (she was also called Adelaide in
Germany), daughter of the Russian Grand Prince of Kiev and
widow of a German margrave, whom Henry had married a year

after Bertha's death in 1087, had been imprisoned for adultery, but
she escaped with the aid of the papalists, made the most horrible
charges against her husband at a synod at Constance and became a
focus of resistance to him. The pope did not disdain to use the most
sordid weapons: the council of Piacenza, over which Urban himself presided in 1095, accepted her charges without investigation.

Morality was lost sight of in a struggle which grew ever wilder
and more personal. A flood of filth and calumny, inspired or at
any rate made use of by the curia, beat against the Emperor and
threatened to engulf him. The charges became more absurd with
every repetition—Henry was supposed, for instance, to have tried
to compel Conrad to commit adultery with his own step-mother.
There are things which it is impossible to fight against. For
nearly thirty years Henry had unremittingly striven to achieve a
position from which he could pass on the monarchy's rights
undiminished to his son. Since the son had now surrendered the
rights and treacherously attacked him, what was the point of
fighting on? It is not difficult to understand why Henry sank
under the blows of fate and wearily laid down his arms, or even
that (according to one account) he turned his weapons against
himself and was only saved from suicide by the chance arrival of
some of his retainers. In vain he tried to find, through Venice and
Hungary, a way to break the ring his enemies had thrown around
him; he was eventually reduced to years of impotence, virtually
imprisoned in the neighbourhood of Verona. As through the
window of a prison cell, he had to watch from a distance a
succession of events which not only deprived him of control over
Italy but destroyed that leadership of Europe and the Church
which his half-priestly character had hitherto given the Emperor.

The success of the wars against the Moslems in the western
basin of the Mediterranean must have suggested the possibility of
enlisting the warlike Christian knights against the heathen in the
east as well, and of utilising them for the extension of the curia's
authority. The Byzantine empire urgently needed effective
reinforcements against the enemies assaulting her eastern frontiers,
where they had already occupied most of Asia Minor. The
distress of the churches in the east, and the oppression and
dangers to which pilgrims to Jerusalem were exposed, awakened in
the west a demand to go to the help of their hard-pressed fellow-
Christians, to free them from the Turks and to take the Holy

Places from the hands of the Infidel. It is difficult to determine how far the crusading movement sprang from religious emotion and how far from political calculation, and to what extent the mercantile interests of the Italian cities underlay both. In Urban's own case, his experience of exile among the Normans also played a part. Count Roger had regained for the Roman Church the territory once lost to Islam in Sicily. In 1098, soon after the conquest, he was rewarded with legatine powers over the new churches, a concession which under the name of 'Monarchia Sicula' played an important part in the history of the island for many centuries before Pius IX withdrew it. Gregory VII's scheme now gradually developed in Urban's mind into a plan for a grand assault on Islam in the east. There cannot be the slightest doubt that Urban fully realised the enormous ecclesiastical and political benefits the papacy stood to gain if it could attach the quarrelsome western knights to itself by means of this idea, and thereby take the last of the wind out of the sails of imperial universality. The improvement in papal fortunes had brought Urban back to Rome in 1093. From there a triumphal progress took him in 1095 to the two great synods of Piacenza (where he received the Byzantine emperor Alexius's appeal for help against the Seljuks) and Clermont-Ferrand (with its promise of a victorious outcome in the cry *Deus lo volt*), through Italy, Burgundy and France and back to Rome again in 1096 on the crest of a wave of enthusiasm: the position of the Gregorian papacy in Europe was secure beyond doubt. The ground was gradually cut from under the anti-pope's feet even in Italy, although Urban himself died too soon to be sure of this or to receive the news of the capture of Jerusalem in 1099. To his successor, Paschal II (1099–1118)— far his inferior in spiritual energy, knowledge of the world and diplomatic skill—fell the credit for the crusaders' success, and it raised his prestige so much that the office of anti-pope lost all meaning when Clement III died in 1100; even the death of King Conrad next year could not restore Italy to the Empire.

The story of the first crusade has no place in an account of German history; only the western parts of the Empire, where Peter of Amiens preached, were affected by it. The first unorganised mass of peasants was viewed with mistrust by the Germans as it passed through on its way to Hungary, for it threatened the peace they longed for. It was followed by new hordes, who began their war against the Infidel by terrible massacres of Jews even before they had left the Rhineland towns. Over a thousand were killed in Mainz alone, and archbishop Ruthard did nothing to save them, although they had paid him protection-money. Soon afterwards, Henry set up an inquiry into the grievances of those who had been robbed or forced to change their faith, and this earned him the hostility of the archbishop, who sought to escape the consequences by fleeing to Flanders. The last of the crusaders to pass through Germany were the Lorrainers—half French in origin, and the only one of the German tribes to take part—whose march was properly organised by their leader, duke Godfrey of Bouillon in Lower Lorraine.

The crusade benefited Henry insofar as it at once diverted clerical resources and lessened the Church's interest in its conflict with the Salian emperor. The harmful alliance of the south German opposition with Italy, which had been the chief cause of Henry's difficulties, collapsed when the Welfs dissolved the unnatural marriage with countess Matilda because she had not produced an heir, and when the old duke, Welf IV, showed his annoyance by allowing himself to be reconciled to Henry in 1096 in return for Henry's recognition of his dukedom. This opened the eastern Alps to Henry. He returned to Germany, where he managed to bring about a settlement in Swabia (almost the only remaining seat of unrest) whereby the imperial fief of Zürich and the title of duke were granted to Berthold II of Zähringen, who had been disputing the duchy with Henry's Hohenstaufen son-in-law ever since the extinction of the house of Rheinfelden. The Salian dynasty was once more made secure by the election and royal coronation of Henry's second son Henry, whom his father hoped to keep from Conrad's evil ways[1] by the moral compulsion of the oath of fidelity which he made him take. The improvement in his position which these actions represented, and the removal of all significant traces of opposition north of the Alps, enabled Henry to claim that he had secured recognition in the whole of Germany without surrendering any of the rights of the monarchy, and to do so at the same moment as the pope was celebrating the Church's victory in the east. He would gladly have gone on to make peace with the Church,[2] but his offer (the way for which

[1] Conrad had been deposed by sentence of the royal court. He died in 1101.
[2] Mommsen and Morrison 176–8.

had been prepared by a number of south German nobles) to undertake a crusade himself as a penance if the sentence of excommunication were lifted was refused by Paschal since it seemed only an evasion of the real issues in dispute. This was a blemish on his success, and it justifies the conclusion that peace in Germany had been bought at the price of concessions by a weakened central government. But even though the Church and the higher nobility had undoubtedly prevented a thorough restoration of royal power and had advanced their own cause, it would still be wrong to write Henry off as a feeble and ineffective old man, whatever blows fate may later have dealt him. By seeking a new social basis for the kingship, the erstwhile reactionary now became a reformer.

Amid the prolonged devastations of the war, one thing in particular had found increasing support among the people: the as yet imperfectly understood idea of a general peace guaranteed by law, an idea that was expressed in the Peace of God. Even Henry's opponents had had to take account of the longing for peace when they held popular assemblies. Henry now put himself at the head of the movement. A general peace of the Empire was proclaimed at the Reichstag of Mainz in 1103 in connection with the projected Crusade, and an amnesty was announced at the same time; this imperial peace was not restricted, like the Peace of God, to banning private war at certain specified times, but was to cover four whole years and to be enforced with the help of the territorial nobility. The social and political importance of the decree lay in the fact that into it, the first of a series of similar peace ordinances, there were inserted new penalties (mutilation and death) applicable to free and unfree alike; there was thus created a means by which the lower classes could gain a foothold in the sphere of law and government. Further measures sought to restrict the lords' excesses and to bring the feudal nobles' growing exercise of criminal justice under the control of the king. The object was to protect the citizens and peasants in their peaceful and productive existence and to involve them in state activity, while at the same time damming up the streams which fed the warlike nobles' love of robbery and plunder and embodying these nobles more firmly in the legal structure of the state. Had it been pursued consistently, a domestic policy like this would have widened the social basis of the German monarchy and strengthened its legal authority, just as similar measures did in England and France later on.

Henry had struggled free of his difficulties once more, and had arrived at a tolerably satisfactory state of affairs. If he had died at that moment, he could have looked back with a certain amount of satisfaction over a life which, though stormy and exhausting, had also been rewarded by some success. In actual fact, his greatest sorrows and worst disappointments were still to come. The desertion of his one remaining son was the severest test he had to face.

The young Henry, a far-sighted but coldly calculating youth, was anxious that his father's peace policy should not alienate the nobility without securing the desired reconciliation with the Church, for in this case it might lead to a new alliance of Church and nobles which could cost both his father and himself the throne. He therefore took the immoral but politically well-considered step of putting himself at the head of the malcontents, seeking recognition from the pope by posing as his father's enemy but without offering any fundamental concessions, with the object of securing his own future at his father's expense through a union of legitimacy and clericalism. But if he did harbour such thoughts, he greatly exaggerated the dangers that threatened the crown, for we have no reason to suppose that Henry would not have been able to overcome them if he and his son had continued to work together. It is essential to see this conflict, like that in which Frederick II and so many other rulers were involved, primarily from the human and personal angle. Friction naturally arises where the mature experience of a father opposes his son's impatience for action in a common enterprise. If, in an age which lacks moral restraint, the tension is not eased by filial respect, then an open breach may easily result. The young king had grown up at a time when morals and family ties had become unusually slack, and under conditions calculated to encourage the early development of jealousy, cunning and selfishness rather than loyalty and generosity. His father, grown suspicious since Conrad's treachery, had tried by means of an oath of fidelity to fetter a character whose natural disposition was to complete independence; the younger Henry felt the oath as a humiliation, and it was therefore only too likely that it would achieve the opposite result from that for which it was designed—particularly when there was no shortage of clerical insinuations to the effect that it was meritorious to break an oath sworn to an excommunicate. The grievances of the discontented nobles who surrounded him, which have been described already, supplied the final impetus for revolt.

Violence and lynch-justice by the lower classes against the nobility was nothing unusual in those days. Because he had infringed their rights, *ministeriales* and townsmen rose against count Sighard of Burghausen while the court was at Regensburg in 1104, and murdered him. Father and son took opposite sides for the first time over this incident. The younger man had supported Sighard, while Henry did nothing to protect him and now allowed his murderers to go unpunished. The Bavarian nobles were indignant; the young king, enraged at his father's attitude, secretly left the court and raised the standard of revolt. Henry was now in an acutely difficult position. For whom had the struggle which had prematurely aged and physically weakened him been fought, if not for the son who was now forcing him to strike the blow which would destroy their dynasty? It was humanly understandable, as well as politically advisable, to try first of all to win the rebels back to their loyalty. The young king, calculating his advantage well, announced that he would have nothing to do with an excommunicate; he even rejected his father's offer of a share in the kingship. The pope refused all Henry's offers of reconciliation, although Henry was prepared to surrender everything except the honour of the Empire and his own crown.

These negotiations gave the revolt time to spread, however, and young Henry established an almost unassailable position for himself among the rebels under Ruthard of Mainz when he moved from Bavaria into Saxony. Although he carefully avoided an explicit undertaking to forego lay investiture, he received immediate support from the pope, who absolved him from the sin of breaking the oath to his father and gave him his blessing. Bishops and lay nobles, both in Saxony and elsewhere, at once seized the opportunity to free themselves from subjection— inconvenient in both spiritual and temporal terms—to an Emperor who had been excommunicated and deposed by the head of the Church. Everywhere, even in south Germany, the glowing embers of old hostility were fanned into new flame. It was an additional misfortune that at this moment there died Henry's most active and reliable supporter, duke Frederick of Swabia.

Young Henry could therefore soon venture to advance from Saxony as far as Mainz to restore archbishop Ruthard. His father prevented him from crossing the Rhine, so he fought his way up the valley of the Main towards Bavaria. There the Emperor suddenly attacked him, drove him out of Regensburg, secured Bohemian and Austrian reinforcements and prepared for a decisive battle on the river Regen. But the rebels disposed of the greater inducements to treason, and were able to persuade the Bohemians and Austrians to desert. The dissolution of his army at first forced Henry to withdraw eastwards. Then he once more showed his tireless resolution by marching speedily through hostile Saxony towards Mainz, although he could not prevent his son from crossing the Rhine further south and hastening to seize the royal treasury at Speyer. When this district too deserted him, he had to retire downstream to Cologne.

The young king summoned a Reichstag to Mainz to decide the succession. Since it was possible that the Emperor would appear in person to defend his rights—for he still had the support of many of the greater nobles, and the citizens of Mainz showed considerable devotion to his cause—the young king moved northwards to stop his approach. The two met at Koblenz,[1] where the son completely outwitted his father, heaping oaths and protestations of affection upon him and giving out that his dearest wish was to see his father reconciled with the Church. On the way to Mainz, to which he had given him safe-conduct, he managed to get his father away from the protection of his guard. With some show of force he conducted him up the river Nahe to the castle of Böckelheim on the pretext of letting him spend Christmas there because he would not be safe in Mainz, and swore that he himself would defend the imperial cause at the Reichstag as if it were his own. When the castle gates closed behind him, Henry was his son's prisoner.

Force now took the place of trickery. Henry still hoped that his words would carry the day, if only he could make a personal appearance at the Reichstag. In order to achieve this, and with the threat of perpetual imprisonment hanging over him, he agreed to hand over the imperial insignia. But he was deceived once more: only his son's supporters came to Ingelheim, whither he had been carried off, and further moving scenes followed. Although he threw himself at his son's feet and begged for mercy,

---

[1] Henry IV's own account of the following events is contained in letters to Hugh of Cluny and others: Mommsen and Morrison 184–200.

pressure was put on him to go through a form of voluntary abdication, which the surrender of the insignia had already symbolised and which necessarily included the renunciation of all imperial property. Just as he had once done at Canossa, Henry tried to secure absolution from the papal legate (who happened to be at Ingelheim) by showing outward signs of penitence. It was suggested that he should read out a prepared confession, which would have completed his degradation. But he refused to lend himself to this, particularly since the legate had declared that only the pope could absolve him. The Emperor's offer to clear himself before a neutral tribunal fell on deaf ears. Now only a private citizen, he was left at Ingelheim—apparently under guard—while his son formally ascended the throne as Henry V in a ceremony at Mainz which was endorsed by the legate's presence although the nobles stood somewhat aloof.

The new ruler's position did not go unchallenged. The Emperor escaped from Ingelheim and for the last time showed his unusual skill in saving an apparently lost cause. It may be doubted whether it was in the real interests of the Empire, and whether it would not have been more magnanimous of Henry to leave things as they were rather than provoke a new conflict. But so feeble a surrender was not to be expected of a ruler incensed at the humiliation he had undergone, who had good reason to fear for his future freedom, and who moreover at that moment could hardly hope that his son would give proper protection to the royal prerogatives he had himself so long defended. From Cologne, where he disembarked, he moved to Liège, making a pilgrimage barefoot to Aachen on the way in order to show his penitence publicly and to demonstrate the injustice of the legate's refusal to raise the excommunication. With Liège as his base, he collected a party round him in Lower Lorraine and recruited troops. Letters[1] which described the recent events in lurid terms and sometimes even exaggerated the terrible facts were sent to the king of France and perhaps also to the kings of England and Denmark, to the Saxon nobles and to abbot Hugh of Cluny, who was begged to undertake once more the task of bringing about a reconciliation with the curia: but Henry still insisted on the proviso 'saving our honour.'[2] The Emperor was even now an adversary not to be despised.

[1] Mommsen and Morrison 189–195, 197–199.
[2] Mommsen and Morrison 190.

Henry V was checked on the Meuse as he advanced hastily into Lower Lorraine, and had to retreat. He lost men and time by fruitlessly besieging Cologne, which had remained loyal to the Emperor, and advanced against his father again when renewed negotiations broke down. The conflict between them would have been settled on the field of battle, had not Henry IV died in Liège after a short illness. As he lay dying, he sent his sword and ring to his son and pleaded for mercy for his supporters and burial for himself in the cathedral at Speyer. His body was given the burial he wished, though only after several refusals on the ground of his excommunicate status—the touching devotion of the citizens of Liège and Speyer was ample compensation, however—at the very moment when his son came into new conflict with the curia.

If the sympathy which Henry's stormy life inevitably arouses be put aside, and if an attempt be made to assess what he had attempted and what he had achieved for the Germany with whose welfare he had so closely identified his own power and interests, it cannot be denied that he threw his whole personality into an unremitting struggle for the rights of the monarchy and the honour of the Empire. He did not defeat the Church, but he never yielded to all its demands; he successfully rejected all the papacy's claims to supremacy, handed over the right of investiture undiminished to his son, and by his stubborn resistance softened the rigidity of clerical claims enough to make his successor's task easier. By so doing, he had made no small contribution towards the fact that the German bishops remained in the service of the crown for another hundred years—even though with occasional hesitation and backsliding—and that to this extent the Ottonian system was not yet completely given up, although it did have to be modified.

On the other hand, although he had defended royal rights against separatism he had been prevented by the attacks of the Church from extending them, and in the long civil war he had been forced to surrender many imperial possessions and to make many concessions to the independence of the greater nobles; but even so he had not yielded the ground upon which in better times the royal authority might be rebuilt. He had shown the way to a future increase of royal power by his new peace ordinances, by giving the monarchy a broader social base and by his favour to *ministeriales* and townsmen, classes which were becoming increasingly important and without whose help no assault on the nobles' position could be mounted.

Henry must therefore be counted among the greatest of medieval German rulers by reason of his natural gifts and his continual striving, not by reason of his successes nor for his complex and contradictory character, the diverse features of which would not all fit together into the heroic mould but only too often blurred with passion the insight of the statesman. His life was more marred by ill-fortune than most, but in it a large part of the German people's destiny was fulfilled.

7

HENRY V AND THE END OF THE
INVESTITURE CONTEST (1106–1125)

Henry IV had defended the monarchy through thirty years of war against the papacy and the nobles. His son had overthrown him by allying with both. Thus the conflict seemed over. But when Henry V became sole ruler it soon became clear that his objectives were really the same as his father's and that he could not remain at peace with his allies for long.

The king had finally brought the papal schism in Germany to an end, but with the assent of the majority of the bishops he had shown no inclination to abandon the decisive influence over episcopal elections which the old law gave him—although he was prepared to restrict his act of investiture to the *regalia* alone. Paschal II was at first under a misapprehension about this, but the next few years made it quite clear that the fundamental conflict of principle remained unresolved: the pope inflexibly repeated the prohibition of lay investiture and extended it to cover all Church property, including the *regalia* with which the Empire had endowed it, and forbade the clergy to take feudal oaths, while Henry stood resolutely for the customs he had inherited. Peace remained nevertheless for a time unbroken. Henry's power was increasing—his betrothal in 1110 to Matilda, the little daughter of Henry I of England, brought him the close alliance of the Anglo-Norman Kingdom—and his demands increased with it. When the chancellor Adalbert was promoted to the archbishopric of Mainz in 1109, he was replaced by a gifted publicist and historian, David (perhaps a Welshman), in whom Henry found an instrument well suited to bring out the harsher features of his own character and encourage him to show them in his attitude to the papacy, just as his father had done. Although prolonged negotiations with the curia had brought agreement no nearer, Henry marched into Italy in 1110 with the army of a united Germany and with the intention of securing coronation as Emperor. Since his relations with the curia were still good enough to ensure that he met with little resistance, the lost territories were regained without trouble. The heavy pressure which the presence of the German army put upon Paschal goes a long way to explain the extraordinary and radical proposals for a settlement in February 1111; but the outlook and character of the pope provide an even better explanation. Paschal recoiled from the prospect of another great struggle and had little understanding of the secular world and its political ways. Like Peter Damian, he sympathised more with the monastic ideal of the desecularisation of the Church than with the Gregorian ideal of power. He made a straightforward attempt to render to Caesar what was Caesar's; the attempt did more credit to his logic than to his statesmanship and it would have needed a far stronger will than Paschal's to put it into effect. The Empire clung fast to investiture, which guaranteed its sovereign rights over the property of the imperial Church. If the German Church now gave back to the Empire all the *regalia*—that is, all the property and temporal rights—which it had received from the Empire since Charlemagne's time, and confined itself in future to living on tithes and private offerings, the acceptance of canonical election and the surrender of investiture would not hit the Empire hard. This was the gist of the arrangements which were now made between Emperor and pope on Paschal's initiative and confirmed in two charters.[1] Imperial coronation was to follow the proclamation of the terms of the settlement in St. Peter's.

The treaty has always been a source of wonder. Did anyone believe that it could be put into effect, or had it some other purpose? In spite of Henry's suspicions, the pope seems to have been completely sincere. He did not entirely overlook the difficulties, for he undertook to compel reluctant bishops to obedience by excommunication if necessary, but he had not in the slightest foreseen the sheer weight of the whole Gregorian party's resistance. That cool realist, Henry V, was not likely to make the same mistake. He had to expect stiff opposition from the German nobles as well as from the clerical extremists: from the clergy because the loss of the *regalia* threatened to destroy the foundation of the prelates' position as lords of imperial territory, and from the lay nobles because they feared that the monarchy would be economically and politically strengthened and were anxious about the future of their own ecclesiastical fiefs. He assessed these

[1] Tierney 89–90.

difficulties correctly, therefore, when he made the consent of the nobles a condition of the agreement, as well as that of the whole Church, and announced at the beginning of the celebrations that he did not for the present intend to deprive the churches of their enjoyment of the *regalia*, that is to say that he wanted to avoid any sudden and violent change in ownership. Thus the execution of the plan was brought at any rate into the realm of possibility, and at the same time criticism was diverted from the king, in spite of the unambiguous recognition of his royal right to the property of the imperial Church.

The storm of protest which broke in St. Peter's on 12 February was therefore directed exclusively against the pope's bull surrendering the *regalia*, which was read out directly after Henry's renunciation of the right of investiture. It became clear at once how far the feeble Paschal was from being in control of the situation. In his dealings with his father, Henry had already shown how inaccessible he was to any stirrings of piety; now, made suspicious by an attack on St. Peter's by the Romans, he promptly seized the pope when Paschal refused to restore the right of investiture and to crown him Emperor, and carried him and the cardinals off into safe custody far away from the rebellious city.

Henry's chronicler David cynically likened the rest of the negotiations to Jacob wrestling with the angel of the Lord—'I will not let thee go, except thou bless me'. Many things probably combined to make Paschal (who was in any case not cut out for martyrdom) and his cardinals agree to the Treaty of Ponte Mammolo on 13 April: exhaustion due to imprisonment, a personal outlook very different from that of the Gregorians, perhaps also the conviction—strengthened by charters of Hadrian I and Leo VIII forged by his enemies—that for peace' sake investiture could be conceded to the Emperor as a privilege, the threat of a schism in the Church, and the Normans' inability to help him because they were weakened by the death of their leader. The treaty granted all the king's demands: investiture of bishops with ring and staff before consecration, the imperial crown, a complete amnesty for Henry's recent actions and in particular a promise under oath never to excommunicate him.[1]

Henry's coronation as Emperor followed hard upon this agreement, which was the greatest victory ever won by imperial power

[1] Tierney 90.

over the reformed papacy. The promises it embodied were so well tailored to the pope's scrupulous and anxiety-ridden nature that he only departed from them very gradually even after he had regained his freedom, and always kept his oath not to excommunicate Henry. Although it was extorted under compulsion and soon withdrawn, the concession of investiture did a great deal to destroy the unity of the opposing party and weaken its cohesion. The unprecedented violence of the act was bound to provoke the bitterest hostility, and events were soon to show that Henry was flatly contradicting ideas which had now finally gained the upper hand. A storm of Gregorian indignation broke over the head of the pope; at first it was weaker in Germany then in Italy, but strongest of all in Burgundy and France. At two synods at the Lateran and Vienne in 1112 the pope's privilege to Henry was denounced as a 'pravilegium'—that is, an act of shame rather than of grace—and declared null and void; lay investiture was condemned as heresy, and the sentence of excommunication launched against the Emperor, who of course refused to surrender it. Paschal confirmed the acts of the synod of Vienne, although they had been directed against him, but recoiled from the thought of proclaiming the sentence himself and did not break off his relations with Henry. He would nevertheless have had to face a refusal of obedience and might have been deposed for heresy if he had not yielded to his opponents inch by inch, while seeking to appease his conscience by equivocal language and a number of reservations. So the old battle, now really an 'investiture contest' in the strict sense, had to be fought over again.

By laying his father's bones to rest in the cathedral at Speyer directly he returned home from a campaign in the course of which he had reconquered the imperial lands in Italy, the Emperor had meanwhile publicly proclaimed that he had completely adopted his predecessor's policy. This naturally re-awakened old enmities, and his German opponents' alliance with the Church was soon to present serious dangers. The nobility's opposition to Henry did not flow from a single source. It can hardly be compressed into Nitzsch's simple formula: that a deliberate renewal of this father's friendship with the towns and of his plans for territorial expansion (the centre of gravity of which was now to be shifted from the Harz to the upper Rhine valley) provoked the nobles to combine against him. At the very least, this basic cause was linked with

I

many other grounds of conflict and coloured by regional, personal and ecclesiastical factors. The Emperor certainly looked for support among the lower nobility and the imperial *ministeriales*, as his father had once done; and if he did not always have the Rhineland towns firmly behind him, his great privileges to Speyer and Worms in 1111 and 1114—which removed the inconveniences of episcopal control—still mark a stage in the emancipation of the German towns. He renewed the attempt to recover the royal estates in Saxony and Thuringia,and tried to extend and strengthen them on the upper Rhine by a programme of castle-building. Elsewhere too Henry sought as far as possible to repair the gaps which years of war had torn in the royal possessions, and was sparing of new alienations. The avarice of which the chroniclers accuse him was from the political point of view rather a virtue, and indeed though morally so repellent Henry possessed in a signal degree the qualities important to a ruler: love of power, calculation, daring and strength of will. But his personality as a whole gave offence to those around him. The ruthless way in which he sought his own advantage everywhere by annexing estates to which there were no heirs, regardless of the claims of collateral relatives, or often used taxation and the threat of punishment simply as a means of bringing pressure to bear—these things and his crafty, calculating, mean and untrustworthy nature raised up enemies against him on all sides; and although their motives differed, these enemies soon found a basis for common action. Personal dislike and friction over territory played the chief parts in Henry's dealings with archbishop Adalbert of Mainz, who resembled him in many ways. As chancellor, Adalbert had at first been Henry's most intimate adviser and the promoter of his plans, but when he became archbishop he had been out of sympathy with the radical tendencies of imperial policy towards the Church and consumed by his own ambition. Henry kept him in prison for three years without trial because he did not immediately hand over the imperial castles when ordered to surrender them, and this turned him into a bitter enemy. Finally, the untamed particularism of the Saxon tribe was still in a class by itself, just as it had been in the days of Henry IV. It was the more dangerous now because after the collapse of the power of Bremen and the extinction of the house of Billung in 1106 the new duke, Lothar of Supplinburg, had united his private estates round Helmstedt with the wide domains of the Billung, Nordheim and Brunswick families through marriage alliances and thus had the whole weight of tribal sentiment behind him. He became Henry's strongest and most determined adversary. Henry had the upper hand at first. Impatient for an heir, he married Matilda in 1114 when she was only twelve and probably too young to bear him one; the Saxon duke appeared at their marriage feasts in the garb of a penitent and seemed submissive. He changed his tune, however, when the successful revolt of Cologne set Saxon discontent going once more. Henry had no taste for fighting and no gifts as a commander—he was often ill, and his first campaigns as king (1107–9) did not succeed in destroying the independence of Poland and Hungary or in gaining more than a slender control over Bohemia. He was compelled to hand over command of the army to the faithful count Hoyer von Mansfeld, who was defeated and killed at the decisive battle of Welfesholze near Mansfeld at the beginning of 1115. A rising in Mainz in the same year set the archbishop free, and increasingly effective clerical intervention secured the defection of a majority of the bishops; soon almost the whole of north Germany was as good as lost to Henry. Yet Henry risked leaving Germany at this very moment, for important affairs called him to Italy, and there was also the chance that he might be able to secure peace through a new agreement with the weak pope.

Countess Matilda had just died; it was essential for Henry to reclaim the fiefs she held of the Empire and to lay his hands on her very extensive private estates as well: for the repetition in 1102 of her previous surrender of them to the overlordship of the Church of Rome seems not to have ruled out her free disposal of them, since they had been given back into her possession. Henry claimed the lands as her private heir, basing his case on a secret agreement probably made in 1111, when he had released her from the imperial ban and appointed her as his vicegerent in Upper Italy. He hurried south in 1116 without stopping to collect troops, skilfully secured the alliance of the neighbouring nobles, towns and churches by means of lavish gifts, and made good his claim regardless of Rome's claims to overlordship—thus notably increasing imperial power in Lombardy and Tuscany at the papacy's expense. Pressure by the Gregorians at the Easter synod of 1116 had already forced Paschal to cancel his grant of lay investiture; Henry's successes now made it impossible for him to suppress discontent in Rome, and he fled to the Normans. Henry had himself and his young bride crowned in St. Peter's in 1117. Paschal returned to Rome on Henry's departure, but his control of the city was still insecure when he died in 1118. Though his intentions had been sound, Paschal's uncertain and changeable behaviour had done the Church more harm than good, and he had brought the already too protracted Investiture Contest no nearer the end for which everyone longed.

Although the next pope (Gelasius II, 1118–9) was peace-loving and moderate, the hostility of the two sides became more bitter. Under him the Roman nobles' faction-strife began to affect the fate of the papacy still more closely. The Frangipani helped the Emperor to raise up another anti-pope, although Henry did not set much store by him. A suitable candidate was found in the Portuguese archbishop Maurice of Braga, who had taken refuge in Italy from plots against him at home. He never exercised any considerable influence, and has remained better known by his nickname Burdinus ('Spanish donkey') than as Gregory VIII. His election reopened the hated schism, however, and this meant that his predecessor's oath no longer prevented Gelasius (who had fled from the turbulence of Rome to the headquarters of the Gregorians in the south of France) from solemnly pronouncing the excommunication of the Emperor. Henry returned to Germany, where the clergy under the leadership of the archbishop of Mainz had raised at least half the country in arms against him. Though all were weary of it, the conflict was renewed on both sides of the Alps, and no end was in sight.

When the extremist archbishop Guido of Vienne, an energetic and strong-willed man, was elected pope after Gelasius' early death, compromise seemed to have been postponed indefinitely. But Calixtus came from a Burgundian noble family and was related to almost all the ruling houses of Europe, including the Salians, and his outlook was that of a statesman instead of being narrowly monastic like that of his predecessors; he saw that the Church needed peace and was suffering because the long conflict had deprived her of it, and he therefore began earnestly to seek a settlement compatible with canonical claims. The Emperor, who had renewed his contacts with the German nobility, began to pay more heed to their desire for peace, so long as the honour of the Empire could be preserved. And the way in which the wishes of both sides could be met had already been marked out for several years by far-sighted canon lawyers. The work of Italian and French publicists, especially the latter, and Ivo of Chartres in particular, had clarified the problem in principle. The transfer of a church itself through the symbols of ring and staff was sharply distinguished from enfeoffment with secular property and sovereign judicial rights: the latter could hardly be denied to the temporal authority, provided it used only temporal symbols to transfer them. Whether or not the enfeoffment should include the act of homage remained a matter of debate. At the same time it had been urged that the ruler, as head of the people, should be permitted a share in the canonical election by clergy and people, and that in addition as the giver of the *regalia* he should perhaps even have the right of consent. Ideas like these had already been given practical effect: the settlement of the Investiture Contest in France in 1098 allowed the king—who, because of different circumstances, was much weaker than in Germany—to hand over the temporalities in most cases only after consecration and upon the sole condition that the *electus* took an oath of fealty, but had at the same time permitted him an influence over the election of those bishops who were dependent upon him. Further, the agreement which ended the short but bitter Investiture Contest in England —an arrangement of more interest to Henry V than the French— had been more favourable to the crown: it granted the Church canonical election and investiture with ring and staff, but allowed the king to be present at elections and required the prelates to take an oath of homage for their temporalities. It was ideas of this sort—already well known to Henry—which now formed the main basis for negotiations between Emperor and pope. After the Church had made a show of strength at the Council of Reims in 1119, Henry put out peace-feelers and Calixtus moved to Mouzon on the frontier of the Empire. But memories of Henry's violence in Rome eight years earlier made him reluctant to meet Henry face to face, and his agents were not yet ready to concede investiture with temporalities by the sceptre in return for the surrender of investiture with spiritualities, although in its desire for peace the Council had not extended the prohibition of lay investiture to cover ecclesiastical property.

Although no understanding had been reached, Calixtus ventured to leave the security of France and return to Italy in 1120.

The schism was brought to an abrupt end by the capture and imprisonment of the anti-pope Burdinus (he spent the rest of his life in a monastery), and this cleared the way for the conclusion of peace. The lay nobility of Germany did not allow armed conflict to break out again. Because their own interests clearly demanded that they reject the prohibition of lay investiture in its severest form, they were able with Henry's assent to take over the task of finding a compromise. After difficult negotiations, the papal plenipotentiary cardinal-bishop Lambert of Ostia (later Honorius II) was at last able to announce the signing of a concordat to a jubilant crowd in the fields outside Worms on 23 September 1122, to give the emperor the kiss of peace and admit him to the Mass.[1]

Henry, who was forthwith released from excommunication, surrendered investiture with ring and staff, but in return was permitted to continue to bestow the *regalia* with the sceptre and to receive homage from the bishops, concessions which were still being refused three years earlier. These ceremonies implied the recognition of his overlordship of the property of the imperial Church; in Germany, as in England, they were to precede consecration, so that they amounted in practice to a right of consent upon which consecration depended. In Italy and Burgundy, where only imperial rights of a more limited nature were in question, investiture with the *regalia* was to take place within six months after consecration, and could thus become merely a matter of form.

The more the disappearance of the full investiture ceremony, with its basis in proprietary church law, destroyed the German ruler's unrestricted right to appoint bishops and imperial abbots, the more important became the question whether canonical election by clergy and people excluded his participation altogether —as the reformers demanded—or whether the old right of consent by the ruler as head of the people (which had been expressly admitted in 1111), or at any rate a right to be present at the election (which of course implied a considerable influence over it), was to be given legal recognition. The compromise could easily have broken down again over this point, but eventually the representatives of the Church yielded a little for the sake of peace. The emperor was granted the right to be present at elections in Germany and—contrary to Gregory's demands of 1080—the

[1] Pullan 157–9, Tierney 91–2.

right to decide disputed elections in favour of the better qualified candidate on the advice of the archbishop and bishops of the province in question, or according to their decision.

Seen from Gregory VII's reforming point of view, the Concordat of Worms plainly bears the stamp of a compromise, and it is easy to understand the extreme Gregorians' deep dislike of it. An estimate of its significance depends essentially upon the question whether the form of the papal bull—which is addressed to Henry personally—means that it was only a temporary armistice, or whether it was intended to be a permanent treaty of peace.

Differences of opinion over this point began at once and have continued down to the present day. An answer based on modern treaty-making practice would fail to take sufficient account of medieval customary law. The facts are as follows: when Henry ceased to invest with ecclesiastical office by ring and staff and thus gave up a practice based on the old proprietary church law, the curia withdrew its objection to the remainder of the customary law, which naturally explained the bestowal of the *regalia* in feudal terms. The curia could declare itself satisfied with Henry's altered practice, since it no longer directly contradicted the revealed law of God. At the great Lateran Council of 1123,[1] which marked the final victory of reforming ideas, this declaration was accepted—although with serious misgivings—by the highest ecclesiastical authority, and at the same time the Emperor's concessions were given legal force by the consent of the nobles. The new practice must before long have become habitual through the tendency of custom not to change, but since German customary law was still developing mainly through oral tradition it was not necessary to take account of the precise wording of the concordat itself. Those who made the agreement are certainly not likely to have thought any more about the chances of its remaining permanently in force than other plenipotentiaries have usually done. The Church silently reserved for itself the possibility of a return to its inalienable rights under canon law at a suitable moment—perhaps under Henry's successor—although of course this was not made any easier by a declaration that deviations from them were acceptable for the time being. The imperial government was soon bitterly conscious of the decline in its influence over appointment to spiritual office. The fact that the wording of the two documents

[1] Schroeder 177–194.

which composed the concordat was far from clear in several places encouraged attempts by each side to encroach upon the other's province; and the success of these attempts depended upon the relative strengths of the two sides. If the Church had the advantage at first, after Henry's early death, the Empire made a new advance under Barbarossa. But the Concordat of Worms provided a legal foundation for a *modus vivendi* between Empire and papacy in the future: the greatest German jurist of the thirteenth century, Eike von Repgow, regarded the wording of the papal bull as valid law.

Thus the long struggle over the Empire ended at last in a compromise. The obstinate resistance of the last two Salians had at least prevented total defeat. Gregory VII's wide-ranging plans, the purpose of which had been to secure feudal suzerainty over the Empire, the complete independence of the German bishops, and free disposal of ecclesiastical property, had not been fulfilled; the realisation of them remained a target for the future. Measured by the situation which had prevailed about the middle of the eleventh century, however, the increased power of the Roman Church, its growing control over the European mind, the development of the papacy as a decisive factor in the Church as a whole and its dominant position in politics—all these were plain to see. The curia could therefore be satisfied with the course events had taken. The Ottonian system had been destroyed in several important respects. German control over the papacy was at an end, and the dependence of the bishops upon the crown could only be maintained in future by the most strenuous efforts and at the cost of constant friction with the curia. But the other half of the Ottonian system, the use of the Church as an instrument of government for the purpose of holding down the lay nobility, had also suffered a severe blow. Wooed by both sides, the German nobles—who were tending more and more to replace the tribal dukes of earlier days—had greatly increased their property and their rights; their share in government, which found its chief manifestation in the election of the king, had become considerably more important; and they had lately taken it upon themselves to defend the rights of the Empire. As the strict dependence of the ecclesiastical nobles on the crown became looser, and as their relation to it approximated to that of the lay nobles, the old distinction between lay and spiritual aristocracy completely disappeared, and the identity of their interests was bound gradually to make the two coalesce into a class of territorial princes who could stand much more completely united against the king than before. In Italy, on the other hand, where the loosening of the bishops' links with the crown deprived them of their chief support in defending the property of the imperial Church, it was the towns which drew the greatest profit from the concordat, since they were nearly all able to secure possession of the *regalia* during the next few years. Barbarossa's struggle with his Lombard opponents was therefore in one sense a renewal of the Investiture Contest, although it was against the claims of the cities, rather than against those of the Church, that he waged it.

In future the Empire was compelled to seek other objectives on both sides of the Alps, and it had to adopt different methods of pursuing them. But the fact that the crown still had at any rate a chance to revive its fortunes was due not only to the tenacity of Henry IV but also to the skill of his son, who had managed to salvage for it everything that was salvageable in the difficult circumstances.

It is impossible to tell how the position would have developed if Henry V had lived on into the period of papal weakness which followed the death of Calixtus II in 1124. While the unpleasant features of his character no doubt aroused much otherwise avoidable opposition, his political gifts might have enabled him to preserve and even increase what remained of royal power: he had for example enlarged the single important office of the central government, the imperial chancery, to cover all three divisions of the Empire. His connexion with the Anglo-Norman court of his father-in-law might have been particularly valuable to Germany. Admittedly, an invasion of France which he undertook in alliance with England in 1124 had to be broken off without success, in face of a remarkable first manifestation of French national resistance, but in domestic affairs Henry had much to learn from his ally. There is mention[1] of a scheme of taxation on Anglo-Norman lines which brought him the bitter hostility of the nobles. We may even consider for a moment the startling prospect which would have been opened up if Matilda had borne Henry an heir, who might then have inherited England through his mother—for this brings a union of England and the Empire into the realm of possibility, and is in sharp contrast with the union of England and half

[1] Otto of Freising, *Chronica*, vii. 16 (trans. Mierow 423).

France, for which her second marriage to count Geoffrey of Anjou in fact prepared the way. Henry's childlessness was a cruel blow for the Empire, and entitles Germans to envy the more fortunate Capetian family. If there was ever a time which demanded a gradual acclimatisation to the new conditions, so that royal power could be slowly recreated, it was now, just after the conclusion of peace with the Church. The disease to which Henry now fell victim raised the spectre of a change of dynasty with its inevitable consequences of disorder and political uncertainty. Henry himself treated his nephew Frederick II, the Hohenstaufen duke of Swabia, as the successor to the kingdom and as joint heir with his brother Conrad to the Salian family possessions. But it was uncertain whether the nobles would use their newly-strength-ened electoral power in favour of Frederick. When Henry died of cancer in 1125, barely forty-four years old, a new conflict with Lothar of Saxony, Adalbert of Mainz and other old enemies was imminent. Had he lived longer, he would probably have emerged victorious, as he had done before. But he died before his time, and he left behind him unhealed wounds, which were made still deeper by renewed ecclesiastical controversy.

The Salian house ended with Henry. It had given Germany four remarkable rulers in the space of almost exactly a hundred years. If the royal power had been noticeably weakened in their time, through conflict with Church and nobility, this was more the result of general tendencies in the country's development and of particular fateful events than of the Salians' incompetence or mistakes. The arts of conciliation and compromise were foreign to the nature of the Salians, which tended towards harshness, violence and hasty decision, but there is scarcely a German ruling house in the whole Middle Ages which can compare with them in sensitivity to the demands of power or natural gift for its exercise.

Moreover, the Empire was very far from collapsing, in spite of the long and exhausting struggle and the decline of the central power. Politically, it was still the leading state in Europe, and its military strength was undiminshed. As the territorial aristocracy began to withdraw from direct economic activity themselves, and as the existing forms of landownership disintegrated, the lower classes made rapid progress by combining together to improve both their legal and their economic status. The *ministeriales* raised themselves above the other unfree classes. Since the more exalted supporters of the central power were being weakened, the *ministeriales* came to their aid and proved capable administrators of the imperial demesne. The increased rents caused by a growth of population, more intensive cultivation, and improved communications were all of less benefit to the lords, inclined to a courtly way of life, than to the peasants—the producers, although they were bound to the soil—who usually managed to improve their lot despite their servile status and to increase their wealth steadily in spite of all obstacles.

The newest element of all among the rising classes, and the one which broke through the existing feudal stratification of society, was provided by the citizens of the towns, whose numbers had grown markedly since the beginning of the century in consequence of new foundations. The lay and spiritual nobles, who had made or encouraged these new foundations in their own interests, could at first scarcely perceive how opposed the new corporate bodies must eventually be to them and to the whole of their economic organisation, based as it was upon landed property. The towns' specialisation in trade and handicraft, with its concomitants of a separate code of law and separate courts, the urge towards the loosening of personal and territorial bonds, the peace guaranteed by the ring of their defensive walls, the essentially adaptable outlook of townsmen who combined energetic action with the careful calculation of ultimate advantage—all this was bound to make the towns demand their economic, administrative and political independence and to bring them into conflict with their lords, particularly with the bishops, whose dioceses were centred in the chief towns. Conflicts of this kind—brought about in the first instance by sworn confederations, and in many ways promoted by the conflict of Church and state—frequently led to brutal reprisals but ended in complete or at the very least partial victory for the towns. Taken as a whole, the movement towards urban autonomy made progress everywhere, but Germany was well behind Italy, Flanders and northern France.

The effects of these changes in social structure upon the growth of a new and freer intellectual life therefore only became apparent in Germany later than they did in the Latin countries. German developments followed mainly traditional channels at first, only later branching out to make significant advances at least in the fields of history and architecture, where work of remarkably high quality was produced. The necessary unity and concentration had been lacking since the beginning of the long and destructive conflict. There was therefore no specifically Salian culture in the sense in which Ottonian or Hohenstaufen culture can be said to have existed. Nevertheless, the hundred years of Salian rule mark an important stage in the intellectual growth of the nation: without them, the lay culture of the Hohenstaufen period would be unthinkable.

8

LOTHAR OF SUPPLINBURG (1125–1137)

We possess a detailed eye-witness account of the election of 1125 at Mainz, just as we do of the elevation of the first Salian. A comparison of the two shows that times had changed. In 1024 what appeared a completely free election had resulted in the choice of the legitimate heir; but on this occasion the claims of Henry's V's Hohenstaufen nephew duke Frederick II of Swabia were almost a handicap, since the German nobility insisted upon their newly-strengthened independence and their right to a free choice. Considerations of ecclesiastical politics reinforced constitutional ideas. Those who disliked the incomplete nature of the Concordat of Worms and the way in which Henry V had operated it could expect no advantage from one who was the heir to his policies, and they had to look round for another candidate. Duke Lothar of Saxony was suitable in every respect: he was powerful enough to rule, but his age and his lack of an heir meant that he represented no threat to the electoral principle, while he was recommended by his hostility to Henry V and his thoroughly clerical outlook. The assembly of the nobles was skilfully manipulated into choosing him by the unscrupulous archbishop Adalbert of Mainz, who had been an opponent of strong kingship since his imprisonment, as well as a political and territorial enemy of the Hohenstaufen. In reply to the difficult question whether he agreed with the other candidates in not recognising hereditary claims in addition to electoral rights, duke Frederick (who had been tricked into delivering up the royal insignia beforehand) gave the only possible answer—an evasive one—and this completely destroyed his chances. A secret agreement with the duke of Bavaria, whose son Henry the Proud was guaranteed the second place in the kingdom by his marriage (it was solemnised two years later, but the engagement was perhaps made at this time) to Lothar's only daughter Gertrude, decided the issue in favour of the Saxon. Even Frederick reluctantly accepted him, though only after some delay. The principle of free election had been victorious.

Had Lothar given binding undertakings which nullified the gains of the last Salian? There is in fact at the end of the account of the election a clearly formulated expression of claims of this kind. We must probably regard them as the programme of the extreme clerical party, but it seems unlikely that Lothar bound himself to them formally, however near he may have been to the position they represented. Apart from this, however, Lothar's past and his whole outlook seemed to offer the reformers sufficient guarantees. He was elected in the presence of two papal legates and entirely under clerical influence. The new ruler repaid his debt at once by showing a thorough understanding of the wishes of the higher clergy and of pope Honorius II, whose confirmation of his office he had no hesitation in accepting. The lawful king now accepted all that the united opposition to the Salians had sought in 1077—the unrestricted right of the nobles to elect and of the pope to confirm.

Although he was barely fifty, Lothar was an elderly man by contemporary standards. He had had a long and active life, filled with the cares of office, fighting and the successful pursuit of power. He was famous in Saxony for his bravery, his love of justice and his plain soldierly attitude. Sudden outbursts of anger and sweeping claims recalled the storms of his youth, but always gave way to the moderation of age and a desire to avoid conflict. Lothar stood out from the other lay nobles as the ablest and the most powerful of them, but like the rest of the exhausted Germany of his day he lacked greatness, and the shortage of information is not the only reason why we know little of his personal character.

It is not only the particularist Saxon chronicles that speak highly of him: Otto of Freising said that if death had not overtaken him his strength and toil would have restored the crown to its former position once more. In sharp contrast with this, most modern historians give a very unfavourable account of him. Their attitude is well founded on the undeniable weakness of his policy of giving way to the Church, but apart from this it is thoroughly one-sided and unjust. Admittedly, Lothar could not deny his origins and did not wish to do so. Particularism and the Church had helped him to the throne. With his Saxon duchy as a base, he had risen to prominence in conflict with the central power, and had no thought of creating an independent monarchy of the Salian type. He was personally devoted to the Church, and his devotion was strengthened by his influential wife Richenza, the daughter of Otto of Nordheim, who often acted practically as co-ruler; he felt himself closely linked with the Church by his own interests, particularly by his need to combat the rival claims of the Hohenstaufen family to the throne. He therefore wanted no new conflict with the Church, but peaceful co-operation with it. In spite of all his concessions, which look like—and indeed for the mostly part actually are—evidence of weakness, his policy was not aimless. He made a noteworthy attempt to discover whether a strong monarchy could be created and maintained even though it gave full recognition to the current development of particularism and clerical independence, just as he had done when he established his authority in his own duchy. The obstacles presented in his first years as king by the interruption in the growth of the imperial chancery, however, and the shortness of his reign, prevented him from going beyond the preparatory stage; he counted on the continuation of his work by his son-in-law. But the ways in which he began to extend the latter's power are reminiscent of the objects of later German rulers—Rudolf I, for instance, or Charles IV, who followed the same lines but out-did Rudolf in ability, cunning and diplomatic skill—and of their efforts to strengthen the monarchy by enlarging their private demesne.

Lothar's attitude towards the Church can only be understood through a proper realisation of the strength and direction of contemporary European spirituality, which was then attracting the best minds of the continent and exercising an irresistible pressure upon the conscience of believers in spite of the schism in the papacy. The fierce, combative and power-seeking Hildebrandine spirit was dying out. After the long, dreary and demoralising struggle, the Church was spiritually barren and its resources were weakened; it needed renewal in both respects. And renewal came once again from the abbeys of France—some of whose monks to be sure were German—though not from Cluny, which was by now thoroughly secularised.

The turn of the century had been a time of new foundations, which were only now beginning to reveal their strength. Bruno, a canon of Cologne, had founded the Carthusian Order as long ago as 1086. More important was the establishment of the monastery of Cîteaux near Dijon in Burgundy in 1098 by Robert of Molesmes, a noble from Champagne, for it was the source from which the

Cistercian Order sprang, although the decisive change in the fortunes of the Order dates only from the entry of Bernard of Clairvaux in 1113, after which its powerful influence was soon extended to the majority of European countries. Bernard himself, who in effect led the Order as abbot of Clairvaux, not only lent it the stamp of his own hard work, simple piety and love of peace, but gave the tone to the whole period between the death of Henry V and the accession of Barbarossa. While naturally wishing to preserve everything that the Hildebrandines had gained, he wanted no further advance along their secular lines, but desired instead to raise the Church high above worldly concerns through the free development of its own special gifts of lively faith, deep mystical contemplation and a herculean readiness to labour in the harvest of the Lord, which might rise in the case of the elect to the personal working of miracles. The roots of this ideal were to be found not least in his own personality, for with the kindly, delicate and even artistic traits of his character there was combined an unusually passionate power to persuade, born of absolute conviction and self-confidence, which awakened belief and guided souls, effected cures and overcame opposition wherever he went. All the threads of western European life came together in Clairvaux. Bernard felt in himself the conflict between asceticism and the imperious demands of the world, and triumphantly overcame it. He advised kings and gave guidance to popes. He was filled with the assurance which comes with recognition as general as he received; intolerant and not without the vanity of the writer or the sensitivity of the artist, but powerful, successful, borne along by the current of the age, he was for thirty years the uncrowned king of Europe.

The Cistercian Order brought religious renewal, economic revival and centralised organisation to the Benedictine monks. When a German under French influence founded the half-monastic Premonstratensian Order (which was also sometimes called the Order of Preachers on account of the special weight it laid upon parish preaching and the cure of souls), the Augustinian canons regular received a similar impulse. Norbert, the son of a count from Xanten, followed Bernard's model: personally harsher and stricter than Bernard, Norbert possessed the versatility and administrative gifts of a man of the secular world, and his Order remained as aristocratic as its founder. The monastery at Prémontré in the diocese of Laon was established in 1120, and the

Order received papal confirmation in 1126; in the same year the curia persuaded Lothar to raise Norbert himself to the archbishopric of Magdeburg. Hence in the conversion of the Slav lands east of the Elbe the Premonstratensians were second only to the Cistercians. Norbert himself lacked the selfless devotion of the missionary, but he was thereby the better qualified to exercise an influence upon the king and the imperial government which lasted until his death in 1134.

Pietistic and mystical tendencies of the Bernardine type were better expressed in the ecclesiastically even severer but personally gentler archbishop Conrad of Salzburg and in Gerhoh of Reichersberg (1093–1169), whom he appointed provost of the Augustinian canons in his diocese. Gerhoh's profound and voluminous writings are full of monastic zeal, but they also contain sharp and independently-minded criticism of the secularised papacy.

It became more and more impossible every year for individuals to swim against the current of this whole movement, but it was nevertheless easier for the monarchy to come to a peaceful understanding with it than with the fiery Hildebrandines of old. It is therefore understandable that Lothar should have paid the greatest heed to a movement in comparison with which the papacy seemed for a time almost insignificant.

His first task was to secure full national recognition for the monarchy, now that it had returned to Saxony. Through the fateful link with the Welfs which was forged when Henry the Proud became duke in 1126, its influence already extended to Bavaria and the Swabian possessions of the Welfic family. Lothar even tried to give the monarchy a foothold in the south by taking action against the Staufen. The private possessions they had inherited from the Salians could not be denied them, but anything they could be shown to have acquired as an accession to imperial territory during the last two reigns—the city of Nuremberg, for example—was declared by a decision of the nobles at Regensburg to belong to the new ruling house as the Salians' legal successors. Neither the thought nor the governmental methods of the time made a sharp distinction between the two, however. When the Staufen denounced the demand to surrender imperial property as an invasion of their rights, their leader Frederick of Swabia was outlawed, and Lothar tried to hold them in check by transferring the rectorate of Burgundy to Conrad of Zähringen, who continued

K

to use his older title of duke. But the successful resistance of the Staufen, which found support in Austria, Lower Lorraine and a number of imperial cities as well as in their own Swabian and Franconian lands, encouraged them at the end of 1127 to set up an anti-king in the person of Conrad III, who—unlike his elder brother Frederick—had not yet sworn fealty to the new ruler, and had been deprived of his East Frankish duchy by Lothar. Although the pope excommunicated him, Conrad made such headway that he was able to invade Italy the next year. There he profited for a time from the conflict between Milan and the curia, and was crowned King of Italy by the archbishop at Monza in 1128. But his resources were too small for him to attain his real object (to contest, as Henry V's heir, the papacy's claims to the Matildine lands) in face of the refusal of Matilda's vassals to accept him, and a reconciliation between Milan and Rome soon cut the ground from under his feet. The whole expedition was shown to be a mistake when Conrad returned to Germany empty-handed in 1130 and found the divided Staufen power in retreat there too, and its own territories threatened. The German civil war was not yet over, however, by the time another great quarrel—one which soon shook all Europe—pushed these merely domestic rivalries into the background and prevented Lothar from crushing his German opponents.

The double papal election of 1130 had grown out of party rivalries in the college of cardinals and struggles for power between the Roman noble families. Supported by the Frangipani, a minority of the college under the leadership of the chancellor Aimerich had raised Innocent II to the throne by hasty and illegal methods. The other party, thus outwitted, chose its leader Peter Pierleoni as Anacletus II in an election the form of which was unimpeachable. One candidate could argue that he was elected first, the other that he had the better right. Europe had to decide between them. It was therefore of decisive significance that although Innocent, the less prominent of the two, was forced out of Rome and eventually (after a short stay in Pisa) out of Italy altogether by his more powerful opponent, he was an upright and moderate man who was able to win the support of Bernard of Clairvaux and the French monasteries, and that reforming ideas were apparently at work in the circles that elected him. This

meant that he was recognised by France and led also to his acceptance by Lothar, who was now wooed by both parties. A strong
and independent monarchy like that of the Salians could have
used this favourable situation to advance the German claim to
control the papacy. Hindered by Staufen opposition and bound
by clerical ideas and sentiments, however, Lothar saw the decision
as ultimately a matter of conscience, and was very glad to be able
to put the final responsibility upon the synod of Würzburg. There
were several among the prelates of the empire who were convinced
that Anacletus's was the better cause, but the majority followed
Norbert's lead and sided with Bernard. Lothar acquiesced,
although Anacletus offered him the imperial crown, and England
followed suit. A great opportunity was missed, and new obligations were placed upon the German king because of his decision.
He was expected to escort his pope back to Rome and to give
permanent protection to 'a Church oppressed by Jewish fury'.

For the position of Anacletus—a cultivated, worldly and
ambitious man, though many of his detractors' charges were
unjust—was indeed weakened by his Jewish descent, which was
enough to make him unacceptable to the Bernardines as pope;
and this was the chief reason for his failure. His position in Italy
was not so easily shaken, however, for he had the support of
Rome, had won the Milanese Church over to his side by well-
timed concessions, and found his strongest protector in Roger II
of Sicily.

The Normans were now demonstrating their capacity as
state-builders in southern Italy as well as in England, France and
Palestine, and in Roger (1101–1154) they produced a leader of
outstanding gifts, the first medieval ruler to have a 'modern'
look. Shrewd in calculating his own advantage and deeply
interested in statistics, geography and national economic policy,
Roger was as versatile as he was prudent, set no bounds to his
ambition and knew how to harness passion in the service of
politics. His father, Roger I, the brother and vassal of Robert
Guiscard, had conquered Sicily from a mainland base in Calabria.
Roger now reversed the process: on the extinction of Guiscard's
line in 1127, he used Sicily as a base from which to invade Apulia.
He had neither talent for generalship nor military inclinations,
but made up for the lack of them by his finesse as a negotiator, by
an unerring certainty of aim and by diplomatic skill. He ruthlessly

subdued the smaller Norman and Lombard states in the toe and heel of Italy and welded them to the stronger and more united island territory which he already controlled, advancing his frontiers step by step northwards at the expense of the feudal claims of Emperor and pope alike. Above all, his genius for administration subjected the motley populations of these petty warring principalities to the authority of a scanty Norman ruling class and hammered them into a solid, unified whole. His Assizes of Ariano (1140), the main body of his laws, have long been over-shadowed by the fuller Constitutions of his grandson Frederick II, which derive directly from them; they have only lately been accorded the recognition they deserve as models of early written law. In Roger's Assizes, Norman-French customs imported into the south were supplemented by ideas borrowed from Roman, Byzantine, Lombard and canon law.

A strong monarchy, enlightened and progressive but with the mystical and absolutist aura of a Justinian upon it, sowed the seeds of a new style of government behind the ramparts of its capital at Palermo. Instead of depending upon the restless Norman feudal nobility, it drew its strength from a disciplined bureaucracy, fortifications and mercenary soldiers, from a fleet which conquered the African coast from Tunis to Tripoli, and from an advanced financial system, based on a money economy and influenced by Arabic and Jewish models, which exploited both the natural resources of the island and its advantageous position in the centre of the Mediterranean to create wealth for the crown by means of taxes and customs-duties. This artificial state, in which a variety of peoples, languages, religions and cultural traditions were held together by the Norman cement, was a disturbing foreign body inside the feudal and ecclesiastical world of its day, provoking unrest and threatening to change the face of the continent. It soon became the most-feared power in the Mediterranean basin: hated by the Italian maritime cities, on terms of hostility with the Greek emperor (at whose expense most of its lands had been won), and distrusted by the papacy (whose rear it protected, but whom it threatened with destruction and whose own plans for dominating the south it had ruined). After renewed disappointments, the papacy had given up the hopeless struggle as early as the time of Honorius II, who enfeoffed Roger with the duchy of Apulia in 1128. Anacletus bought Norman assistance with still greater concessions: in 1130 he made Roger's papal fief into a hereditary kingdom, enlarged it by the gift of the principality of Capua and suzerain rights over Naples and Benevento, confirmed the king's legatine powers over the Sicilian Church (which dated back to Urban II)—thereby making him still stronger and better able to exclude all rival authorities—and rearranged the ecclesiastical organisation of the southern part of his mainland possessions.

If he yielded to the demand that he accompany Innocent back to Rome, Lothar risked serious conflict with Anacletus's friend and vassal. Could concessions be secured in exchange? When he met the pope at Liège in 1131, Lothar did in fact ask that the old right of investiture be restored, but he showed his inexperience of great affairs by unhesitatingly performing the service of the stirrup, after the fashion of a servant or a vassal. Hitherto he had given every sign of wanting to meet the Church half-way over appointments to bishoprics, and had never attempted to exercise the full extent even of his rights under the Concordat of Worms in regard to his presence at elections and his right to decide disputed cases. Now that he was king, he was uncomfortably aware of the restrictions which the royal power had undergone. Innocent, on the other hand, now had no further need to be conciliatory, and he found solid clerical support for his attitude. Lothar gave way at once when confronted with the hostility of his own bishops and the force of Bernard's eloquence. Since he had ruled out the possibility of conflict from the start, resistance could bring him no advantage, and he was soon compelled—though perhaps against his will—to allow the newly-elected bishops of Trier and Regensburg to be consecrated before he had invested them.

He had planned an Italian expedition to secure himself the imperial crown and to mark his final victory over the Hohenstaufen pretender, and it was still in his own interests to execute the plan; but the way in which he did so in 1132-3 showed that he had no mind to pull anyone else's chestnuts out of the fire. Since he dared not denude Germany of troops because of Hohenstaufen enmity, he took only weak forces with him. He crept cautiously past the hostile Italian cities, but kept the interests of the Empire carefully in mind and did not let himself be side-tracked. Even when he reached Rome in 1133, he made no effort to drive out Anacletus (who held St. Peter's and most of the city), but contented himself with receiving the imperial crown from his own pope in the Lateran, which was not the usual place for the ceremony.

His short stay in Rome showed once more the contrast between his indifference to ideological damage and his keen sense of material advantage. He let it pass without comment when a bull of Innocent's used words which threatened the traditional relationship of the two powers: 'We confer the fulness of imperial authority upon you'. Another move to re-establish the old right of investiture came to nothing, like his previous attempt in Liège, and this time he was opposed by his own arch-chancellor for Italy, Norbert. He gained a small advantage in the matter of episcopal appointments, however, when he secured from Innocent an explicit declaration against several recent cases where consecration had preceded royal investiture. Norbert seems to have taken the position that previous royal investiture was equivalent to the giving of the king's consent and that it therefore amounted to a right of veto: incidentally, as will be seen, it was with Norbert's help that papal approval was unexpectedly won for the claims of the German Church in the northern and eastern territories.

Another success was important for the extension of imperial power. The Emperor and the papal curia were at one in their desire to prevent the Matildine lands from falling into the hands of the Hohenstaufen in their capacity as the private heirs of Henry V. The pope lacked the power to act, however, and Lothar —for whom Matilda's vassals declared their support—had no legal title to possession. Lothar therefore signified the Empire's acceptance of the papal claim to ownership and himself accepted the lands as a fief in return for an annual payment. Outwardly, this was a very considerable gain. Lothar did not take the regular oath, which was associated with vassalage, but was invested instead with a ring, the ecclesiastical symbol. It would be very easy, however, for the legal position to become obscured, and for the Emperor to be represented as the pope's man, the Empire as a fief of the papacy in the sense which Gregory VII had desired: Innocent's words, quoted above, and Lothar's holding his stirrup both pointed in the same direction. In point of fact, this reading of the situation was soon given pictorial form: a painting in the Lateran showed the emperor doing homage to the enthroned pope before he was crowned by Innocent, and the accompanying verses explicitly described him as the pope's vassal. This shows clearly how dangerous Lothar's short-sighted acceptance of the external forms of subordination was for the future of the Empire. The material advantage which the occupation of the Matildine lands represented was on the other hand undeniable, and the subtlety of Lothar's demesne policy was shown when he immediately transferred possession of them to his son-in-law, Henry the Proud, who admittedly then had to become a vassal of the pope in the full sense. This action of Lothar's laid the foundation for Welf predominance over central Europe from the North Sea across southern Germany and into central Italy.

Lothar could be content with the profits from his Italian expedition, if he weighed them against the little that he had ventured. That he had gained so much, however, was largely attributable to the fact that domestic troubles had hampered Roger's foreign policy, although Lothar refused the pope's urgent request to take advantage of Roger's embarrassment by attacking him. But when Lothar withdrew over the Alps and Roger began to recover his strength, Innocent's position soon became intenable. Disappointed of his hopes, he was forced to take refuge in Pisa. Shortly after Lothar's withdrawal, it became clear that if the schism was to be ended, a new and larger expedition would have to be mounted against Anacletus's chief supporter Roger, who was now regaining power.

The task of the next few years was to prepare the ground for such an operation by promoting the cause of peace. Bernard here achieved his greatest diplomatic success, mediating even in the negotiations between Lothar and his German opponents. The two Hohenstaufen brothers—who could not in fact have held out much longer—submitted in turn. At the Reichstag at Bamberg in 1135, where a ten-year Landpeace was proclaimed, they secured a full pardon in return for recognising Lothar as Emperor and promising to take part in a new Italian expedition. Apart from Bernard's share in all this, there were other grounds as well for Lothar to be grateful to the Church for support at home and abroad.

These were the prosperous and peaceful years to which the chroniclers looked back with longing from the period of renewed disorder which soon followed, and in the light of later German history they were certainly not unjustified in doing so. For this was the time when peasants began to migrate eastwards from the

relatively densely populated Low Countries and the Rhine valley
to seek new ploughlands among the marshes and fens between
Weser and Elbe; later they moved on across the frontier to colonise
Wendish territory, while at the same time the more enterprising
clergy and higher nobility sought new fields of activity in the same
areas. It was therefore bound to be a matter of great significance
that, under Lothar and because of the location of his duchy, the
monarchy carried through a change of front from south-west to
north-east and began once more to follow the lines of development
which had been so suddenly cut off after the death of Otto the
Great. Lothar gave less attention to west Germany than his
predecessors had done, but a lifetime's experience had made him
adept in Saxon affairs. Some of his appointments—that of the
Ascanian Albrecht of Ballenstädt to the Nordmark of Brandenburg
in 1134, for instance, or the union two years later of Lausitz with
the Mark of Meissen under Conrad of Wettin (who had already
held the latter as a fief since 1123), and the transfer of the Schauen-
burgs from the Weser to the counties of Holstein and Stormarn—
show that he knew how to put the right man in the right place;
several well-known families can in fact trace their later importance
back to the favour shown them by Lothar. It must not be forgotten, moreover, that considerations of Saxon policy were
prominent in Lothar's mind even during the coronation ceremony
in Rome: he secured from the pope confirmation of the archbishop
of Bremen's metropolitan rights over the northern lands (it was
only later on, when the Danish archbishopric of Lund was
created, that they were surrendered), and he supported Norbert's
efforts to get similar recognition of Magdeburg's claims over
Poland, which dated back to the missionary dreams of the Ottonian
period. But here, as in Scandinavia, national resistance was too
strong to be overcome by a sheet of parchment. The subordination
of the Pomeranian Church was never achieved, although the
missions promoted by the kindly and self-sacrificing bishop Otto
of Bamberg (which Lothar warmly supported, even diverting the
Polish tribute to Otto) substantially paved the way for later
Germanisation by increasing the regard in which the Germans
were held. In the feudal dependency of Wendish Wagria (in
eastern Holstein) Lothar encouraged the missionary activity of the
priest Vicelin, and at his suggestion founded the castle of Segeberg,
round which the first Saxon settlements grouped themselves.

The increased prestige which Lothar gained for the Empire in the north and east was reflected in his relations with the rulers of the neighbouring states. Although he suffered a severe defeat in Bohemia in 1126, at the beginning of his reign, the old dependent relationship of the duke was soon re-established on a remarkably friendly footing. Eric, king of Denmark, obtained imperial recognition at the Reichstag of Merseburg in 1135, as soon as he emerged victorious from a long succession dispute. After mediating in a war between Hungary and Poland, at the same Reichstag Lothar enjoyed the triumph of seeing the unruly duke Boleslaw III of Poland carry the sword before him in procession as a sign of his subjection, pay the arrears of tribute which had been outstanding for twelve years, and accept enfeoffment with Pomerania and Rügen, which he had succeeded in conquering. The emperor even promoted trade in the north-east by giving a privilege of protection in imperial territory to the merchants of the Danish island of Gotland. It is not too much to say that in the Baltic lands Lothar foreshadowed the part that his grandson Henry the Lion was to play more thoroughly and more permanently a generation later when he encouraged the first large-scale German colonisation.

The period of prosperity and peace for Germany lasted but a short time, however. Even at Merseburg all the opponents of King Roger—the Greek emperor, Venice, south Italian refugees, and above all Innocent II and his partisans—had forced the reluctant Lothar to undertake a new Italian expedition. The unity and solidarity of Germany (manifested by the size of his army), clerical propaganda, and Bernard's successful preparatory work (which won Milan for Innocent and ensured naval support from Pisa and Genoa), all made this 1136–7 expedition a very impressive affair. It was explicitly directed at Roger of Sicily. The emperor marched through northern Italy from the western Alps to Ravenna as an accepted ruler, before whose advance all resistance melted away; he was once more a legislator when he issued a feudal law forbidding the *valvassores* from dividing or alienating their fiefs in order to build up resources for private war.

The army moved south from Ravenna in two columns: Lothar with the main body along the Adriatic coast, Henry the Proud, at the head of a detachment which included the pope, by a westerly route through Tuscany. The two columns converged on the Norman kingdom, met at Bari, and won several victories still further south in 1137. So far the campaign had been successful, but what was to come next? Roger had treated the invasion like a torrent which swells at flood time but is bound to subside in the succeeding drought, and was clever enough to surrender part of his kingdom in order to overcome it. To secure peace, he even offered to separate Apulia from the rest and give it as a fief of the Empire to one of his sons, handing over another son as a hostage: for Lothar this was a chance, never likely to recur, of ending the difficult campaign with honour and the outward semblance of victory. But Innocent, whose objective was the total destruction of the Norman kingdom, persuaded him to reject it and himself pressed on further south. There impassable limits were set to his actions by the return of his German troops, who feared the effects of the July heat and rose against pope and cardinals. Permanent occupation of the conquered territory was out of the question, so the old policy of division was revived. The principality of Capua was re-established, and Roger's old enemy Rainulf of Alife was enfeoffed with the duchy of Apulia; it was hoped thus to hold the Sicilian king in check on the mainland. Here the papal and imperial claims to sovereignty collided. Lothar, who had no documentary proof of imperial rights to hand, accepted a feeble compromise, and an uncertain legal situation was thereby created, which was later to prove seriously disadvantageous to the empire: pope and emperor both held the ducal banner and as joint overlords together handed it to Rainulf.

A dispute over the occupation of the old imperial abbey of Monte Cassino led to the first occasion on which Lothar stood upon his rights (he had written evidence for them this time) against Innocent and Bernard, and threatened a rupture if they were not admitted. The events of this period leave the unmistakeable impression that the lines of papal and imperial policy had begun to diverge. The curia's grasping disregard of legality was bound to cause the emperor misgivings, however anxious he was for peace. The pope, on the other hand began to fear that the empire might fall into the ruthless hands of Henry the Proud (with whom he had had several sharp differences) and become oppressive. Furthermore, his desires were in no way satisfied when Lothar and his army turned back northwards. He found himself almost completely dependent upon the prestige and the oratory of Bernard, and was forced to concede Roger (who now advanced again) the position of judge between himself and the anti-pope— a concession which nevertheless brought no result. Only the death of Anacletus (who had held out in Rome to the end) in 1138 at last gave him breathing space and heralded the end of the schism.

By that time Lothar was dead. He was already a sick man when he reached German soil, and died in a peasant's hut on the slopes of the Alps soon afterwards, in December 1137. If increasing influence is the mark of political success, then Lothar's reign was by no means without it, even though it was not distinguished. But his was essentially a preparatory role. A short time before he died, he had made Henry the Proud margrave of Tuscany; his last actions were to appoint him to the duchy of Saxony in addition to his own Bavaria and to designate him as heir to the throne by sending him the imperial insignia as he lay dying. Henry thus directly ruled vast territories, 'from sea to sea, from Denmark to Sicily'. If, instead of the Hohenstaufen, the Welfs had secured the crown, historians would have praised Lothar as the far-sighted founder of the dynasty. But cunning plots and the accidents of fortune nullified this aim and destroyed a large part of Lothar's work, as well as throwing the Empire into a state of confusion and weakness.

9

CONRAD III (1138–1152)

It is strange that a family whose main task was to be resistance to the hierarchy's claims over the Germans should have ascended the throne under papal patronage. The curia had repaid Lothar for his mildness by determining to profit ruthlessly from the advantage it had given them and by preparing, at the end of his life, to frustrate the succession of his son-in-law. Their chief instrument was the cleverest and most energetic of the German prelates, archbishop Albero of Trier, a Frenchman by birth. The sees of Mainz and Cologne being vacant at the time, Albero took the lead in the election proceedings; aided and abetted by a cardinal legate, he mismanaged them in a quite extraordinary way. The election of the former anti-king, Conrad III, in March 1138, was reminiscent of the way in which the pope himself had been chosen; it was both illegal and unexpected, and was carried through by a small minority of the nobles some time before Whitsun, the date which had been set for the meeting. The proceedings had sinister consequences for the whole history of Germany for one reason above all others. By the 1130's the monarchy was well on the way to a revival; under the Welfs it had certainly been far from abandoning its Italian possessions, but the location of its German territories had given it close contacts with the vitally important affairs of the whole of central and eastern Europe. Now it moved back to the south-west, and the perpetuation of Welfic power prevented it from being in a position to arrest the separate development of north-east Germany. Although the 'parson's King' or 'crowned noble', as the chroniclers call Conrad, gained ground with remarkable speed and later legalised his position by a regular election, these satirical descriptions nevertheless point directly to the two foundations upon which his authority rested. Church and nobility, which had raised Lothar up, turned away from his house as soon as it became strong and when the character of its new head—the ruthless Henry the Proud—seemed to offer them no guarantee against a change in policy. Henry soon had to abandon his hopes of the crown, although he could continue to expect that the recognition of his full rights to Saxony and Bavaria, the two most firmly established duchies, would make him the real ruler of the Empire. For this very reason, Conrad could not possibly give him that recognition. To unite two duchies in one hand contradicted the whole concept of the ducal office; and even if it was not expressly forbidden by the law, political considerations alone were enough to decide the matter. After hesitating long enough to ensure that Henry handed over the royal insignia, Conrad refused to enfeoff him with Saxony, outlawed him when he refused to do homage, and gave the duchy to margrave Albert the Bear, who had claims to it as the grandson of the last Billung in the female line; soon afterwards, in 1139, he gave Bavaria to his Babenberg step-brother, margrave Leopold IV of Austria. Actions like these could only be made good on the field of battle. Germany at once split into two rival camps, and the bitter feud between Welf and Hohenstaufen began.

At first it was a struggle between the nobility of the middle rank, backed by the Church, and the full strength of the monarchy. For Conrad by himself was nothing. As the younger of the Staufen brothers he did not even control Swabia: he could only rely on his old East Frankish duchy, and his personal standing did not make up for his lack of real power. As anti-king he had shown more energy than skill. He was in the full strength of his manhood, a handsome, knightly figure, a valiant warrior who sought danger, was capable of clumsy practical jokes, and shared fatigue and privation with his men. Friendly and cheerful, he mixed easily after a layman's fashion in the learned conversation of his clerical courtiers, and laughingly envied the philosophers the calm way in which they could make out that the impossible could be done. But in spite of these attractive characteristics, contemporaries and later historians are unanimous in their opinion of him as a states-man: not one of them has very much to say in his favour. He did not so much lack adaptability or enterprise—after all, he twice undertook the burden of the crown in the most difficult circum-stances—as shrewdness, caution, the calculation to prepare and the steadiness to persist in any course he chose to adopt. Like so many others he was captivated by the ecclesiastical ideals of the time and filled with a sense of his own sins, as his correspondence with the visionary Hildegart of Bingen demonstrates. Easily moved and credulous, he was no more readily persuaded by the eloquence of a Bernard of Clairvaux than by the belief that an eclipse of the moon was the work of Antichrist, and allowed himself to be drawn unreflectingly into ill-prepared schemes, only to surrender to new influences and countermand his own orders, so that even his intimates complained of his instability. As a result, his reign was unproductive; every expected success petered out between conception and realisation, and at the end he was little further on than he had been at the beginning. Meanwhile disaster flooded the land, the king's prestige sank low, and even if this very misfortune was instrumental in hastening the change, the total reversal of public opinion which was the chief result of his reign can hardly be called his own achievement.

It may well be asked whether Conrad would have made any headway at all if Henry the Proud had not died suddenly in 1139, at the beginning of the civil war and shortly after gaining the upper hand in Saxony; it speaks volumes for the strength of the opposing party that they were able to secure Saxony for the ten-year-old Henry the Lion in spite of his father's death, although Bavaria, where his brother Welf (VI) was in command, remained hotly disputed. Peace was patched up when, on the death of Leopold of Austria, his brother Henry (nicknamed Jasomirgott) gained possession of Bavaria by his marriage to Henry the Proud's widow Gertrude in 1142, but it proved short-lived. When Gertrude died soon afterwards, Henry the Lion renewed the claim to Bavaria which Welf had never quite dropped, and the conflict began again.

The paralysis of royal authority meant that private war broke out all over Germany and a period of instability and lawlessness set in. Its external consequences were soon evident. In east and north the prestige gained for the monarchy by Lothar was lost, though similar disturbances in the neighbouring countries removed all danger of invasion. In the west the French crown had extended its demesne to the Pyrenees by Louis VII's marriage with Eleanor, the heiress of Aquitaine, in 1137; when its resources, thus doubled, came under the guidance of the statesmanlike abbot Suger of St. Denis, it really began to dominate France. Conrad did have some success in Italy; after Henry the Proud's death he was able to secure recognition from the feudal tenants of the Matildine lands, who saw advantages in holding directly of the king, and tenure by three German rulers in succession gradually began to engender a customary-law right to lordship over them. But in the Middle Ages, more than at any other time, rights were only of any use when they were actually exercised. Since Conrad never dared leave Germany, the Matildine lands gradually fell apart and served only to enrich the neighbouring authorities. But this was not all. The fifteen masterless years after Lothar's death happened to coincide with a period of remarkable growth on the part of the cities of Lombardy and central Italy; for this reason they were fatal to imperial rights, which gradually fell either into the hands of others or into oblivion. The Italians lost the habit of subjection and became accustomed to a freedom which knew no limits save their neighbours' greed. From the south the pent-up power of King Roger overflowed into Rome and the central provinces as soon as it was released by the death of his adversary Rainulf in 1139.

It was therefore a piece of gross self-deception when Innocent II, over-confident because unity had been restored to the Church, thought he could win new laurels by a campaign in the south. He failed, as Leo IX and Honorius II had done. Defeated and taken prisoner, in the treaty of Mignano (1139) he had to confirm all the concessions Roger had extorted from the anti-pope. For the grant of Apulia and Calabria as fiefs to Roger's two sons was only a face-saving sham, and so was the drafting skill of the curia when it made no mention of Anacletus's privilege and traced the recognition of the Sicilian kingdom back to Honorius II. His total disregard of the Empire's claims over southern Italy could easily have brought the pope into collision with the German king, but his agreement with Roger had only been made under duress and did not reduce their mutual hostility. For as Roger now began to transform his state into the centralised institution described earlier, he extended without more ado to the mainland the legatine rights which only applied to the island of Sicily, and even tried to advance his frontiers with the papal state when the curia delayed the ceremony of enfeoffment. As long as Roger lived the papacy found the empire an indispensable counterbalance to threats of this kind.

Over and above all this, events in Rome soon made Conrad's intervention very desirable. The movement for urban self-government, which had already spread from Milan into central Italy, first reached Rome shortly after the death of Innocent II in

1143. The divisions among the leading men which the schism had caused now began to turn to the advantage of the hitherto weak bourgeoisie and to mingle with the quarrels of the noble families and with memories (never quite lost, and now reviving strongly) of the former greatness of the city. A senate, calling itself the instrument of the popular will, met on the newly-restored Capitol under the leadership of the *patricius* Jordan Pierleoni, a brother of Anacletus, and demanded that the pope renounce secular dominion over Rome—exactly the same demand as the Lombard cities had made of their bishops. In the bloodshed and confusion which followed, the popes's efforts to assert themselves were in vain. Eugenius III (1145–1153) who wore the habit of a Cistercian beneath his papal vestments and greatly promoted the influence of his master St. Bernard, was forced to flee northwards in March 1146 after fruitless attempts to arrange a settlement. At that moment, he was expecting Conrad to march down into Italy. A series of important events prevented this.

Nothing would be wider of the mark than to deduce a general decline in regard for the papacy from occasional examples of local opposition to it. North of the Alps, its influence had never been stronger nor its intervention in all spheres more profound. Even under Innocent II, clerical legislation had increased this influence by permitting unrestricted appeal to the curia (1135) and had worked against that of the king by encouraging the tendency— first noticeable at the Second Lateran Council of 1139,[1] which triumphantly celebrated the restoration of unity within the Church— to exclude the laity from episcopal elections. A new wave of exemptions to monasteries widened the meaning of papal protection to include proprietary rights and the payment of tribute. Soon after 1140, the *Decretum* of Gratian, a Camaldulensian monk of Bologna, developed canon law even beyond Pseudo-Isidore. Although it was originally made only for private use, the *Decretum* soon drove the older collections of canons out of the ecclesiastical courts and the law schools and became the basis of the *Corpus juris canonici*. It gave papal claims a permanent form in which they were soon being spread abroad by the religious movements which, in spite of an undercurrent of opposition, still ruled unchallenged over men's minds. Even those who noted bitterly how the development of the Church was sapping the strength of the

[1] Schroeder 195–213.

German monarchy regarded this development as something fore-doomed. Conrad's step-brother, bishop Otto of Freising, gave this idea striking expression in his 'Chronicle of the Two Cities' (of God and of the Devil). He saw the Roman-German Empire gradually fading away, and (since it was the last of the four great world-monarchies, according to Daniel's interpretation of Nebu-chadnezzar's dream)[1] expected the world to end after its dis-appearance, and this to be followed by the coming of Anti-Christ and the Last Judgement. But the stone which broke the feet of clay to pieces and became a great mountain which filled the whole earth he took to be a figure for the papal Church. Raised to eminence by the Emperor's generosity, the Church had begun to attack his secular authority from the time of Gregory VII and, according to Otto, had won a great victory in the Concordat of Worms. Now it was spreading over the whole world. Would it bring the longed-for Kingdom of God to pass? Was the fulness of time now come, and was only one last violent effort needed to compel the stubborn Gentiles to come in? Otto of Freising expressed the thoughts that were in all hearts. It is only against this background of religious emotion that the fantastic successes of the new crusading move-ment can be properly appreciated.

The stimulus was provided by the armed resistance of Islam to the progress of the Franks, which began with Imadeddin Zenki, the ruler of Mosul. Zenki profited from the disunity of the crusading leaders to capture their eastern outpost of Edessa in 1144. From here he could threaten Antioch, the key to the Syrian coastal plain. Had God himself given this as a sign that he was about to exalt the Cross over the whole globe? When at the end of 1145 Eugenius III followed the example of Urban and appealed for help to the French, the people of the first crusade, he did not foresee the effect his words were to have. Louis VII, still young and active, declared himself ready to set out in fulfilment of a vow of pilgrimage, and this awakened the spirit of emulation. But it was of even greater consequence that Bernard of Clairvaux accepted the pope's invitation to undertake the preaching of the crusade, for his burning eloquence and the miracles which convinced the multitudes of his divine mission drew his hearers after him like men in a dream. At Vézelay at Easter 1146 he had to cut up his habit, because there were not enough crosses for the

---

[1] Daniel ii. 31-5.

L

crowds who demanded them. A single purpose dominated all minds. 'Suddenly,' says Otto of Freising, 'such a hush came over the whole West that it was counted as sacrilege to fight or even to carry weapons openly.'

The expedition thus took on a more universal character than the first crusade, to which Urban had really managed to attract only the feudal nobility of France. This time 'the kings of the earth were themselves to lead the armies of the Eternal King against the enemies of His Cross'. Soon the flood burst over the frontiers of Germany. The first object of attack was the unbeliever near at hand, and there were massive pogroms against the Jews until Bernard appeared and halted them. Conrad was caught in a serious conflict of duty. Every rational argument was against his joining the crusade, for if he was really determined to turn his back on the unfinished struggle in Germany, then the pope's distress, the imperial crown, the disregard of imperial rights and Roger's encroachments all summoned him urgently to Italy. He refused to take the Cross. But how much did the counsels of cold reason count for at a time like this? At Speyer soon after Christmas Conrad had to face a final eloquent appeal from Bernard, who threatened his indifference with the terrors of death and the judgement-seat of Christ and praised his change of heart as a miracle of miracles. In his own interests the pope sought to release Conrad from his vow, but in vain. Nothing could stop the movement in Germany now. Excited crowds followed Bernard wherever he went, although they understood neither Latin nor French. On one occasion Conrad himself had to drag Bernard away from a church to protect him from the crowd which pressed towards him. At Bernard's instance, a general land-peace spread over the Empire. When duke Welf took the cross, even Henry the Lion swore to stop prosecuting his Bavarian claims for a while. The pacification of the country apart, the preaching of the crusade brought the Hohenstaufen house another substantial advantage: Conrad's ten-year-old son was elected and crowned king, and under the guardianship of archbishop Henry of Mainz was to represent his father during the latter's absence. Thus a first step had been taken to revive the tradition of hereditary succession which had been broken after the end of the Salian line. In later times, a crusade was often to serve as a means to the same end.

The events of the second crusade can only be sketched lightly here. It was indicative of the general objectives of the movement and of the excessive numbers of participants, as well as of the lack of unity in the Empire, that few except the south Germans followed Conrad. The Saxon magnates were disinclined for an expedition to the Levant, and on their own account—though also with the approval of St Bernard and the pope—undertook a crusade nearer home into the Wendish lands as far east as Pomerania, with the scarcely-concealed purpose of roughly disturbing the peaceful progress of the missions in those areas. They soon departed from Bernard's solution—conversion or death to the heathen—in pursuit of their own advantage, preferring token baptisms and the payment of tribute to the devastation of the land. But Flemings and Lower Lorrainers joined Englishmen and Normans in the sea-passage to Syria, and won the only lasting success of the whole crusade when *en route* they helped the king of Portugal to capture the Moorish city of Lisbon. Other Lorrainers travelled with the French army which followed Conrad's ill-organised forces through Hungary into Byzantine territory.

Here the German king's relationship to and friendship with the crafty and cunning emperor Manuel stood him in good stead, as did Manuel's liking for the knightly culture of the western courts, while their common hostility to Roger of Sicily formed a political bond between them. Manuel's own desire to get rid of the Germans before the French arrived, his unlimited resources and the great superiority of Byzantine over western technology all made it easy for him to shift the German crusaders (who probably numbered several tens of thousands) across to Nicaea. He advised them to advance by the longer but safer coastal route. However, the onward urge made them decide on a march through the interior of Asia Minor. A disciplined, well-mounted and well-fed army could have reached Iconium in about three weeks. Conrad therefore determined to send the disorganised and ill-provided masses by the coastal route, accompanied by a small detachment of troops under bishop Otto of Freising; but most of them, fearing that they were to be sacrificed, refused to let themselves be separated from the main body. Only their absolute trust in the direct guidance of God made them risk such a march in ignorance of the route and with totally insufficient supplies. After ten days in a land desolate by nature and laid waste by the enemy, abandoned by the Greek nobles whom they mistrusted and abused and beset on all sides by clouds of light Turkish cavalry, they had reached the limit of their endurance. Safety, if it was to be found at all, lay only in immediate retreat; an eclipse of the sun struck terror among them and seemed a sign of God's anger. Hunger, sickness and the attacks of the enemy turned the retreat into a terrible catastrophe, and Conrad—who devotedly shared the danger, toil and privations of his men—managed to bring only a scanty remnant of the army back to Nicaea.

Joining Louis VII's crusaders, who had arrived meanwhile, Conrad marched with them part of the way along the coast, but he was exhausted by the time they reached Ephesus in January 1148 and took ship for Constantinople to recuperate in Manuel's care. Shortly before this, Otto of Freising's detachment, which had marched from Ephesus up the valley of the Meander, was overwhelmed by the Moslems near Laodicea and cut to pieces, so that only a small part of it reached Syria. The French suffered severe losses at the same spot. Louis, accompanied by as many knights as could bear the expense, only reached the Holy Land because he chartered Greek ships and left the main body of the poorer crusaders to their fate. Conrad made the journey by the same means, and now that the scattered fragments of the original expedition were at last gathered together they composed a force which in spite of everything was still strong enough to have attempted something worthwhile. But the first enthusiasm had gone, and there was no clear objective now that Zenki's son Nureddin had razed Edessa to the ground. The sorry quarrel between Louis VII and his vassal Raymond (who had just broken up the king's marriage) hindered essential reinforcements from reaching Antioch. Since the remainder of the crusading states were not directly threatened, the newcomers soon felt themselves to be rather a burden than a blessing to the Latins, whose aim was colonial independence and separation from the mother country. An unsuccessful thrust towards Damascus only drove its friendly prince into the threatening arms of Nureddin. In order to have at any rate something to their credit, the crusaders tried to take Ascalon, which was still occupied by the Egyptians, but they were simply left in the lurch by the Latins. Nothing remained but to return to Europe. After incalculable loss of life, health and property the great movement ended in angry discord and spiteful recriminations. Islam raised its head more threateningly than ever.

Nitzsch aptly compared the catastrophe of the second crusade with the destruction of Napoleon's Grand Army in Russia. Just as in the one case Napoleon's designs on world-empire received, because he had over-extended himself, a decisive blow which annihilated French 'glory' and ushered in an age of nationalism and resistance, so the passionate conviction that the Kingdom of God would be realised on earth under papal direction perished in Syria and Asia Minor. The shortcomings of clerical government were seen in future with a keener eye, and secular tendencies dominated the next half-century.

Bernard grasped the possibility of such a reversal at once. Not that his own faith in the objectives of the expedition was shaken—he even let himself be elected leader of a new French crusade in 1150, but it never set out. After all, Moses too had been prevented by their own sins from fulfilling his promise to lead the Children of Israel into the Promised Land. Bernard's own sensitiveness to the shortcomings of the Church became sharper, and he saw a thorough purge of the Temple by the scourge of Christ as the best means of blunting the force of complaint. The purge took the form of the scathing criticism, grounded in piety and devotion, of what has sometimes been called his 'Testament'—his book the *de Consideratione*,[1] which he dedicated to the pope. The *de Consideratione* remains entirely within the framework of hierarchical—if not exactly Gregorian—conceptions: through its own inner purity, the papacy—whose duty it is to judge sin, but not to meddle with earthly property or worldly affairs—will exalt itself still more securely over the kingdoms of this world. But other voices had already been raised in bitter complaint against the Church's presumption in claiming superiority over the state, and they took up the struggle against the legalism and greed which prevailed at Rome in deadly earnest and with blistering scorn. The praise of the holy martyrs Rufinus and Albinus (gold and silver) whose relics opened every door in Rome, was nothing new, but before the century ended the terrible satire of the 'Gospel according to the Silver Mark' was passing from mouth to mouth: at the pope's command, the doorkeeper rebukes the impoverished petitioner with the words 'Friend, thy poverty go

[1] Extracts in Pullan 63–66, Tierney 92–94.

with thee into damnation. Get thee behind me, Satan, for thou
savourest not of the things that be of gold. Verily, verily, I say
unto thee, thou shalt not enter into the joy of thy Father until thou
hast paid thy last farthing'.[1] The demand for the clergy to return
to apostolic poverty was in the air, and it found its first influential
mouthpiece in Arnold of Brescia.

In the Lombard cities the religious radicalism of the Pataria
had long ago joined hands with civic democracy to oppose the
increasing secularism of the Church. To these two elements there
was added a third during Arnold's student days in Paris: the
influence of the rationalist theology of Peter Abelard, with its
emphasis on logic and its refusal to prejudge debatable questions.
On his return to Brescia, Arnold received priest's orders and
became a canon regular; soon he was prior of the Augustinian
convent in Brescia. His strength of will and puritanical outlook
made him set the strictest standards for his own personal conduct,
but they inflicted chastisement no more severe than the compelling
eloquence with which he denounced the worldliness and moral
degradation of the clergy and the desecration of the Church by
wealth and power. When the bishop of Brescia persuaded Innocent
II at the Lateran Council of 1139 to banish the unwelcome critic
from Italy as a schismatic, Arnold turned to Abelard once more.
At Abelard's side he came into violent conflict with the all-
powerful Bernard of Clairvaux, whose sensitive nostrils smelled
danger in the reason-based theology of Abelard and his Lombard
squire. After the justifiable condemnation of Abelard's teaching
at the Synod of Sens in 1140, Bernard managed to get a sentence
of life-long imprisonment in a monastery imposed on both his
opponents. When Arnold sharpened his attacks after Abelard's
death in 1142, Bernard enlisted the aid of the king and had him
expelled from France. Bernard's influence later drove him out of
Zürich too. His personal connexion with a cardinal took Arnold
in 1145 to Rome, where humble submission gained him a pardon
from Eugenius III.

He spent the next few years doing penance in the catacombs,
until he was caught up in the currents of Roman popular agitation
and carried by them back into politics. The small circle of ascetic

---

[1] G. G. Coulton, *Life in the Middle Ages*, i. 112–3. For a rather different
view of anti-clerical satire in the twelfth century, see R. W. Southern, *The Birth
of the Middle Ages* 154.

supporters, the so-called 'Lombards', which had surrounded him hitherto, was now replaced by excited popular assemblies on the Capitol. Arnold was genuinely moved by ideas of ancient Roman greatness when he inflamed the people with his oratory against the cardinals' greed and the pope's lust for power, and told his hearers that they were the only legitimate source of imperial authority.

Though he held no official position, Arnold was at the centre of a movement which comprised a mixture of Church reform, urban democracy and political Utopianism, just as Hus and Savonarola were later in Prague and Florence. What an impression the news that the crusade had failed must have made in such surroundings! The lower clergy of Rome were themselves already full of the revolutionary spirit when Eugenius III came back from Germany and France (where he had been during the crusade) in 1148 and excommunicated Arnold not only as a relapsed schismatic but also as a heretic because he had failed to respect the ordained status of evil-living priests, and threatened him and his clerical supporters with deprivation. But the senate protected its prophet, and the pope's efforts to make himself master of the obstinate city were in vain, in spite of a transient rapprochement with the king of Sicily.

This was the position when Conrad landed at Aquileia in May 1149, after a protracted sojourn in Constantinople on his way back from the crusade. The Romans hoped, both then and later, to win his support for themselves against the pope. Eloquent letters from the senate, sometimes even in verse form and always inspired by Arnold's ideas, invited him to the Eternal City. The unfortunate state of affairs which had prevailed since the time of Gregory VII, which meant that the clergy bore the chalice in one hand and the sword in the other, would come to an end, they proclaimed; the Roman people themselves were offering him the imperial crown, in accordance with the ancient rights which Vespasian had recognised in the Lex Regia, and they would restore to him the unlimited power of Constantine and Justinian, untrammelled by clerical pretensions. Attractive as this prospect might be, and correct as some of its historical justification undoubtedly was, these vainglorious proposals so naively ignored prevailing political facts that Conrad could not possibly commit himself to them, although his current mood prevented him from rejecting the idea of an association with the Romans out of hand. Since he also either could not or would not help the curia, the situation in Rome remained extremely critical for the pope, although he made a short-lived attempt at a compromise solution.

Politics on the grander scale were not determined by events in Rome, however, but by the friction between the Sicilians and the Greeks. Roger, the only European ruler who in this age of religious excitement never for one moment left political calculation out of account, had turned the emperor Manuel's embarrassments to his own advantage and attacked the Byzantine Empire. The crusade was hardly over before both sides began to look for allies. Conrad's interests coincided very closely in this respect with those of Manuel, whom he encouraged to attempt the reconquest of the former Byzantine possessions in southern Italy, completely disregarding the feudal claims of the papacy in order to bring Roger down. The facts that so soon after the crusade he attempted to raise the sunken royal prestige wherever he could, and that with his pitiful resources he was prepared to make an offensive alliance against Roger and precipitate new strife in Italy, amply confirm the impression created by the rest of his career—namely, that although under heavy pressure (Manuel's, in this case) Conrad could be induced to support well-prepared and wide-ranging plans, he lacked real political force and an eye for the possible. Insuperable obstacles barred the way to the enterprise. Roger in his turn had allied with returning crusaders against both empires: with the French king and the Welf duke, who was planning a new rising in south Germany for the same moment. As soon as this countermine went up, Conrad was forced to beat a hasty retreat.

The foreign policy of Conrad's last years, heavily influenced by abbot Wibald of Stablo, is a picture of complete powerlessness. Wibald's talents were mainly academic; as a politician he tacked anxiously, always seeking friendly relations with the curia, and his work does not bear comparison with the constructive statesmanship of his contemporary, Suger of St. Denis. Policy was hampered, too, by the king's frequent illnesses—the crusade had broken Conrad's health—and hindered by a lack of resources so serious that it sometimes even prevented the despatch of envoys abroad. An Italian expedition, to secure coronation as Emperor and bring about a joint Greco-German attack on Sicily, was postponed as often as it was planned, even when its departure had been finally fixed for 1151.

Conrad's domestic policy was more successful, in so far as he was able to defeat the restless Welf and use the mediation of Frederick (III), the young duke of Swabia, to induce him to make peace on generous terms in 1150. But Henry the Lion soon renewed his claim to Bavaria and openly defied the king, who continued to favour his Babenberg step-brother; war broke out afresh, and all the advantage lay with Henry. Further, the whole northern part of the kingdom began to escape from central control and go its own way; the gains made by Saxon territorial policy were by far the best things in the whole of German development at this time, and held out most promise for the future. In the north-eastern frontier lands, peaceful missions to the heathen— the results of which had been almost completely wiped out by the foolish crusade against the Wends—were gradually giving way to a deliberate policy of colonisation by plough and sword. As early as 1143 count Adolf II of Schauenburg had called for Germans from the north-west to settle the devasted Wendish lands beyond the frontier, and in the same year or the next he founded the city of Lübeck on the site of an abandoned Wendish royal settlement whose favourable location his keen eye had noticed. Soon after this, and partly in competition with Adolf, Henry the Lion began to extend his Slav dominions in almost complete independence of the Emperor; concerned only with power, he did not permit his purely secular interests to be in the slightest degree influenced by the metropolitan rights of the archbishop of Bremen, but thrust them roughly aside and followed the example of King Roger of Sicily by treating the occupants of the sees which he founded or re-established as his own officials. During Conrad's last years, margrave Albert the Bear secured compensation on the east for the loss of the Saxon duchy by inheriting the Brandenburg possessions of his friend the Christian prince Pribislaw in 1150, and thus began through the labour of hardy peasants the task of Germanising lands which were to be so important for the future.

The monarchy played no part in all this. Elsewhere in Germany there was scarcely a trace of the grasping, secularist, and in some senses anti-clerical policy revealed by these developments: instead the rest of the country looked back nostalgically to the past and yearned for a new and just leader to appear. It was felt to be a humiliation when, at the time of the crusade, Eugenius III held court in Trier during the winter of 1147–8 as the real ruler of the Empire; and still the pope and his legates continued their interference: the regent Henry of Mainz (the most distinguished of the archbishops) and the archbishop of Cologne were suspended when they disobeyed the pope's summons to the Council of Reims and offered no excuse. If in these and similar cases a quick and humble submission prevented more serious consequences, Germany was nevertheless full of dissatisfaction. The ground was being prepared for a new alliance of monarchy and episcopate along the familiar lines of the old dispensation. Even Conrad III himself, who had always been far more feebly complaisant than even his predecessor in matters affecting the rights or powers of the Church, had moments during his last years when the example of Byzantium, where things were so very different, inclined him to kick against the pricks. But he could not shake off the past, and his spirit was broken by the sudden death in 1150 of the young King Henry, the son on whom all his hopes rested. Henry's death meant that the solitary success of his reign, the securing of the succession for his family, had turned to dust.

Conrad bore the same name as his ancestor, the first Salian, but his nature and his career are more reminiscent of the inconclusive and unsuccessful struggles of the first Conrad, whom he resembled also in his kindliness and his knightly qualities. Like Conrad I, too, he performed on his death-bed the one great action for which Germany owes him gratitude. It was no light matter for him to pass over his own eight-year-old son Frederick and designate his nephew Frederick of Swabia, who was already a fully-grown and experienced man, as his successor by sending him the royal insignia. In this act there lay hope for the future, if the princes' election coincided with his own desires, for it is hard to think of anyone better suited than Frederick Barbarossa to deal with the two chief problems which awaited the new ruler—how to settle the conflict between Welf and Hohenstaufen in Germany, and how to restrain the growth of papal and ecclesiastical power in Europe.

10

THE FIRST YEARS OF FREDERICK I
(1152–1157)

Frederick Barbarossa has secured a place second only to that of Charlemagne in the regard of the German people, and this is due less to his policy, which was not exactly original, than to his heroic personality, the fullest expression of the springtime of German knighthood. He embodied the highest secular ideals of his time; that he was thus typical of his age meant not that he was a weakling but that his own character was strengthened by the obstacles his age forced him to encounter. The powerful personality which resulted was scarcely ever weakened by inner conflict. Frederick had stormed through life until his middle twenties,[1] bold and self-confident, early to mature. His outward appearance —a strong and well-proportioned figure of medium build, a cheerful manner, fashionably-dressed reddish hair and beard which earned him the nickname 'Barbarossa' from the Italians— corresponded much more to the new knightly ideal than to the uncouthness of the old Germanic warriors. In upbringing and outlook the contrast was still greater. Since he was not heir to the throne, he had been given no literary training and understood Latin very imperfectly; but he had a patron's interest in German poetry, history and architecture, won hearts easily by his ready tongue and his memory for faces, was a master of courtly conventions, and above all held strictly to the supreme knightly virtue of '*mâze*'.[2] 'His countenance reflects the serenity of his soul,' an Englishman once wrote, describing him from personal observation, 'It is always calm and unruffled, never darkened by sorrow nor distorted by anger, and he is not given to excess of joy.'[3] This serenity was the chief source of his success, although it made him a less 'interesting' character than his son or his grandson.

Strong-willed and active, his hand ever on the sword or the

[1] He was born in 1125 or 1126.

[2] *Mesure* in contemporary French and later English—'moderation and self-control'.

[3] Richard of London, in MGH. SS. xxvii. 204.

judge's wand, Frederick travelled untiringly across the face of his empire. He was brought up as a warrior, and well into middle age he still took pleasure in personal combat, with its ever-present dangers and its occasional wounds, emerging unshaken even after defeat. He contemptuously dismissed a straightforward expedition into Lombardy as 'child's play, not man's work'. During forced marches he ate his simple meals in the saddle. Once, when his siege-works were set on fire, he took his part in putting out the flames, and after the surrender of Crema he was seen helping one of his retreating foes, who was sick, to carry his pack. But outside such knightly deeds, he was the bold and canny general, and a strict disciplinarian.

The idea of justice was foremost in his mind, and was the guiding light of his policy. He was deeply impregnated with the old Germanic concept of the king as the guardian of peace and the upholder of law. As judge, he was no respecter of persons and set no store by family connections; even the pardon he issued on the day of his coronation seemed to him an infringement of justice. In all doubtful cases he was careful to avoid innovation, and thus ensured that he always had the support of such 'public opinion' as could be sensed in aristocratic circles. There was a rapidly growing regard for law at this time, and Roman jurisprudence was being revived in Bologna. This was bound to promote the idea of the dignity and independence of the Empire and to provide the intellectual weapons to defend it. In Frederick's case this perfectly suited his own efforts to re-establish ancient royal and imperial rights. This is in turn led him away from his immediate predecessors and back to Charlemagne (whose canonisation he secured from his anti-pope in 1165) and the Ottos. Out of this combination of Roman legal concepts with a desire to revive the past, there grew a body of thought which has been none too happily described as 'the Hohenstaufen idea of Empire'. Yet at bottom it sought only the old objectives: the Emperor's absolute temporal supremacy—under God alone—and his unlimited universality; his right to protect the Church and to expect loyal co-operation from the papacy; and the union of the whole might of central Europe under German leadership. The only novelty is that these claims are now increasingly emphasised and more strictly defined, are seen as more closely related to the Roman imperial past, and are given a religious flavour. This new form, which had already been slowly developing for two generations, became prominent during Frederick's reign, while Frederick himself became more identified with it as he grew older.

How could he have thought less of his own position, when the Archpoet celebrated him as king over all other kings, and even a ruler of the standing of Henry II of England addressed him humbly in 1157 with the words 'To you, as the superior, falls the right to command; we shall not lack the will to obey.'[1]

Ideas like these were bound to make a personality as determined as Frederick's intensely aware of his monarchical authority. Once a right decision had been arrived at, Frederick felt it his duty to carry it out whatever the opposition. The stubbornness with which he refused to change his mind led him into frequent difficulties, but it very greatly increased his prestige, for all men knew that it was no light matter to oppose the royal will. In fact, as one of his intimates wrote, Frederick 'had never quite learned to love his enemies'. A feeling that his majesty had been insulted kept him from wearing his crown from the moment of the Milanese rising until the destruction of the city; the same feeling made him stern towards rebels, who had to face terror and reprisals often carried to the point of brutality. But since Frederick scarcely ever gave judgement without the advice of his court, this did not take away from contemporaries' impression of his '*mâze*'.

This conclusion was reinforced by his life-long resistance to the temptations of absolute rule, and more particularly by the fact that he behaved towards the German nobles as if he were merely the first among equals. He may have begun by giving an impression of weakness, since he often suited his actions to their advice, several times gave up expeditions which he thought important because they refused to join them, and frequently made do with inadequate military support. But his compliance arose from a true estimate of the realities of the situation. Great care was required if the effects of the Investiture Contest, which had brought the nobles to power, were to be overcome; a premature effort was bound to throw the kingdom back into its old state of confusion. Frederick had been one of the secular nobility, and he sympathised with them. They could see in him the chief representative of their own special interests. He won the whole of the knightly class over to his side by foreign enterprises which provided new

[1] *Gesta Friderici* iii. 7 (trans. Mierow 179).

objectives for their love of adventure, and by legislation which accepted the exclusiveness of their own caste and its separation from the lower classes. The feudal policy which he thus pursued was naturally more closely related to the power-structure of his own day than to that of later times, but its ultimate purpose was always to strengthen the monarchy by concentrating whatever force was available to it.

His remarkable gift for man-management became more and more apparent as every change in his varying fortunes brought him fresh experience. Almost every time he intervened in person —persuading, reconciling and making peace—he gained the ends he sought. He often began by yielding to the opinions of his advisers, but his ascendancy over them can be seen increasing steadily until it is he alone who can secure his opponents' adherence to his plans. In his later years, Frederick practised to perfection the art of handling men and guiding their decisions. He gradually acquired mastery in the fields of politics and diplomacy, and learned to distinguish confidently between the possible and the unattainable. In spite of every reverse, but not without some surprising changes of direction, he managed to increase his political prestige throughout his long reign. The more personal his rule, the greater became his prestige until, a grey-bearded hero, he was suddenly removed from the scene and the recollection of his successes began to illuminate the darker parts of his reign.

The unanimity of his election on 4 March 1152 is explained by the fact that he, the Hohenstaufen designated by Conrad III, was also closely related to the Welfs through his mother (she was Henry the Proud's sister), and had disagreed with his predecessor's pro-Babenberg policy. He was himself therefore the cornerstone which held the fabric of the Empire together, and he alone could offer the prospect of a peaceful settlement. He directed his chief efforts towards this end at the beginning of his reign, and his willingness to come to terms with strong lay forces which his predecessor had opposed recalls the early years of Henry I. Just as Henry had once had to tolerate territorial power in Bavaria, so Frederick admitted the extensive claims of his cousin Henry the Lion, duke of Saxony, to sovereignty in the Slav lands beyond the Elbe, including the investiture of bishops, and recognised his claim to the duchy of Bavaria by a decision of the princes in 1154. This hit the Babenberger Henry Jasomirgott hard, but after two years of painstaking negotiation Frederick eventually secured a compromise acceptable to both.[1] By completely separating Austria from it, he reduced Bavaria in size and made it an entirely German territory. Henry the Lion's position—now recognised by the Empire—remained very strong in spite of his losses; the crown was able to tolerate it in future only because king and duke struck out in different directions, south-west and north-east, and could therefore lend each other cousinly support for a number of years —Henry by participation in Italian expeditions, Frederick by occasional pressure on the secular and ecclesiastical nobles of Saxony, among whom Albert the Bear was already converting the recently-conquered Slav lands of his Mark of Brandenburg into a territorial authority closely resembling that of Henry the Lion on the eastern bank of the Elbe.

There were other claimants to Bavaria too, and they had to be satisfied. Frederick's uncle, duke Welf VI, had already been won over in 1152 by the grant of the imperial fiefs of Tuscany, Spoleto, Sardinia and the Matildine lands in addition to the Italian claims of his house which originated with Lothar. Henry Jasomirgott eventually accepted the new arrangements, although only after a good deal of resistance, because of the very special privileges granted to his newly-created duchy of Austria: here, as along the whole eastern colonial frontier, such privileges promoted the development of territorial sovereignty.

The crown had made concessions in both directions in order to secure the peace which all desired. Frederick's first steps had been painful, but how could he have turned weakness into strength overnight? His first need was to gain room for manoeuvre by careful consideration of the princes' views, and it was in deference to them for instance, that he abandoned expeditions against Hungary and Bohemia. This combination of internal peace and firmer direction slowly began to have an effect abroad as well. Within a decade the Empire had regained its preponderance in north and east. When Sven I, whom Frederick had put on the Danish throne, was killed in a rebellion, his supplanter Waldemar I sought enfeoffment from Frederick. Barbarossa's victorious campaign against Poland in 1157 was to have even more important consequences for Germany, since although the duke did not at first fulfil all the conditions imposed upon him the final peace

[1] The key documents are in Pullan 160–164.

settlement of 1163 led to the introduction into Silesia of princes
from the house of Piast who were friendly to Germany, and
prepared the ground for the latter colonisation and Germanisation
of this important territory. Henceforth Silesia formed a wedge
between Poland and Bohemia, whose duke Wladislaw II was
given a crown by Frederick and remained his loyal supporter.
Even Hungary was again reduced to the position of a dependent
kingdom before 1160, and sent contingents to Barbarossa's Italian
expeditions.

Inside Germany too, despite all the caution of his early steps,
Barbarossa's own kingship was by no means the 'phantom' von
Sybel made it out to be. A multitude of royal rights still existed,
and they could raise the king high above the nobles and make
him far more than a first among equals—if he knew how to use
them. Frederick was just the man to take advantage of them.
With careful husbandry, he began at once to concentrate the
direct possessions of the crown and to extend them in all directions.
He had grown up familiar with the nobles' territorial policy, and
he now began to apply their methods on a larger scale to the
development of the Staufen estates: he secured the transfer of
advocacies to himself as fiefs of ecclesiastical princes; he made use
of purchase, exchange and every other peaceful means to enlarge
and consolidate his possessions, and he proceeded to protect them
by building castles, to enrich them by founding new towns, and to
administer them not through feudal machinery but through
imperial *ministeriales* in strict official dependence upon himself.
The *ministeriales* played a particularly important role in the
eastern districts, where they led the work of clearing new areas for
cultivation and settlement. This went so far that in the course of
time an almost complete chain of royal possessions stretched from
the old Staufen-Salian estates in Swabia, Alsace, Franconia and
the Palatinate north-eastwards through Nuremberg and Eger
right across into the Vogtland, Thuringia and Meissen. A particularly significant gain was the old Lotharingian palatine county—
now finally shifted southwards and centring on Heidelberg—
which Frederick gave to his step-brother Conrad in 1156. From
Alsace he pushed still further south and south-west; after the
dissolution of his first marriage, he married the heiress to the
county of Upper Burgundy, Beatrix, who thus became the ances-
tress of all the later Hohenstaufen. The direct possessions which

Beatrix brought him were of particular importance, and Frederick was able to draw the north-western part of it completely into the Hohenstaufen sphere of influence by diverting the attention of the rector of Burgundy, Berthold of Zähringen, eastwards into Switzerland. In a sense, therefore, Frederick secured Burgundy to the Empire for a second time.

But the German monarchy was not yet entirely dependent upon the power which Frederick wielded as the possessor of the Hohenstaufen family estates, nor had it yet finally surrendered the regalian rights which gave it a foothold in every noble's territory. A king with sufficient force of personality could still ensure that the crown received its due. The energy and perception with which Frederick fulfilled his royal duties in this respect was shown in these same years when he released the shipping on the Main from unlawful tolls. His strict and just management of the king's court gave it once more an authority which was feared and respected; even the greatest of the nobles came to feel that disregard of the obligation of military service would be punished as severely as breach of the peace. It seems probable that shortly after his accession Frederick followed the example of Henry IV and issued a general land-peace, and that the standards it laid down, even though without practical effect until reaffirmed in sworn provincial peaces, were nevertheless the embryo of a new type of imperial legislation. His efforts soon showed results, and they were increased by the settlement with the Welfs: as early as 1157, after all the miseries of recent times, an annalist could speak of the 'fulness of peace'.

The most significant indication of the monarchy's new strength, however, was the fact that it succeeded in reconstructing the old foundations of government, laid long ago by Otto the Great but by now half ruined: the close relationship of crown and bishops. Frederick's sense of his own rights fitted in here with the temper of the times. The words which a later chronicler puts into his mouth could well have been his in reality: he would pay proper regard to the concessions over episcopal appointments made by previous emperors, since they had willed them, but he would hold stubbornly to the state of the law as he had found it. This 'state of the law' was, of course, nowhere exactly written down. It was simply the customary law which had grown up round the Concordat of Worms, and it still left plenty of room for the energetic

M

exercise of the royal influence on elections, since customary law always tended to give way under the pressure of force and personality. During the last few decades the crown had been the weaker party, but Frederick now reversed this tendency.

He utilised every foothold the crown still had in order to regain for it the decisive voice in the appointment of bishops. The last two rulers had paid careful heed to clerical misgivings about the restriction of electoral freedom caused by the practice of election in the presence of the king; Frederick, on the other hand, was usually able to bring his influence to bear heavily at a still earlier stage—the nomination of the candidate. If nevertheless there was a double election, he often intervened ruthlessly and ensured the recognition of his own candidate by the device of a new election. Right at the beginning of his reign, for instance, he won an impressive victory over the reluctant curia in the case of the appointment of archbishop Wichmann of Magdeburg. Soon he took further steps by getting the nobles to agree that he had a 'right of devolution' in such cases—that is to say, a right to set both candidates aside, with the nobles' consent, and to appoint a third of his own choice—although in actual fact he only made occasional use of it in later years. He successfully disputed the recent efforts of the curia to replace the king's influence by its own[1] by protecting the voting rights of the lay members of electoral bodies and by restricting appeals to Rome. He held firmly to the principle that only investiture by the king conferred enjoyment of the *regalia* upon the man elected, and that this must precede consecration; and at once took severe measures against contraventions of this principle which the crown had tolerated in the province of Salzburg.

Just as he treated the bishops primarily as imperial officials, so also Frederick gave priority to political requirements. It was to his advantage here that the victorious progress of feudal law began to affect the imperial Church at about this time. The *regalia* were now regarded as fiefs of the Empire, investiture with them by the king as full feudal investiture; consequently bishops and imperial abbots formed the second rank in the *Heerschild*,[2] behind the king, and the way was gradually being paved for them to amalgamate with the greater lay nobles in a single class of territorial

[1] Cf. p. 142, above.
[2] 'Military order of precedence.'

princes. Meanwhile, their stricter incorporation into the structure of the feudal state helped to bind the prelates more closely to the crown, and Frederick was able to take advantage of the fact. He could now make increased demands for military and political services from the bishops, whose contact with their lord (unlike the lay nobility's) could not be broken by the process of inheritance. Further, the ancient and profitable rights of *regalia* and *spolia* (the right to enjoy the income of a see during a vacancy and to take a bishop's movable property when he died), which originated in proprietary church law, now seemed to be feudal incidents and were more energetically exploited by Frederick than they had been by his predecessor. This complete transformation of the higher clergy was carried through without serious friction and with remarkable speed. The death of Bernard of Clairvaux in 1153 brought to an end the period associated with his name. The German bishoprics were no longer occupied by ascetics of his stamp, but by worldly and practical administrators, business-like politicians and diplomats, wherever possible the products of the imperial chancery who frequently even possessed military abilities actually proven in the field. Piety and devotion to clerical ideals were no longer decisive in choosing them. Men like provost Gerhoh of Reichersberg—who in fact reflected the change after his own fashion by increasingly sharp criticism of the Church— became rarer and rarer among the higher German clergy. Since their independence was far more seriously threatened by the absolutist tendencies of the curia than it was by the German monarchy, the bishops gladly grouped themselves behind the young king, whose own self-confidence strengthened their morale; before long, they constituted a circle of bold and secular-minded men, highly educated and ready for action in defence of their country. Pride in German power and the German spirit breathes through the clerical drama 'Antichrist' (depicting the last revival of the Empire before its final destruction at the end of the world) which, next to the verses of the Archpoet, is the finest poetical fruit of this period. Some even among the older and more moderate prelates, who had borne the cares of conflicting loyalties in the recent difficult times, were cheered by the freshness in the air of the new age. Only a few years earlier, Otto of Freising had found his own melancholy expressed in the course of world history, but

now in the *Gesta Friderici* (1157–8) he praised the king who
brought peace and a new dawn after the dark and stormy night.

Could this peace be lasting so far as the curia was concerned?
For a time it was preserved by a community of interests in Italy.
Eugenius III realised that he was still dependent on German help
against rebellious Romans and hostile Normans. Frederick was
the more ready to give it because he needed the imperial crown.
He had no mind to receive the crown at the hands of the Roman
revolutionaries, who offered it to him in proud and haughty terms;
now as always he held fast to established law, and he could after
all expect coronation from the pope only in return for services
rendered. He finally met the curia's wishes by reversing his predecessor's policy and refusing to tolerate a new Greek landing in
Italy by the emperor Manuel. The treaty of Constance in 1153
expressed the coincidence of interests. Frederick undertook to
defend the rights and possessions of the Roman Church against all
comers and to lend the pope his support in regaining them when-
ever necessary; there was to be an early imperial expedition to
Italy, in order to give him security from his Roman and Norman
enemies. In return, the pope promised Frederick the imperial
crown and spiritual help against the enemies of the Empire, as
well as support in protecting imperial rights. Eugenius III did not
long outlive his promise—he died the same year—but his successor
observed the agreement.

Frederick's first Italian expedition (1154–5) was not outstandingly successful, and indeed recalls Lothar's both in its
objects and in its results. With Germany still in an unsettled
state, only 1,800 knights answered his summons. On the other
hand, the king's demeanour betrayed a pride and a confidence
which had not been seen for many years. The main themes of the
coming drama were revealed as soon as he reached Lombardy: a
feudal law, based on Lothar's, and aimed retrospectively against
the cities' usurpations; friction with the defiant Milanese, which
led to the siege and destruction of Milan's ally Tortona and to an
offer of protection to the smaller neighbours it had overpowered;
and finally in Bologna the establishment of friendly relations with
the representatives of the reviving study of Roman Law. The
outline of the policy was already unmistakeable: all that was
lacking was the power to enforce it. As far as Rome was concerned,
too, it was very doubtful whether Frederick's scanty forces would

have sufficed even to secure him entry for the coronation, had there not been a shift in the balance of power in favour of the curia shortly beforehand.

The change in the character of the age affected the papacy too, and brought able politicians to the leadership of the Church. Hadrian IV, still the only Englishman to become pope, was an energetic man who had risen from great poverty to the cardinalate by his own abilities and had since been occupied in creating an independent organisation for the Church in Norway. As pope, he was convinced that the revival of the secular powers required the Church to return to the lines laid down by Gregory VII, and to adopt severer measures and a sharper tone—although his actions were in practice often restricted by resistance in the college of cardinals. Behind him stood—like Hildebrand behind Alexander II—his chief adviser, cardinal Roland, a Sienese of outstanding gifts and education who had for many years been a famous teacher of Roman Law in Bologna and was now papal chancellor with wide responsibilities in all fields. Fiery and austere, quick to make up his mind and absolutely determined, Roland was the leader of a party among the cardinals which was calling for a forward policy.

This party gained its first important success at once: by means of an interdict—an extreme measure which had never been used against the city of pilgrims before—Hadrian forced the Romans to expel Arnold of Brescia at the beginning of 1155. Complete agreement between curia and citizens could of course not be attained immediately, and the threat from the south seemed to be growing when, after Roger II's death in 1154, his son William I attacked the papal state on the pretext that he had been refused investiture. It was therefore essential that Frederick should intervene. As he approached central Italy, he demonstrated his goodwill towards the papacy and his intention of fulfilling the treaty of Constance by having Arnold arrested at the Tuscan frontier and handed over to the prefect of Rome. Arnold was sentenced to be hanged, but the steadfastness with which the bitter foe of the secularised papacy met a martyr's death helped to give his ideas a still wider influence.

Did this useful service which Frederick had done the pope lead to further friendly relations between them? It is impossible to mistake the deep distrust which prevailed at their first meeting at Sutri. It was apparent at once, when Frederick baldly announced his election and received in return the pope's approval, for which he had not asked. It became more marked when the king at first refused to go through the ceremony of holding the pope's stirrup and leading his horse, on the ground that it was degrading, and only gave way when the pope expressly confirmed a decision of the nobles that the ceremony betokened only honour to St Peter and humility towards him, and did not imply the performance of vassal-service. Thereupon the imperial coronation in the Leonine city followed without further incident in June 1155; the hostility of Rome itself grew sharper, however, when Frederick roughly repulsed the citizens. But then the unexpected happened: without making any serious attempt to carry out the treaty of Constance—although the domestic confusion of Sicily invited attack—Frederick yielded to the insistence of the nobles, heeded the warning given by the summer heat of Italy, and against his own will led his troops back over the Alps. It was here that the bravery of count Otto of Wittelsbach rescued him from serious danger as the army crossed the Brenner.

The non-fulfilment of the treaty of Constance was to have very serious consequences. Since the Emperor was not in a position to give the help he had promised against the Normans, the curia had to leave him out of their future calculations over Sicilian affairs. Instead, Hadrian sought through an alliance with the emperor Manuel to take advantage of the disorders which the serious illness of the king were causing, and to conquer William's lands himself. Then, when William recovered, gathered strength and beat the Greeks decisively, Hadrian—thus left in the lurch by both emperors—and a few cardinals deliberately carried through a complete revolution in papal policy by concluding the concordat of Benevento in 1156. He accepted William as his tributary and feudal vassal, recognised him as lawful possessor of the crown and of the enlarged kingdom—since he could no longer dispute its unity—and granted him (for the island of Sicily at any rate) the legatine powers already exercised by Roger, which included the decisive influence over appointments to bishoprics. This one-sided agreement, which disregarded all the Empire's claims in southern Italy, was undoubtedly inconsistent with the treaty of Constance, even if it did not directly contradict it. At the same time, it would be idle to talk of breach of faith—treaties cannot be valid for ever. The expectation that the new German king would, like his predecessors, be a convenient tool of the curia had not been fulfilled; it was rather support against him that was needed. Thus from the papal standpoint the revolution is certainly understandable, and was perhaps essential. But it undoubtedly involved a breach with the imperial court, and was understood there in this sense. There was an immediate increase of tension. On the one hand, it became necessary to take account of the possibility that under the present pope or one of his successors the strong imperial party in the college of cardinals might gain the upper hand and bring about another reversal of policy. On the other, Frederick was determined to resist, and here it was of the greatest significance that he found at this very moment an assistant who had the strength and the will to meet papal hostility with violent aggression should need arise.

11

IMPERIAL POLICY UNDER THE INFLUENCE OF RAINALD OF DASSEL
(1157–1167)

Rainald of Dassel was the second son of a count whose family claimed descent from the Nordheims and had settled on the Weser. Destined for the Church from an early age, he had been trained in theology and philosophy at Hildesheim and Paris and had gained experience in administration as the provost of several religious houses in his native land before being raised by Frederick to the responsible position of imperial chancellor in 1156. One of the most striking figures in the whole of German history, he came to the fore at a time when tension with the curia was increasing. For the next ten years the Swabian Emperor had at his side this blonde, thick-set Saxon: a man of cheerful and secular temper, blunt but affable, decisive and generous, a great builder and a lover of literature, familiar with the prose and poetry of the ancient world but delighting also in the lively verses of the Archpoet, whom he took under his patronage.

His manifold gifts and his active and impetuous nature were placed unreservedly at the service of the imperial cause. As a skilful and persuasive negotiator, he was given the most difficult diplomatic missions to conduct; his reputation for thorough and careful organisation brought him heavy administrative responsibilities, while his clerical station did not prevent him from gaining notable success as a general. Fear and irresolution were unknown to him, danger stimulated his disconcerting audacity. With only ten knights at his back he once surprised and captured a detachment of some three hundred Ravennese, no doubt himself taking a hand in the fighting at the decisive moment. No blow could shake him; 'he grew greater daily', says a chronicler, until death removed him at the height of his power and influence.

The suddenness of his disappearance spared him the humiliation of seeing his authority wane, but it can easily mislead us into judging him too favourably. His influence on Frederick's policy cannot be regarded as entirely beneficial, although it must be admitted that it will never be possible to know with certainty how strong it was, nor whether and how far Rainald ever became the effective maker of policy rather than simply its executive agent. A ruler like Frederick would hardly have let himself be overruled by his own chancellor in the way which his clerical opponents repeatedly chose to claim, freely as he might be content to let him speak. It must be assumed that they were in complete agreement on the general lines of policy. Rainald had no time for radical and Utopian schemes, like the separation of Germany from Rome in ecclesiastical affairs. Like Frederick, he wanted to make the maximum use of the legal rights and the actual power which the German monarchy still retained, in order to win back for it, if possible, the position of the Ottos and the first Salians. He planned to do this primarily by the reinvigoration of the imperial Church through military control over Italy, and by bringing pressure to bear on the papacy. His tempestuous nature certainly carried the Emperor farther along this path than Frederick would have gone on his own, however, and farther than a sober appraisal of the obstacles would have permitted. In his downright way he then tended to follow the chosen course by more violent means, just as his boundless optimism made him adopt a more ruthless and haughty tone, than was either tactically necessary or could be welcome in detail to his master. And as the natural reaction grew, as the Gregorian papacy's defence of its independence found its most powerful support in the national sensibilities of western Europe and in the Lombard cities' desire for freedom, his tough Low German obstinacy succeeded to the end in holding Frederick to the path he had chosen—although Frederick's moderation would perhaps have made him hesitate if he had been left to himself. We cannot tell what new ways Rainald's inventive mind would have found to escape from the serious situation which the catastrophe of 1167 suddenly revealed; but he left the Emperor an unenviable legacy. In spite of all this, however, it must be stressed that his policy was a form of defence as well as of attack, and that two offensives met each other head-on.

As early as 1157 the Reichstag at Besançon was the scene of a violent skirmish. Archbishop Eskil of Lund had taken the anti-imperial side in the dispute over the Danish throne and had looked

for protection against imperial vengeance to the pope, who confirmed his metropolitan claims over the northern lands and thus harmed
the interests of the see of Bremen. Eskil was set upon in the
imperial territory of Burgundy on his way back home, and thrown
into prison. Hadrian sought to turn these chance events to good
use. He sent two cardinal legates (one of them was the chancellor,
Roland) to complain to Frederick. They were at the same time to
try to negotiate a reduction in the tension which had strained the
curia's relations with the Empire since the concordat of Benevento,
and to ensure a satisfactory outcome of the complications to be
expected in consequence of the Emperor's new Italian expedition.
Finally, they had the task of undertaking a comprehensive visitation of the Church in Germany with the object of reforming it and
bringing it into stricter dependence on Rome. The letter which
was handed to Frederick at Besançon contained a phrase to the
effect that the pope nevertheless 'did not regret crowning Frederick
and would even rejoice if he could confer greater *beneficia* upon
him.'[1] This ambiguous expression had plainly been chosen as a
cautious revival of the ancient claims to universal rule and to
feudal supremacy over the Empire which Barbarossa had emphatically rejected at Sutri, so that its legal force as a precedent might
be used in any future conflict. The German court already had
good reason to mistrust the curia's intentions, however, and
chancellor Rainald translated *beneficia* not by the harmless word
'benefits' but by the menacing 'fiefs', and thus raised such a storm
of German indignation in the Reichstag that only the intervention
of the Emperor saved the legates' lives. Instead of immediately
rejecting Rainald's translation as incorrect, the pope tried by
means of an evasive letter to get the German bishops on his side
in what he described as a dispute frivolously conjured up out of
nothing. But the consequences of the transformation of the
German episcopate which Frederick had begun were soon plain
to see; he skilfully prevented the planned visitation from being
carried out, protected the German Church from any diminution
of its independence, and made appeals to Rome depend on the
consent of the bishop concerned. All these measures strengthened
the bishops' attitude. In a series of manifestoes the force and bite
of which betray Rainald's authorship, Frederick abruptly rejected

---

[1] Pullan 173, Tierney 105. Extensive extracts from the account of the
incident in the *Gesta Friderici* are printed in Pullan 172–6 and Tierney 105–9.

the presumption of the pope. 'In the chief city of the world', runs one of them, 'God has, through the power of the empire, exalted the Church; in the chief city of the world the Church, not through the power of God, we believe, is now destroying the empire. It began with a picture, the picture became an inscription, the inscription seeks to become an authoritative utterance. We shall not endure it, we shall not submit to it; we shall lay down the crown before we consent to have the imperial crown and ourself thus degraded. Let the pictures be destroyed, let the inscriptions be withdrawn, that they may not remain as eternal memorials of enmity between the empire and the papacy.'[1]

The German bishops' complete agreement with such phrases as these showed the curia that it had chosen the wrong battle-ground. Hadrian found himself compelled to pour oil on troubled waters (he was already under pressure to do so from Henry the Lion), and at long last explained the objectionable words away. The curia's defeat delayed an open breach once more. But the episode had both heightened the tensions in the college of cardinals and raised the confidence of the imperial court. New grounds for dispute were added to those that already existed when the Emperor intervened in Lombard affairs.

Frederick's Lombard expeditions, directed towards a revival of imperial rights neglected since Henry V's time, have often been condemned. They have been contrasted with an ideal picture, with the policy of a nation-state restricted to the pursuit of narrower and more purely German interests and directed towards the east. It has been suggested that such a policy could have led to a gradual enlargement of the royal power, as it did in France, and could thus have prevented the later collapse of the central authority. Such a suggestion, however, leaves the dominant ideals and the decisive loyalties of the time far too much out of account, and measures past events by standards which were still in all essentials quite foreign to those who made the policy in question. To give up traditional Italian claims, when to defend them might raise the Empire's lately sunken prestige again, was quite unthinkable at that time. Moreover, Frederick's attempt at reconstruction can be understood well enough from the stand-point of practical politics alone. The compromise settlement with the Welfs had set bounds to the necessary enlargement of

---

[1] *Gesta Friderici* iii. 17 (trans. Mierow 193); Tierney 108–9.

Staufen territory, and in particular had barred the way to the east. But any advance in south Germany could only be achieved one step at a time, and the considerable financial resources required could not be provided within a Germany which was still largely confined to an agricultural economy. Further, it was impossible without large sums in bullion to manoeuvre in wider political fields—to oppose the power of Sicily and Byzantium, for instance, or to join the growing movement which aimed at founding monarchical power on salaried state officials instead of on feudalism. Lombardy seemed to offer vast riches. Her cities had developed entirely new forms of economic life and had risen, together with Sicily, to the position of the chief financial power in Europe. The imperial authority had not profited at all from this, however, because by far the greater part of the relevant sovereign rights had not for many years been under direct imperial control, but had been granted out to bishops and feudal lords. The outcome of the Investiture Contest had been to make the Italian bishops more independent of the crown but also, by virtue of that very fact, to leave them without support: there had been no royal intervention in Italian affairs for several decades (it had been notably absent in Conrad III's reign). The rising cities, which had by now almost everywhere won from their episcopal masters the right of self-government under elected consuls, therefore became in large measure the inheritors of the *regalia* as well, not through lawful grant but through usurpation. To the extent, therefore—and it was a great extent—to which the Investiture Contest had been a struggle for a material end (namely, influence over the property and rights of the imperial Church), in the later contest too the very same objects were in dispute: the only difference was that their proprietors had changed. Furthermore, Piedmont had been brought very close to the Emperor by his recent acquisitions in Burgundy; the broad lands of the Piedmontese demesne offered a secure foundation for imperial power, and one which was capable of extension in the future. Thus when the plan for a large-scale reclamation of imperial rights in Italy took shape in Frederick's mind and became from now on the chief objective of his policy, he was governed by thoroughly material considerations of the advantages to be gained for German power.

He must of course have realised that such a policy was almost bound to lead to renewed conflict with the curia, for it could not be reconciled with the political objectives which the papacy had pursued since the time of Gregory VII. Rome held firmly to the wide claim upon territory in central Italy to the possession of which it believed the ancient promises of the Carolings and the Ottonians gave it an indisputable title. Hadrian could only contemplate the re-establishment of imperial power in northern and central Italy with the greatest apprehension. Would it not of necessity lead also to a collision with the Norman kingdom (itself only recently allied with the curia again), and how were the temporal possessions of the Church to maintain their independence in the face of such a threat? Barbarossa was not blind to the dangers that loomed at this point, and in earnest discussion with pious men sought to make sure of the justice of his cause before the expedition set out.

The immediate excuse for the new enterprise was given by the stubborn defiance of the powerful city of Milan. Disregarding every imperial warning, Milan continued to abuse its economic, political and military superiority to impose an unparalleled oppression upon its weaker neighbours, destroying their commercial competition and extending its own territory. Justice demanded the breaking of the burdensome Milanese yoke, and to do so was a prerequisite for any rearrangement of the legal situation in Lombardy; hence Milan was the chief objective of the Italian expedition of 1158–62. The chancellor himself (who thus at once emerged as the driving force behind Frederick's Italian policy) and the count palatine, Otto of Wittelsbach, went ahead of the main body like the imperial heralds of former days and everywhere skilfully prepared the way for it.

This time the Emperor, with an army said to have numbered more than ten thousand knights as well as strong Lombard reinforcements, set out directly for Milan. Before many weeks had passed, he enjoyed the triumph of seeing the consuls of the city stand before him bare-footed and with their swords hung about their necks. The thick walls could have resisted longer, but hunger and disease demanded surrender, if this could be made on reasonable conditions. The treaty seemed in fact to make possible a compromise between opposed interests, since it guaranteed to the Emperor the sovereign rights he claimed but permitted the city a certain measure of self-government (notably the free election of its own consuls, although subject to confirmation by the emperor).

Before long, however, new disputes were to arise about the force of this right of confirmation. Meanwhile, Milan was reduced to the same level as the other Lombard cities, and the chief obstacle to a complete and general remodelling of the Lombard situation had been removed. Frederick now began to set about this task with all his customary thoroughness and strong legal sense.

It was first necessary to establish the value of the imperial rights, the *regalia*. Among them were the appointment of the chief officials and the building of imperial castles, supreme jurisdiction and a share of fines and confiscated goods, extra-ordinary taxes and services on the occasion of Italian expeditions; above all in potential value stood a whole complex of rights which were important in view of the highly-developed Lombard economy —those concerned with jurisdiction over roads and the control of commerce, including market-dues, tolls and the rights of coinage and safe conduct. But how were the details of each one of these rights now to be discovered? The old charters had mostly perished, new ones had not been issued, circumstances had changed in almost every respect. New norms were required, and the task of laying them down was handed over to the four famous doctors of Bologna who were invited to the Reichstag of Roncaglia[1] and appointed to preside over a commission of twenty-eight city judges. Here, for the first time, the influence of the reawakened study of Roman Law on practical politics is plainly visible. Ranke acutely noted that 'the opposition to the papacy which was one of the facets of the development of speculative theology had a political effect favourable to popular freedom, but the work of the jurists on the other hand favoured the Empire in its struggle with the papacy and the towns'. There was in actual fact to be found in the law-books of Justinian the concept of a sacred and absolute majesty, unlimited by any associated spiritual power, which was entirely foreign to the German notion of monarchy. His whole background and his whole idea of justice made it scarcely possible for Frederick I to do anything but reject it for his own person. When Rahewin makes him say at Roncaglia 'But we, though having the name of king, desire to hold our authority under the law and for the preservation of each man's liberty and right rather than—in accordance with the saying 'to do all things with impunity, this is to be king'—to become arrogant through freedom

[1] The Diet of Roncaglia is described in extracts printed in Pullan 179–185.

from responsibility and to transform the task of ruling into pride and domination',[1] he puts his finger on the essentials of Frederick's attitude, in spite of the phrases borrowed from Sallust. At the same time it is easy to understand that the Emperor and his advisers could not fail to be affected by Roman concepts so favourable to monarchical power, and traces of the outlook of the Bolognese jurists are to be found in the legislation issued at Roncaglia in November 1158, which represents the results of the commission's work. The language in which the laws are expressed often shows the influence of classical models, but besides this Roman Law ideas are also occasionally taken over—notably that of a direct imperial tax, although it was not in fact to win acceptance in the following years. The influence of Roman Law has been much exaggerated, however. For when the *regalia* were now promised to the Emperor with the assent of the Lombard magnates and the urban consuls, it was at bottom simply the rights of the earlier Frankish and German rulers which were in question —that is, Italian law was being restored to the form in which it had been in force up to the time of the Salians. And in as much as it was now for practical purposes laid down that the whole of this vast mass of explicitly-named rights belonged to the crown unless charters were produced to prove that they had been granted away, the cities were deprived of their purely *de facto* possession of the *regalia* and the way cleared for a complete reshaping of imperial authority in Upper Italy—though this of course could not be put into effect without bitter opposition from those most involved.

What was at stake in the struggle which followed? It was certainly not simply a conflict between feudalism and civic independence, between medieval and modern. This still popular misconception would only fit the case if, after regaining them, the Emperor had regranted the legal titles as fiefs—something which he in fact did only exceptionally, and not as a common practice. On the contrary, the decrees of Roncaglia led to a serious attempt to establish direct rule through imperial officials. After Roncaglia, Frederick only granted to a very few friendly cities the enjoyment of the *regalia* in return for a fixed payment, contenting himself with investing their elected consuls, who also had to secure authorisation from him through the ceremony of *Bannleihe* before

---

[1] *Gesta Friderici* iv. 4 (trans. Mierow 234). The phrase about 'each man's liberty and right' comes from Gratian's *Decretum*, and the quotation in parenthesis from Sallust.

they could administer justice. In the remainder of the cities he himself appointed one or more *podestàs*, at first Italians, but later Germans as well. These *podestàs* were appointed for a period only and were removable, and they were to exercise the regalian rights not as feudal fief-holders but as officials acting for the Empire: the same applied to the counts who were installed to rule the county districts. The Emperor may again have had the restoration of the past particularly in mind—after all, the empire of Charlemagne had known officials of this kind appointed from the centre —but his attempt looked as much to the future as to the past and pointed the way to the modern bureaucratic state which was to replace the feudalism of the Middle Ages. Reaction and progress went hand in hand.

National opposition—that is, the protection of Italian freedom from barbarian oppression, of which so much is heard in Italy later on—did not play a significant part in the twelfth century. The Lombard people welcomed Barbarossa joyfully. Italian poets sang his praises as loudly as did the Germans. A native king with the same objective of unifying authority in himself would have met exactly the same resistance, for opinion was decided not by national sentiment (only the seeds of which yet existed, at any rate so far as politics were concerned) but by the independence and prosperity of the common life of a particular city, the consequence of which was that rival neighbours were even more fiercely hated than the Emperor and his German *ministeriales*.

Modern historians like Nitzsch and Lamprecht have emphasised economic opposition: they see the peasant-based agricultural economy of the Germans interfering brutally with the higher, commercial money-economy of the Lombard cities and seeking to subordinate it wherever possible. This explanation is equally unacceptable, at least in so extreme a form. Lombard life looked very strange to a foreign observer, as can be clearly seen from Otto of Freising's famous description:[1] it seemed monstrous to Otto that the Lombard craftsmen shared the honourable profession of arms with the knights. Moreover, the German aristocrats and *ministeriales* who were suddenly entrusted with the government of Lombardy can hardly have understood the complex commercial procedures of their new subjects. It is true, too, that in Piedmont —where city life was not so fully developed—deliberate and

[1] *Gesta Friderici* ii. 13 (trans. Mierow 127–8), Pullan 176–8.

successful efforts were made to enlarge the great imperial demesnes and to rule them in the German manner. More than this cannot safely be asserted. For if in the end Frederick tried to destroy the city life of Milan, it was a purely political measure, by which he may indeed have sinned against the holy spirit of historical development, but in which he had been instructed by none other than the Milanese themselves. As for the rest of Lombardy, it is the opposite of the truth to suggest any suppression of financial and commercial enterprise: on the contrary, this enterprise was in the interests of the imperial treasury itself, and Frederick even for some time successfully promoted a plan to mint imperial *denarii* of high value as a unitary coinage for the whole of imperial Italy— another sign, too, of his centralising tendencies.

The heart of the great conflict remains, therefore, the confrontation between two opposing tendencies: on one side a strong monarchical power, which was already beginning to break with feudalism and to consider the communal independence of urban society a restriction upon its freedom of action, its rights and its income; on the other side, powerful urban organisations, grown great through self-help during the period when state control had been absent, and proud of the autonomy they had won through civil conflict, who now treated the ancient and lawful demands of the Empire as novel and insupportable exactions. The simple fact that formal law was on the Emperor's side, while the cities could claim a considerable measure of historical right on theirs, was bound to make any compromise difficult.

It is easy to see that the criteria laid down at Roncaglia— which, after all, the Milanese consuls had accepted—should have helped to make the separate treaty with Milan assume a severer form in the eyes of the Emperor (in that they defined the Emperor's authorisation of the chief officials as a simple act of appointment, following a purely nominal election), but it is just as easy to understand why the Milanese saw this as a breach of the treaty, renewed their preparations for defence and found allies among those who were also reluctant to surrender the customs of electing their own consuls freely. Further: in the exercise of his sovereign rights it was from the first quite impossible for the Emperor to steer clear of party conflicts and group interests; favour to one awoke the opposition of another. Lombardy was split between supporters and adversaries of the Emperor, and this

N

division corresponded closely with that between the rival cities of Cremona and Milan. Frederick felt himself compelled to take firm action in order to avoid losing face; the siege of little Crema (maintained by Milan as a fortress outpost for the subjugation of Cremona), which was razed to the ground in January 1160 after a heroic seven months' defence, marked the real beginning of the struggle for imperial Italy. The papacy now took a hand in this struggle, side by side with the kingdom of Sicily, which was of course already hostile to the Emperor.

The execution of the Roncaglia decrees touched the interests of the Church on a sensitive spot, for they threatened it with the loss of most of what it had gained from the Investiture Contest. In so far as the Italian bishops were still in possession of the *regalia*, they were reduced to a position of strict dependence upon the Empire through the demand for homage and for the performance of important services and even through control of Church property and the Emperor's intervention in elections. No gift of prophecy was required to foresee the rapid extension of this sort of control to central Italy. What would become then of the curia's freedom of action and of its own territorial claims in the same area? Could it even hope to preserve unharmed the territorial authority which centuries of struggle had secured for it in the states of the Church, where it claimed that sovereign power and all the regalian rights belonged to St. Peter? Had not Frederick's reply to the pope's complaint already made it plain that he intended to widen the meaning of his claims to sovereignty over the city of Rome, hitherto limited to the provision of supplies and accommodation on the coronation journey: 'Since by divine decree I am Emperor of Rome and am so styled, I should have merely the appearance of ruling and should bear a completely empty name if authority over the city of Rome were torn from my grasp'.[1] If intentions like this were put into effect, the pope would soon be no more than simply one among the bishops of the Empire.

The threat of a coming storm hung over the relations of Empire and papacy during Hadrian IV's last days. Hard words— 'sharp as spears', says a contemporary—were exchanged between the two sides. Under Rainald of Dassel's spirited direction, the imperial chancery became for the first time at least the equal of the papal in diplomatic skill. Promoted at this very time through

[1] *Gesta Friderici*, iv. 36 (trans. Mierow 271).

his imperial master's favour and without the formality of consecration to Cologne, the second senior archbishopric of the Empire,
Rainald did not thereupon adopt a hierarchical outlook—as
Thomas of Canterbury did soon afterwards—but remained true
to his former loyalty and as arch-chancellor for Italy exercised a
decisive influence over the chancery and the policy of Barbarossa.
This influence can be detected in the proud, blunt way in which the
curia's mistaken forms of address were countered by setting the
Emperor's name before that of the pope in letters to Hadrian and
in the use of the familiar 'Thou' instead of the more formal 'You'.
The whole situation recalls the last years of Alexander II. Once
again the curia refused the Emperor's offer of arbitration, made a
close alliance with his enemies—the king of Sicily and the
Lombard rebels—and contemplated excommunicating him, while
Frederick sought an understanding with the citizens of Rome.
Affairs stood thus upon a razor's edge when Hadrian died suddenly
in September 1159.

In the prevailing circumstances, as well as because there was
a deep division in the college of cardinals, a unanimous, or even
an orderly election was not to be expected. To the majority, it was
obvious that the chancellor, Roland, should be raised to the papal
throne. This meant an open breach with the Empire. For this
very reason, therefore, the imperialists sought to influence the rest
of the cardinals. Frederick's envoy Otto of Wittelsbach secretly
supported the imperially-minded minority, who elected one of
themselves (Octavian, who was descended from the counts of
Tusculum and was related to the Hohenstaufen family) as Victor
IV at a tumultuous meeting. Thereupon the other side by a
better—though not by any means an indisputably legal—procedure
elected Roland as Alexander III. With Roland there emerged a
man of the rising urban democracy to challenge the representatives
of the feudal and dynastic aristocracy, so that the two rivals
embodied the two great social forces whose conflict occupied the
whole century.

Frederick's purpose, in the struggle which at once broke out,
was not really to renew the old dependence of the papacy upon the
Empire which had prevailed a hundred years earlier. He had
scarcely ever tried to intervene in normal papal elections in the old
way, and he would almost certainly never have come to blows with
the papacy if it had refrained from obstructing his Italian plans.

But he felt himself bound to combat, even on the throne of Peter himself, a papacy which openly opposed the Empire and its legal claims, and he believed that a disputed papal election gave him the chance to exploit his rights as *advocatus Petri*. On the other hand, as soon as imperial Italy was firmly under his control the *de facto* dependence of the pope upon the Emperor would follow inescapably. Thus by the very nature of the case the freedom and independence of the curia were called in question: the political sovereignty won for it by the reformed papacy was now to be tested in the ordeal by fire. Alexander III, upon whom this duty fell, showed deep reflection and patient determination as well as bitterness and cunning, and fought with spiritual rather than military weapons, retaining a dignified bearing for all his passion and making the least possible use of personal calumny. In this respect he stands half-way between the aggressiveness of Gregory VII and the political calculation of Innocent III. He survived the anxieties and the dangers to which he was subjected with unshaken courage and growing prestige, and gained lasting recognition for the independence of the papacy.

By summoning a General Council to Pavia for 1160 in his capacity as protector of the Church, Frederick at first sought to preserve the appearance of neutrality and to secure a European decision. Although most countries either sent envoys or signified their support, the preponderance of German bishops made it difficult to regard the Council as a meeting of unprejudiced representatives of the whole Church, and it was obvious that it would either decide for Victor or declare the election of both popes irregular. Alexander III was clever enough to refuse to recognise the Council on the ground that as pope he was subject to no earthly tribunal. The Council was made aware of his hostility to the Empire through the capture of letters he had sent to the Milanese, and promptly decided to excommunicate him and recognise Victor; but it thereby merely widened the schism, for Alexander's reply was naturally to excommunicate the anti-pope, the Emperor and his chief advisers. Moreover, the decision of Pavia was far from being the verdict of the whole of Europe. It was soon plain how far the vast changes in the whole situation since the days of Henry III had removed the independent territories from imperial leadership, and how all-pervasive the papacy's influence on the destinies of Europeans had become. If the papacy became dependent upon the Empire once more, other countries too would thereby become indirectly subject to imperial control. The Englishman John of Salisbury spoke for many when he cried 'Who made the Germans judges over the nations? Who gave this coarse and barbarous people the right to set a lord of their own choice over the rulers of the children of men?'[1] In fact not only did Sicily, the Lombards (with whom Venice associated herself), Hungary, Castile, Norway, Ireland and the Latin East recognise Alexander III as the lawful pope at the Synod of Toulouse in 1160, but France and England did the same—a success which was the more welcome to Alexander because his prospects on imperial soil (which for this purpose included the dependent lands of Denmark, Bohemia and Poland) were poor because the German bishops followed Rainald of Dassel's lead and stood firmly behind the Emperor, either declaring themselves openly for Victor IV or (with the solitary exception of the bishop of Salzburg) reserving their judgment between the rival popes. On the other hand, Alexander at once lost his first line of defence in the Empire's Italian territories.

The campaign against Milan was renewed with mounting violence and growing cruelty, and reached its goal without a proper siege but instead through the destruction of the harvest and the cutting off of supplies. The starving populace insisted on unconditional surrender in March 1162. Punishment was at once mercilessly exacted. The communal existence of the now defence-less city was obliterated, by the judgement of its Lombard neigh-bours, in revenge for its own action in destroying Lodi and Como. Its inhabitants were resettled in four unwalled villages, where they were reduced to a peasant existence and subjected to labour-services, villein dues and the officers of the imperial demesne, whose jurisdiction was extended from Piedmont into Milanese territory. Severe measures like these, which flouted both natural circumstances and historical development, were only accepted by the proud Milanese under duress, and could scarcely be enforced for long. For the moment, however, terror of his army preceded the Emperor's advance and brought the remainder of his Lombard enemies to their knees. Swollen with pride, Frederick now announced that he would 'direct his armies and his victorious eagles to new undertakings and to the full re-establishment of the

[1] Tierney 112.

Empire'. His intention was to extend his Lombard system of government over the whole of Italy. In the Romagna he succeeded without difficulty, and in Tuscany Rainald of Dassel, the prime mover in this whole policy, managed in spite of Welf's nominal suzerainty to secure at once a similar subordination both of the towns—which had developed more slowly than those in Lombardy —and of the feudal magnates, who counted for considerably more in that part of the country. Comprehensive promises of naval assistance were secured through treaties with Genoa and Pisa. Rome and Sicily, the one torn by party strife and the other seriously weakened by internal unrest, were the next objectives of the triumphant imperial advance. It seemed, indeed, as if Frederick might succeed where even Charlemagne had failed, and bring a united Italy under imperial control.

Alexander's only success during this period was to escape from the ring which was tightening round him by fleeing to France. This deprived the enterprise of its designed objective, and since friction between Pisa and Genoa was also endangering it, Frederick broke it off in the summer of 1162 and turned to the west, where an opportunity of ending the papal schism seemed to present itself. Louis VII's allegiance to Alexander III had never rested on a particularly firm foundation, and was now very shaky. Tension with England, and the personal influence of his brother-in-law Henry, count of Champagne, who was related to Victor, inclined the king to a rapprochement with the Empire. The count, empowered to negotiate on his behalf, concluded an important agreement with the Emperor: both rulers, accompanied by their bishops and counts, were to come to the bridge over the Saône at St.-Jean-de-Losne in September 1162 and to confer about the schism at a meeting to which representatives from Aragon, Provence, Hungary and Denmark would be invited. If either of the popes refused to appear, he would be deemed to have forfeited his claim; otherwise, a court would be set up to decide between them. Alexander's cause seemed lost when he refused to take part; nevertheless he stood unshakeably if anxiously by his determination not to admit that he could be judged by anyone. The imperialists had clearly reckoned on this, and made no secret of the fact that they took the transfer of Louis VII's support to Victor IV for granted. Under the pressure of Alexander's partisans Louis soon began to regret his excessive haste, however, and looked for a way out of his undertakings. The turning-point was reached when, urged on by Alexander, Henry II of England stiffened his will to resist the Emperor. He waited only for an excuse to justify the breach of his engagement, and the imperialists seem to have offered him this when they gave up all hope of winning him over. The German bishops had come to the meeting in great numbers, and in order not to send them away without any settlement of the schism, Frederick summoned them to a synod in the neighbouring town of Dôle (where Rainald of Dassel himself followed up a speech of Frederick's by roughly and sharply forbidding any interference by the western European 'reguli' in appointments to the see of Rome on the ground that it belonged to the Emperor as overlord), got them to insist once more on the legitimacy of Victor's election, and dissolved the synod without waiting for the arrival of the French king. There was an angry exchange between Rainald and Louis on the Saône bridge, but high words could not disguise the fact that the disappointment of his hopes of ending the schism represented a most unwelcome set-back for Frederick. It was the first sign that there was insuperable opposition to Rainald's extreme power-policy: Frederick himself is said to have remarked that he experienced the caprice of Fortune for the first time at St.-Jean-de-Losne.

The death of his anti-pope in 1164 was another blow for the Emperor. It was arguable that Victor's disappearance should be made the occasion for an understanding with Alexander, but Rainald at once cut the ground from under any move in this direction by getting the imperialist cardinals to elect a new anti-pope, Paschal III. Frederick permitted this because he still hoped for success. But what chance would there have been of negotiating acceptable terms for those who had been consecrated by Victor, as well as over all the other disputed matters, if from the start victory had been conceded to Alexander all along the line by surrendering the opportunity of a new election? Frederick had no real choice, but the change of popes was none the less to his disadvantage: not all of Victor's supporters declared for his successor.

The Emperor's position in Italy was seriously threatened at about the same time. He returned to Germany from Burgundy for a short time in the autumn of 1162, to punish the rebellious city of Mainz for the shameful murder of archbishop Arnold of Selenhofen two years previously and to nip in the bud a conspiracy against the growing power of Henry the Lion, who was at that time still closely allied with Frederick. Since a new expedition found no favour with the German nobles, Frederick returned to Italy in 1163 without an army, to resume the designs on Sicily which he had abandoned the year before. Rainald had acted as his vice-gerent in Italy during the interim, and had held the land on a tight rein in spite of occasional signs of discontent. The complete restoration of imperial control had led Venice to feel herself threatened ever since the fall of Milan. Allied with Sicily and the Greek emperor Manuel, and the frequent refuge of Alexander's cardinals, Venice had become the centre of hostility to the Empire and had enlarged her sphere of influence by bribing the imperial cities of Verona, Vicenza and Padua to form the League of Verona. The League was openly directed against the Emperor, and successfully resisted the attacks he made with insufficient forces; all the oppressed in Lombardy looked to it in hope, and it gave them a dangerous example of self-help through co-operation.

All the failures of the last few years began at last to shake the foundations on which Frederick's power rested. Alexander's secret partisans among the German bishops raised their heads more boldly, and some of the neutrals joined them. Hitherto, Frederick had been mild in ecclesiastical matters wherever he found political obedience, but it now seemed that the continually growing pressure of the schism could only be met with severer repression. This was connected with a new political development which seemed to offer yet another opportunity to end the schism to his own advantage.

The strong and centralised Norman kingdom of Henry II of England, which—like Sicily—already had one foot outside the medieval feudal scheme of things and allowed no authority independent of itself, not even the ecclesiastical, had just come into sharp conflict with advancing clerical claims to independence in the sphere of law. When the Constitutions of Clarendon struck at them in 1164 and explicitly laid down the royal rights over the Church by means of a direct appeal to the customs of previous rulers, the king's former chancellor Thomas Becket, whom Henry had made archbishop of Canterbury, placed himself at the head of the clerical opposition. He soon had to flee to France to escape Henry's anger, and the ecclesiastical dispute in England grew into a serious rift between Henry and Alexander's adherents, although the pope himself avoided a final pronouncement upon it. Rainald of Dassel at once tried to turn this to his own advantage. As ambassador to the English court at Rouen, he sketched out a political alliance, which was cemented by the betrothal of one of Henry's daughters to a son of Frederick and of another to his cousin Henry the Lion.[1] At the same time he secured Henry's recognition of the imperial anti-pope.

Rainald came to the Reichstag at Würzburg at Whitsun 1165 fresh from this triumph. Its significance can only be grasped when it is remembered that the Plantagenet kingdom included a full half of France and therefore unquestionably counted as the second great power of the west, that Louis VII's direct demesne was only a petty province in comparison with it, and that even all the rest of Louis' feudal territory was less than the continental possessions of his greatest vassal, the king of England. The alliance of England and the Empire therefore immediately constituted an irresistible force and seemed to herald a victorious end to the schism. Carried away by his success, Rainald drove the Emperor and the Würzburg Reichstag to some fatal decisions. Frederick, the English ambassadors and all the lay and clerical nobles took the most binding oaths never to recognise Alexander and to remain absolutely loyal to Paschal or to a successor elected by his party. Magnates who did not take the same oath within six weeks were to be outlawed and to lose their offices, fiefs and property. Thus the German Church was to be thoroughly purged of Alexander's adherents and of all doubtful elements, and to be established in a political orthodoxy which would deprive Alexander of all hope of compromise.

The decision was executed with all severity: even the first archbishop of the Empire, Conrad of Mainz, was deposed because he supported Alexander; he was replaced by Frederick's chancellor, the worldly Christian of Buch, an outstanding statesman and general. Heated conflict broke out in the diocese of Salzburg, and made the aged provost Gerhoh of Reichersberg fear for the reconciliation of Church and state for which he had always striven. Such violation of the individual conscience was bound to create resistance, however. Moreover, Frederick scarcely showed political wisdom in restricting his future freedom of manoeuvre, the more so because his new English ally was always ruthlessly

---

[1] Only the second of these marriages actually took place.

opportunist in foreign affairs and had from the outset regarded his
co-operation in these matters of ecclesiastical politics as simply a
means to an end, and was in any case unable to realise it in full
because of the unanimous resistance of the English clergy. Henry
used the new alliance mainly as a means of bringing pressure to
bear on Alexander in subsequent negotiations, and was always
ready to recognise him if he received enough concessions in
return.

Frederick's understanding with England and the division
between the western powers which resulted from it brought him
at any rate some success, for it increased the uncertainty of
Alexander's position and hastened his return to Rome (upon
which he had already decided) at the end of 1165. In Rome he
was far more open to attack by the imperialists, for the expectations
which had led him to return there were in no way fulfilled. He
was practically beleaguered in the city: in the north a skilful
campaign by the chancellor Christian had carried the anti-pope
as far as Viterbo and threatened the Patrimony; Sicilian support
slackened during the regency after the twelve-year-old William II
succeeded to the throne in 1166; and finally the curia was torn
between hope and fear for the outcome of the adventurous policy
of the Greek emperor Manuel, whose capture of Ancona had made
a modest start to his plans for reconquering the western half of the
Roman Empire and reuniting the churches, plans which in their
awkward predicament the curia dared not reject outright. Every
circumstance urged Frederick to advance on Rome and compel
his opponent to submit. A new Italian expedition was decreed.
It was of course first essential to resolve all manner of disputes in
Germany, particularly to mediate in that between Henry the Lion
and his Saxon opponents. Once again the Emperor was able not
perhaps to bring about a full settlement but at any rate to demand
and secure an undertaking to keep the peace in return for excusing
both parties from the Italian expedition, although he did this
reluctantly. Thereupon he set out to Italy for the fourth time in
1166, with a force which was imposing in size in spite of these
absentees and which he reinforced with large numbers of trained
mercenaries.

The oppression of his officials and the burden of taxation had
meanwhile brought Lombardy to a dangerous state of ferment, but
the Emperor did not allow this to delay him. His further march on

Rome proceeded like Lothar's last expedition, in two separate columns. Just as on that occasion, the Emperor led the main body southwards from the Romagna along the east coast, and after a siege of several weeks recaptured Ancona from the Greeks. Meanwhile archbishops Rainald and Christian with the rest of the knights and the Brabantine mercenaries marched through Liguria and Tuscany, forced their way into the Patrimony, and by skilful tactics defeated a numerically far superior Roman army at Tusculum in May 1167. Alexander found himself encircled in a Rome whose loyalty he could not trust, and Paschal called on the Emperor to 'cut the standing corn and harvest the grape'. Frederick set his troops to storm the walls directly they arrived, captured the Leonine city, enthroned his pope in St. Peter's and had himself and his wife Beatrix crowned again on 1 August 1167. He was within reach of his objective; but Alexander disguised himself as a pilgrim, escaped out to sea just before the Pisan galleys closed the mouth of the Tiber, and fled to Benevento. The end of the schism was once more relegated to the distant future. Nevertheless, when the Romans themselves opened their gates to him as well and accepted his authority unconditionally, the long-desired occupation of the city seemed to mark a victory for the Emperor which only Henry IV before him had equalled. At once a fearful natural calamity struck him down suddenly in the moment of triumph, and contemporaries saw it as divine punishment for his persecution of the true pope. The day after the coronation a cloudburst brought an unprecedentedly heavy fall of rain within the space of a few hours, and this was followed by a deadly sickness which raged among the citizens and the imperial troops alike and carried off all and sundry. Two thousand of Frederick's knights died—great magnates like Conrad III's son Frederick of Rotenburg and the young Welf VII, prominent officials like bishop Hermann of Verden and bishop Daniel of Prague, but above all others the greatest of his servants, the man who had led him to the heights and whose counsel would now not aid him on the downward slopes: Rainald of Dassel, dead in the full flood of his creative powers. Reluctant as Frederick had lately sometimes been to follow Rainald's genius and its power-politics, strongly as his own temperament inclined him to the more moderate and cautious policy which was to bring him such success in later years, yet the courage and buoyancy, the inventiveness and the organisational talent of his faithful servant had never failed to impress him, and his disappearance seemed to leave a gap which could not be filled. He heaped honours on the dead man and eulogised him for having 'always set the honour and the increase of the Empire before his own advantage and pursued with ardour all that would promote the Emperor's renown.'

There could be no thought now either of continuing the campaign against Alexander and Sicily or of a longer sojourn on the plague-stricken soil of Rome. The Emperor hastened northwards through Tuscany with the remnants of his army and crossed the Appennines to Pavia with difficulty. In Lombardy there had meanwhile been a complete reversal of opinion, and this was greatly accelerated by the impression created by the 'divine punishment' of Rome, although not caused by it. Because the arrival of the Emperor had brought greater severity instead of the relaxation of control for which the Lombards had hoped, four cities (encouraged by Venice and Alexander's party) had secretly leagued together during the spring shortly after Frederick had moved south towards Rome. Among them was Cremona, which had been disappointed over its wider claims although Frederick had shown it much favour, and the league had made contact with Milan (which gave an undertaking not to resume its old oppressive sovereignty) and in open rebellion had begun to rebuild the city which Frederick had destroyed. Since then the alliance had been extended (not without some violence) to eight cities in all, whose territory formed the heart of Lombardy, and had received enthusiastic support from the League of Verona. Their expressed object was to throw off the rule of the imperial officials and to re-establish self-government and the exercise of the regalian rights. The benefits which the Emperor had originally brought to Lombardy by overthrowing Milanese sovereignty and bridling mutual conflict were in future to be assured by the League through a body of rectors, to which each city was to send one of its consuls and which was to form both the supreme military authority and the final court of appeal. The League was therefore intended to be permanent, not limited to the needs of the moment alone, and was conceived as an independent federal state inside the Empire.

If Frederick had returned to Lombardy with undiminished prestige and an army which was still strong, he would have been able to destroy the hostile alliance; in the actual situation, however, everything went wrong. His hesitant attempts to change his fortunes by quick successes gained from a base in loyal Pavia were fruitless. Rebellion soon took a hold in western Lombardy as well, and threatened to cut his line of retreat by closing the Alpine passes. For a moment he seemed completely isolated and at the mercy of his enemies. At the last minute he succeeded in persuading the count of Savoy to change sides; disguised as a servant and threatened with imprisonment and death in Susa, the Emperor at last regained Germany in March 1168.

The Lombard League, now grown to twenty-three cities by uniting with the League of Verona, could consolidate and develop in peace. Acceptance of the anti-pope vanished along with imperial rule. The Lombards formed a close alliance with Alexander, and in honour of the pope they gave the name Alessandria to a new commune they founded in 1168 between Tortona and Asti: it grew out of the combination of a number of villages, extended the development of city life westwards, and was designed to serve the ends of both attack and defence against what remained of the Emperor's support and against the imperial demesne lands.

A remarkable change had occurred in the space of a few months. The end of the schism was farther off than ever, and the proud imperial structure which Frederick had erected in Italy with Rainald's help lay in ruins. Frederick seemed back almost at the point where he had started. The collapse, coming at the same time as the death of his most important adviser, marks a turning-point in his life. Yet a character like his was more fitted to survive misfortune than to exploit success. He immediately set about building anew but by better methods.

12

FROM THE DEATH OF RAINALD TO THE END OF THE SCHISM
(1168–1177)

It is tempting to compare Frederick's prospects after the disaster of 1167 and the Lombard rising with the situation of Henry IV when Italy went over to Urban II. In each case it became impossible to persist with the schism and an antipope. European support and Italian resistance gave backing to the independence of the curia. When the death of Paschal III made it necessary to choose a new antipope, the possibility of abandoning his successor, Calixtus III (who was little more than the creature of a Roman party) in return for concessions by Alexander was not far from Frederick's mind and certainly led to negotiations which were serious enough to be prolonged for several years and broke down in the end mainly because Alexander insisted that the rebellious Lombards should be included in them. Frederick's authority both north and south of the Alps was very considerable, however, and far greater than Henry's had been a century earlier. Nevertheless, in Italy a new-style combination of self-governing cities had been driven like a wedge between the two blocks of imperial territory and prevented any union between them. The enemies of the Emperor had gained ground in central Italy too, but in general his authority was not so seriously shaken here as in Lombardy, and Christian of Mainz did his best from about 1170 onwards to restore it by diplomacy and arms. He intervened as a mediator in the party struggles of the Tuscan cities, and was even more successful in the duchy of Spoleto, the March of Ancona and the eastern Romagna. Even parts of the Patrimony itself, including the city of Rome, remained in imperial hands throughout the following years. Finally, Frederick secured a decisive advantage when about 1174 he persuaded the old duke Welf VI (whose only son had been a victim of the epidemic of 1167, and who had consequently lost interest in his Italian fiefs) to cede him his rights in Tuscany, Spoleto, Sardinia, Corsica and the Matildine lands in return for a money payment. Thereby Frederick gained new bases not only in central Italy but in Lombardy as well, and with them the possibility of reconstructing his Italian policy on new foundations.

The German consequences of these advances were unfortunate in as much as they increased the German nobility's reluctance to engaged in Italian adventures. In other respects, however, Frederick soon managed to strengthen his greatly weakened authority in Germany by skilful, cautious and well-calculated measures. Henry IV had only managed to regain at any rate political control of Germany by concessions to the Saxon and south German opposition, and the power of Henry the Lion now showed that a similar solution was called for. But Welf and Staufen power had not yet become completely separate, and the stability of German domestic politics was for some time yet to depend on their unbroken friendly co-operation. It was just at this moment that Frederick gave his cousin the protection of the Empire against a league of his territorial opponents and imposed peace upon them; yet while thus benefitting his most powerful duke he managed also to group the other great nobles round his throne by just and careful measures and the exercise of imperial authority, and secured from them—apparently without resistance— the election of his second son Henry (who was only three years old) as king in 1169. It was plainly a deliberate move on the Emperor's part to set the younger brother above his eldest son Frederick: the nobles, jealous of their electoral rights, would have been far less willing to accept succession by strict primogeniture, particularly since the younger Frederick had recently received the duchy of Swabia, whose duke—the young Frederick of Rotenburg, the son of Conrad III —had been another victim of the malaria epidemic. By avoiding the union of duchy and crown in the same person, Barbarossa followed a custom which had prevailed since the Hohenstaufen had mounted the throne, and thereby made it easier for the nobility to accept the succession of his house.

What made the authority of Barbarossa in Germany at this time so incomparably greater than that of Henry IV, however, was that he also held the reins of Church government firmly in his hands and even drew them tighter. In pursuance of the Würz- burg decisions, he everywhere compelled the clergy to accept ordination from the anti-pope's bishops, and thereby bound them securely to himself. He even breached the defences of the province of Salzburg, the fortress of the Alexandrines, and at the head of a united Germany successfully defended imperial interests in east and west. The murder of archbishop Thomas of Canterbury in 1170, which had horrified the whole of Christendom and aroused its anger against the guilty king Henry, led to an unexpected change in political alignments, for the removal of the obstinate Becket nevertheless helped to reduce the tension between England and the curia. When hostilities between Empire and papacy broke out again, therefore, the Emperor replaced the lost English alliance by a *rapprochement* with France; the close connexion between Staufen and Capetian lasted well into the next century, while blood-relationship continued to hold England and the Welf family together.

The next six years, all of which Frederick spent on German soil, saw few great events but much quiet and lasting progress. Could the papacy and its Italian allies resist his might, when he came to gather it for a final annihilating blow? Pope and Italians had successfully defended their position in recent years, but had scarcely improved it. The Lombard League had certainly been somewhat widened, but it had also become considerably looser. Venice was in practice outside it, involved in bitter strife with the Greek emperor and therefore on occasion even driven to co-operate with the German forces against a renewed Greek occupation of Ancona; and old rivalries were reawakening in the heart of Lombardy itself, where the reviving power of Milan threatened Cremona's leadership.

The eight-thousand-strong army with which the Emperor set out on his fifth Italian expedition in 1174 was not remarkable for its size—memories of the treacherous Italian climate were still vivid, and it had unfortunately not been possible this time to secure the presence of the most powerful prince, Henry the Lion— but the first successes could be expected to bring powerful reinforcements, and Frederick's diplomatic skill was faced with the task of separating the pope from the Lombards as far as possible.

The weight of the German attack, which speedily regained the western parts of Lombardy for the Empire, fell first upon the fortifications of Alessandria, which had been called a 'city of straw' in mockery of its village-like unpreparedness but now proved itself rather a city of iron by a stubborn defence which lasted six months and caused the emperor's army serious losses. The protracted siege decided the fate of the campaign and more besides, for it showed Frederick his enemies' capacity for resistance and decided him to restrict his political objectives in Lombardy. Thus when a powerful relieving force of the Lombard League approached his lines, he preferred negotiation to armed conflict, and the Lombards—caught between the undefeated Emperor and the archbishop of Mainz's advance from the Romagna, and mistrustful of their own solidarity—were glad to accept his overtures although for the moment they had the upper hand. This was the origin of the treaty of Montebello of 1175: formally, the Lombards threw themselves upon the Emperor's mercy, but in reality it was an agreement to accept judicial arbitration between the opposing claims, putting both sides under such binding obligations that it deserves to be regarded not merely as an armistice but as a real treaty of peace. For the points still in dispute were to be settled by the consuls of Cremona, whose decision was to be unconditionally binding—an arrangement which incidentally shows that because of her recent cautious hesitation both parties were prepared to treat Cremona as a neutral power despite the fact that she retained her position at the head of the League. In accordance with these provisions, Frederick dismissed the mercenaries who formed a large but costly part of his army, and the cities disbanded their forces.

An honourable observance of the terms of the treaty seemed now in fact to give promise of a peace acceptable to both sides. For with one of those sudden shifts which were so characteristic of his later personal policy Frederick abandoned the enforcement of the Roncaglia decrees, that is to say the imposition of direct rule by imperial officials upon northern Italy. He was prepared, while recognising the League, to content himself with the exercise of the sovereign imperial rights which previous German rulers had held before the heavy losses which followed the death of Henry V. The compromise which eventually emerged from the negotiations in the shape of the decision of the Cremonese consuls was not very different from the later provisions of the treaty of Constance. Why, then, had there first to be new conflict? The reason was that Frederick's change of policy was directed solely at settling with one opponent in order to leave his hands free to deal with the other. The struggle with Alexander III, whose ecclesiastical

o

cause the Lombards might again espouse, was to be prosecuted, while not only was the League's fortress of Alessandria (which enjoyed the special protection of the pope) not to be recognised as such, but it was to lose its municipal status as well. But this ran as contrary to the ecclesiastical conviction of the Lombards as it did to their awareness of a close community of interest between themselves and the papacy. By at once bringing pressure to bear on an Emperor who was short of soldiers, they ensured that papal plenipotentiaries were brought into the negotiations, though admittedly this did not help to heal the schism. The imputation that they would be prepared to surrender heroic Alessandria was bound to be felt as a deliberate insult to the League. When the consuls of Cremona gave way to the Emperor's wishes on both points, it seemed almost as if they were preferring the advantage of their own city to the common interests of the League, and as if they were not living up to their associates' expectations of them in this respect. The announcement of their decision was therefore immediately followed by the outbreak of a popular movement in Lombardy which was encouraged by the bishops and led to an open infringement of the treaty of Montebello—understandable enough although it cannot be excused. It is debatable which side began hostilities anew, but immaterial. Politically, the new situation was not unfavourable to Frederick, for Cremona felt herself insulted and after holding back at first soon began to incline to his side; but from the military point of view the small size of his army presented a considerable danger. It was thus a piece of good fortune when the defection of Como to him opened important Alpine passes to the passage of reinforcements from Germany.

In this situation Frederick turned to Henry the Lion as well. North of Lake Como, at Chiavenna, there had taken place early in 1176 that memorable encounter which some historians would still like to strike out of the record because there is no mention of it in the scanty pages of the directly contemporary chronicles. Other accounts, however, only slightly later in date, are sufficient to establish the fact of the encounter, its location and the essence of what took place with sufficient certainty—medieval sources often permit no more than can be arrived at in this case. Frederick could not demand military support as his lawful right, since his cousin had not sworn to give it, but the sight of his imperial overlord in need might seem to lay an obligation on the loyalty of a vassal, and the memory of their earlier friendship could perhaps bring moral pressure to bear. Furthermore, Frederick seems to have pleaded so passionately that he even went on his knees to his own vassal. However, the duke, who had taken no part in Italian expeditions since 1161 and whose policies had in recent years diverged widely from the emperor's, was unaffected by this display of emotion and with his usual sober opportunism demanded as the price of his help the strategically important imperial city of Goslar and its silver-mines, over which he appears occasionally to have exercised rights of protection earlier on. The Emperor held this demand, which almost amounted to blackmail, to be improper and incompatible with the honour of the Empire, and angrily broke off the interview. The busy hand of popular fancy soon added colourful touches to the story, and still does: it is impossible to remain entirely unmoved by an occasion on which the two leading men of their country, widely different in position and outlook, broadly representative of the two great motive forces which affected German history from its beginnings down to Bismarck and beyond, faced each other and parted in disagreement. Yet to ascribe to the occasion an influence on the later legal proceedings against Henry is to miss its significance, for it did not lend itself to that sort of exploitation. Rather than an open breach, it involved a change of mind on the part of the Emperor, whose feeling of personal humiliation led him at the same time to recognise that in the long run it was not feasible to preserve, in the interests of the Empire, the prevailing equilibrium in Germany.

The effect of German particularism upon the outcome of the Lombard campaigns, and so upon the great conflict of Church and state, was here manifest and was to prove decisive. For the troops which now came up secretly by the little-used Lukmanier pass were not numerous enough to give the Emperor the upper hand in Lombardy; while he was leading them in person on a daring march to join up with his forces round Pavia, the German knights were shattered on the shields and pikes of the numerically superior Milanese infantry at Legnano (northwest of Milan) in a battle which was important not in itself but only for its consequences. Frederick could only attain his objective at the cost of serious losses. His first defeat in the field forced him to admit once more his north Italian enemies' capacity for resistance; once again he offered them a peaceful settlement. The provisions of a new 'decision of Cremona', with which Frederick declared he would be satisfied, went well beyond those of the previous year in the concessions they made to the Lombards. They offered more than was actually granted by the later treaty of Constance, and Frederick remained firm only on the question of separating the Lombards from Alexander III. Yet the Lombards threw away the fruits of their own victory when they over-estimated the extent of their success and at Milan's suggestion rejected peace out of consideration for the pope. The outbreak of rivalry between Cremona and Milan brought the League's dissensions into the open.

Frederick now changed course again and successfully opened negotiations for a separate agreement with Alexander. The pope refused to conclude a permanent peace without his allies, but it was a real success for the Emperor when the issues which divided Empire and papacy were settled (provisionally at least) by the treaty of Anagni in November 1176.

At long last Frederick declared himself ready to break the oath he had sworn at Würzburg, to drop the anti-pope, and to recognise Alexander—a difficult decision after seventeen years of strife, but by now a necessity. There had not for a long time—certainly not since the defection of England—been any prospect of his gaining a European victory, and the German Church was isolated even if it was solidly behind him; even Frederick's closest advisers felt the need to bring the abnormal situation to an end. On the other hand, the pope's position was more secure than it had been earlier. A Hildebrand in his position might perhaps have refused to give way; but Alexander had grown grey in the defence of the freedom of the papacy, his influence in the Empire was seriously diminished, the Church and its possessions thrown into disorder and its finances exhausted, the bonds of obedience loosened as much as those of belief. He welcomed the opportunity of bringing the conflict to an end without abandoning his position. It was a simple matter to release the repentant Emperor from excommunication and to recognise him. Acceptance of schismatic ordinations was a more difficult matter. While the pope retained a free hand in Italy, which was predominantly on his side, he made far-reaching concessions to the opposition party in Germany and thus left Frederick's links with the German Church unbroken. Even the violently Alexandrine cardinal Conrad of Wittelsbach was to

resign the province of Mainz in return for a promise of the first
vacant archbishopric—which in the event proved to be Salzburg.
Alexander's demands in terms of the temporal authority of the
Church were more serious: the surrender of imperial sovereignty
over the Patrimony, the restoration of the temporal possessions to
the situation of Innocent II's time, and the recognition of clerical
claims to the property of countess Matilda—the last of these was
unacceptable to Frederick in his need for a new power-base in
Italy, and he only entertained it in order to get the peace negotiations under way.

The treaty of Anagni smoothed over all disputes and skilfully
surveyed every possibility. It shows the diplomacy of both sides
at its best, but it was only the preliminaries of peace and was not
to come into force until an agreement with Sicily and the Lombards
had been concluded. Alexander intended to assist in person with
the removal of the difficulties which were likely to arise, particularly in northern Italy, by holding a peace congress there; it met
in Venice.

The extent to which Frederick had improved his position by
this separate peace with the papacy was soon evident. Mistrust
arose between the pope and the Lombards, and the Emperor
encouraged it. The Lombards' complaints about the pope's
unilateral action are reminiscent of the attitude of the German
opposition after Canossa. The Emperor's demands escalated at
once: not even the concessions offered at Montebello were left
untouched, let alone those proposed after Legnano.

It was now in the pope's interest to induce his allies to yield; if
they refused, they could be charged with being the sole obstacle to
the peace of the Church. When, in spite of this, no basis of agreement could be found, Alexander proposed a six-year truce instead
of a final peace treaty. In itself, this was not to the Emperor's
disadvantage, for until the six years were up he could widen the
rifts in the League—Cremona and Tortona had left it already—
and in future negotiations he faced a Lombard party which was
completely alienated from the curia. Yet with astonishing diplomatic skill he was at the same time able to secure modifications of
the treaty of Anagni in his own favour in return for acceding to the
pope's request for this change. An indefinite declaration covering
the mutual restoration of occupied territory replaced a precise
definition of the Church's territorial claims. Over and above this,

Frederick made it a condition that the Matildine lands (the income from which probably represented a temporary replacement for the Lombard tribute which he could expect from a future peace settlement) should remain in his hands until a court of arbitration pronounced upon their ownership. His intention is clear: to accept Lombard self-government only if the rich Matildine lands gave him alternative bases for imperial rule. Since Alexander gave way to this demand, the negotiations ended with a very valuable and entirely personal success for Barbarossa, and one which was to be decisive for future developments. Lastly, a truce was to be arranged with Sicily as well as with the Lombards, but since this was to be for fifteen years it was almost the same thing as a peace-treaty and helped to promote friendly relations between Empire and kingdom after a long period of hostility.

These were in all essentials the foundation upon which the treaty of Venice was concluded in the summer of 1177 after lengthy negotiations in which the German archbishops Christian of Mainz and Wichmann of Magdeburg played a prominent part. There was a remarkable scene when the Emperor disembarked from the doge's galley near the gaily-decorated Piazza San Marco, mounted the steps of a papal throne erected in front of the cathedral doors, knelt and kissed the feet of his ancient enemy and was raised by Alexander with the kiss of peace. This and other ceremonies during the next few days certainly represented no intolerable humiliation for Frederick, but they did bring out the fact that the papacy had won a victory in principle and that its painful struggles had brought it victoriously through the ordeal which had tested its freedom. When soon after the conclusion of peace Alexander assembled the Third Lateran Council in Rome in 1179—following the example of Calixtus II after the Investiture Contest and Innocent II after the schism—not only did the distinguished representatives of Latin Christendom remove the last vestiges of ecclesiastical dispute and strengthen the storm-shaken edifice of the Church, but they also secured the head of the Church as far as possible from future external dangers by passing a decree on papal elections which required a two-thirds majority of the cardinals and called for the exclusion of all outside influence.

But the papal victory had only been won because Alexander's careful moderation had for the time being replaced the wider-ranging Hildebrandine political objectives. The recognition of ecclesiastical independence was far from implying the subordination of the Empire. Instead, the Empire stood over against the papacy as an equal, a power in its own right, and from the political point of view the peace of Venice can in no sense be considered a defeat for the Emperor. His completely undisputed authority in Germany formed a secure foundation for his power. In the kingdom of Burgundy—where, as in Germany, the object of his policy was to renew the old links between crown and episcopate and above all to bind the great churches more closely to the imperial cause by bestowing privileges upon them—it was just at this time, after the peace of Venice, that he again personally resumed extensive sovereign rights and had himself crowned king at Arles in 1178 as a sign of his authority over the southern part of the kingdom. In Lombardy he stood by the decision (announced in 1175) not to execute the Roncaglia decrees, but his most recent diplomatic successes had so altered the course of events in spite of this that they had opened up a possible route towards the achievements of his real objective—imperial authority in Italy—on other foundations and by different means. He was safer than he had been quite recently in relation to the Lombard League, now divided against itself and increasingly immune from papal influence, and above all there was nothing to fear from Sicily. The full scope of imperial authority over central Italy had finally been asserted, and here the development of direct rule by officials, with all that this implied, was soon renewed with great energy. This meant, however, that the danger of political and military pressure on the curia was also renewed. Alexander was only brought back to Rome in 1178 by imperial troops, and he was unable to maintain himself there. Soon there was new friction between papal and imperial claims. Alexander preserved the peace by calculated moderation, but by the time he came to die in 1181 he could scarcely look to the future with as much satisfaction as he could to the struggles with which his life had been filled. For Frederick Barbarossa was by then without question the greatest ruler in Europe, and with the overthrow of his mighty German vassal he soon entered the period of his last great successes.

13

BARBAROSSA'S LAST GREAT
SUCCESSES (1178–1190)

The union of Bavaria (still the strongest duchy, if reduced in area) and Saxony (always remarkable for the strength of its separatist spirit, although the extent of ducal authority was restricted) would alone have made Henry the Lion's power immense. But the peculiar quality and the historical significance of Henry's position derived from the fact that he had managed to divert to his own advantage the waves of German colonial settlement which for a generation past had been beating upon the Slav lands to the east. His ruthless and violent action—which made him more feared than God among the Abotrite chieftains—had brought about the subjugation, Germanisation and conversion of the Wendish territory of eastern Holstein, Lauenburg and western Mecklenburg, and by about 1172 had (in Helmold's somewhat exaggerated words) already made them into one vast Saxon colony with towns, villages and a steadily growing number of churches and clergy. Henry's policy of urban settlement was marked by violence but conceived on a grand scale; although its objectives were naturally confined to his own political and military advantage, it nevertheless showed a far-sighted realisation of the economic and governmental requirements of the rising bourgeoisie. Certain aspects of it in particular seem already to foreshadow the great days of the Hanse—for instance, his concern for the prosperity of Lübeck, which he had painfully wrested from the Schauenburg family and practically refounded, and his commendation of its market to the Danes, Swedes, Norwegians and Russians; his confirmation of the charter his grandfather Lothar had given to the men of Gotland, the addition to it of a reciprocity clause and his related action in redefining and securing the rights of the German merchants who visited the island; his clearing of Wendish pirates from the Baltic; his intervention in Danish succession disputes and the dependence of the kingdom of Denmark upon him. The Empire too benefitted from this advance of his frontiers and the respect it compelled abroad. On the other hand, he can no more be credited with a consciously German national policy than can the rulers of Brandenburg-Prussia until well into the nineteenth century. The recently-conquered Slav areas were valuable to him chiefly because in these new lands the supreme authority of the territorial ruler was not broken up by the existence of semi-independent lay and ecclesiastical lordships, as it was in the older parts of the Empire, but could be planned and organised as a unity. In them the duke possessed, besides his territorial rights, authority over the law-courts and military service which extended to all inhabitants of the frontier provinces alike; he controlled markets and coinage, and exercised the right of taxation. An early attempt to put all these territorial powers into the hands of an independent official body, like that which the Emperor was trying to establish in northern and central Italy, admittedly came to nothing in the end. A substitute for it was to some extent found in the ecclesiastical authority over the three colonial sees which he kept firmly in his own hands along with the right to appoint bishops and invest them with the *regalia*; these great churches, incorporated into his system of government and not withdrawn from ducal control through exemptions to the same degree as was the case with the imperial churches which were escaping the Emperor's supervision, gave him a secure foundation and also— particularly when a parish organisation had been set up—provided the framework for further colonisation. Thus there developed on the frontier of the Empire a state organisation of an entirely new pattern, the first—as has rightly been pointed out—with full territorial authority. Henry thereupon sought to transfer this novel concept of territorial authority to his German lands, Bavaria and Saxony. To this end he could utilise many of the traditional rights of the old tribal dukes, although he did not simply try to revive them, since the time for such an attempt was long past. Instead, he used the conventional family policies of the nobility, but went far beyond them towards modern methods of establishing royal power.

Thanks to a long and unbroken tradition, ducal authority in Bavaria was firmly enough rooted to serve as a useful foundation for a claim to leadership of the whole tribe. But since the Welf possessions there were too few to serve as a basis for a policy of acquisition and extension, Henry regarded Bavaria rather as an outlying territory and only visited it occasionally. He seized control (partly by force) of the ancient salt road from Reichenhall to Augsburg and endeavoured to install his men at vital points in the network of Bavarian trade-routes, but although his motives may have included the old idea that it was the duke's duty to keep the peace and ensure the freedom of the roads, his objectives were primarily economic: Bavaria was to provide him with the financial resources which his forward policy in Saxony required. But in Saxony—where the frontier dukedom of the Billungs (small in spite of the addition of Lothar's family lands) had almost regained the standing of a tribal duchy—the duke's powers could only to a very limited extent be used as a foundation for supreme authority or even as a starting-point for claims to it; moreover, the magnates —men like the margraves of Brandenburg and Meissen, the count palatine of Saxony, the landgrave of Thuringia, the arch-bishops of Cologne, Bremen and Magdeburg or the bishops of Halberstadt and Hildesheim—directly opposed any enlargement of the duke's authority. On the other hand, most of the private lands of the house of Welf lay just in this part of east Saxony, between the Weser and the Elbe, and Henry directed his main efforts towards a planned extension of them. He did this by a variety of forceful measures: he confiscated property to which there were no direct heirs (roughly setting aside the claims of daughters and other kindred) and the estates of nobles who opposed him, accumulated advocacies and countships, and even turned the schism to his own advantage by securing the promotion of his creatures to episcopal sees and then compelling them to transfer important ecclesiastical fiefs to himself. All this led to a vast increase in his power, raised him high above his peers, and practically made him a sovereign prince. In a number of respects Henry's intellectual and political attitude seems hardly dis-tinguishable from that of one who rules in his own right, and many features of his government suggest the new type of ruler which had been developing in the Norman states during the last few generations—a type of which Frederick II was to be the supreme example. He held court for instance, in a palace at Dankwarde-rode in Brunswick which he had built after the pattern of the imperial palaces at Goslar and Aachen; he deliberately encouraged art and literature and used them to increase his own prestige, and his more rational methods of government show the beginnings of an escape from the fetters of feudalism.

True to the settlement they had reached at the beginning of his reign, the Emperor put no obstacles in the way of his cousin's progress, and indeed often gave it valuable support. As late as the sixties, when Henry was already standing aloof from his Italian enterprise, Frederick mediated several times between Henry and the Saxon nobles (whose hostility to the Lion's plans was already threateningly evident) to Henry's advantage. As time passed, however, the friendly relationship between the cousins gradually gave way to an estrangement. Henry, increasingly pre-occupied with his schemes of domination, perhaps felt that he could do without the protection which the Emperor had hitherto afforded him. His second marriage to Matilda, daughter of Henry II of England—after Barbarossa the greatest ruler in the west—increased his dynastic pride, and the close connection with an Anglo-Norman court whose political ambitions in Italy collided with the Emperor's in more ways than one was hardly likely to have a favourable influence upon his attitude to Frederick. It is not necessary to assume that Henry was actually conducting an international policy outside his own sphere of influence, but his disinclination to lend further support to his cousin's policy in Italy could only be reinforced by this connection. Thus he became accustomed to a neglect of his links with the Hohenstaufen which reached its peak when he refused help at Chiavenna; and when he worked feverishly to increase his power in Germany at the expense of the lesser princes, upon whose support the Emperor was increasingly dependent, there began to loom a danger that he might do the Empire permanent harm or even break it up and to a large extent put himself in its place.

Even if, taking a modern and nationalist point of view, one wished to argue that this need not have been altogether a misfortune for Germany, it would still be easy to understand why the Emperor opposed it. But it is essential to avoid regarding the Welf as a national hero locked in combat with the universalism of Barbarossa, and vital not to explain as a difference of political conviction something which was no more than the result of differences in historical and geographical background. As a duke, regularly protected by the Emperor's power, Henry had been able to pursue his more limited objectives undisturbed. There is every reason to believe that, had he been Emperor himself, he would, like Otto I, Lothar and Otto IV, have been compelled by the nature of things to adopt an imperial policy and that he would then very likely have prosecuted every claim with even more violence and lack of scruple than his adversary. For a comparison between the two personalities and particularly during this last conflict, shows up to advantage the greatness, the maturity and the confidence of Frederick by contrast with his cousin's pride and passion; it is easy to understand that when he had realised his life's ambition—the strengthening and extension of his power as duke —Henry should have determined to protect it against every tendency to disintegrate, yet his very wilfulness and blind recalcitrance were themselves the causes of the disaster which overtook him. Frederick's approach was slow and cautious, and his recollection of the old Welf-Hohenstaufen feud that he had himself settled with so much difficulty was still far too vivid for him to have begun by contemplating either a renewal of the feud or a fight to the death with his powerful cousin. It was only the unfolding of events which gradually carried him beyond his original intentions.

The first sign that Frederick was no longer prepared to consider Henry's interests came in the treaty of Anagni, with its provision that the archbishop of Bremen and the bishop of Halberstadt, schismatics whom he had promoted, should be deposed. New conflicts arose in Saxony as a result. If Frederick once more restrained his cousin's opponents, this was less because he was again taking Henry's side than because he had decided to force Henry back into legality through the processes of the law instead of by disturbing the peace. Henry's contumacy in persistently refusing to face the charges brought against him can only be explained by supposing that he had at once noticed the change in the atmosphere when he met Frederick at Speyer at the end of October 1178 and had sensed that he could expect no benefit from these proceedings. Furthermore, the area of friction between the cousins' interests was enlarged about this time. Old duke Welf VI, whose extravagance kept him constantly short of money, had originally offered his rich private estates in Swabia to the Lion at a price which Henry thought too high. Welf now closed with an offer from his other nephew, Frederick, and thus gave Henry one more ground for disenchantment by suggesting the threat of a double offensive against him through an alliance between the emperor and his enemies among the nobility. A more calculating opportunist would have accepted the inevitability of some relatively slight sacrifice; his hot Welf pride could not stomach the idea and, overestimating the security of his position, Henry felt that he could make a success of open resistance to the Emperor's judicial authority. It was this alone which caused his fall.

The details of the proceedings against Henry the Lion have only been freed from the contradictions and bias of the fairly extensive sources by the painstaking researches of recent years. They are of more interest, however, to the legal than to the political historian. The proceedings could not be made to rest upon Henry's refusal of help at Chiavenna, which had no legal significance, although its political importance could be exploited for purposes of propaganda. The injured nobles complained, under the *Landrecht*, that the peace had been broken and, like Otto of Nordheim a century earlier, Henry obstinately disregarded the summons. He was thereupon declared an outlaw at Magdeburg in June 1179 on the purely formal ground of contempt of court. Even at this point he dismissed, at a meeting with Frederick at Haldensleben, the proposal that he might buy his way back into the Emperor's favour with a payment of five thousand marks, on the ground that 'the discharge of so great a sum seemed too hard' and further losses to his accusers would almost certainly have followed; at the same time he avoided the offer of single combat made by one of his enemies, margrave Dietrich of Lausitz. Though an outlaw, he continued to encroach violently upon the rights of others; and for this reason, and more particularly on the ground that his refusal to answer the *Landrecht* summons had broken his obligations as an imperial vassal, he was now summoned anew under feudal law. After failing to meet the three successively appointed dates he was sentenced to the loss of his imperial fiefs at Würzburg in January 1180. Once he had persisted in his outlawry for twelve months the ban of the Empire came into force at Regensburg in June 1180; with it went complete dishonour and the loss of all legal rights.

The redistribution of Henry's imperial fiefs which at once took place marked the end of the process by which the tribal duchies were destroyed. The dioceses of Cologne and Paderborn were cut off from Saxony and given as the duchy of Westphalia to the archbishop of Cologne, whose power was thereby considerably increased. The ducal title to what was left of Saxony—shorn of all recent usurpations and thus reduced almost to the old Billung

territories and the Wendish marches—was handed over to the
Ascanian Bernard of Anhalt, the youngest son of Albert the Bear,
in April 1180.[1] Bavaria was similarly dismembered. Another new
duchy, Styria, was carved out of it, and the count of Andechs was
made independent and given the title of duke of Croatia, Dalmatia
and Merania. The remainder was the reward for Otto of Wittelsbach's loyal support of the emperor; Otto resigned the palatine
county to his younger brother, and in September 1180 became the
first of the long line of Wittelsbach dukes of Bavaria.

The chief result of all these changes was to strengthen the
middle rank of territorial princes who had been the principal cause
of the fall of Henry the Lion. The emperor himself gained no
direct benefit from his victory. It is not unlikely that he had at one
time or another contemplated the possibility of annexing Saxony
to the Empire or handing it over to one of his sons. A project of
this sort would have fitted in quite well with the rest of his territorial
policy; be that as it may, the obstacles to its realisation were in the
event bound to be insuperable. In the course of Frederick's
reign feudalism had increasingly become the leading principle of
the imperial constitution. The nature and definition of the status
of prince of the Empire was feudally determined, and henceforth
emerged clearly as the decisive factor in the life of the state, side
by side with the central authority; the *Heerschildordnung*[2] was
likewise feudally determined, and in it the relationship of
individual groups of free nobles to each other and to the kingship
found an ordered pattern. The consequence of the legal proceedings against Henry the Lion was therefore a victory of feudal law
over the older conception of the tribal duchy. But in so far as the
ruler threw the whole weight of feudal law into the scales against
an insubordinate vassal he was thereby precluded from seeking to
escape from the same law himself, and had to recognise the
fundamental principle of *Leihezwang*[3]—according to which the
king had to re-grant a vacant fief within a year and a day—which
now began to take firm root in German feudal law. Further,
Frederick's royal authority was not in fact strong enough for him
to turn against the middle rank of territorial princes (hitherto his
allies) directly after the fall of the Welf, and to deny them their

[1] The Gelnhausen charter, which recorded Henry's sentence and the
partition of Saxony, is in Pullan 165–7.
[2] 'Military order of precedence'.
[3] 'Compulsory re-enfeoffment'.

expected reward. It is one of the characteristics of his domestic policy that he always took a moderate line towards the rising princely families. If his private dynastic policy was always calculated to form a counterweight to their nascent pursuit of independence, on the other hand he made concessions to their attitude in particular cases (for instance, Austria in 1156 and Würzburg in 1168) which markedly advanced the development of the territorial sovereignties of the future, notably in the sphere of law. Now, after the fall of Henry the Lion, he could hope to be able to deal more easily with a multiplicity of territories than with the huge unyielding power of the Welfs. It is in any case certain that the proceedings against Henry did not finally decide the way in which the balance of power inside Germany would in future be determined.

Frederick's most urgent task now was to slay the lion whose skin he had already given away. He did not relax his menaces. But he had now linked the interests of the princes with his own twice over, and with their assistance he appeared in Saxony to execute the sentence against Henry, using the prestige of the imperial crown and dislike of Henry's regime of force combined to bring about an unprecedented series of desertions by Henry's supporters. With this support, the emperor's superior strategy deprived Henry of his lands almost without a blow; the English and Danish assistance, on which Henry may have counted, came to nothing, and Henry was soon (towards the end of 1181) compelled to throw himself humbly on the emperor's mercy at Erfurt, where the only clemency shown him was a modification of the princes' decision which left him his family lands in Brunswick and Lüneburg. He was exiled, moreover, and was not to return to Germany for at least three years, and then only with the emperor's consent. He and his supporters took refuge in Normandy at the court of his father-in-law Henry II. His dominating figure disappeared entirely from the scene for a time, and his powerful influence was gone for ever, to the great loss of the lands beyond the Elbe. For although branches of the Ascanian house now controlled the duchy, the Mark of Brandenburg and the archbishopric of Bremen and thus held a preponderant position in Saxony, the fragmented authority of rival princes could not take the place of the concentrated power of a single ruler. Lübeck, for instance, enjoying the freedom which it claimed and won from

Barbarossa as a vacant imperial fief, undoubtedly made great strides as a market and embarkation port for emigrants, and the waves of German colonists had not yet died down; but German political influence over the Slav lands along the Baltic soon declined, and Denmark proclaimed her independence of the Empire and inherited Henry's position of leadership. Frederick was by no means indifferent to these developments; he sought— though in the end vainly—to make Pomerania a fief of the Empire and gave privileges to Lübeck, but his other commitments were so wide that he could not spare enough regular attention to a frontier province in the far north-east.

For Frederick himself, however, the sudden and total defeat of a widely-feared adversary was an important success, even if he shared his victory with the princes; his prestige grew fast both inside and outside the Empire. The brilliant courts of the next few years radiate an air of secure peace and confident power, particularly the Whitsuntide feast of 1184 at Mainz, renowned of the poets. A domestic festivity of the ruling house—the knighting of Barbarossa's two eldest sons and the ceremonial coronation of the emperor, the empress and the young king Henry (who henceforth appears as co-regent with his father in Germany)—was turned into a national celebration. Tens of thousands of guests were housed and fed—an astonishing feat of organisation—and the parade of the German knights was a menacing demonstration of military power. Over and above this, however, the Whitsun feast at Mainz marked the beginning of a great new cultural epoch. The handshake which the troubadour Guyot de Provins and the German poet Heinrich von Veldeke exchanged was a symbol of the penetration of Germany by French knightly culture. That culture signified the revival, for the first time since the ancient world, of an ideal of beauty and of an appreciation of the sensual and material world alongside the stern demands of Christian morality: in short, the first lay culture. It combined the wealth of the Islamic intellectual heritage and the revived memories of antiquity with the peculiar characteristics of the Celtic and Germanic peoples. It brought with it a refinement of perception and of form in life and art and an enrichment of the imagination. Knightly virtue and heroic verse, love-lyrics and a new-found respect for women, were its chief glories. As they flowed into Germany, these influences Gallicised the ruling classes as at no other time except the eighteenth century, but with the great difference that now a strong nation, far too self-assured to become submerged by the foreign elements, grafted the novelties on to the sturdy stock of its own character and bore fruit which was often sweeter than anything in the harvest of its French masters. In the period shortly after the festival at Mainz Walther von der Vogelweide began his poetical career, the Nibelungenlied assumed its present form, and Wolfram von Eschenbach matured into a thinker and poet. It was only when Germany's political predominance gradually disappeared under Frederick II that German knighthood fell back into a state of cultural torpor, that sentimentality, formalism and frivolity appeared and that a slavish imitation of foreign models became the rule. But for the present, the cultural revival played no small part in the glory of Barbarossa's last years. The early Minnesang crowns the greying head of the Emperor with a halo of romance as he leaps down, still a vigorous sixty-year-old, into the tumult of the lists at the 'incomparable feast' and is likened by the poets to Alexander, Caesar and King Arthur.

By this time the increased standing in Germany which Henry the Lion's fall gave him had already brought further Italian success in its train. As the six-year truce drew to an end, the Lombards did not dare risk a new conflict. Negotiations were opened, and led to the conclusion of the peace of Constance in June 1183.[1] An understanding was made much easier through the removal of one particularly disputed point by a special agreement beforehand. Alessandria felt it advisable to ensure her continued existence as a city by throwing herself upon the emperor's mercy. She was formally refounded and rechristened Caesarea, and served in future as an imperial stronghold for the protection of western Lombardy—both a moral and a material victory for Frederick, and also a sign of his strength. The peace of Constance itself sought to link the recognition of the Lombard League and of its members' territorial status with imperial sovereignty and with the utilisation of the League's forces to strengthen imperial authority in other parts of Italy.

Within the city walls, Frederick handed over the *regalia* in their entirety, but outside the walls only if they were proved by the courts not to be imperial rights or if instead the communes

[1] Pullan 185–190.

P

redeemed them by paying an annual tribute. Moreover, the single lump-sum payment which the cities made as the price of peace was of considerable benefit to the imperial treasury. But imperial sovereign rights were interpreted far more widely than the Lombards wished: it is true that, instead of being installed as the emperor's officials, the consuls were to be the freely-elected representatives of the cities, but they were bound to obtain investiture from the Emperor within a given time and to do homage to him, and all citizens had to swear the oath of fealty. The right of appeal to the Emperor in important cases was retained (it was facilitated by the appointment of imperial representatives in the cities) and the traditional supplies for the army were still to be rendered—not only when the Emperor went to Rome to be crowned, it seems, but every time he passed through Lombardy.

The treaty of Constance, which brought the protracted battle for Lombardy to an end for the moment, must be judged in much the same way as the peace of Venice. Just as on that occasion the papacy had managed to secure its independence and so to keep the upper hand on the main point of principle, so now the Lombards could boast that they had asserted their right to self-government against the Emperor's officials and that they had thereby promoted the free development of their cities' economy. But the impossibility of enforcing the Roncaglia decrees had already been apparent before Frederick's defeat at Legnano. Compared with the proposals which he had been willing to accept then, however, the provisions of the treaty of Constance marked a new increase in imperial rights which corresponded to the growth of his power, although now—as at Venice—the Emperor's continuing diplomatic skill provides part of the explanation. So far as control over Italy was concerned, the concessions made at Constance were in no way decisive. A private league within the state was of course still bound to be a matter of concern, and the independence of the Italian cities was comparable to the independence of the German princes. But here, just as in Germany, Frederick's skilful policy gave him foothold enough to make his will prevail; the peace of Constance not only secured a rich source of income to the Empire in the shape of the Italian cities, but also ensured it the necessary minimum of sovereign rights, even if in practice there was to be little question of the consuls actually being invested. The fierce rivalries within the League, moreover, left plenty of opportunity for adroit diplomacy to bring the emperor's weight to bear. Finally, in between the cities there still remained everywhere small secular and ecclesiastical territories and scraps of imperial property which were bound, because of the rise of the cities, to lean more heavily on the imperial authority, and it was one of the more remarkable successes of Frederick's policy that he compelled the Lombards to accept the obligation of defending the scattered imperial possessions. In addition, Piedmont and the Romagna— one to the west and the other to the east of the Lombard plain— were now far more under his control than they had been at the beginning of his reign, and his wider plan to extend in another form to the central Italian countryside the imperial bureaucracy which he had been forced to withdraw from the League's territories had already begun to take shape. Thus although it represented the abandonment of exaggerated hopes, Frederick could regard the treaty of Constance as a basis for further advance.

The chief question for the immediate future was whether it would be possible to carry the new Italian policy through without a second breach with the curia. Since Lucius III (1181–85), a friend of the Cistercians, showed goodwill towards Frederick and needed peace, the outlook was not unpromising. If no agreement was reached, the explanation lay in the Emperor's unshakeable determination to keep firm hold of the Matildine lands, the chief basis of his power, and never to surrender at any rate the strategic-ally and economically most important areas, while on the other hand the aged pope (who had once been chosen by the Emperor to arbitrate in this dispute) was hindered by a strong opposition party among the cardinals. Hence Frederick's repeated offer to give firm guarantees for the payment of a tenth of the whole imperial income in Italy to both pope and cardinals in exchange for the lands the curia claimed met with no response, because it would have turned the curia into a pensioner of the Empire. The proposal to determine the rights of both sides and then to provide the Church with some other substitute for the strongholds which the Empire could not surrender was equally unsuccessful. The legal position was in fact very far from clear and the evidence of charters was contradictory; but the Emperor, as the sitting tenant drawing the income, was in the stronger position and could better afford to await the outcome of events.

New grounds for conflict also appeared. Should the papacy,

which at the Lateran Council of 1179 had already tried to strengthen its influence over episcopal elections, let Frederick's control over the German Church go unchallenged? There had been a double election in the archdiocese of Trier in 1183. In accordance with current practice, the Emperor had recently invested the majority's candidate, but his defeated rival had appealed to the curia. On the other hand, like Charlemagne and Otto the Great, Frederick wanted to see his son Henry crowned in his own life-time in order to prevent any interruption of government if he should die, and sought the pope's agreement. Yet this seemed almost to imply the heritability of the Empire and to threaten the curia with a further increase in the imperial pressure which it was already finding so burdensome.

The two heads of Christendom hoped to settle these and other points of difference most effectively by a personal interview, which took place at Verona in the autumn of 1184. Left to themselves, Emperor and pope would perhaps have found a solution, since their personal relations were still as friendly as ever. Frederick met Lucius III (who was completely dependent upon imperial help for the restoration of order in Rome) several times, declared himself willing to add secular outlawry to clerical excommunication as a means of combatting heresy, discussed with the pope a new plan for a crusade and at the pope's intercession (which itself rested on English initiative) even allowed Henry the Lion to return to Germany. No solution was found to the real issues in dispute, however—the Trier election and the Matildine lands— perhaps because of deliberate delaying tactics by the curia, and although it seems that Lucius himself was prepared to crown Henry VI the project foundered on the opposition of the cardinals.

The curia's opposition to the pope's accommodating attitude was perhaps determined by the changes which were already coming over Italian politics and which reached their climax in the betrothal of Frederick's heir to the Sicilian princess Constance at Augsburg on 29 October. It was an event of fundamental importance for the history of Europe, but its origins are almost completely obscured by the scantiness of the sources. Frederick had already contemplated a treaty and a marriage alliance with Sicily in 1173, but could not secure his end while conflict with the papacy lasted. Friendlier relations had begun with the cessation of hostilities after the peace of Venice. Sicilian policy, which was now no longer focussed on Italy, had rapidly changed its direction back to the ancient overseas objectives of Robert Guiscard and Roger II. The main purpose of King William II (1166–1189) was an expedition of conquest against the Byzantine empire, which had fallen into decay after the death of the Emperor Manuel in 1180, and closer relations with the western Empire would protect his rear. If, according to the custom of the time, an alliance between the two states was to be given visible expression by a marriage relationship between the two courts, the Norman royal family was so small that only Constance, the posthumous daughter of Roger II, could make a suitable bride for the barely eighteen-year-old heir to the German throne. At nearly thirty, she was considerably older than her future husband, but as the closest relative of a king who was still childless (although he had been several times married) she had a recognised claim to succeed to the kingdom of Sicily on his death. Her nephew William II, who was the same age as herself, could of course hope to have children, and for the same reason the pope did not attach too much importance to Constance's expectations of succeeding. For Lucius did not oppose the marriage, although he must have known about the negotiations which prepared the way for it; but it is difficult to believe that he proposed and negotiated both treaty and marriage, as one of the chronicles asserts. Clearly, the pope expected that the establishment of a lasting peace between the Empire and the Norman kingdom would promote the crusade which he had so much at heart, and he evidently accepted what he presumably regarded as the not yet very serious risk that the papal state would be encircled through the union of Empire and kingdom. It can hardly be doubted, on the other hand, that Frederick Barbarossa took this possibility very much into his calculations. It was quite in conformity with his recent policy that he should seek to unite Sicily with imperial Italy by peaceful means, if fortune should favour his dynasty, now that it seemed impossible to achieve the same end by force. A close connexion with the best-organised state of Europe, one which had ample financial resources and a powerful fleet at its disposal, could compensate for the most obvious deficiencies of the imperial government; only such a connexion could make really secure the control of Italy at which Frederick was aiming, and even in the looser form of a political alliance it was bound to promote this. These were advantages

which no statesman could afford to overlook—least of all Barbarossa, who always understood how to unite a prudent and careful
domestic territorial policy with far-reaching universal aims. Even
though its prospects had to depend upon the accidents of birth
and death, this marriage was therefore one of his greatest political
triumphs, and was judged to be so by contemporaries.

Hindsight cannot of course avoid dwelling upon the fateful
consequences which this new plan was to have for the history of
Germany. The attempt to hold together permanently two such
very different lands as north Germany and Sicily was bound
sooner or later to show itself to be unnatural and incapable of
realisation. The heavy weight which was now put on the southern
arm of the imperial scales was bound to tip the balance against
Germany, especially at a time when an energetic and methodical
expansion of German royal power was necessary and still possible.
Finally, the papacy, deprived of its support in the south and with
its feudal overlordship there threatened for the future, hemmed in
by the Empire and restricted in its freedom, would be compelled
to fight to the death. If Lucius III really underestimated the
danger, it seems to have been fully realised in the college of
cardinals: it was in protest against his naïve peace-policy that on
his death the majority of the electors chose a determined representative of the hierarchical point of view as his successor. Urban
III (1185–7)—a member of a Milanese family which had suffered
severe loss through Frederick's earlier actions and who had
himself been archbishop of Milan until his election as pope, a
man of great gifts, eloquent and trained in the law yet of a passionate temper—must have been known by the cardinals as a bitter
enemy of the imperial policy and of everything German. He had
the courage to withstand the Emperor, but soon learned that the
curia was no longer a match for Frederick's growing might.

The last phase of Frederick's Italian policy had meanwhile
begun with renewed operations over the Alps in 1184. In
Lombardy, the peace of Constance led to a complete reversal of
party alliances. Cremona, which had grown too powerful, fell
under the ban of the Empire, and Frederick made a firm alliance
with Milan. Won over by far-reaching concessions, Frederick's
ancient enemy counted it an honour that the wedding of the heir to
the German throne with the heiress of Sicily was celebrated within
her walls and that Henry was crowned king of Italy by the

Patriarch of Aquileia soon afterwards, in January 1186: more than a mere ceremonial coronation, the act was intended to symbolise the actual taking over of the government of Italy by the young king. The claim of the archbishop of Milan to crown the king was passed over, and the chroniclers of the time record that Henry was addressed as Caesar in the Roman and Byzantine fashion. This seems to show that Henry was to rank immediately as co-regent and representative of his father, without reference to the imperial coronation by the pope, although this was already under consideration: pope and archbishop were at that moment one and the same person.

The agreement with Milan, which had the support of the bulk of the Lombard League, meant a further strengthening of the imperial supremacy in northern Italy and had repercussions in the middle of the peninsula as well. At Constance, the cities of the League had already taken an oath to protect imperial rights and property in Lombardy; in the Milanese treaty this was extended to the March of Treviso and the Romagna, and special emphasis was laid on the fact that it also covered the Matildine estates. It is clear that the Emperor set great store by the new territorial policy as well as on securing his sovereign rights. The central Italian lands now gained a special importance which they had not had hitherto; since the death of Christian of Mainz in 1183 imperial rule had become enfeebled in this area, and one of the most important tasks of the Emperor and his son in these years was to re-establish it more securely. Tuscany, Romagna and Matilda's lands were now grouped into unified administrative districts under the control of German nobles or *ministeriales*, just as had been done in Spoleto and the March of Ancona after 1177. The communes, whose struggle for autonomy had begun to be evident, particularly in Tuscany, were forced to accept far-reaching restrictions on their self-government, and the feudal and episcopal authorities enjoyed royal favour instead; the whole area was secured by castles and garrisons and brought under a planned system of control. The boundaries between the papal territories and some of these newly-secured imperial districts, now the centre of gravity of German power, were by no means undisputed.

Nevertheless, it is not necessary to attribute the early collapse of the negotiations which Urban III at once opened entirely to the pope's hatred and anger; there were plenty of grounds for the curia's apprehensions. But the precipitate way in which Urban threw himself into the conflict betrayed a certain lack of foresight. He gave the signal by recognising the minority candidate for Trier and by consecrating him archbishop although he had not been invested with the *regalia*: this may have been in conformity with the direction which the recent Lateran Council had given to the law, but it also showed an open contempt for German custom and for his own previous undertakings. War being thus declared, Frederick abandoned all restraint and ordered King Henry to march through Tuscany into the papal state, most of which he conquered and occupied after first pillaging it. The inhabitants had to take the same oath of submission as those living on imperial territory, and imperial authority over Rome was again restored. Deprived of his last reliable ally by the speedy subjection of Cremona (which Frederick compelled to sue humbly for peace in June 1186), almost shut up in Verona by the imperial troops and with his influence in Italy paralysed, Urban rested his hopes on Germany. If the links between Frederick and the German Church could be broken, the foundations of the imperial power would be shaken. The claims the pope now made were soundly based on canon law, but the fact that he made them at this moment reveals their hostile purpose with great clarity. He demanded the abolition of the royal rights of *regalia* and *spolia*, Frederick's severe enforcement of which the German bishops had found burdensome and unreasonably oppressive although they had never declared them unlawful. Further, he wanted to ensure the better protection of Church property against the frequent complaints of the lay power's interference by forbidding the latter to receive Church advocacies or clerical tithes, since each had often led to illegal alienation. These claims, which spread the conflict into other fields and sought to create an opposition party among the German bishops, were perhaps not entirely without effect.

Real danger began with the defection of the most powerful of the ecclesiastical princes, archbishop Philip of Cologne, although the Church-state conflict only served him as a pretext. Since the time when his authority had been greatly extended by the acquisition of the duchy of Westphalia, this formerly devoted and influential supporter and adviser of the Emperor had become more and more concerned with the particular interests of his own see: the rounding off of its territory, an increase in the number of its feudal dependents and the promotion of the city's growing trade. His efforts conflicted with similar Hohenstaufen plans to extend and strengthen the imperial estates along the lower Rhine, met everywhere with competition from the royal towns and customs-posts, and led to personal friction with King Henry. The arch-bishop sought and found allies, notably Henry the Lion, but the threads of his diplomacy led to France and England, and the Empire suffered particularly damaging loss from the attitude of the young Danish king, who refused feudal homage and soon claimed the whole coastal strip between Ditmarschen and Pomerania for himself.

These dangers recalled Frederick to Germany; but if he harboured fears about the German Church the Reichstag of Gelnhausen in 1186 banished them. The overwhelming majority of the German bishops, including the most ardent of Alexander's former supporters, joined the secular princes in rallying round the ageing Emperor, confirmed his proclamations and the conviction of the justice of his cause with which they were filled, and despatched a letter to the pope bidding him retract and make peace. The correctness of the assembly's ecclesiastical tone, and the moderation of its language, are a measure of the moral defeat administered to the curia. Urban III did not long survive it. Forced to yield by his own powerlessness and the pressure of the cardinals (a majority of whom had completely reversed their attitude), but torn by conflicting emotions and apparently himself inclined to the extreme step of excommunicating Frederick, he died in 1187 at Ferrara on the way to safety in Venice, scarcely a year after the Reichstag of Gelnhausen.

Affairs in the east, where the fall of Jerusalem seemed imminent, now added to the feeling that a compromise with the imperial court was necessary and made it urgent that the leaders of Christendom should come to an understanding. Under this pressure, two men—both friendly towards the Emperor—were elected pope in quick successsion; Gregory VIII (1187) continued the work of peace-making which Urban had begun, Clement II (1187–91) brought it to a conclusion. The victory was Frederick's all along the line. The order for a completely new election in Trier corresponded with one of his own suggestions; Henry was promised imperial coronation, and in return Frederick enabled the pope to return to Rome and agreed to evacuate the papal state, although he reserved all the Empire's rights and thereby left open the possibility of re-occupying it at any time. We hear nothing of a settlement of the disputes about any of the other territories. The legal position can hardly have been resolved, and this meant that the Emperor continued to occupy them. He had at last gained the prize which he had been pursuing for so many years. The concessions he had made at Constance had not prevented the whole of imperial Italy from coming under his sway—on the contrary, the power of the Lombard League had lent him valuable assistance —and the papacy too had been forced, willy-nilly, to accept the situation.

Because these developments had been clearly discernible since the end of 1187, the archbishop of Cologne had no reason to continue his opposition. His rear exposed by Frederick's alliance with Philip Augustus in May 1187, without other foreign support, and isolated in Germany by the Emperor's counter-moves, he was too calculating a politician to follow the example of Henry the Lion's furious resistance and wholly disregard the legal proceedings which had been opened against him. At the last moment, he secured his position by throwing himself on the Emperor's mercy, purging himself by oath and paying a fine; the unresolved conflict of real interests was disguised under the appearance of friendship. The archbishop's humiliation and Frederick's pardon were alike made easier by enthusiasm for the crusade, for the settlement was reached at the 'Court of Christ' at Mainz in the spring of 1188, at which Barbarossa and his eldest son both took the cross and spurred on many of the nobles and other magnates to emulate them.

The decision to lead the great expedition himself, while France and England were held in check by their quarrel with each other and the papacy stood impotently aside, sprang equally from Frederick's religious feelings and from his awareness of the obligations of his universal position. In the conviction that after outlawing Henry the Lion once more he could safely leave the Empire to be guarded by the energetic hands of his son and co-regent (soon also to be crowned Emperor), believing too that the sacred undertaking itself provided a further guarantee of peace, he reached out towards greater goals for the Empire and raised it once more to the position from which it had been driven since the days of Urban II—the leadership of European affairs.

If he were to succeed in fulfilling the longings of Christendom by wresting the Holy Places from the infidel once more, the prestige of the Empire would be immeasurably enhanced. It was the last triumph of the heroic Emperor that, unbowed by the weight of years, he shouldered this gigantic task and bore it triumphantly on until the very moment of his death.

Just as, a century earlier, the divisions of the east had simplified the crusaders' task and ensured the stability of the states they founded, so now the union of Egypt and Syria under sultan Saladin threatened them with extinction because he was so vastly their rulers' superior in force, drive and moral energy. Light-heartedly challenged by them, Saladin had defeated the army of the Latin states at Hattin in 1187 and had recaptured one after another of their strongholds, Jerusalem included. Fears that even the last coastal cities like Tyre would fall before the crusaders arrived, together with the imperialists' slender acquaintance with the sea, persuaded Frederick to choose the land route. It was a serious mistake. In spite of the experience of the second crusade, the difficulties of the march were grossly underestimated; better preparations, it was hoped, would easily overcome them. Organisation was in fact incomparably more far-sighted and energetic than it had been in the days of Conrad II: an excited and disorderly mob was replaced by a well-trained body of knights whose numbers were deliberately restricted because of the difficulty of provisioning them, but which was therefore easier to feed and command, high in morale and kept under iron discipline; transit and supply were apparently guaranteed by agreements with the king of Hungary, the Great Zupan of Serbia, the Byzantine emperor and the sultan of Iconium; and at the head stood a man well-tried both as general and as diplomat, a ruler universally respected, whose unfailing activity and unshakeable confidence enabled him to overcome the obstacles which the faithlessness of foreign princes created for him and his followers.

Difficulties began as soon as the Greek frontier was reached, after the passage through Hungary and Serbia: at first only shortage of supplies, robbery, the intrigues of officials and friction with the local populations, but after a painful crossing of the Balkans there was open hostility on the fertile plain of Philippopolis, Frederick's envoys were thrown into prison and the Greek emperor even allied with Saladin. Isaac Angelus' policy was a mixture of stupidity and mistrust. Suppose that in spite of the guarantees they had given each other Frederick were to reveal himself as heir to the Norman lust for conquest and to harbour the old plan of giving the crusade a firmer foundation by capturing Constantinople? Ideas which later occurred so easily to the western barons during the fourth crusade might not be far from Frederick's mind. Had Isaac Angelus been able to look into Frederick's heart, he would of course have seen there only the mark of the crusading cross. Nothing but the hostility of the Greek emperor made him consider the capture of Constantinople for a moment, only to reject the idea at once when Isaac Angelus at last accepted, in the treaty of Adrianople (February 1190), the minimum demands on which Frederick had insisted with moderation but also with dignity and firmness. Was this not to miss a great opportunity? Did not the situation invite the establishment of German rule or a German dependency on the ruins of the decaying Greek empire in order to restore the divided unity of Rome and to serve in future as a bulwark for Europe against the pressure of the east? Whether the administrative resources of contemporary Germany were anything like enough for a task of such gigantic dimensions, and whether the Germans could have created a stronger and more lasting structure than the French managed to erect in the Latin kingdom, must remain more than doubtful. As always, here too Frederick showed his renowned moderation and moral strength: he remained true to himself and to the crusading ideal.

The passage of the Hellespont was made without further incident, but on the march through the barren interior of Asia Minor the crusaders suffered far greater privations and losses from the attacks of masterless Turks and through the sultan of Iconium's failure to keep his word. In spite of this, the weakened and exhausted army was still vigorous enough to put the sultan's troops to flight, to take Iconium and to dictate peace. The Cilician mountains had been traversed with difficulty, Christian Armenia was spreading before the longing eyes of the crusaders and offering to supply their every want, while its prince, Leo II, was asking a royal crown of Frederick, when the worst blow of all fell: the Emperor was drowned while bathing in the chilly waters of the river Saleph on 10 June 1190. 'At this point, and with this sorrowful report,' says the royal chronicle of Cologne, 'our pen fails us and we fall silent'.

Frederick's death sealed the fate of the German crusade. The brave duke of Swabia, Frederick, proved himself a capable leader when the army marched on, but confidence in victory was gone and he too soon died. Beside the fresh armies of England and France, which now arrived by sea, the Germans fell into the background, and for this reason the events of the crusade need concern us no further. Its results were feeble indeed in contrast with the effort expended: only a narrow coastal strip saved for three years, and the main objective—the recovery of the Holy Places—unattained. No great reversal of popular feeling followed, however, as in the case of the second crusade. In particular, the prestige of the Empire remained undimmed, for only an untimely death had removed the heroic Emperor like a second Moses from the scene of his triumphs, and the fact that he had died in the mysterious lands of the distant east was itself enough to surround him with the romantic lustre of devotion to a great ideal.

His memory was never extinguished among the German people, but the national feelings which are aroused today by his name are due only to the later link between him and the legend of the hidden German Emperor who shall one day come again. Rückert's poem of 1813[1] eventually gave him the place in folk-lore which belonged to his grandson Frederick II, and half a century of longing for a new unified German Empire linked his name inseparably with imperial tradition. After the glory of the old Empire had been revived in a new form, a search was made for his bones in Syria, in the hope that they might be brought back to Germany as a sacred national relic, but in vain. Meanwhile learned investigation had distinguished the original form of the old legend from its modern poetic elaborations. The acceptance of its conclusions by a limited circle of scholars will, however, scarcely prevent the further growth of legend in the popular imagination. Yet this does not matter, for imagination properly takes precedence over reason in this case: it has rightly linked national aspirations not with the person of his half-Sicilian grandson but with the heroic figure of the wholly German Barbarossa.

[1] Friedrich Rückert (1788–1866), Orientalist and Romantic poet. His vast output of mainly mediocre verse includes poems famous in their settings by Schubert, Brahms and Mahler. His poem 'Der alte Barbarossa . . .', sung to a tune by J. Gersbach (1787–1830), has become a German folk-song.

14

HENRY VI (1190–1197)

Henry VI's personality presents a strange contrast to his father's: a precociously mature youth succeeded a king who never grew old. Frederick had introduced his son to politics at an early age and given him great responsibilities, had made him co-regent and had left him behind as his deputy when he set out for the east; at twenty-four Henry was already ripe with experience. His thin and weakly build and his pale, serious and almost beardless face, dominated by an imposing forehead, betrayed the statesman's care but did not proclaim the warrior's might. One side of his father's richer and more harmonious nature—a feeling for power and a gift for decisive action—was developed to an extreme in him at the expense of every other characteristic. If a conclusion may fairly be drawn from so short a reign, then Henry VI possessed to a greater degree than any other medieval German ruler the ability to seize his opportunities, to calculate his actions to a nicety and to attain the greatest results with the least expenditure of effort; in these respects he somewhat resembled Henry V, although he far outstripped him in grandeur and refinement of character. A burning ambition 'to make the Empire greater and more powerful than under his predecessors' drove him on, denied him rest and enjoyment and made him unlikeable, severe and (when it was to his advantage) ruthless, cruel and insensitive. He lacked the knightly feelings, the just moderation and the moral greatness of his father; there was no one of equal authority to restrain him, and his love of power was felt in ever-widening circles of European politics until death removed him at the high-tide of success.

What the treasure of the Nibelungs was to the heroes of legend, the wealth of Sicily was to the Hohenstaufen: it cast its spell over their imaginations, until in the end it lured them to destruction, and Germany with them. The policy of Henry VI himself was governed by the purpose of winning and holding Sicily to a far greater extent than was once realised, and even the imperialistic designs of his last years showed strong Norman and Sicilian influence.

On the death of William II at the end of 1189, Henry had to make good his claim to the Sicilian inheritance. He had just taken the field against Henry the Lion, who had broken his oath and returned to Germany. Instead of crushing Henry in July 1190 he quickly made peace with him, so as to leave his hands free to invade Sicily and to compel the pope to fulfil his promise to crown him Emperor—imperial coronation having become much more urgent on the news of his father's death in the east. Towering obstacles beset his way towards both objectives. Determined to reject German rule, a nationalist party in Sicily had placed a bastard member of the Norman royal house on the throne in January 1190. Tancred, a physical weakling of no particular significance although he was brave and energetic, was certain in advance of support from the pope, who was bound to grasp at any means of saving himself from encirclement by Hohenstaufen power and claimed that as feudal overlord he had the right to a share in deciding the royal succession. Further support for Tancred came from an alliance with his relative Richard I of England concluded (after some friction and hostility) in 1190 or 1191 while the crusaders were wintering in Messina; this alliance was directed against Henry. Emboldened by this backing on his southern frontier, the newly-elected Celestine III (1191–8) refused to fulfil his predecessor's promise of coronation. Celestine was an old man of eighty-five who had been a cardinal for fifty years, a peace-lover and of great integrity, but a man whose actions were determined by the fluctuations of circumstance. His nature made it in any case unlikely that he would take heroic decisions to safeguard ecclesiastical freedom, and the Emperor's preponderance of power ensured that he continued to limit himself to passive resistance, delaying tactics and secret intrigues.

Long delay and a temporary surrender of his demand would have been equally hazardous to Henry because of the opposition of Sicilians and Germans. In any case, he was not the man to let the main issue be obscured. He reached his goal not, like Henry V earlier, by brutally taking the pope prisoner—that would only have created opposition—but by a shrewd use of his adversary's weak points. He exploited Celestine's Roman origins and sympathies by evacuating the protective imperial garrison from

Tusculum, which the pope then immediately handed over to his Roman compatriots, who regarded the town as a dangerous rival and destroyed it utterly; and by attaining his object—imperial coronation—in this fashion he revealed for the first time the cold political calculation which is so typical of him.

Misfortunes followed one upon another as soon as he advanced to the conquest of Sicily in the spring of 1191, and they seriously endangered his authority. The city walls broke his attack on Naples because Pisa sent too little naval support; a terrible sickness in the army gave a last-minute warning that the union of the two countries was unnatural, and when it attacked the Emperor himself Henry was forced to raise the siege. False news of his death caused his wife to fall into the enemy's hands at Salerno. Even before this, Henry the Lion's eldest son, who had been brought along as a hostage, escaped from the camp, made contact with Tancred (who was now given formal recognition by the pope, as feudal overlord of Sicily, in return for the almost complete surrender of the Norman kings' special relationship with the Church) and began trying to stir up revolt in Germany. In spite of this the Emperor, hastening back to Germany and still prepared for wide concessions where Sicily was concerned, might have managed to restore peace if an outrage had not fanned the sparks of dissension into fire.

Henry followed the same course in the ecclesiastical politics of Germany as his father, but in accordance with his nature he did so in a rougher and more ruthless way. Thus when there was a double election at Liège he enforced the right of free imperial decision (which Barbarossa had already claimed) very sharply. At the end of 1192, during the resultant confusion, the papal candidate Albert, a brother of the duke of Brabant, whom Henry had outlawed, was murdered by German knights. The memory of the fate of Becket was still fresh, and was perhaps not the least of the reasons for immediate—though unjustified—suspicions that the Emperor was an accessory to the crime, particularly since he rightly did not punish the murderers, as they were simply executing an imperial ban. Revolt began among the dead man's many relations but soon involved the whole area of the lower Rhineland and made contact with the Saxon and Welf opposition. Behind both stood England, bound to Cologne by trade and to the Welfs by the tie of blood. If we remember that the English king was in alliance with the Sicilian usurper and that in the background stood the pope, more or less openly supporting any enemy of the emperor, it becomes clear that Henry found himself faced with an extensive and powerful international coalition.

Good fortune and his own mastery of diplomacy enabled him to break the noose before it was drawn tight. He had long had an understanding with Philip Augustus of France to look out for their common enemy Richard I on his way back from the east. Duke Leopold of Austria had the additional motive of revenge for a wrong done him in Palestine; he took Richard prisoner as he tried to pass unrecognised through the Empire in the guise of a pilgrim, and handed him over to the Emperor. The general outcry over the imprisonment of a returning crusader at first increased the number of Henry's enemies by adding the south Germans to them. Henry extracted the maximum advantage from possession of his valuable prize, however; he kept Richard well guarded at Trifels in the Palatinate, and used him as a means both of imposing peace in Germany and of preparing a new Sicilian expedition. The large ransom which Richard had to pay for his freedom provided ample resources for the campaign, while his influence over the Welfs and in the lower Rhineland stifled the German revolt. In addition, Richard had to abandon his ally Tancred, and to bind himself to provide troops for service against him by doing homage for England. When Richard emphatically rejected any such humiliation, a more acceptable plan to make him feudally dependent upon the Empire by giving him southern Burgundy as a fief was for a time considered. Richard's position became still more difficult when his brother John raised the standard of rebellion against him at home, allied with Philip Augustus, and in concert with Philip offered to pay the ransom to the Emperor if Henry would keep Richard in prison for another year or even hand him over to them. Henry thereupon returned to his earlier and more burdensome demand and in 1194 used it to extort an oath of homage for England from his prisoner and a promise to pay an annual tribute of five thousand pounds sterling. Richard was excused only from taking part in the campaign against Tancred in person.

By acting in a way which cannot be described as either knightly or honourable, Henry VI had given further proof that he allowed sentiment no influence if it conflicted with reason of state. Tremendous success was the result. The hostile alliance was destroyed

Q

and Germany pacified. A hasty love-match between the younger Welf, Henry, and a cousin of the Emperor, the only child of the count palatine Conrad, ran against the grain of high politics but also seemed likely to satisfy the Welfs by giving them the expectation of succeeding to the Palatinate; and in the following year (1195) the hostility of the implacable Henry the Lion was ended by his death. With the securing of feudal lordship over England a significant step had been taken, though one with a questionable future: and in addition to large sums of money an English fleet of fifty ships had been gained for the conquest of Sicily.

The Sicilian plan came increasingly to dominate Henry's policy from this time forward. With his rear far better protected, with the restoration of peace in Lombardy securing his communications from interruption, and with naval assistance ensured by agreements with Genoa and Pisa, Henry made elaborate preparations and was setting out in 1194 for his second campaign in his wife's realm when a notable change in the situation there made his task easier. Tancred, who had meanwhile made steady progress in the continuous fighting and had strengthened his position by an alliance with the Greek emperor, died suddenly at the beginning of the year, together with his eldest son. Against his second son, William III, who was still a minor, victory was certain from the start. After a short campaign marked by calculated moderation, Henry made a triumphal entry into Palermo before the end of 1194. The young king and his chief supporters were at first taken into his protection, but were banished to Germany soon after a conspiracy was discovered. Henry had reached the desired goal.

His conquest had now to be secured and united permanently with the Empire. It was therefore an event of the first importance when on 26 December 1194 his forty-four-year-old wife bore him their first and only son, who received the prestigious names of Frederick and Roger to signify the union in him, their cornerstone, of two dynasties and two traditions. So far as the future was concerned, however, there was the difficulty that in Germany the elective principle had consistently gained ground on the older blood-right, whereas hereditary succession was the rule in Sicily. A lasting union of the two realms was therefore certain only if dynastic succession were equally guaranteed in each. To begin with Henry believed that it would be enough if the union was ensured for another generation by the usual election of his young son as king. Although Adolf of Altena, the archbishop of Cologne, held back, the plan might well have succeeded, for his power was great enough to overawe the princes. After all, on several occasions —most notably when he even passed over a relation in the Mark of Meissen in 1195—he successfully broke the principle of *Leihezwang*, now established to the disadvantage of the central power, and thus increased crown property in the way the Capetians had begun to do in France. Feudal law could in fact be moulded by the pressure of power, and could have been reshaped again in the German monarchy's favour. Two valuable counterweights to the separatist spirit of the princes were at his disposal: the imperial *ministeriales*, who were just rising to the pinnacle of their importance and provided Henry with his two principal assistants, the *Reichsmarschall* Henry of Kalden (of the house of Pappenheim) and the seneschal Markward of Annweiler, who could turn his hand with equal skill to diplomacy or war; and the growing towns, which he sympathetically encouraged on the German crown lands, just as he managed to keep them on his side in Lombardy by judiciously continuing the policy of his father's last years. He therefore felt able, in the spring of 1196, to set on foot a far more ambitious plan for a German hereditary empire.

If the immediate origin of this plan was the difference between the rules of succession in Germany and Sicily which has already been mentioned, it must not be forgotten that more general considerations also suggested a change in the constitution of the Empire. Hereditary succession had already become widely accepted in the western European countries, France and England: in contrast, the electoral right of the princes in Germany seemed an anomaly. The intense self-assurance of a Henry VI was bound to regard the preponderant influence of the princes upon the succession as scarcely tolerable, and the idea of hereditary succession was a natural outgrowth of the heightened Hohenstaufen belief in the dignity and majesty of the ruler's person. If the great plan succeeded, so Henry calculated, the ground would once and for all be cut from under both the princes, with their selfish and separatist tendencies, and the popes, with their interference in the succession to the German throne. Had it been successful, it must however be added, it would at the same time finally have stamped the Empire as Roman and universal instead of mainly German, for by it the union of the Empire and Sicily would have been firmly and permanently established.

Soon after the capture of Palermo Henry had proclaimed his decision to lead a new crusade, and with his own fleet and fifteen hundred picked knights he renewed the struggle for the Holy Land as soon as the three-year truce with Saladin came to an end. The crusade was preached in Germany too. It is possible that at this moment (as perhaps earlier in the negotiations over the election of the young Frederick as king) the princes put into words their desire for legal recognition of feudal succession on a wide scale and its extension to include the female line, and that Henry skilfully turned this to account and in his turn demanded hereditary succession to the Empire as the price of his agreement. At the same time he tried to ensure the assent of the ecclesiastical princes by declaring that he was prepared to give up in exchange the burdensome right of *spolia* which the crown had exploited so fully. Although the Emperor's demand—which sought to do away with the princes' most valuable privilege, one by means of which they could strengthen their power—was felt to be unprecedented, a majority of the princes at the Reichstag in Würzburg was none the less prepared to accept it and to put their acceptance into writing. On the other hand the archbishop of Cologne—who had to fear a reduction in the value of his right to crown the king at Aachen as well as the loss of his right to play a part in electing him—soon lent his support to the resistance of a group of Saxon and Thuringian princes, with the consequence that the execution of the agreement could no longer be free of trouble.

In this situation Henry turned to Italy again. If he managed to get the pope (without whose co-operation success was unattainable, partly because of his feudal claims over Sicily and partly because of his undisputed right to crown the Emperor) to accept the plan and even to give his acceptance visible form by baptising the young heir to both realms and anointing him king, he would hold the trump card in Germany too. It was certainly asking a lot of the curia—acceptance of perpetual encirclement, surrender of the claim to overlordship in Sicily, and the blocking of all the channels through which the succession in Germany could be influenced. But it was necessary first of all to resume the relations which had been broken off since the pope had sided with Tancred. Here the planned crusade served its turn. In the interests of Christendom, Celestine could not refuse to begin negotiations again. Yet the unsolved territorial problems stood in the way of an understanding of any kind. Henry did not even contemplate any weakening of his territorial power in Italy, which the Sicilian connection made doubly important; on the contrary, imperial claims reached far beyond the frontiers of the papal state (which had never been completely evacuated) and did not even stop at the gates of Rome. On the other hand, the curia had begun to examine the ancient privileges, and had found documentary evidence entitling it to territory far beyond the confines of Matilda's lands and right into central Italy. There could not be any open opposition to the Emperor's pressure, but the passive resistance of the embattled curia could scarcely be overcome. Henry measured the value of the districts which the curia claimed largely by the income they provided, and proposed a financial settlement on even better terms than his father had suggested. A proposal for which the evidence is unreliable seems to belong in this context: according to it, the archiepiscopal and the richer episcopal cathedrals of the Empire should in future always hold their best canonries at the disposal of the pope, and the lesser sees should provide for the curial clergy in a similar way; an extension of this system to all the states of Catholic Christendom was envisaged. Since in fact the fiscal development of the Roman Church took this kind of course during the next hundred years, this proposal cannot be dismissed as simply Utopian. On the other hand, the curia never regarded the Matildine lands simply as a source of income, but prized them as a power-base too; thus its rejection of purely financial compensation is readily comprehensible. If, then, no understanding even over the territorial issue could ever be reached, how much less likely was it that the pope would fall in with the idea of a hereditary Empire? Even Henry's offer to take publicly the cross which he already wore in secret, and to go on crusade himself, could not shake the curia's stubborn resistance.

Henry therefore angrily broke off the negotiations; mounting German opposition, fostered by the curia, forced him to abandon his plan for the moment. By releasing from their promises the magnates who had given it their support, however, and by returning to customary procedures, he easily secured the election of his son as king at Christmas 1196, even the archbishop of Cologne assenting. He seemed thus to have ensured for at any rate another generation something he would have liked to settle for ever—the union of both kingdoms under the rule of the Hohenstaufen house. He may well have secretly harboured the intention of returning to the wider plan at a more suitable moment.

The union of the two kingdoms was also seriously threatened from the Sicilian side. There, Henry had gone some way towards satisfying the nationalist party by leaving the administration unchanged: but his rule still depended so much upon the German knights who had been given rich fiefs in Sicily that it was regarded by the Norman nobility of the island as alien domination. Further discontent was bred by a high tax-assessment and by Henry's attempt to subject all previous royal privileges to severe scrutiny. A conspiracy grew up; its object was nothing less than to murder the Emperor and every German in the land and to set a native king on the throne. Its threads are supposed to have led as far afield as Lombardy, and the pope seems to have been informed of it. The Empress herself, a proud woman of independent spirit and passionate temperament, seems to have stood close to the nationalist party, so foreshadowing her later attitude; how far she was privy to the conspirators' intentions cannot be established with confidence, in view of the uncertainty of the rumours which came to the chroniclers' ears. The Emperor managed nevertheless to take safe refuge in Messina and to crush the conspiracy in bloodthirsty fashion during May and June 1197. The cruelty of the punishments, which extended to the outlaws in Germany as well, has drawn severe criticism upon a man who had hitherto acted with moderation: but it was not out of keeping with its time and place and it matched the horrors which the conspirators themselves had planned. Inasmuch as the nationalist party was now powerless, however, the conspiracy had helped the Emperor to a further triumph and had strengthened the union of Sicily with the Empire.

The crusading host began to assemble on the Apulian and Sicilian coasts at about this time. The expedition was conceived on the grand scale and its outlook was universal, but only Germans undertook it: a core of imperial mercenaries was supported by numerous contingents led by nobles and princes from Germany. A leading part was also to be played by the German Order of the Hospital, which had been founded outside Acre in 1190 and possessed valuable lands and rights in Sicily; next year, at Henry's command, it became the Teutonic Order, after the model of the

Templars and Hospitallers, who were predominantly recruited in France and the other Romance countries. The Emperor, who could not be spared to leave home, had entrusted political leadership to his chancellor, Conrad of Querfurt, bishop of Hildesheim, and military authority to the *Reichsmarschall* Henry of Kalden, reserving the most important decisions to himself in Sicily.

The organisation, advance planning, and prospects of the crusade gave rise to higher hopes than any previous expedition. Since navigation was now fairly well understood, simply to use sea-transport offered enormous advantages over the hardships of a march through barren and hostile territory. For in particular, Henry's relations with Byzantium had not improved since his father's death. From his Norman ancestors he had inherited the extensive claims and the piratical designs upon the Greek empire which had never quite disappeared during the whole period between Robert Guiscard and William II and which as recently as 1185 had led to a large-scale invasion of the Balkans. Moreover, he had not forgotten the Greeks' alliance with Tancred, and he could add recent hereditary claims on the part of his own family. He had discovered the Byzantine princess Irene, the widow of Tancred's eldest son, in the palace at Palermo, and had married her to his brother Philip. Irene's father, the Greek emperor Isaac Angelus, had been violently deposed by his brother Alexius III in 1195. If Henry wished to intervene and to secure the throne for himself or his brother, who could prevent him? It is impossible to guess whether he harboured such plans for the future or whether the course of events would of itself have led him to such a conclusion. Meanwhile, in negotiations conducted with his customary skill, he contented himself with using his superiority to compel the usurper to pay a large annual tribute, and was thus able to conduct his eastern policy at the expense of the Greek emperor in the same way as he had conducted the Sicilian campaign at the expense of the king of England. The decaying Byzantine empire still stood, but its power and its prestige had vanished. Oriental princes were already looking towards the western Empire. Leo of Armenia asked Henry for a crown as his vassal, just as he had asked Barbarossa; Amaury of Lusignan, king of a Cyprus which Richard I had freed from Byzantium, offered homage, and since he shortly afterwards secured the crown of Jerusalem as well he would thus have brought the crusaders' chief objective into direct dependence upon the Emperor.

Everything seemed therefore to promise great success to the expedition, and at the same time events in the Mohammedan camp—the death of Saladin in 1193 and quarrels among his sons —also seemed favourable to it. But the imperial fleet had scarcely reached the Holy Land when Henry, whose most cherished hopes accompanied it and for whom the harvest of careful preparation seemed about to ripen, fell victim to the Sicilian summer at the age of thirty-two on 28 September 1197. His bones still rest in Palermo cathedral.

His early and unexpected death was the greatest of the catastrophes which overtook medieval Germany. The chance operation of blind natural forces played a decisive part here, as so often, in determining the course of history. But this was not all. It would be quite unjustified to credit Henry with a boundless urge to world-mastery and to speak of a flight of Icarus which was bound sooner or later to end in disaster. For if we take only the known facts into account, and not the intentions which it is so easy to ascribe to the young Emperor, we must conclude that he had not in any single respect aimed at more than the German dominance in central Europe which had been the objective of his Saxon and Salian predecessors and of his father as well, and that he gave no hint of setting about unlimited world conquest. The establishment of new tributaries and feudal suzerainties in east and west and the occupation of Sicily, long desired by his predecessors for the sake of the security of imperial Italy but only now attained—these had certainly accentuated the universalist traits in his rule, but they had not led to any extension of actual imperial control beyond central Europe. It is impossible to tell whether Henry, had he lived longer, would have been induced to widen the basis of his power significantly. In the same way, the shortness of his reign and the unusual degree to which he was favoured by fortune make it difficult to estimate his quality as a statesman: for we cannot know how he would have stood up to a protracted struggle with a foe of equal ability. Above all, however, the narrowness of the real foundations of his power must be emphasised. Only a section of the ecclesiastical and secular nobility of Germany were truly committed to supporting Henry, together with the solid ranks of the *ministeriales*. Elsewhere, serious tensions had to be overcome by pressure or craft, as they had been in Germany, Italy and the curia since before the time of Barbarossa; Henry had added the Sicilian national party, the western powers and Constantinople to the list of hostile interests. A system of government of this kind needed a genius at its head; its great weakness was that it could not survive under a minority, and the course of nature could bring this at any moment.

At hardly any other time—not even on the death of Henry III in a somewhat similar situation—did everything depend on the life of one man so completely. Even the contemporary German chroniclers showed the liveliest sense of irreparable loss and guessed at an impending upheaval. It was reported in Cologne that Theodoric the Ostrogoth had reappeared in Germany, his warrior's face lined with care; his giant figure, riding a coal-black horse, had been seen along the Moselle. It was a portent of miseries to come.

15

INNOCENT III AND THE GERMAN SUCCESSION (1198–1216)

The Empire was already moving towards dissension and civil war when, three months after the death of Henry VI, there succeeded to the papacy a man who was perhaps the most gifted of all the great political popes. It was this which ensured a complete reversal in the fortunes of the two institutions. The mere fact that the youngest of the cardinals, Lothar of Segni (a member of a comital family from the southern Campagna later known as the Conti) was elected shows how dominant a position he already held.

Innocent III was of slender build, and his delicate features reflected the acute intellect and pent-up energy within. He was a stranger to leisure and enjoyment. He immediately cut down the expenditure of the papal court, yet he never counted the cost when the prestige of the Church was at stake. His indifference to personal comfort did not leave those around him unscathed, and gave rise to some discontent. The exertions which he imposed upon his physique gradually undermined his health; as birds for flight, he was wont to say, so man was made for toil. This incessant but deliberate activity is as characteristic of him as is the passionate urgency of Gregory VII with its sudden fits and starts. His nature held no fathomless depths and hid no sudden and astounding lightning-strokes of genius, but perhaps for that reason was better able to preserve his life-work from destruction.

Innocent had assimilated to an uncommon degree the scholastic education provided by the universities of his time. Every one of his pronouncements shows the sharpness of dialectic. By modern standards he was neither a profound theologian nor a moving orator, but the rhetoric of the 'Abraham of the Faith' made a deep impression upon his contemporaries. As a lawyer he was unsurpassed. Since he spent a large part of his time hearing cases in person, the papal tribunal under him became in very truth the judgement-seat of all Europe, where the admired decisions of the 'second Solomon' were given on legal and moral problems of every kind.

To Innocent himself, such comparisons scarcely seemed too exalted. He was used to being credited with direct converse with the Almighty. Right from the day of his election, he was filled with the lofty conceptions which had been associated with his office since the time of Nicholas I and Gregory VII, and regarded himself as the embodiment of hierarchical ideas. He stood as mediator between Heaven and earth, 'less than God but more than man', the anointed of the Lord, in whom Christ had once more put on mortal flesh. The story that he once tried on the seamless robe of Christ which was preserved in the Lateran, in order to discover whether Jesus was smaller than he, is but a satirical version of his real claims. These were not merely confined to the position of mediator between this world and the next, but extended to dominion over this world too in the widest sense of the term. To the representative of Christ on earth, who like Melchizedek was king and priest at once, belonged in his view the right to intervene in earthly government; if he passed on to secular rulers one of the two swords which had been entrusted to him, he still retained the authority to take power into his own hand in special cases—particularly in matters of mortal sin, like breach of the peace, for example—and to make kings bow to his command. There was of course nothing in all this which had not already been at least foreshadowed by Gregory VII; but in the imposing phrases with which Innocent drove into the European mind the images and metaphors upon which papal supremacy was founded, traditional ideas were often given lasting form for the first time. Furthermore the force and logic with which he defended them gave them a new and increased weight.

When he solemnly set himself to translate these ideas into practice, Innocent was helped not only by the general situation (conflict in the Empire, the minority of the heir to Sicily, anti-German tendencies in Italy, the mutual hostility of France and England), but also by his outstanding gift for administration and finance, by a remarkably keen critical sense (it enabled him to lay down criteria for testing suspect papal bulls which are almost those of modern research, for example) and above all by his masterly diplomatic skill. Many quite unexpected pieces of good fortune made his path easier, but Innocent knew how to make the most of them as well as being flexible enough to adapt himself when things went badly: always keeping the final objective in view

though prepared to change the route towards it, sometimes ready
to be content with only a small gain or even to take one step back-
wards in order to take two forwards later on. Ruthless, therefore,
and untroubled by nice moral scruples, he always managed to
perceive where his advantage lay—the advantage of Church and
world, as he understood it—and like a true statesman he always
weighed and judged things in the light of his own immediate
intentions. No charge which can be brought against him from the
moral standpoint involves much outside the normal run of
politics—what attracts attention is simply that it concerns a pope.
But that the highest religious and moral authority on earth should
come down to the level of ordinary politics, welcoming today what
he had rejected yesterday, using ecclesiastical punishments for
purely secular ends and thereby depriving them of their force,
careless of the truth and applying to his own political activity the
proverb 'He who touches pitch is defiled'—all this meant a step in
the growing secularisation of the papacy which took it far beyond
Alexander III and set the standard for the following centuries.
In any case, how could world domination be achieved without
recourse to political means? Innocent III, the most skilful of all
the popes in using them, perhaps also came nearest of all to the
ultimate goal. For the unity of western history has never been so
manifestly embodied in one man as in this pope.

His first task was to free the Church from the stifling grip of an
Empire united with Sicily, and to rest its independence firmly on
foundations of its own. Even in its days of powerlessness under
Celestine III, a future recovery had been prepared inside the
curia through a collection of the papacy's economic and political
rights. From among the ancient privileges of the Emperors there
had been extracted the comprehensive Carolingian promises
which quite obviously contradicted the more limited charters
which had replaced them, and the widest conclusions for the
enlargement of the papal state had been drawn. When even so
moderate an official as the chamberlain Cencius remarked that
whole duchies and margraviates belonged to the Patrimony of St
Peter, a complete programme can already be seen growing out of
a renewal of the traditional claims of papal territorial policy since
Gregory VII. The boldest demands arose, as they had done in
the middle of the eighth century, from the severest oppression.
How far they had been revealed in the latest negotiations with the

all-powerful Emperor is unfortunately not clear, and in consequence there is nothing against which Henry's so-called Testament
can be measured with confidence. It is certain, however, that on
his death-bed Henry looked anxiously to the future and sought to
preserve a dominant position for his son by reducing existing
tensions. According to an unreliable source, he released Richard I
from vassalage and offered him compensation for the ransom he
had paid, and he seems also to have tried to link the interests of the
curia to the future of his dynasty by wide-ranging concessions. In
return for the recognition of Frederick II as Emperor and king of
Sicily—that is, for the maintenance of the union of the two realms
—the feudal dependence of Sicily upon the papacy was to be
modified greatly to the popes' advantage, and their territorial
wishes in Italy were to be met in large measure even though the
exact degree was dependent on the goodwill of the imperial
government. Scarcely any doubt is cast nowadays on the authen-
ticity of the fragments of this Testament which have come down
to us, but it had almost no practical effect; for by the time a
strange chance brought it to light events since Henry's death had
completely changed the situation.

Immediately upon his election Innocent secured his sovereignty over Rome against the claims of Emperor and Roman
people alike. Next he gained recognition for his rights over the
papal state in its narrower sense, as far as the disputed frontier
area of southern Tuscany, and by encouraging and making use of
the anti-German reaction against foreign oppression which had
broken out all over Italy on Henry's death he managed to replace
imperial by papal officials in the duchy of Spoleto and the March
of Ancona. By these conquests—which in reference to the
disputed and obscure Carolingian promises were deliberately
called 'recuperations'—the papal state was turned into a barrier
cutting Sicily off from the north altogether and extending across
central Italy from sea to sea. It was rather different in Romagna
and Tuscany, over which similar claims were made; the imperial
yoke was broken there too, but the cities did not want to
see the pope's lordship imposed on them instead, and the urban
usurper could not in most cases be evicted from the Matildine
lands between Mantua and Lake Garda. Similarly, while the
Lombard League took up an attitude hostile to the Empire
('Caesarea' became 'Alessandria' again at this time) it also asserted
its independence.

Meanwhile Innocent had won other victories in Sicily. On Henry's death the national party gained the upper hand, with the Empress at their head. The Norman kingdom was to arise again, German rule to seem but a passing phase. Constance cut the connection with the Empire, expelled the Germans from Sicily, renounced the Kingdom of the Romans in her son's name and had him crowned king of Sicily. A policy of separating the two realms in this fashion was a policy after Innocent's own heart. But only after first forcing the proud Norman princess to accept a concordat (which limited the Sicilian crown's ecclesiastical privileges even more than Tancred's concessions had done, and only left it vestiges of the royal right of consent to episcopal elections) did he re-establish the old feudal ties between Sicily and the papacy— just in time, as it proved: for on the Empress's unexpectedly early death in 1198 he was able, at her wish and as her overlord, to secure the guardianship of the young Frederick and by so doing to ensure himself the decisive voice in the fate of Sicily. The kingdom soon gave him trouble enough, for the German commanders did not evacuate the strong mainland castles and were in constant touch with the Hohenstaufen government through Markward of Annweiler, who had risen to freedom from the ranks of the imperial *ministeriales*, had been charged by the dying Emperor with the execution of his Testament (which had of course been overtaken by the rapid course of events) and now with some justice claimed the regency for himself. Frederick's kingdom seemed for a time lost amid these obscure struggles. In the short space of twelve months the political situation in Italy had been completely transformed; there remained only fragments of Henry's once supreme authority, and over the local anti-German factions there rose the papacy, free and dominating now although closely confined only a short time before. A change of such magnitude would have been impossible but for the dissensions in Germany.

The unhappy double election of 1198 was the most fatal event in the medieval history of Germany, the turning-point as much in the influence of the Empire abroad as in the internal conflict between crown and particularism. In the threatening situation of the moment it was at once clearly seen to be quite out of the question to save the throne for the young Frederick since, now they were free from the Emperor's pressure, many of the nobility did not feel themselves bound by their action in electing him. Only a grown man could hold the empire of Henry VI together. Out of genuine concern for imperial interests and not from personal ambition, Philip, a brother of the dead Emperor, let himself be persuaded to accept the crown and was elected 'to the imperial authority'[1] by a large number of princes—the influence of Roman Law concepts and the closer union of imperial territory under the Hohenstaufen had led to an assimilation of the terms 'kingdom' and 'empire'. The full imperial rights given by the princes' election lacked nothing but the title, and only papal coronation could provide this.

Common interests had been gradually drawing England, the lower Rhineland and the Welfs together since the fall of Henry the Lion, and they now allied to resist the seizure of the crown by the Hohenstaufen dynasty; they were joined by all the nobles who feared a hereditary Hohenstaufen Empire. Richard I saw the chance to take his revenge and to shake off the feudal yoke; at the same time he must have intended to make trouble on her eastern flank for France, the ancient enemy of his house. He therefore took the lead in promoting with money and influence the candidature of his favourite nephew Otto, the third son of Henry the Lion. Foremost among the German princes to take the same line was archbishop Adolf of Cologne, whose territorial interests linked him with both England and the Welfs; the absence in the Holy Land of the archbishop of Mainz and other loyalists increased his influence. More than any other, Adolf bears the heavy responsibility of having brought about the election of Otto. At a time when there was more need than ever for a concentration of effort against a strong pope and foreign threats on all sides, Germany's old wound opened again—the hostility of Welf and Hohenstaufen. The civil war which now began was the more exhausting, the more devastating and the more demoralising because it brought no quick decision on the battle-field. Germany's greatest political poet, Walther von der Vogelweide, who now threw all the force of his passionate conviction on to the Hohenstaufen side, thought he could detect in it the first signs that the Day of Judgement was at hand.

The two claimants to the throne, both young men of little more than twenty, were very different in character.

---

[1] 'in imperaturam Romani solii', which Pullan (193) translates 'to the Emperorship of the Roman dominion'.

As the youngest son of Barbarossa, Philip was originally destined for the Church and was educated with this end in view; but when death thinned the family ranks Henry VI withdrew him from it in 1193 and enfeoffed him first with Tuscany and the estates of the countess Matilda in 1195 and next year with the duchy of Swabia as well. Because he had trespassed on the papal sphere of interest in the course of conducting his affairs in central Italy, Philip fell under a general sentence of excommunication which Celestine III had pronounced against all who invaded papal territory. Although he agreed with the general lines of Henry VI's policy, he almost entirely lacked his brother's energy and states-manlike stature. The qualities which the father had combined in his single person seemed to have been separated and made more extreme when they were passed on to his two sons. Philip was a slender youth with curly blonde hair, refined alike in appearance, demeanour and education, the most attractive of the Hohenstaufen, gentle, cheerful and courteous, of blameless character, 'a sweet young lord', as Walther called him. Beside him stood his wife, the Byzantine princess Irene, the 'rose without a thorn, the dove without gall', and Germany could not have wished a nobler or a better royal couple to reign over an era of peace. But neither as statesman nor as soldier was Philip equal to the problems of these stormy times, at any rate to begin with: he became stronger and more mature through his bitter experiences during the next decade, and it was because of this that the future began to look brighter after all.

The opposite was the case with his rival. Otto had followed his father into exile while still a boy and was brought up at the Anglo-Norman court. His uncle, Richard I, whom he resembled in many ways, had enfeoffed him with the county of Poitou and given him the title of duke of Aquitaine; in Germany he only held a third of the Welf allod of Brunswick-Lüneburg. He was tall and of powerful physique, eager for war and adventure, brave and foolhardy after the Norman style, but haughty and uncouth, lacking in the confidence that comes with education, and torn between vanity and despair. It is typical of his coarse greed that he was credited with a plan to make the brothels of the Empire a source of income. Such a man was not made to be a sober politician, for he had no trace of diplomatic skill. His greed and ruthlessness could be dangerous if he had power in his hands, but he did not possess the qualities needed to establish himself permanently. He could batter his way through his adversary's snares by main force, but he lacked the adroitness to escape from them in the long run.

Neither king was elected or crowned in a manner entirely free from objection. Philip had by far the greater number of princely votes and he was in possession of the imperial insignia before the archbishop of Tarantaise crowned him in Mainz: but Otto was crowned in the right place, Aachen, and by the right man, the archbishop of Cologne. Only the sword could decide the issue. The princes hesitated between the Hohenstaufen south and the Welf north, inclining to the side which was for the moment prepared to surrender more royal rights and possessions. Landgrave Hermann of Thuringia, by completely disregarding all political principles, secured the means to build the Wartburg, his palace of the arts at Eisenach. Foreign influence played its part as well as the lure of land and gold. Family ties and the trade connections of Cologne, his chief base, inclined Otto towards England, whose king supported him with large grants of money. Philip drew all the closer to France, renewing the old alliance for mutual defence against the Anglo-Welf combination directly after the election of Otto.

All these divisions increased the pope's influence. Although Philip showed that he was not at all unwilling to come to an understanding with the Church and seems to have been ready to make sacrifices in Italy in order to reach it, right from the start there was no doubt which side Innocent favoured. Philip stood for the Hohenstaufen tradition of the German monarchy's independence of the Church, while Otto's supporters went some way towards meeting the curia's claims by explicitly asking the pope to confirm his election. As the weaker party, Otto was much more thoroughly dependent on the curia's support, and he at once bound himself by oath to recognise all the rights and possessions of the Roman Church and hinted at further concessions by surrendering the right to the *spolia* in Germany as well. Meanwhile Innocent was wise enough not to hurry his decision: the civil war was serving his ends by weakening German power and leaving his hands free to realise his territorial plans in Italy. Yet from the first he quietly tried to help Otto by arranging a truce between England and France so that the English troops which had

R

been pinned down in France could be released to support him. In the spring of 1199 he began secret negotiations with Otto and openly claimed the right to decide between the rival candidates for the German throne. While Innocent was demanding, like Gregory VII, that claimants should recognise this right, and asserting that the validity of their authority depended on papal confirmation, a brilliant assembly of Philip's princely supporters (including almost all of the bishops, still unshaken in their loyalty to the Hohenstaufen) issued a furious protest against papal interference. It breathed a thoroughly imperial spirit, expressly rejected the papal policy of regaining Italy, and indicated that Philip would shortly come to Rome to receive the imperial crown. This Declaration of Speyer of 28 May 1199[1] and the somewhat later Halle protest of January 1202[2] (which was equally firm against the curia though its form was different) are worthy to rank with the pronouncements of Besançon, Würzburg and Gelnhausen, and they close the series which these had begun. Germany saw nothing like them again until the time of Rhens and Frankfurt.[3]

Soon after the Speyer meeting the Hohenstaufen party was further strengthened by returning crusaders, while Otto was forced into complete dependence on the pope when the sudden death of Richard I on 6 April 1199 deprived him of his chief support.

It was not until the end of 1200 that Innocent finally made his attitude clear and explained the grounds on which his decision was based in a secret speech to the cardinals (the *Deliberatio*).[4] Although he discussed the rights of the three claimants (Frederick II had also to be considered) with ostensible impartiality, his careful sophistry was designed to hide the fact that it was the political advantage of the papacy which weighed most with him. Naturally he decided in favour of Otto, who soon afterwards had to pay the price of papal recognition. The charter Otto issued at Neuss on 8 June 1201 meant his total subjection to the will of the pope, for in it he not only explicitly surrendered imperial rights in central Italy and Sicily but also promised to make peace with France in accordance with the curia's wishes—that is, to follow

[1] Pullan 192–194.
[2] Pullan 201–203.
[3] i.e. the anti-papal pronouncements of princes and Emperor in 1338.
[4] Pullan 194–200.

the curia's directions in the most important question of foreign policy.

The pope now took up the struggle in earnest, excommunicated Philip and his supporters and deliberately tried to undermine his position. Just as Gregory VII had worked on the bishops who were loyal to the Empire, so Innocent now assailed the clerical signatories of the Speyer declaration with skilfully graded rewards and punishments, jurisdictional pressure, compulsory oaths of obedience, citations, suspensions and excommunication. He played unscrupulously on the consciences of some and drove others to desert or even—like Philip's own chancellor—to betray their Hohenstaufen master; Philip, naïve to the point of weakness, only accustomed himself gradually to this duel with poisoned weapons. By ruthlessly intervening to ensure victory for the Welf partisan in every new appointment and every double election (as in Mainz, for example, after the death of archbishop Conrad), Innocent found another way of thinning the ranks of the Hohenstaufen prelates. The pillar which had carried the weight of the German monarchy since the days of Otto the Great, cracked during the Investiture Contest but shored up by Barbarossa, now collapsed for good.

Several other factors helped to increase Otto's power greatly during the next two years, 1202–3; other secular princes— Bohemia and Thuringia, for instance—joined him, he came to terms with the king of Denmark by surrendering Nordalbingia and Slavinia, and England renewed its support when King John made an offensive and defensive alliance with him on the outbreak of his war with France.

It soon became evident, however, that Otto's success was more apparent than real. The English king's defeats, leading to the loss of Normandy in 1204, had repercussions on the German civil war. The general breakdown of loyalty worked against Otto too; his growing power made him enemies and drained away his supporters from 1204 onwards. His own brother Henry abandoned him, and so did even Adolf of Cologne, who had brought about his election, as soon as he found justification for his fears that Otto was preparing to re-establish the old Saxon stem-duchy. When Philip advanced to the Rhine, the archbishop recrowned him on 6 January 1205 at the proper place, Aachen, after a new election. It was an unprecedented invasion of imperial rights

when the pope thereupon deprived Adolf of secular and ecclesiastical office and set up a new archbishop against him. But this
could not stem the tide of defections from Otto. Hohenstaufen
successes in central Italy and another attempt to occupy Sicily
were already threatening the foundations of papal policy. When
Otto lost his chief base, Cologne, in November 1206, had to leave
Germany, and was reduced to dependence upon English and
Danish support, the pope thought it better to abandon his protégé's
lost cause and to save what he could from the wreck by coming to
terms with Philip.

Innocent's change of front, prepared in lengthy negotiations,
was facilitated by two things. The conflict between royal rights
and the Church's claims in England, which had never been really
settled since the time of Henry II, had widened into a serious
struggle between Church and state in consequence of the double
election at Canterbury in 1205, which made King John's Welf ally
an enemy of the pope too. In Sicily the approaching end (26
December 1208) of the young Frederick's minority would discharge
his uncle's rights of guardianship and confirm the separation of
kingdom from Empire. It therefore cost Philip nothing to
surrender it. Similarly, Innocent could maintain his fundamental
position over ecclesiastical disputes in Germany like those in the
provinces of Cologne and Mainz while at the same time making
small concessions of detail. On the other hand, Philip does not
seem to have been prepared to surrender the independence of his
kingdom; it is clear that he never admitted the pope's right to
decide the succession, although he was ready to accept his
mediation in the dispute with Otto, and the prospect of imperial
coronation was held out to him although nothing was said about
formal confirmation of his election. The evidence for the settlement of the territorial issues in Italy is very obscure; it appears
that there was talk of a marriage between one of Philip's daughters
and a nephew of the pope, who was to be given land in the empire
—perhaps part of the disputed territory—and that Philip had to
reconcile himself to other concessions as well. Each side had
yielded a little, and the agreement which was finally reached in
May 1208 left neither victorious.

At this moment one of the unexpected strokes of fortune which
was so frequent in the pontificate of Innocent III transformed
everything and turned the situation in the papacy's favour. Just

as he was about to advance in overwhelming force to stamp out the remains of Welf resistance in Brunswick, King Philip was murdered in the episcopal palace at Bamberg on 21 June 1208, the victim of an act of private revenge by the count palatine of Bavaria, Otto of Wittelsbach. It was another fearful blow struck by fate at Germany: Philip had no sooner cleared the way to unity, after years of painful toil, than this evil deed seemed to throw the Empire back into chaos again.

But the German princes were tired of strife. Even during the last stage of the negotiations it had been suggested that Otto should be betrothed to one of Philip's daughters and that—since Philip had no sons—he should be compensated thus with the prospect of the succession or perhaps become king of the Romans alongside the Hohenstaufen Emperor. Philip's partisans, and particularly the imperial *ministeriales*, now declared themselves for this saving solution, since it prevented further conflict. Otto thereby abandoned the role of anti-king and united the two hostile families in his person, rather as Barbarossa had done at the beginning of his reign. The effects of this union were immediately evident in the king's considerably increased prestige and in an improvement in peace and order.

Only in one respect was the new united kingship bound by its past. In a charter drawn up at Speyer on 22 March 1209, Otto renewed and extended his earlier concessions to the pope, who joyfully recognised him as king.

Otto once more surrendered all the disputed lands in Italy, and expressly confirmed the pope's rights to the Patrimony with the addition of frontier territory in southern Tuscany, the March of Ancona, the duchy of Spoleto, the estates of countess Matilda, the county of Bertinoro, the exarchate of Ravenna and the Pentapolis. But he also drew the necessary conclusions from the ecclesiastical politics of Germany during the last decade. By tying episcopal elections to a majority decision of the cathedral chapter alone, and by silently passing over the king's presence and his right to decide disputed elections, he left none of the previous royal rights remaining except simply that of investing the bishop with the *regalia*; by conceding unrestricted appeals to Rome in ecclesiastical cases and by yielding to the spiritual princes the rights of *spolia* and *regalia*, hitherto so valuable to the crown, he cut the ancient bonds between the monarchy and the German Church and accepted every advance Innocent had made in this field during the last few years. Control over ecclesiastical electors and scrutiny of elections gave the curia a decisive influence and secured for it the authority over the bishops which had formerly belonged to the monarchy.

Since he was now ruler of a united Empire, Otto was no longer under any compulsion to make such concessions, and it is hardly likely that he quite failed to grasp the monarchy's needs. It is probable that they were empty promises, to be forgotten as soon as Otto had received imperial coronation in return for them. He crossed the Alps the same year on his way to Rome, and it was at once clear that he did not take his concessions very seriously. He saw things with the eyes of the Hohenstaufen bishops and the imperial *ministeriales* who were his advisers: to add the surrender of the rich income from the Italian possessions he had promised the pope to the serious losses of royal property which Philip's necessities had compelled him to accept and to those which had followed from the transformation of much demesne land into service tenures—this seemed almost suicide for the German monarchy. Otto therefore left the clerical claims to be settled by process of law. He received the pope coolly at their very first meeting: his promises had not had the prior consent of the German princes, he said, and they contradicted his coronation oath, in which he had sworn always to seek to enlarge the Empire. Innocent crowned Otto nevertheless in Rome on 4 October 1209, but made another attempt to tie him down by inserting into Otto's public oath a promise to respect the rights and property of the Church. But the Emperor paid less attention than ever to the curia's territorial claims, even its claims to the Matildine lands. The pope's displeasure was increasing, but in spite of this an acceptable settlement (as in the case of the negotiations with Philip) could probably still have been made.

A surprising turn in Otto's policy now made a breach with the curia unavoidable. In Pisa at the end of November 1209, several weeks before the coronation, he had already considered the idea of attacking Sicily. Tempting appeals from the German commanders who were still holding out because Frederick's control was so weak, suggested that it would be easy to conquer the Norman kingdom; the promises of the Pisans, who hoped to receive from him the freedom to trade anywhere on the coast of Sicily, at the expense of their Genoese rivals; and lastly the example of Henry VI, whom he now increasingly tried to emulate—all these drove him to a decision from which the German princes dissented and which was bound to have fateful consequences. Conversations with the Sicilian rebels on the frontier, together with military and diplomatic preparations, made it clear during the next few months that Otto planned to seize the kingdom and thus to re-establish the dominion of Henry VI in its entirety.

This plainly involved an open breach of the promises he had given in his coronation oath. Furious, Innocent saw his own creature brutally trampling on every sense of obligation and respect, and seeking to destroy his life's work, the separation of Sicily from the Empire. He realised at once that there was now no further chance of an understanding with him. While Otto continued his preparations and at the same time began to reoccupy the disputed Italian territories, Innocent—together with the king of France, Otto's chief enemy—tried secretly to induce some of the German princes to desert him and to create an opposition party. When Otto crossed the frontier in November 1210 with a large army, Innocent at once excommunicated him. He did his best to stir up the weak resistance which showed itself in the Terra di Lavoro, if only as a means of gaining time. For how could the divided kingdom possibly defy so heavy an attack for any length of time? The whole of the mainland, including Calabria, was in the Emperor's power by the end of the following year. Otto planned to cross the straits of Messina, and the island seemed ready to fall into his hands: a galley stood by in Palermo harbour to take the young king to Africa should it come to this. But the pope's counter-scheme was now ready: he offered Frederick a rescuing hand.

During the months when Otto had been campaigning, French and papal influences had together managed to persuade the leading princes of south and central Germany to desert Otto and agree to set up an anti-king. Their candidate was no other than Frederick of Sicily; in November 1211, just as he saw his south Italian kingdom about to vanish, a German embassy informed him of his election as future Emperor. The pope had already signified his assent. Innocent had only accepted the French proposal of Frederick's candidature with a heavy heart, however, for it brought with it the one thing against which he had always fought—the union of Sicily and the Empire. Yet who else could have faced the Welf Emperor with any prospects of success? Powerless as Frederick might appear at the moment, his claim to the throne was firmly based on his descent and on the fact that he had once been elected king, while the traditions of his house and the glory of the Hohenstaufen name were strongly in his favour. He recognised the feudal supremacy of the papacy over Sicily, and confirmed his acceptance of it and of Constance's concordat;[1] by implication, something like them might be transferable to the Empire. Guarantees against a personal union of the two realms could be devised, and a first step in this direction was taken when, on the pope's instructions, Frederick's twelve-month-old son Henry was crowned king of Sicily. At worst, the young ward of the papacy, ruling (as he once said) 'by grace of God and the pope', was certainly not as dangerous as the ungrateful and faithless Welf who was threatening to repeat Henry VI's pressure on the curia. The shift in papal policy, which was the source of serious future complications, becomes on these grounds at least understandable. Contemporaries saw only that the pope was faltering again, however, and began to doubt the moral authority of the Vicar of Christ. 'Thy words are the words of God, but thy works are the works of the devil' shouted a Roman party leader in the middle of one of Innocent's sermons, and Walther von der Vogelweide spoke for others too in Germany when in bitter verses he accused the pope of being two-faced and branded him as Judas, the wolf in sheep's clothing.

Papal counter-measures scored their first success when Otto gave up the certain prize of Sicily and hurried back to Germany in October 1211. But his troops continued to occupy the mainland, and the threat would be renewed if Frederick failed to answer Innocent's call. It was the desperate position of his Sicilian kingdom, however, combined with a consciousness of his rights, dynastic pride and personal ambition which compelled Frederick to attempt the risky enterprise against the advice of his counsellors.

He reached Rome accompanied by only a small guard and almost without resources. There he took an oath of homage and fealty to his papal overlord, was provided with money and with the pope's assent was accepted by the Romans as the future Emperor. He marched from Genoa through Lombardy like a soldier of

---

[1] Above, p. 236.

fortune, disappeared into the Alps to reappear again at Chur, and eventually reached Constance. Here, in September 1212, he succeeded in getting a firm footing; his supporters grew in number, and civil war broke out in Germany again. Once more, as Walther wrote, the pope had 'put one crown on the heads of two Germans to bring discord and desolation to the Empire'.

Otto had by now managed to restore his position in Germany. At the same time Frederick was elected in the traditional fashion as king of the Romans by a number of princes at Frankfurt, and crowned (because of the archbishop of Cologne's hostility) in Mainz in December 1212. He extended his authority over the whole of south and central Germany and began to move against Saxony. Several forces, working together, explain this surprising success. Hohenstaufen tradition and Frederick's skill on the one hand, a revulsion against Otto's violence and fears of his centralising tendencies on the other, but above all the effectual support of the pope, which Frederick repaid on 12 July 1213 by the Golden Bull of Eger—largely a repetition of the promises Otto had made at Speyer, but this time confirmed and given legal force by the consent of the princes. The enlargement of the papal state and the surrender of the old royal rights over the German Church thus received their authorisation in law. Finally, the influence of France—with which Frederick had at once made an alliance— counted for a great deal: French money, the political and military success of Philip Augustus, and a French victory of immense significance for the whole of Europe, brought the German civil war to an end at one stroke.

This is not the place to describe how the complicated feudal and geographical relations of England and France demanded a solution, how their alliance with the Welf and the Hohenstaufen respectively and the effects of ecclesiastical disputes aroused the sympathies of all Europe and split it into two great coalitions, and how finally France had to face the terrible threat of a double Anglo-Welf offensive in 1214. The decisive battle of Bouvines (south-east of Lille) on 27 July 1214, which made the French monarchy secure and ensured the success of the anti-monarchical forces in England, settled the future of Germany as well. When Philip Augustus put the Emperor's superior forces to flight, he sent the golden eagle from the captured imperial standard to his Hohenstaufen ally as a gift, signifying thereby the transference of rulership but also the continually growing influence of France over German history, which steadily increased from this time onwards. 'From this moment,' wrote the Lauterberg chronicler, 'the renown of the Germans fell in foreign lands'.

Nothing went right for Otto after his defeat. He was soon driven out of the lower Rhine valley, and Frederick had himself crowned a second time in the traditional coronation city of Aachen in 1215. Otto was soon restricted to his family lands round Brunswick, but was threatened even there by a new alliance between Frederick and the king of Denmark—purchased, admittedly, by the surrender of imperial control over Nordalbingia. After a few years of ignominy he died in the Harzburg in 1218, conscious of failure and already half-forgotten. His end marks a stage in the history of the Empire. For he was the last to assert (at any rate in his final years, and admittedly without the requisite political skill) all the old imperial rights against princes and pope. Frederick II made no attempt to do so.

Of all the powers involved in these complicated events, the papacy came off best. It had managed to learn valuable lessons from its disappointments and to wring its own ultimate advantage from the changing situation. It had secured recognition for its protégé in the Empire; it had maintained its feudal supremacy over Sicily, its territorial claims in Italy and its ecclesiastical demands in Germany. In other respects too it stood high in the world's esteem. It had on the whole worked in friendship with France, still the only political power capable of independent action, and had just forced England into feudal dependence. The extent of its power had been increased by the progressive liberation of Spain from Moslem rule, by the ecclesiastical union with the newly-established Latin empire of Constantinople, and by the conversion of Livonia and Estonia, while in the rest of Europe and even as far away as Armenia either its feudal superiority had been admitted or it had gained significant political influence.

The structure of Church organisation had been made stronger. Not only in Sicily and the Empire, but almost everywhere—particularly in England—breaches had been forced in the ruler's rights over the Church, and at the same time the pope's absolute power inside the Church had been greatly extended at the expense of the bishops and every other intermediate authority.

The centralisation of ecclesiastical jurisdiction in Rome, which threatened to suffocate the spirit of true religion under the multiplying cares of business; the irresistible advance of these jurisdictional claims in the secular sphere, with its consequence of endless conflicts with the lay powers over even the smallest details; the growing fiscal demands of the curia, which needed an income sufficient to support its universal policies and to maintain its increasingly numerous staff; the excessive use of spiritual penalties, which could easily blunt the edge of religious feeling—all these were characteristic of the most recent developments in the papal Church, and they also nourished the growth of heretical sects.

A fierce war of annihilation was begun under Innocent against the Cathari and the Waldenses, these enemies within the Church; a gruesome triumph was won in the south of France, and the ground was prepared for the later Inquisition through the first measures for the deliberate tracking-down of heretics.

New forces to reawaken true religious feeling were also coming to the fore within the Church, and after some hesitation the pope welcomed them. Francis of Assisi had already been living and preaching the self-sacrificing gospel of poverty and love for several years. He and his remarkably different contemporary, the determined and rational Spaniard Dominic, asked Innocent III to confirm their new Orders, although these were only in the first stages of their development. Far-sighted observers already saw in them the pillars to hold the Church up amid the general collapse, as in the Franciscan legend of Innocent's dream the night before he gave his confirmation to Francis and his first companions. For the two Mendicant Orders, the Franciscans and Dominicans, together with the later but similar Augustinian and Carmelite friars, provided the papacy with an army directly subordinate to it and constantly ready for battle, able to by-pass the whole hierarchical organisation and by embodying the old high ideals and by popular preaching to win the masses back to the Church and bend them to the curia's will. The example of labour which they offered, and the new depth which they gave to the spiritual and intellectual life of the Church, went a long way towards meeting the critics' charges and stealing the heretics' thunder.

All these triumphs and cares for the future came together in the great Fourth Lateran Council of 1215, which brought the pontificate of Innocent III to a striking close. A new crusade, under papal direction, was envisaged. Even Frederick II, in an unusual mixture of emotion and political calculation, had taken the cross at the time of his royal coronation at Aachen, and this kindled the council's hopes. The German succession dispute was finally settled at the council when Otto IV was declared deposed and Frederick II recognised—a decision which had scarcely any effect at the time but provided an unfortunate precedent for the future. When he opened the Council with a sermon on the text 'With desire have I desired to eat this passover with you, before I suffer', Innocent seemed already to sense his coming death. Six months later, on 16 July 1216, he died at Perugia while preparing for the new crusade.

Europe had been under his influence for two decades. A secular figure held the stage for a generation after him and filled contemporaries with admiration or hate. With the death of Innocent III there began the age of Frederick II.

16

THE RISE OF FREDERICK II, TO THE
PEACE OF CEPRANO (1216-1230)

The names Frederick and Roger, which Henry VI's heir received at baptism, signify the two traditions—Norman and Hohenstaufen —whose influences met discordantly in his person. Events had restored almost the whole of his inheritance to him, but a vast discrepancy in power underlay the surface similarity. The terrible destruction of the last twenty years could not be made good, and an insuperable task lay before him. His remarkable talents enabled him to maintain himself for a whole generation, but the results of his struggle were bound to be negative—except in so far as all Europe was profoundly affected by the firm resistance to an omnipotent papacy which the secular state put up under his leadership.

The positive consequences of his work lay in the continuation of the inheritance he received from his mother's side. By education and inclination, Frederick was a Sicilian through and through. 'The God of the Jews', he is supposed to have said in Palestine, 'could not possibly have praised the land he gave his people so, if he had seen my Sicilian kingdom.' Frederick's character cannot be grasped without an understanding of the extraordinarily rich and cosmopolitan culture of the land where it developed. Many of the traits in him which have been praised as peculiarly modern or individual were in fact taken over from his Norman forbears, and some which have been condemned were no more than Sicilian custom. To develop the kingdom he had inherited was but to re-establish and complete the work of his grandfather Roger II, but it was at the same time Frederick's most tangible and most lasting achievement. His own universal personality was simply the crucible in which were fused the various elements of the mixed Arab-Sicilian culture—Roger was his model here too—but since he was also the embodiment of the imperial tradition and an Emperor who held the world's attention for thirty years, he was a most successful propagator of that culture and had a profound effect on the intellectual life of the west and of Italy in particular. Many aspects of the early Renaissance find their source in him. The influence he wielded in these ways can easily be underestimated by those who concern themselves only with Frederick as a German Emperor.

From the time when, after her husband's death, his mother Constance had taken the three-year-old boy from Foligno to Sicily so that he should be brought up as a Sicilian, Frederick had spent the whole of his childhood in Palermo. There the mingling of Italians, Arabs, Normans and Jews was at its most striking in custom and law, in language and art; and in the 'capital city of the Moslems', where Mohammedan cultural influence was strongest, in a large urban community, where daily contact with developed city life was natural, the boy could hardly remain unaffected by what went on around him. For Frederick did not grow up in the polite obscurity of an ordered court, but under truly chaotic conditions—and this in spite of the outwardly satisfactory arrangements made by his papal guardian and the 'college of advisers' composed of Sicilian secular and ecclesiastical magnates which he established. As a fatherless and motherless orphan, without any blood-relation to support him, the child was passed from hand to hand, treated simply as a property to be exploited by greedy and conscienceless Germans and Italians; when others' squandering of the crown estates reduced him to poverty, the burgesses of Palermo took it in turns to provide for his maintenance.

By the time he was seven years old unusually precocious signs were appearing that his inherited pride and sense of authority were deeply wounded by the unmerited weakness of his position. As he grew older, these became a burning desire for revenge, and he prepared himself with steely determination for his future career as a ruler. When he came of age at fourteen, the hard school of adversity had already taught him worldly wisdom, but it had also sown the seeds of mistrust and misanthropy. A description of him written at that time by one of his tutors gives an incomparable picture of his restless genius and dominating will.

The young king soon began to establish his authority along the northern and eastern shores of the island, although his plan to cross over to the mainland with an army provided by Constance of Aragon, the wife the pope had chosen for him, was ruined by plague. Soon after this, Otto IV's invasion threatened his very existence. We have already seen that the natural gifts and the precociously mature skill of the young king played no small part in the subsequent events which brought him to the German throne. He soon familiarised himself with the imperial idea of universal rule, but possession of his new territory could not turn him into a German.

He has been severely blamed for neglecting the responsibilities he had now assumed and for preferring an easier task in the south although, even at this last minute, a restoration of the German monarchy was still possible. But his connexion with Germany was purely dynastic; he felt at home only in Sicily. This is hardly likely to have decided his attitude, however: political calculation took first place. Even if he neither could nor wished to go back to Henry VI's scheme for a legal union of Sicily and the Empire, simply to survive as a ruler he still had to treat the whole of the territory which had come down to him as a single entity. If he now considered which part of his inheritance—Germany, imperial Italy, or Sicily—he could rely on most if he wanted to turn his present merely nominal rule into a reality, then a sound political judgement would necessarily suggest Sicily: although the strong Norman monarchy had been undermined for the last two decades, it had surrendered none of its rights apart from the concessions made to the curia, and local resistance appeared in no way insuperable. To restore his position in Italy would be far more difficult, for his losses there were in large measure gains for the papacy and the great communes and could hardly be won back without a collision with both. The situation in Germany offered fewest prospects, for feudalism and a natural economy were still overwhelmingly prevalent there and Germany thus presented an alien appearance to a more progressive Italian. It may be granted that a policy of restoring the German monarchy still held possibilities and that during the remaining years of his stay in Germany Frederick in fact regained many lost royal estates (particularly in Switzerland, Swabia and Alsace) and strengthened the imperial hold on the south-west by establishing towns. But princes and popes had profited from the events of the last generation, and therefore an attempt to reverse this movement could only succeed by conflict with these two powers—the very powers through whose assistance Frederick had come to the throne and to whom he had given legally binding undertakings. Such conflict was clearly quite out of the question. It is therefore clear from the situation itself why Frederick's work of reorganisation proceeded from south to north. It followed that in order to secure freedom to pursue his Italian enterprises through peace in Germany he continued to work hand in hand with the German princes and thereby made it more difficult to change his attitude later on because he had meanwhile surrendered still more royal rights.

This broad political outlook of Frederick's ran counter to the curia's efforts to dissolve the personal union of Sicily and the Empire, since if it lasted any length of time this could be as dangerous to the papacy as a legal link between them. Hence Innocent III, who still held the trump card of imperial coronation, took certain precautions shortly before his death. Frederick had had in 1216 to promise that from the moment when he was crowned Emperor he would abdicate the Sicilian throne in favour of his infant son Henry and a regency council to be established by agreement with the pope. It is not clear whether Frederick ever took this promise seriously. It seems likely that from the first he hoped to withdraw it later on, and he did in fact gain the upper hand over Innocent's successor.

Honorius III (1216–1227), the former chamberlain cardinal Cencius Savelli, and one of the curia's most remarkable financiers and administrators, felt it his duty to follow up his predecessor's achievement in greatly increasing the Church's authority in the outside world by continuing the work of internal reconstruction which he had begun and by setting the Church on a sound economic footing. Moreover, the great task of organising the new crusade had now fallen to him, and he took it very much to heart. Lastly, he was an old and sick man, and his honourable and conciliatory nature made him disinclined for the deceptions of high politics, while Frederick at once showed himself the willing pupil of his papal guardian. His insight showed him the weak point of the treaty. He had renounced the personal union only for himself; a renewal of it under his son did not conflict in the least with the wording of the agreement. Frederick now strove for this goal quite openly. Once the union of the realms was assured for the future in Henry's person, could the curia find grounds for objecting to it under the boy's father, who would thus be able to keep the valuable prize of Sicily under his direct control?

To bring Henry to Germany (1216), to enfeoff him with the

duchy of Swabia (1217) and the rectorate of Burgundy (1219) were preparatory steps, giving him a foothold north of the Alps; his title as king of Sicily disappeared from the charters. The next question was whether the German princes would be prepared to elect him king before his father was crowned Emperor—a proceeding which although not unprecedented was somewhat unusual. If it be remembered that election was only a preliminary to the establishment of a subordinate government in Germany which would guarantee them the chief influence during the long years of Henry's minority, then the princes' consent becomes comprehensible in spite of the support it lent to hereditary right. Only the spiritual princes, torn between the king's blandishments and the pope's warnings, had to be won over by extensive new concessions which mark an important stage in German constitutional history.[1]

Having already surrendered all decisive voice in the selection of the spiritual princes, the crown now gave up to them a generous measure of its ordinary sovereign rights. The central power began to withdraw from these ecclesiastical territories and lost for ever the possibility of influencing their internal affairs; the last vestiges of the Ottonian ecclesiastical policy vanished away. The establishment of new customs-posts and mints was made dependent upon the consent of the spiritual lord; the incidence of the right of *regalia* when the king was present in person was restricted to occasions when a meeting of the court had been formally proclaimed; outlawry, the supreme expression of royal justice, was limited by the provision that it had to follow excommunication automatically; and the ecclesiastical princes' property was protected in future from compulsory transfer of fiefs such as the crown had been in the habit of demanding when it founded new towns. At the same time the Empire undertook to protect spiritual territory against the incursions of lay powers—usurpation of the rights of *spolia* given up by the crown, abuse of their authority by advocates, the erection of fortresses in the spiritual princes' lands against their will—and to limit the attraction exercised by the towns over the unfree population in their neighbourhood: all in all, a valuable body of concessions which the spiritual electors found irresistible.

Thereupon Henry's election to succeed him in the Empire went through so smoothly that Frederick could even suggest to

[1] Pullan 208–211.

S

the pope that the initiative came from the princes themselves. It was also justified, he said, by his need to leave behind a deputy while he went on crusade. The curia had to accept the *fait accompli* and change its tack. Since the complete separation of Sicily was now out of the question, Honorius III had to rest content with new guarantees against a closer actual union of the two lands arising from the ancient imperial claims to sovereignty in lower Italy—a concession which Frederick was reluctant to make, in view of his independence in Sicily—and on Frederick's return to Italy crowned him Emperor in Rome in November 1220. The good relations of papacy and Empire, which nothing had yet marred, found expression in the decrees issued at the time of the coronation. Frederick put the secular sword largely at the Church's disposal for the suppression of heretics—by cutting themselves off from the established order they were rebels against the state as well—made outlawry follow upon excommunication and (mainly at the expense of the cities) pronounced the Italian clergy free from secular taxes and lay jurisdiction. At the same time he renewed his crusading oath and promised to fulfil it during the next twelve months. The crusade now became the focus of politics for a whole decade.

The impulse had not slackened in the west since the failure of the fourth crusade to reach its original objective, and had led to monstrosities like the childrens' crusade of 1212. Hence it was right that the Lateran Council should have tried to bring it within bounds again, and Innocent III would perhaps have led in person the expedition then foreshadowed. His successor, who was not the man for so huge a task, certainly gave the enterprise every support, but he could not make all the separate streams flow together into one great river. The decision to attack Egypt because it was the chief Moslem power was in itself perfectly reasonable. The port of Damietta was captured in November 1219 by an army composed largely of Germans led by the papal legate Pelagius, and a very favourable treaty, providing for the restoration of Jerusalem, might have been obtained from the Egyptian sultan al-Kamil. But Pelagius wanted more and pressed on with the advance inland towards Cairo although this was not feasible without considerable reinforcements. Frederick's expedition was therefore definitely announced for 1221 and the legate was told to suspend warlike operations until then.

But how could Frederick go off at once to the east, leaving Sicily in the state of anarchy in which he had found it when he at last returned there after his coronation? The success of his crusade would in any case largely depend on the resources the island could provide. Yet when he now threw himself energetically into the task of reducing Sicily to order, he became involved in a new undertaking which would not easily let him go free again, however good his intentions. It was something that he was able to send two fleets in quick succession to Egypt with large troop reinforcements during 1221; with the tacit consent of the pope he himself still remained behind. Disaster meanwhile overtook the crusaders. Casting caution aside, the legate did not wait for Frederick's second fleet but involved himself in an expedition of conquest into the interior of Egypt which delay had made still more risky, was at once surrounded by the waters of the Nile when the Egyptians cut the dykes, and was only saved from total annihilation by al-Kamil's wise moderation. Success was at an end: the withdrawal of the crusading army was purchased at the price of the surrender of Damietta and an eight-year truce was agreed, which could only be cancelled by a crowned Christian king.

Frederick did not go quite unscathed by this humiliation. From his point of view, however, the outcome was not unsatisfactory: all hopes for the future rested in him, and since the need for haste had now disappeared and a new crusade would require far more thorough preparation, he gained a respite for the pursuit of his most pressing tasks in Europe.

Sicily urgently demanded his attention. The work of the Assizes of Capua (December 1220) and Messina (June 1221) was one of restoration rather than of innovation, but the way was cleared for this particularly by the law concerning the revocation of privileges, which was based on Norman precedent: it called for documentary evidence of all privileges given since 1189, permitted the king to cancel or vary them, and extended the royal estates by large-scale resumptions. Briefly put, the consequences were: to reduce the extent to which feudalism hindered royal intervention by greatly lessening the independence of the feudal nobility and by allowing them in future to gain advancement only in the personal service of the ruler; to enable the state to enforce its will through a chain of strong fortifications (some newly built, some taken over from the baronage), through the creation of a standing army (when he had reduced the numerous mountain tribes of Arab Sicily in a series of campaigns, Frederick transported the garrisons to the military colony of Lucera in Apulia and established there a completely loyal body of Saracen troops which was proof against papal excommunication), and through the re-equipment of the efficient Norman fleet; to increase his resources by revoking the privileges of Genoa and Pisa, by abolishing all new tolls and markets and by extending state trading monopolies; to restrict the exercise of royal judicial rights to royal justiciars, and to build up the requisite body of lawyers at the state university of Naples which he founded in 1224, which became a *studium generale* in the full sense (embracing all faculties except that of medicine, which was reserved to Salerno) and which was designed to provide a central focus for the intellectual resources of the kingdom and to protect them from the Bolognese spirit of communal independence as much as from the encroachments of the Church.

The Norman monarchy of Sicily was all the more remarkable because it was established without the use of external force and exclusively from the resources of the land itself—some of which it had at the same time been compelled to suppress. The result justified the general lines of Frederick's policy; he could not have achieved it had he not bought peace in Germany for these years by leaving the princes alone.

Henry (VII), still a child, had been allowed back into Germany as the representative of the Emperor. His government was from the start the rule of the princely class, and this was not at first changed in any way by his election and coronation as king of the Romans at Aachen in 1222—apparently on the princes' initiative, but probably not without Frederick's consent—although this strengthened the independence of the royal authority and created the possibility of future conflict between father and son over the boundaries of their jurisdiction. If none the less this government did not altogether lack a sense of the wider national interest, the explanation lay entirely in the personality of the man whom Frederick's happy choice had made regent and guardian of his son. Archbishop Engelbert of Cologne was a remarkable figure; still quite young, he was ruthlessly active in his own lands to protect the general good against the selfish interests of greater and lesser lords alike, but he stands out among his contemporaries for his

ability to raise his eyes from the narrow horizons of a territorial
prince and think of Germany as a whole. At this moment the
opportunity to gain a great national advantage in the north
presented itself. Ever since the unfortunate succession dispute the
unnatural prominence of Denmark's power had burdened the
Empire: the Danes occupied the German colonies from the Eider
to Rügen, had even gained a footing in Samland and Estland and
advanced into Livland, and were on the point of turning the
Baltic into a Danish lake. During a period of peace, king Waldemar
II fell through treachery and cunning into the hands of count
Henry of Schwerin, whom he had grievously ill-treated; however
unjustified his capture may have been, the German leaders were
in no doubt that, like Richard I's, it could be exploited to the
advantage of the Empire and perhaps used to compel the return of
the German eastern territories. Engelbert went farther in this
direction than the Emperor, who though fundamentally in
agreement with him, was prepared, in view of his universal policy
and the pope's interference, for modifications of the treaty. The
swords of the nearest German magnates were able to protect their
own and the Empire's interests better than high diplomacy. When
Nordalbingia had been liberated from Danish rule by force,
Waldemar at last agreed, at the end of 1225, to a treaty under
which he was released from captivity in return for a large ransom
and the cession of the territory from the Eider to Pomerania. As
soon as he was out of prison, however, he denounced the treaty on
the ground that it had been signed under duress and got the pope
to absolve him from his oath to observe it. Thereby he simply
gave his German opponents the chance to confirm more honourably in battle on the plain of Bornhöved (southwest of Kiel) in
July 1227 the gains already won by the treaty they had extorted.
The Danish defeat marked the decline of Waldemar's over-
extended power all along the line, and gave the signal for renewed
German penetration into the whole area along the southern and
eastern shores of the Baltic. However, the Empire had no direct
share in this great national victory. The Emperor—at this time a
little less preoccupied with the curia—followed the events of the
year with great interest from a distance and furthered them,
raised Lübeck to the status of an imperial city in 1226, and accepted
the new situation they had created. The fresh advance of German
influence in the Baltic lands significantly coincided with the

establishment in Prussia of the Teutonic Order, which was destined in the course of the next decade to join up with the Knights of the Sword in Kurland and Livland. To Kulmerland, which had been promised them by duke Conrad of Masovia, Frederick now added all their future conquests in Prussia, and assured the Grand Master of a wide measure of autonomy within the Empire for the new state he was establishing. Had there been no other reason, his close relations with the Order and its remarkable head, Hermann of Salza, were enough to ensure Frederick's lively interest.

The regent Engelbert would perhaps have welcomed these latest developments even more than his master, but he was not to see them. Relations with the imperial court were a little strained throughout the years 1224 and 1225, for although Engelbert directed German policy, Frederick always reserved the final decisions to himself on the principle that wherever the Emperor and a few of his princes came together, there was Germany. Differences of opinion arose in particular over the question of the young king's marriage: with Cologne as his background, but also from a nationalist and anti-French point of view, Engelbert wanted an English connection; Frederick, holding fast to the Capetian alliance, eventually decided for Margaret, the daughter of duke Leopold of Austria. The grim news of the violent death of the archbishop came in the middle of the young couple's wedding celebrations: his own relations and their accomplices, resenting his strict rule as territorial prince, fell upon him and struck him down on 7 November 1225. He had already bowed to Frederick's will and, barely forty, had placed his further services at the Emperor's disposal, when the hand of a murderer cut short the career of a statesman who had hitherto served Germany with distinction and success. It is easy to understand why the ageing Walther von der Vogelweide pronounced a terrible curse upon the evildoer.

The dominance of the princely class continued unchanged, but duke Ludwig of Bavaria, who succeeded Engelbert, had neither the gifts nor the broad vision of his predecessor. When the outbreak of the struggle between Emperor and pope began to complicate matters, the eighteen-year-old king at once thrust the incapable duke aside and in 1228 himself took over sole responsibility for the conduct of German affairs.

In the meanwhile the date of Frederick's departure on crusade had been several times postponed with the reluctant assent of the curia. Friction in central Italy, where the papal 'recuperations' awkwardly interrupted the Emperor's lines of communication, and quarrels over episcopal appointments in Sicily, where papal confirmation and the royal right of consent often came into open collision, had already been the cause of irritation and mistrust from time to time. Another agreement was made at San Germano in 1225. It laid Frederick under the most binding obligation to sail with a stated number of ships and men in August 1227, under penalty that any further delay would bring upon him the excommunication with which he had already been threatened, together with the confiscation of a large sum which he was compelled to give as security. But when in the same year the Emperor, who was already a widower, married Isabella of Brienne, the heiress to the kingdom of Jerusalem, his own personal interests became closely linked with the enterprise and he moreover gained two further invaluable years.

In the treaty of San Germano he had already indicated how he intended to use them: by the restoration of royal rights in central Italy, which had fallen into serious decay during the last twenty or thirty years, an essential link was to be established between his direct rule over Sicily and his indirect control of Germany. When he summoned a Reichstag to meet at Cremona the following year, 1226, to determine on measures for the recovery of royal rights as well as to prepare for the crusade and take steps against heresy, he probably had nothing more in mind than to restore the law to the situation laid down in the treaty of Constance. But he mistook Lombard opinion, which was very distrustful of him because of his absolutist tendencies in Sicily, underestimated the strength of the resistance to which the unrestricted freedom of the last generation had given rise, and did not attach sufficient importance to the quiet but enduring community of interest between the Lombards and the pope. These errors led to his first disagreeable political failure.

Most of the north Italian cities, led by Milan, immediately renewed the old Lombard League, took up a hostile attitude, closed the gorges of the upper Adige to German reinforcements under king Henry, and demanded unacceptable and humiliating terms before they would open them again. Frederick was quite unprepared for war and had to confine himself to outlawing the members of the League for the crime of *lèse majesté* and for hindering the crusade, and to cancelling all the privileges which had been granted them. It was only the intervention of the pope, who because of the approaching crusade undertook to mediate once more, that brought about a condition of wary peace. By restoring the pre-1226 situation, this failed to satisfy the Emperor, but at least no irrevocable decisions had been taken and the dispute was left for the future to settle.

The arrangement of this truce was Honorius III's last action. He died shortly afterwards, in 1227, hoping that the long-desired crusade would go forward without further hindrance. But the necessity of electing another pope created new unrest. As so often, it put the opposition in control. In spite of his sixty years, Gregory IX (1227–1241), a near relative of Innocent III, was a handsome and imposing figure, respected for a generation past as 'a model of eloquence and an ornament of the pure life', renowned for his retentive memory, his legal acumen and his learning. As cardinal-bishop Hugo (Ugolino) of Ostia he had already been regarded as one of the pillars of the Church. In him, as in scarcely any other of the long series of popes, the deep internal contradictions of the hierarchy lie quite openly and naturally side by side. He was the friend and promoter of the religious orders, particularly the Franciscans, and although he forced St. Francis' glowing ideals into a cooler and more realistic mould, he showed thereby a true grasp of their practical value and the conditions under which they could survive; and he not only had personal experience of the silence of religious contemplation, the self-mastery of the ascetic and the mystic's deep inner ecstasy but showed an artist's ability to express them in the written and the spoken word. Yet as pope he loved outward show and the striking pose, made favourites of his nephews and furthered the interests of his family, and conducted the struggle for universal dominion by the most wordly means to the point of secularisation and decline. Contradictions as apparently irreconcilable but as firmly rooted in one and the same nature are familiar from their recurrence in many of the leading figures of the Counter-Reformation. Inwardly as well as outwardly, he embodied in almost heightened measure the contradictory tendencies towards reform and towards worldly dominion which had marked the papacy under Innocent

III, whose pupil and assistant he had been. But whereas reason and cool reflection had always guided Innocent's actions and ensured him success, Gregory IX shared some of the volcanic temperament and mountain-moving will-power of the great pope whose name he chose for his own. His passions were uncontrollable and easily aroused, and his nature inclined equally to love and hate; this may be the explanation of many of the unpleasant aspects of his conduct and it certainly denied him complete success. Like Gregory VII, he was a man of absolute singleness and power of vision who could take the initiative explosively but who could not carry it laboriously through to its appointed end. Twice he took upon his shoulders the dreadful responsibility of world-wide conflict. His fiery temperament stamped itself on the fatal struggle he unleashed and made future reconciliation impossible; yet despite the fury of his onslaught he was not Frederick's most dangerous enemy.

It was not the chance events of the year 1227 which provoked the new strife: they were merely the occasion for the attack on Frederick II which the curia had deliberately prepared. Gregory IX's paternal solicitude for the young ruler had turned to disillusion and even dislike with Frederick's growing independence. He had observed with anxiety and displeasure how his predecessor's gentle rule had enabled the Emperor to entrench himself firmly against the policies of Innocent III, and how Frederick was already moving into central Italy from his strong Sicilian base and was letting it be known, in many high-toned pronouncements, that although he desired peace he still retained the outlook of a Hohenstaufen and kept the old political objectives in view. What availed all the Church's concessions, then, if the encirclement of Rome was to be renewed? All the old disputes arose again in their most acute form. The papacy, which regarded independent territorial rule as a necessary pre-condition for its freedom of action, tried to extend its ecclesiastical influence in Sicily and its political influence in Lombardy. For the Emperor, who wanted to remain master of his own house in Sicily, the possession of central Italy was essential to the firm government of his separated territories; as far back as 1222 he had incautiously let it be known that he wanted to reoccupy the 'recuperations' which cut his lines of communication. Even more clearly than in Barbarossa's time, Italy was the chief object of the dispute between

the two heads of Christendom. There was therefore bound to be
an increasingly violent struggle over the fundamental principles
of world-rule. Gregory was the first to realise that the knot would
have to be cut; with remarkable logic and decisiveness he began a
war to the death.

The curia had planned for the crusading fleet to set sail during
the heat of August. Frederick increased the consequent danger by
going beyond the terms of the treaty of San Germano and
announcing that he would provide ships for all the pilgrims as
well. Plague wrought havoc among the crowds collected on the
plain of Brindisi. The Emperor himself fell ill shortly before the
embarkation-date, and his companion, landgrave Ludwig of
Thuringia, died at sea. Frederick turned back to convalesce at the
baths of Pozzuoli. Since he had not fulfilled his promise, Gregory
IX excommunicated him at the end of September—completely
disregarding the fact that his failure to keep it was due to circumstances beyond his control—and declared his illness to be feigned;
he utterly rejected Frederick's offer to do penance for his neglect
and to repair it the following year, basing the excommunication on
new complaints, this time about Sicily. Further sinister allega-
tions, which Frederick calmly denied, and a hostile alliance with
the Lombards, made it clear that the papacy wanted either to
annihilate the Emperor or to humiliate him and weaken him
permanently. It was therefore a master-stroke on Frederick's part
to set out for the east next year in spite of the excommunication,
thus demonstrating publicly the seriousness of his intentions and
putting the pope in the wrong.

The fifth Crusade (1228–9) differed from those that preceded
it in two ways: the excommunicated Emperor had dynastic
schemes—his wife had borne him an heir to the kingdom of
Jerusalem, his second son Conrad, although she died in childbed
—and from the beginning he intended to secure victory by peaceful
diplomacy, for he was on as friendly terms with sultan al-Kamil
of Egypt as he was with the large number of Mohammedan
scholars whose respect he enjoyed. The Islamic world, into
which he was now penetrating further, was familiar to him from
his Sicilian experiences, and only a man with his personal qualities
could have made the treaty of Jaffa (1229); the Holy Places of
Jerusalem, Bethlehem and Nazareth and the land between them
and the coastal strip (itself enlarged by the transfer of Sidon)

which was all that remained of the kingdom, were ceded to Frederick as the new king, while the Moslems obtained a ten-year truce, a guarantee of neutrality if they were attacked by a third party, and freedom of worship in the mosque at Jerusalem. This treaty had undeniable weaknesses. Although they attracted more obloquy than they deserved from Christians, the concessions just mentioned were of less significance than the impossibility of defending the narrow strip of territory. But a settlement had been secured in extraordinarily unfavourable circumstances. Al-Kamil had recently strengthened his position against Damascus and occupied Jerusalem itself. Frederick was weakened by the small size of his army, and by dissension and treachery in his camp. The pope treated him not as a crusader but as a pirate, the patriarch of Jerusalem preached open resistance and even worked against him at the sultan's court, the Hospitallers were unreliable, and the Templars were perhaps not even above scheming to betray his person into the enemy's hands. Finally, the news of a papal invasion of Sicily warned him to make all possible haste and to limit his commitments. And in spite of all this more had been gained than by decades of heroic sacrifice. The lamentations of the Moslems spoke more in favour of the treaty than even the joy of the pilgrims, to whom the Holy Places were open again; but Frederick's realism and toleration were out of keeping with the crusading spirit, and the pope closed his eyes to the Emperor's success.

So the sentence of excommunication was not lifted when the Holy Places were freed, as had been expected. Instead, when Frederick placed the crown upon his own head in the church of the Holy Sepulchre—an action which derived from respect for the excommunication because it dispensed with consecration, but which could at the same time be regarded as a sign that the kingdom was now free from the Church—the patriarch placed Jerusalem under an interdict and began to raise an army against Frederick. Without delay, Frederick returned to Europe by way of Acre, where the mob pelted him with filth as he embarked, and landed unexpectedly at Brindisi in June 1229.

Frederick had had to plan for the open hostility of the pope before he set off on crusade. Duke Rainald of Spoleto, whom he had left as vicegerent in Sicily, had received instructions to answer any attack by invading the papal states and reoccupying the 'recuperated' areas. He exceeded his powers and crossed the frontier as soon as Gregory released the Emperor's subjects from their fealty, declared him deposed, tried to set up an anti-king in Germany and allied with the Lombards. But in so doing he gave the pope an excuse to attack Sicily with a hastily-gathered army in order if possible to bring it under the direct rule of the Church as an escheated fief. The structure of the kingdom was not yet strong enough to withstand attack in its ruler's absence; more than half of the mainland was already in the pope's hands by the time Frederick returned.

The inactivity of the papal commanders gave him time to gain strength; hurriedly collecting troops, in a rapid series of victories he soon drove the invaders out. On the frontier he dismissed his army and offered to discuss peace terms. If Gregory had only been concerned to secure satisfaction for the breach of the treaty of San Germano, he would have grasped Frederick's outstretched hand with joy. But he held out a long time before he did so, and only accepted it when his soldiers' incapacity, his own shortage of money, the ill-success of the Lombards and the failure of his propaganda in Germany had put him in a very awkward position. The negotiations, conducted in San Germano and concluded in Ceprano, were marked by the greatest obstinacy on the pope's part and the greatest moderation on Frederick's: prevailing opinion in the curia did not consider the treaty as one between equal powers but only as the submission of a penitent son to the will of the Church, which was to dictate the terms of the settlement and modify them simply of its grace. Even when the Emperor accepted the pope's draft without significant alterations, the curia was so reluctant to believe that it would be honourably executed that agreement was only reached when generous guarantees were provided by the German princes, who wanted peace in their own interests. The Emperor received absolution, but in return had not only to restore all conquered territory and issue a comprehensive amnesty, but in addition to make important concessions in the Sicilian Church.

Opinion is still sharply divided on this treaty, as it is on the whole of Frederick's ecclesiastical policy. His submissive attitude has been likened to Canossa as a humiliation for the Empire, and he has been accused of entirely misunderstanding the curia's real intentions. This, however, is to go too far towards treating the two sides as equals in power and to take too little account of

Frederick's fundamentally hopeless situation vis-à-vis the papacy. It would be difficult to say what other course he should have followed. In the ecclesiastical sphere the papal power was immovably entrenched until the nation-states or the masses should mobilise themselves against the curia. The time for this was still far off. Frederick's aim could therefore only be to delay the papacy's war of annihilation against him as long as possible by diplomacy and concessions, and meanwhile to strengthen his political position as much as he could. The peace of Ceprano gave the Church valuable concessions in Sicily, but they were not enough to shake Frederick's absolute sovereignty there and hence did not bring the papacy the advantages for which it had hoped. And in return for this sacrifice, without which peace could apparently not have been made, Frederick everywhere gained a thoroughly impressive moral victory in the eyes of the contemporary world: the sentence of excommunication against him was raised, in spite of the pope's reluctance; the results of his crusade were recognised, although it had been branded as piracy; the invasion of Sicily had failed miserably and all attempts to arouse resistance to him in Germany had proved vain. Europe owed its peace to Frederick's wise moderation alone. The situation was the contrary of that at Canossa: there, momentary political success was bought by lasting moral sacrifice; here, material concessions bought a huge increase in imperial prestige, as the next ten years clearly demonstrated. As evidence for just this, the chief impression which these events made in more distant perspective on a contemporary Arab observer should perhaps not be underestimated. The Arab Abu al-Fadayl wrote of Frederick: 'There has been no prince in Christendom like him since the time of Alexander, not only in respect of his might but also because of the skill with which he dared to confront the pope, their caliph, make war on him and put him to flight.' A western writer, William of Andres, also described the peace as a humiliation for the Church, and he was none the less correct in his judgement because he went on to say that the harmony which had been attained was more pretence than reality. The first attempt at annihilation had been beaten off, the Empire had regained its place alongside the papacy, but the unhealthy hostility between the two had been in no way removed. Nevertheless, Frederick had laid the foundations for a further strengthening of his authority.

17

FREDERICK II AT THE HEIGHT OF HIS POWER (1230–1239)

Frederick was now at the height of his power. His appearance was not specially imposing in itself—a figure no taller than the average and inclining to stoutness in his later years, auburn hair and a clean-shaven chin—but the impression he created was one of inexhaustible energy and the confidence of majesty. The pomp that surrounded him—the strange figures of Moors and negro pages, Saracen maid-servants, dancing-girls and singers, together with the elephants, dromedaries, lions and panthers of the imperial menagerie, all animals seldom seen north of the Alps—caught the imagination of the Germans but also showed how little they could regard their Emperor as one of themselves. Whether in good taste or bad, all this luxury (it was far more intoxicatingly manifest in his Apulian castles) was in fact as Sicilian as the exuberant sensuality of his whole way of life, and something very like it had been common among his Norman ancestors. It cost vast sums of money and gave considerable offence, but Frederick's character, strong beyond the ordinary, was not in the least debilitated by it.

He shouldered the multifarious and exhausting responsibilities of his office without fatigue. Imperial, Norman and Moslem traditions, supported by the doctrines of the Roman Law, combined with his native genius and a hard schooling to make him a true autocrat, capable of taking every important decision himself. His political gifts were undoubtedly at their strongest in the fields of organisation and government—like his grandfather Roger, upon whom he largely modelled himself, although he was by no means content to copy him slavishly. Shackled to a politically hopeless cause, and constrained in many ways by the traditions of his family, he nevertheless combined firmness of purpose with flexibility and inventiveness in the means he adopted. He often did himself harm as a diplomat by his impulsive way of showing his hand too soon, by the biting sarcasm which sprang too readily to his lips and by the furious rages which often darkened his vision, made him needlessly depressed, and sometimes prevented him from perceiving all the possibilities the situation offered. He was on the whole no match for the diplomacy of the curia, particularly under the two Innocents, but this was to some extent compensated for by his shrewdness of wit, by his gift for surprising changes of front and his flair for original strategy. The talents of a soldier did not come naturally to Frederick, but he was not entirely without them; if he can hardly be called a great general he had such a gift for organisation, was so technically accomplished in constructing fortifications and conducting siege-operations, so decisive and so untiring that he never met his equal in this field.

Occupations like these, forced upon him by his position, were not enough to exhaust the riches of his character. His significance cannot be fully understood by taking account of them alone; the stimulus which he gave to cultural life was at least as fruitful. Although much of this had been foreshadowed in Sicily since Roger II, it took on an altogether different aspect once it spread, under the Emperor's powerful influence, beyond the shores of the island and held the world in suspense for a whole generation. Frederick's marvellously receptive mind affected the future principally because it freed itself from inherited ecclesiastical mysticism, showed a penetrating insight into the reality of things and an instinctive certainty that nature was governed by a necessity impermeable even to divine intervention, and insatiably desired to uncover everywhere the workings of that intrinsic rationality and purpose.

Arabic texts now came to the fore as the work of translation was resumed at the Sicilian court. Learned Italians, Spaniards, Greeks, Mohammedans and Jews surrounded Frederick. He himself was carried away by his love of falconry to spend years in earnest zoological study, of which the highly significant product was his book *On the art of hunting with birds*, marked by close observation and a remarkable acuteness of reasoning. Over and above this, he showed a lively interest in and understanding of the whole field of science, medicine, mathematics and optics, astronomy, astrology and above all Aristotelian and Averroistic philosophy, and he awakened the same in others. He corresponded and disputed in a wide variety of languages with the most important thinkers of his time—the mathematician Leonardo Fibonacci, the polymath Michael Scot, even Arab philosophers in the Middle East and North Africa, putting technical problems to them all.

It is easy to understand that with this breadth of interest he could not stay within the narrow and circumscribed bounds of the western Church. Although he never freed himself entirely from the usual cosmological ideas of the Middle Ages, his quest for knowledge did not prevent him from approaching close to the most sacred mysteries—as, for instance, when he inquired how God sat upon his throne and in which of the Heavens, or how the saints and angels around him spent their time—and he showed at least a tendency towards scepticism when, under the influence of his Aristotelian studies, he questioned the divine creation of the world and demanded proof of the immortality of the soul. But to commit himself to a set of philosophical beliefs other than those accepted in Christendom would have been as much at variance with his totally undogmatic turn of mind as with his historic role as a Christian Emperor. He was at pains to emphasise that he belonged to the Church, and he never thought of breaking with the Christian religion. On the other hand, he was not sparing with the sarcastic mockery which his scepticism of all authorities suggested and which was provoked by his dislike of the hierarchy which opposed him. Above all, the whole process of lay education which he originated and promoted—the lawyers at his court were particularly prominent in this—presented a serious threat to the continued spiritual domination of the Church.

If concern for knowledge occupied Frederick's restless energy only during his leisure hours, he must have regarded his artistic interests as still more of a luxury and a recreation. Yet these too exercised a significant influence. As the instigator and leader of a school of Sicilian poets, he was the first to use the vernacular instead of Latin for the verses he wrote in the Provençal style but in the Sicilian dialect which he had spoken from childhood. He played a leading part in raising it, when refined and enriched with Latin, Provençal and Italian elements, to the rank of a court language, and so Dante could praise Frederick as the father of Italian poetry. In the plastic arts there are traces of the influence of French Cistercian Gothic or of the Lombard style which was just gaining prominence. But everything else depended upon the quite personal encouragement, inclination or needs of the ruler—

the solidity and functional simplicity of his numerous fortifications; the charming decoration of country retreats like Castel del
Monte, west of Barletta; the novel because completely secular
masterpieces of Frederick's protégés, the Capuan sculptors (their
feeling for nature and late classical models was well fitted to serve
the cult of the Emperor and reached its climax in the triumphal
arch at Capua); the delicate reliefs of his golden *augustales*,[1] and
the classical statues which he collected. It was a hot-house
culture, with all the consequent good and bad characteristics, and
although it did not grow out of the life of the community but was
closely bound up with the person of its inspirer, it still had a
lasting influence on the Italian renaissance.

The strongly personal note in this whole range of activities
shows that immersion in them did not make Frederick into a
dilettante or cause him to lose his own individuality. This was
prevented by an exaggerated pride in his position as ruler, by his
immovable will and by his easily wounded self-esteem. So long as
these were untouched, Frederick could be affable, generous and
magnanimous; but directly anyone encroached upon them wild
and primitive forces were unleashed and demanded their way
whatever the cost: a ruthless and arbitrary will, merciless cruelty,
the crooked cunning which seemed permissible when dealing with
rebels and traitors, and the passionate thirst for revenge which
was expressed by his saying of Viterbo when it deserted him 'that
even after death his bones would not find rest until he had
destroyed the city, and that if he had already set foot in Paradise he
would come back again to revenge himself upon it.'

It is easy to see that the very rapidity of these changes in a
character which lacked any settled warmth, and the unpredictable
anger which no feeling of piety controlled, were quite enough to
arouse misgiving and distrust in those around him, and that even
if the savage struggles of his later years had not occurred he would
still never have attracted the admiration and affection which were
freely given to his grandfather, Barbarossa. Opinions about him
differed violently; hatred and admiration are both still current
today.

The most urgent task facing Frederick after the treaty of
Ceprano was to rebuild his shattered authority and to make his
dominions more capable of resistance. His plan was the same as it

---

[1] Frederick II's gold coinage, which was based on classical models.

T

had been ten years earlier; first to reorganise Sicily and Germany, though along completely different lines, and then to establish imperial power in Italy, but so far as possible to do both without endangering the settlement with the curia.

The Constitutions of Melfi of 1231[1] (in all essentials Frederick's own work, although he was assisted by a number of eminent jurists), together with the new financial and other provisions, went far beyond previous arrangements and put the Sicilian state on a firm basis for the first time. Much was borrowed from the Assizes of Roger II, which had already combined Byzantine bureaucratic despotism with Norman emphasis on the authority of the feudal lord; but nevertheless it was in essence new, creative legislation. This novel organisation of the state did not lack a metaphysical basis—the omnipotence of the ruler who, as the 'image of God' is necessary if cosmic order is to be restored in the chaos caused by Adam's sin. But since everything was traced back to the natural necessity which governs all things, the earthly state was deprived of its transcendental mystique and was placed firmly in this world rather than in the next. The sacred ruler at the head of the central government, 'the living law on earth', was as infallible in matters of justice as the pope in matters of belief, and was therefore empowered to overrule every law which stood in his way. No important decision could be taken without him, and thus Gregory IX could complain that 'No man dare move hand or foot in your realm without your command'. The chancery —the most important government office from the subject's point of view—had already been influenced by Rome during the period of papal rule; but now, under Peter della Vinea, a man of bourgeois origins and lively mind who had risen to the position of supreme judge and protonotary, it gained greatly increased significance and a form that was almost baroque in its ceremonial. In the ranks of its officials—trained in the law, salaried, appointed for a fixed period and arranged according to a strict system of subordination—the urban element began to be preponderant, while the influence of the nobility was restricted even in the army by the employment of mercenaries. The new legal code, which used the inquest procedure and dispensed with the ordeal, may have used Innocent III's practice as a model, and the same is true

[1] Pullan 219–231.

of the bureaucratic paper-work in the law-courts and in government. But this absolutist system had a very different content, however similar its external form. The coldly calculating Norman spirit shows itself in the emergence of economic, statistical, hygienic and educational policies, in land-improvement schemes and in far-sighted trade treaties (even with Moslem sultans) and in the whole rationalist outlook with its emphasis on nature. Its roots were in the similar tendencies that created the states of Roger II and Henry II of England, but the monarchy of Frederick II points the way beyond these to the *signorie* of the Renaissance and in many respects to the enlightened despotisms of modern times as well.

Faced with a monarchy supported by officials, fortifications, an army and a navy, all other formerly independent bodies sank into insignificance: the assemblies of the great vassals at formal meetings of the royal court; the cities, whose chief magistrates the ruler appointed and to which he almost certainly denied the permanent right to political representation, although he sometimes called their citizens in as expert advisers; even the great ecclesiastical foundations, which could not escape the pressure of the state machine in spite of the Ceprano concessions and papal protests. This pressure, the surveillance of suspects and a growing number of denunciations at first burdened the upper classes more than the mass of the population, who were better welded into national unity by the official bureaucracy and by the justice and the care of the king than they had been by the fragmented feudal state of earlier times.

The welfare of the people could of course only be given relatively little attention, since the concentration of state powers was primarily a preparation for defence against the future enemy. Above all, it was essential to secure productive sources of wealth against the two great financial powers of the west, the pope and the Lombards. Here too lessons were learned from Norman experience, particularly in England, but Arab and Jewish influences also led to innovations. Besides the land-tax imposed on all land-owners and the ingenious extension of indirect taxation, there was a very profitable state trade in corn and an even higher yield from monopolies granted mainly to Jews. By means of the huge income thus derived, the ruler of Sicily became the leading financial power in the world. But these results were achieved by a system of exploitation, amounting to robbery, which was bound to

exhaust the overstrained resources of the country within a fore-
seeable future. The population, unremittingly taxed, was restive;
the artificial system of tolls and duties raised food-prices to a
critical level; state dealings in corn had a ruinous effect on private
trade and made corn production outside demesne lands scarcely
worth while; monopoly economics ended by strangling enterprise
in a number of important fields. Frederick, who declared his
conviction that 'the safety and well-being of his subjects is the
foundation of a king's glory', was not in the least blind to such
ill-effects; he followed them carefully and tried repeatedly—for the
last time in his testament—to lighten the burden by reducing
taxes. But the terrible struggle for existence which filled
the last third of his reign forced him to take risks
against his will. Nevertheless, it was his financial system which
contemporaries admired more than anything else, and it was
widely copied—not only in the small Italian city-states and in
Aragon, but also farther afield in the lands of the Teutonic Order.
In Sicily itself, however, Frederick's constitutional arrangements
outlived Hohenstaufen rule by many hundred years without
serious change.

Frederick sketched out the main lines of his new state organisation with astonishing speed. Even before the end of 1231 he
was in a position to turn his mind to imperial affairs again.
Between the absolute monarchy in the south and the feudal
German state in the north, he had to give his attention, now as
before the crusade, to the imperial territory of Italy in the centre,
which differed widely from both the others and was very difficult
to control. At the Reichstag of Ravenna he for the second time set
himself the task of reducing the self-willed society of the Lombard
cities, with their free, republican and democratic spirit, to subjection. The events of 1226 were at once repeated: the Lombard
League was renewed, the Brenner was closed to the German
princes whom he called to his assistance, the sentence of outlawry was proclaimed, and once more the pope's mediation was
accepted because of the unfavourable military situation. During
the succeeding years it was particularly the need to take account
of the curia's attitude which made it difficult for him to concentrate all his strength on the task in Lombardy. Outwardly, pope
and Emperor were on friendly terms at this time and spoke of
single-minded co-operation by the two universal powers: in

secret, they were still deadly enemies, driven only by their own embarrassments to show courtesy and consideration to each other. Thus while Gregory was forced by his struggle with the rebellious Romans to depend on the Emperor's military support, it was on the other hand in Frederick's interest not only to keep the pope from openly taking the Lombard side for as long as possible but also to prevent him from interfering in the affairs of Germany, where his son Henry was giving him cause for concern.

Important changes in German history were beginning to occur at this time; they were bound to bring the narrower interests of the German monarchy into conflict with the wider interests of the Empire. During his first stay in Germany, as has already been shown,[1] Frederick had begun a policy of building up his power similar to that which any ruler who took a German view-point was bound to adopt, but which collided in many respects with the territorial interests of the princes whose lands bordered his own. As soon as he took over the reins of government in 1228, Henry (VII) was forced to move in the same direction. Moreover, the revolutionary movement in the towns had taken a hold in Germany too, though not to the same extent as in Italy, so that there was a standing temptation to look to the towns for support against the bishops who were their lords. The more the Emperor concerned himself with universalist policies, however, the more necessary was it for him to restrict any increase of his power in Germany, since he was dependent there on the good-will of the German princes. As early as 1220 he had given way to the bishops over the price to be paid for his son's election as king. Now he had secular as well as ecclesiastical princes to thank for their mediation and backing, and had perhaps already given them new assurances in return for it But King Henry—who had energetically supported the imperial cause during the recent conflict and had brought the pope's ally, the duke of Bavaria, to his knees by a skilful campaign in 1229—overlooked the compulsions of his father's universalist policies, and under the influence of advisers drawn from the ranks of the *ministeriales* tended more and more to steer a course which would bring him into collision with the princes. On their return to Germany, the princes faced the young king at Worms on two occasions in January and May 1231[2] and extorted from him

[1] Above, p. 253.
[2] Pullan, 211–3.

considerable privileges which had the effect of admitting their claim to territorial sovereignty and restricting the towns' pursuit of independence. The very thing Henry had set out to prevent— a strengthening of the princes' power—had thus been brought about. At the same time, it is true, a counter-weight was being created within their own territories by the provision that general regulations and new laws (specifically any which concerned taxes) were to be approved by the higher Estates of the territory: this was the source of important later developments, but its full effect was only to be felt in the distant future.

Since the Emperor could not forsake the lines fixed by his universalist policies, which required a peaceful understanding with the German princes, he had to confirm his son's concessions, although with a few modifications advantageous to the crown. This was accomplished particularly by the 'Statute in favour of the Princes', issued in May 1232 at Cividale in Friuli.

The crown had already in 1220 given up most of its sovereign rights in the ecclesiastical territories, and this was now extended to the lands of the secular princes as well. Each prince was recognised by the Emperor to have the sole right of coinage and of granting safe-conduct within his lands. The vital element in the process by which these nascent territorial states were gaining their independence was the exclusion of all external jurisdiction, particularly the king's. By withdrawing from princely territory and by surrendering to the princes the authority to appoint the presidents of lower tribunals (even where they were still dependent upon the *Gaugraf* and functioned in the king's name), thus ensuring them against usurpation from lower down the scale and at the same time subjecting the knightly class to the princes' jurisdiction, the crown went far beyond its previous concessions; the charter gave involuntary expression to the significance of this new alienation of royal rights when it coined the term 'territorial authority'[1] to express it. The rise of the secular and ecclesiastical princes to territorial sovereignty had long been foreshadowed, but the Emperor's acquiescence now greatly accelerated it.

The flourishing imperial cities, hitherto the chief opponents of such tendencies, had to bear no small part of the cost of this policy. Henry (VII) had to atone for the feeble attempts he had made at a Capetian-style policy of friendship with the towns by

[1] The phrase 'dominus terrae' occurs in two clauses.

the most humiliating concessions to the princely interest in this respect as well. It is the provisions hostile to the towns, almost more than those directly aimed at raising the status of the princes, which are the distinguishing mark of Frederick II's confirmatory privilege.[1] Since the towns were at that time the most progressive element in the country, often allowing themselves to go beyond the law as they tested their new-found strength, the provisions are strongly conservative in character.

The imperial government frequently assisted princely policy against the towns in other ways too at this time, for instance by dissolving the first league of Rhineland cities in 1226 and by following this up in 1231 with a general prohibition on city leagues. Similarly, it helped the bishops against their own cities' desire for independence by forbidding all demands for self-government, whether through the creation of a city council, through workmen's organisations or through other manifestations of communal feeling. A number of individual measures pointed in the same direction.

It would be easy to exaggerate the effect of these hostile regulations, as the continual later repetitions of them demonstrate. The importance of the imperial cities was constantly growing, and their natural interests drove them to take the Hohenstaufen side in the great struggles of the 1240's in spite of all that had happened earlier. Moreover, it would be entirely wrong to see a fundamental hostility to the growth of the towns in all this, whether on the part of Henry [VII], whose contrary desires are often apparent, or on that of Frederick II, who, as an Italian, cannot have been blind to the economic importance of the towns. Wherever no princely interest stood in the way, Frederick never failed to show favour to the royal cities by facilitating trade, establishing fairs, repairing roads and building walls. Still clearer evidence is provided by his numerous new foundations, which continued well after 1240 in spite of the concessions embodied in the privileges of 1220 and 1231. Through them, the direct royal estates gained an economic advantage over the princes' lands, the effect of which lasted for centuries. In combination with many other measures directed towards the strengthening of the monarchy's power during the years which followed, this urban policy might very

---

[1] Pullan 213–15 prints Henry (VII)'s charter of May 1231. Frederick's confirmation repeats it substantially word for word.

well have proved a suitable counterbalance to the princes' federalist ambitions, and it can hardly have been Frederick's intention to accept the latter without reservation. Moreover, there was no lack of complaint during the period that followed about the actual practice of the royal officials, who were accused of continuing to follow the old policy contrary to the princes' demands. It was only the continual hindrance caused by his last titanic struggle with the curia, and the final collapse of his work, which ultimately decided the issue and made the statute of 1232 a fatal landmark on the road from monarchy to princely aristocracy, from imperial unity to federal fragmentation.

Henry's independent policy, which in the end led only to a further weakening of royal power, had aroused serious misgivings in the Emperor. When they met at Aquileia in 1232 a reconciliation was achieved by the king's complete submission to his father's will, but the mistrustful Emperor only renewed Henry's authority in Germany after imposing humiliating restrictions upon it. Henry swore obedience and promised to show favour to the princes, who would be released from their fealty and bound to act against him if he broke his word. The pope, who was more dependent than ever on Frederick's help against revolutionary activity in Rome, even persuaded Frederick to threaten Henry with outlawry as the penalty of disobedience.

These restrictions had the same effect on the touchy and restless young king as the oath of homage had once had on Henry V. The pressure of the princes and the censures of a father who had become almost a stranger to him seemed now unbearable and drove him into rebellion. In addition to certain *ministeriales*, the rising dynasties of counts and *Freiherren* in the south-west (who hoped to gain from conflict between crown and princes) probably exercised a bad influence on Henry.

The religious excitement which seized Germany at this time could hardly have a calming effect; on the contrary, it stoked the fires of conflict between king and Emperor. The influence of the new Mendicant Orders was beginning to be felt in Germany. Franciscan convents had multiplied with remarkable speed since the 1220's, and the image of St Francis shone more brightly than ever after his death in 1226 and his canonisation only two years later. Many who could not join the Order were filled with his ideals of poverty, self-sacrifice and highly personal religion. The sterner and more dogmatic spirit of the Dominicans was influential too, and in 1231 they had been given an independent commission, alongside that of the usual ecclesiastical authorities, to combat heresy. Elizabeth, wife of the landgrave of Thuringia, and Master Conrad of Marburg (a secular priest, but endowed with a full measure of Dominican intensity) are typical representatives of the two influences, and their destinies were closely linked. Elizabeth, daughter of the king of Hungary, was gentle, impressionable and completely devoted to the Franciscan ideal of poverty. After the death of her husband in 1227 she joined the Franciscan Third Order. Devoting herself more and more to a life of total renunciation, to extreme ascetic practices and to works of charity, she soon undermined her health; when she died in 1231 her body was almost torn to pieces by the crowds, eager for relics, who already regarded her as a saint before her formal canonisation in 1235. Her confessor Conrad, a hard, narrow, gloomy and fanatical figure, directed her religious life according to a plan of his own, alternately driving her on and reining her in; if his was the world of torment portrayed in the art of the Spanish Counter-Reformation, she was a Madonna from the school of Cologne. Empowered by the pope to take charge of the Inquisition, after Elizabeth's death he launched the first great persecution of heretics in Germany. Particularly in the Rhineland, a monstrously extended series of trials gave rise to an orgy of half-crazed fanaticism, blood-lust and greed, which lasted for several years; about the same time, religious tension expressed itself in Italy through the devotional movement of the 'Great Alleluia' led by the Dominican John of Vicenza, who for a short time held in the March of Treviso a position of spiritual and secular dominance like that of Savonarola later on.

Shortly before John's eclipse in September 1233, Conrad of Marburg, raging ever more furiously in Germany, had fallen victim to his enemies' hatred in the open street; the high tide of the movement now began to recede. The peasants of Stedingen on the lower Weser had still to pay the price of their 'heresy' in refusing tithes to the archbishop of Bremen; they were wiped out after a brave resistance in 1234. But the persecutors' excesses had already provoked profound disgust in influential German circles. King Henry made himself the instrument of a general desire when in Frankfurt in February 1234 he put an end, at the princes' wish, to all preaching of crusades and to all campaigns of violence against alleged heretics on the ground that they overturned civil order; a general land-peace was proclaimed and accusations of heresy were again to be subject to the sober judgement of the ordinary courts.

However justified and well-intentioned this decision may seem to us, it agreed very ill with the policy of the Emperor at that moment: in 1232 Frederick had renewed and sharpened the proclamation he had made against heresy at his coronation, and had extended it to the whole Empire. At this point Frederick was laying great weight upon agreement and co-operation with the pope, to whom he had once more offered the position of arbiter in the Lombard question. Moreover, even if full weight is given to the fateful tensions which formed the specific background to a conflict between father and son which grew steadily more acute, the conclusion still imposes itself that while the ill-advised young man may indeed have been moved by humane considerations, his actions were not for that reason any the more justified. Self-willed and unstable, dissolute in his private life, given to hasty advances and sudden withdrawals, he possessed neither the fixity of purpose nor the clear vision of the possible which alone would have made him capable of pursuing an independent policy. At odds with the strongest forces in contemporary Germany, the princes and the Church, and supported only by a handful of bishops, abbots and towns in addition to numerous lesser lords and *ministeriales*, he dared to rebel against a father who was just about to reach the height of his power; he blocked all avenues to a reconciliation not merely by an alliance with France but also by making a treasonable agreement with the Lombard League under which he light-heartedly contravened every Hohenstaufen tradition by closing the Alpine passes to imperial troops.

But Frederick, who had observed these latest developments with remarkable calm, had no need of an army; he came alone, though surrounded with all the majesty of an Emperor. Everything was in readiness; he needed only to draw the net tight. Within a short time the incautious rebel found himself deserted by his followers, deprived of all assistance, and forced to surrender. He was imprisoned in Apulia until he found an early death by his own hand in 1242. The father did not find it easy to take this course of action, but the statesman had no choice. To improve the prospects of his dynasty (which, aside from Henry's young sons, now depended on a single life) he shortly afterwards contracted a new marriage with the English princess Isabella. This shift in foreign policy away from the old alliance with France—it was partly the consequence of French encroachment in Provence—led in domestic affairs to a final reconciliation with the Welfs when their family possessions in Brunswick and Lüneburg were enlarged and raised to the status of a duchy. The brilliant meeting of the court at Mainz in 1235, at which this occurred, was significant for Germany in other ways as well.

The easy suppression of the revolt and an unusual readiness to co-operate on the part of the curia—which, perhaps not without ulterior motive, had lent Frederick a great deal of assistance against Henry—had much increased the Emperor's prestige and had thereby simplified the task of re-establishing the order which had been greatly upset by the disturbances of recent years.

The great land-peace of Mainz in 1235, which accomplished this task, stands high in importance above all similar imperial decrees of earlier or later times—even in its outward form, for it is the first law of the Empire of which we possess, in addition to the operative Latin text, a German version which was probably intended as a preliminary announcement. It is still more important because of its comprehensive nature. It repeated older provisions and added new, decisively extended criminal law and the punishment of crime and tried thereby to give new life to the ordinary processes of the courts, to prevent future disturbances of the peace, to secure communications and to protect from usurpation the imperial rights of toll, coinage and safe-conduct which had not been surrendered in principle although their exercise had been much restricted by the two great privileges to the princes. Later ages often repeated these provisions, which re-emphasised the sovereign rights of the Empire after earlier concessions to the principle of federalism, and they became the foundation for all future developments. A final significance lies in the more or less clearly visible transference to the Empire of Sicilian legal concepts and institutions. This is most obvious in the establishment of a justiciar of the Empire,[1] a man of free condition appointed for a fixed period and according to administrative law, to be the king's permanent representative in the supreme court, and also in the

[1] By clause 28 of the land-peace of Mainz: Pullan 215–6.

importance attached to a regular written system of record and the
collecting of precedents, shown in the appointment of a special
notary with exactly defined functions.

These and similar examples are not cases of the forcible trans-
plantation of alien law, but of the entirely beneficial influence of
advanced Sicilian constitutional practice—although, like other
tendencies towards the strengthening and revival of imperial
power contained in the same law, only careful cultivation could
have made them bear fruit in Germany. There may have been
more cases of this kind than the accidental preservation of evidence
allows us to ascertain. Similar favourable influences seem at any
rate to have operated in the field of taxation. The lucky discovery
of a list of tax-receipts from royal cities for the year 1241 has
shown that, contrary to previous belief, the royal exchequer had a
single central organisation and a considerable regular income
which might on occasion he supplemented by extraordinary
assessments.

Frederick's last visit to Germany (it extended from 1235 to
1237, with an interval from August to December 1236 for the
Italian campaign) showed indications of an increase in the power
of the monarchy in other respects as well. The royal estates were
being enlarged once more. The Emperor sought, for instance, to
secure the northern approaches to the Gotthard pass (which had
only recently been opened, at any rate for trading purposes), and
used Sicilian money to buy up the claims of the king of Bohemia
(son-in-law of his own uncle Philip) to extensive Hohenstaufen
estates in Swabia. Nothing shows better the degree to which his
power had grown than the fact that he persuaded the princes,
without compensation, to elect his nine-year-old son Conrad IV
as king of the Romans and Emperor-to-be in 1237. Future
attempts at independence, like those Henry (VII) had made, were
forestalled this time by withholding royal coronation; nominally
under the control of a prince as imperial procurator, in practice
guided by trustworthy men like Godfrey of Hohenlohe, the young
king was simply to be the vicegerent of the Emperor in Germany
and Upper Burgundy. Moreover, Frederick was already attempt-
ing the bold stroke—far more important than Henry VI's efforts
in Meissen—of securing direct imperial rule in the south-east by
acquiring Austria and Styria (which had been united with Austria
since 1192 by a dynastic agreement). In conjunction with the

considerably enlarged and well-organised imperial estates in Alsace, Swabia and Franconia, this could have formed the nucleus of a revived central power north of the Alps. The last Babenberger, duke Frederick II the Quarrelsome, an impetuous and ambition-ridden young man, had come into conflict with the Emperor in 1236 and 1237 on personal grounds and because of the hasty way in which he had used Barbarossa's charter to build up his territorial authority; the revolt of his brother-in-law Henry VII was only loosely connected with this dispute. The next steps in this affair are very reminiscent of the events which led to the fall of Henry the Lion—the way the Emperor moved against him only after constant consultation with the other princes, received insolent replies to his repeated summons, outlawed duke Frederick and entrusted the execution of the sentence to Austria's princely enemies before taking action himself, the widespread desertions among the duke's supporters, the raising of Vienna to the status of an imperial city. Frederick wanted more than his grandfather had sought then: he aimed at incorporating the two duchies permanently into the direct administration of the Empire, contrary to the prevailing customary law. But whereas Barbarossa had concentrated his whole force upon a more limited objective (admittedly against a far stronger opponent) and had gained a complete victory by doing so, his grandson believed that he could at the same time also fulfil a grander design, and so squandered his chances of lasting success. The duke put up a stubborn defence in one part of his lands, and the fighting dragged on. Nevertheless, Frederick here directed the German monarchy along a profitable path which he himself followed again later, but which Rudolf of Habsburg was the first to pursue to its appointed end.

If the Emperor failed at this moment to persist long enough in a task the importance of which he had correctly estimated, the explanation lies in the far greater struggle in which he now became involved. For the Lombards' participation in King Henry's treasonable plans had created a new situation in northern Italy too, and presented the Emperor with a long-awaited opportunity to declare war on the League. The outbreak of hostilities made the pope's recent commission to mediate superfluous, and swept the German princes into a unanimous decision in favour of war against the Lombards at Mainz in 1235. The Emperor used the cere-monies surrounding the reburial of the bones of his relative St

Elizabeth at Marburg to give religious sanction to the start of the campaign of 1236.

These events had put the curia into an extremely delicate position. The Emperor's power—rather than the justice of his cause—warned Gregory against openly supporting the rebels. Would not the crushing of this last element of resistance, however, make Frederick strong enough to extinguish all freedom, that of the papacy first and foremost? The curia therefore began to work against him in secret. Scarcely veiled support for the Lombards and long lists of complaints against the Emperor (which alleged practically everything except the real grounds of conflict) alternated with new but vain attempts at conciliation. All efforts failed in face of the Emperor's refusal to agree that the peace of Constance could still be regarded as valid law.

A decision could only be reached on the field of battle. Frederick's brilliant victory over the Lombard troops at Cortenuova (south-east of Bergamo) on 27 November 1237 gave him at one stroke the chance of securing a solution in accord with his wishes. At the peace negotiations which the Milanese opened under the shadow of their terrible defeat, the victor could have secured everything that the honour and the advantage of the Empire required, well beyond the provisions of the peace of Constance. It was Frederick's tragedy that he was unable to show in victory the skilful moderation which had brought his grandfather so much success after the defeat of Legnano, and that memories of the 1162 policy of force prevailed instead. He was possessed by a passionate hatred of the Milanese which distorted his vision and led him into politically ill-advised action; he demanded unconditional surrender from them, as he had from his son. The Milanese and their allies could not bring themselves to accept this final humiliation. The war went on. It was the most critical moment in Frederick's life. Instead of agreeing to an honourable and advantageous peace in Lombardy, which would have left him free to concentrate his forces against his chief enemy, the Roman curia (which was at that time completely isolated), he risked everything for a formal satisfaction of his pride which would have changed nothing substantial, and conjured up the endless struggle which was to bring down both the Empire and the house of Hohenstaufen.

The striking successes of the previous years seem however to have created in the Emperor an exaggerated feeling of Caesarean omnipotence which he showed in a growing torrent of boastful manifestoes. He thought himself strong enough to crush not only the Lombards but the papacy too if necessary, should it oppose his ultimate aim, the revival of the Empire in the Eternal City itself, its ancient seat. From Rome as its centre, government by Sicilian-style officials was to extend over the whole of Italy. He enlisted the help of the Roman aristocracy, collected a body of supporters by distributing money, fiefs and privileges, and even scored some success in his attempts to divide the college of cardinals. The triumphal despatch to Rome of the Milanese standards captured at Cortenuova and the display of them on the Capitol must have seemed an open challenge to the pope. Frederick could not but feel himself a truly universal ruler when he appealed to all kings to show their solidarity with him in the common cause of legitimism against the rebellious Lombards, and there came in answer, not only English, French, Castilian and Hungarian troops but also contingents from the Greek Emperor of Nicaea and even from the sultan of Egypt to join the campaign of 1238 and to fight under his banner. This certainly showed the universal acclaim Frederick had secured; from the military point of view, however, it was little more than pageantry, calculated to create alarm and despondency in the enemy's ranks but scarcely capable of facilitating the siege of a strongly-fortified city like Brescia, which was the first objective. The failure of this undertaking, after heavy losses in two months of fighting, was the signal for the pope to break off relations.

Gregory IX had long been making secret preparations for this moment. The Emperor had most incautiously let his aims be known, and they threatened everything which the curia had won during the last two hundred years. What would become of the pope's freedom and independence if Italy were subject to a centralised imperial government in Rome? He would have to be content to play the part of an imperial bishop once more, and would be even more subservient than in the days of Henry III. Rather than accept such a prospect, the ageing Gregory heroically chose a struggle to the death. Opinion in the college of cardinals had been changeable as long as Frederick was victorious, but his failure at Brescia gave the opposition party the upper hand even before Frederick provided new grounds for complaint. He married his natural son Enzio to the heiress of part of Sardinia and created him king of the island, over which the curia had long claimed sovereignty. It was Gregory who now organised the Lombards' resistance on the grand scale, won Genoa and Venice over to their cause, and extended their support throughout Italy by means of the Guelf party. Finally, on Palm Sunday, 20 March 1239, he excommunicated Frederick for a second time. On the same day there died Hermann of Salza, the sincerest mediator between the papal and imperial courts. The time for conciliation was past.

18

THE FINAL STRUGGLE BETWEEN
EMPIRE AND PAPACY (1239–1250)

The final conflict between the two universal powers which now began had grown out of purely political opposition: control over Italy was the prize for which in the last resort both were fighting. It was therefore essential for the Emperor to put the country on a war footing. His first care was to ensure the safety of his Sicilian base and to increase its productivity. The kingdom was protected against the infiltration of papal influence from outside by draconian frontier regulations, and was purified from suspect elements already within by the expulsion of the Mendicants; the papal enclave of Benevento was taken over and the Sicilian Church reduced to a state of weakness—such benefices as were not left vacant were filled by creatures of the Emperor. The whole administration was placed firmly in the hands of two supreme justiciars (one for the island and one for the mainland) who were themselves under the direct orders of the perambulatory imperial court; a severe system of collection under the control of a supreme exchequer saw to it that the tax-yield was increased. The 'recuperations', territory annexed to the papal states and forming a wedge between imperial Italy and Sicily, were spared no longer. Spoleto and Ancona were re-occupied without serious resistance, then southern Tuscany and its centre at Viterbo, and finally even the Patrimony and Rome itself were threatened. This cleared the way for the union of Sicily with imperial Italy; in future the governments of the two are indistinguishable. If the tendency towards centralisation and absolutism had at first only been apparent in piecemeal measures since the defeat of the Lombards, Frederick now of set purpose abruptly transformed the whole Italian administration, and under the pressure of war-time necessity carried his changes through with astonishing speed.

Here too the vital political motive force was the arbitrary and unrestricted will of the Emperor, who took all decisions in both civil and military affairs. Immediately next to him stood the

U

supreme justiciar—guaranteeing the link with Sicily—the unified imperial chancery, feverishly active under Peter della Vinea and Thaddeus of Suessa, and the imperial court of justice. The country was divided into some ten districts, each ruled by a vicar-general or a captain-general with a fixed tenure of office; like their subordinates the vicars, garrison commanders and city *podestàs*, they were appointed by the Emperor and responsible directly to him. Frederick's son and vicegerent Enzio, with the title of legate-general, alone had the duty of overseeing the government of all Italy without regional restriction. Experienced Sicilian administrators soon far outnumbered Italians or Germans in all these offices. Frederick was mistrustful—he studied physiognomy in order to probe the character of his servants—and he only felt sure of those whose property and families he held hostage. There was no room in this strict centralisation for feudal rights of suzerainty or even for the independence and long tenure which had hitherto characterised the royal offices of duke and margrave; still less for urban self-government, in respect of which Frederick went far beyond the aims of Barbarossa and Rainald of Dassel—he never allowed the loyal cities to elect their own *podestàs* but laid down regulations for their conduct, continually demanded new war-taxation, required absolute obedience in everything which concerned the Emperor and if necessary overruled anything which stood in his way, including laws which he had made himself. It was a system built on force and suspicion, and it required a genius at its head. Yet the object which Frederick had long set himself to achieve—the restoration of the ancient Roman Empire, based on its Italian homeland and lacking only its capital, Rome—was now secured at one blow: a triumph of organisation which, although less highly developed than the Sicilian monarchy and peppered with hostile territories in many places, yet exceeded Sicily in area and extended even as far as Burgundy and the bishopric of Trent. It represented Italy's sole opportunity for several centuries to throw off her tormenting and destructive divisions and attain the status of a unified national state, efficiently organised and peaceful at home and capable of securing recognition abroad. More even than in the Roncaglia decrees, progress was here linked with reaction. In all the Italian cities the common people were thoroughly tired of the bloody blessings of a century of freedom. Longing ardently for peace, they gazed indifferently upon the varying fortunes of the noble factions as they exhausted themselves in battle, and were just as ready to accept imperial domination as clerical, so long as it brought to an end the perpetual threats to their peace and quiet. As in antiquity, the process of development was from aristocratic self-government to democratic Caesarism, and thus it took the same direction as Frederick. The most convincing proof that Frederick was not aiming at something unhealthy or impossible of achievement is the way in which his creation still continued to develop after his death, even though the circumstances could not have been more unfavourable. The vicariates-general took root in some places, and out of them grew the later *signorie* (which were certainly no more tolerant of free elections than were their predecessors), and not only the last Hohenstaufen, but Charles of Anjou and the German rulers who later invaded Italy all utilised the remains of Frederick's administrative organisation because it was the only living element in the governmental structure and the only one capable of development.

However, the Italian communes' desire for freedom and independence was not yet extinguished. They rose in determined and often heroic resistance to the rule of the imperial officials, which suited the north and centre of Italy (where Germanic influence was stronger) far less well than the mixed population of Sicily, with its Byzantine traditions. The hostile cities, at first few in number, would certainly have been broken by the concentrated force of Frederick's power if the curia had not repeatedly stiffened their resistance with the implacable resolution which the Emperor's ambitions compelled it to adopt. For there was in the long run no room, in this unitary and absolutist Italian state, for the independent territorial sovereignty of the pope, which had for so long seemed the only guarantee of the Church's freedom of action. Frederick's schemes collapsed only because of the resistance of the papacy, which gathered all his enemies around itself and opposed his centralised system with one equally well-organised and far wider in scope.

For the pope was very much more than simply a political opponent. He was the head of an ecclesiastical community which comprised the whole of the western world, and as such was in a position to intervene in every situation, to influence it from within, and to secure new allies and new resources at every turn, while himself remaining to some extent immune from the extremes of

violence—since martyrdom would only have made his cause
stronger and since a new head grew on the body of the Church as
soon as one was struck off. This situation (completely hopeless
from their point of view) must be kept clearly in mind if the policy
of all the Emperors after the great Church reforms of the eleventh
century, and particularly that of Frederick II, is to be judged
correctly. Since complete victory was impossible so long as the
enemy stood firm, Frederick had long tried—sometimes by
exerting pressure, sometimes by making concessions—to reach a
peaceful and acceptable understanding with pope or cardinals,
until he was forced to give up the attempt during the last dreadful
life-and-death struggle. Up to that point—and rather because of
his cool appraisal of the facts than because of any lack of determination—he always appears as the flexible negotiator, anxious
for peace and holding firm only to certain minimum political
demands.

Since the pope as territorial sovereign now found himself in
direst need, and since the encirclement of Rome threatened the
independence of his spiritual authority as well, there were in
reality two offensives colliding with each other. Gregory had
declared war because, entirely in the spirit of Innocent III, he
denied the Empire and all the other states an independent right to
exist, appealing to the Petrine commission and the Donation of
Constantine as support for his own claim to supreme authority.
Frederick, on the other hand, would always have been content to
regard the papacy and the Empire as equals, and this is the reason
why he never considered setting up an anti-pope. Moreover, he
was also clever enough never to stress the Roman Empire's claim
to superior rank over the 'subreguli' as Rainald of Dassel had
done, although in the last analysis he was firmly convinced of it.
Instead he suggested that it was now as much the concern of all
monarchs to ward off papal interference as it had been earlier to
combat rebellious heretics, and he presented himself as simply the
foremost fighter in the common cause. His skilful diplomacy did
in fact ensure that in spite of all the pope's efforts to involve them
in the struggle, every foreign power remained at least neutral.

In the furious manifestoes which (contrary to what had been
the case during the Investiture Contest) now issued almost
exclusively from the chanceries concerned, views like these were
put forward belligerently by both sides. Frederick directed his

attack solely against the person of Gregory, whom he denounced as a disturber of the peace and unworthy to be the head of the hierarchy because he neglected the obligations which his office laid upon him. He had some success in breaching the solidarity of the college of cardinals by awakening oligarchical ideas and inducing some of its members to desert Gregory. Accusations like these were admittedly only made in reply to the mischievous rumours and violent slanders with which the papal chancery had opened the literary campaign against the Emperor—he was even accused of murder, of poisoning the landgrave of Thuringia, for instance, who had in fact died during the plague at Brindisi in 1227. Well-worn ecclesiastical punishments like excommunication, interdict and the dispensing of subjects from their allegiance no longer had their former effect, even though the papacy had acquired a tremendous army of propagandists in the shape of the new Mendicant Orders. Still stronger forms of terror were needed. The curia's publicists competed with each other to arouse horror of the Emperor among the superstitious masses. Lauded by his own supporters as the Messiah-Emperor who would come at the end of time and bring back the days of Christ and Augustus, Frederick was represented to the terrified people as the Beast of the Apocalypse who would rise out of the sea, as the incarnation of Antichrist who abandoned his faith and plotted the destruction of Christendom. His heretical beliefs were proved, asserted Gregory, by his remark that 'The world had been led astray by three deceivers, Moses, Christ and Mohammed, two of whom died honourable deaths, but Christ in shame on the cross, and that only fools believe that God, who created nature and all else, could have been born of a virgin'. Frederick immediately rejected this famous charge, and it is unlikely that he really made the remark in that form. In spite of his sceptical outlook, it would have been simply a matter of self-preservation for him to appear an orthodox Christian even if inwardly he had been more estranged from the medieval Church than could in fact possibly have been the case. As late as 1246 he voluntarily underwent an examination in the faith, in order to proclaim his acceptance of Christian doctrine to the world.

Only a few incidents in the changing fortunes of war deserve mention here. Frederick wanted to clear himself before an impartial general council summoned by the cardinals, and to put

his case against the pope; but such a scheme was too far ahead of
its time to be practicable. A synod of a very different kind was
summoned to meet in Rome at Easter 1241 by Gregory, who had
only with difficulty managed to maintain the shaky loyalty of the
citizens when the Emperor made his first attack in 1240. It was
plain before the council met that it would bow to Gregory's
influence; the Emperor was not accorded equal standing, but like
Otto IV was to be condemned and deposed. Frederick made it
clear that he would do all in his power to prevent such a council;
when a number of Spanish, French and Lombard prelates risked
taking passage for Rome in a Genoese fleet, Frederick had a
Sicilian and Pisan squadron fall upon them south-east of Elba in
May 1241. Many ships were sunk; over a hundred prelates
(among them three papal legates, two archbishops and six bishops)
were captured and consigned to Apulian gaols, where they were
roughly handled. This success increased the fear which the
Emperor's power inspired and hindered the plan to depose him;
but it caused much bad feeling in the Mediterranean world, and
the apocalyptic dread which had become attached to his name
seemed to be confirmed by his act of violence.

Further agitation was caused about this time by the savage
hordes of Gog and Magog, foretold in the Bible, who were breaking
in from the east. Rumours about the Mongol emperor Genghis
Khan and his conquest of almost the whole of Asia had reached the
west some time earlier, and the tremendous possibilities of
alliance against the common Moslem enemy which they suggested
had even caused Genghis to be taken for the mythical Christian
priest-king Prester John or the Messiah-David of the Jews. The
Mongol flood rolled westwards after his death. The Russian
principalities fell to his grandson Batu between 1237 and 1240,
and Hungary in April 1241; another army overwhelmed Poland,
crushed duke Henry II the Pious of Lower Silesia at the Wahl-
statt near Liegnitz on 9 April 1241 and devastated Moravia.
Terror seized the Empire and made the danger seem perhaps even
greater than it really was—for the Mongol onrush would surely
have been stemmed by the walls of Germany's fortified cities, even
if only after fearful carnage and destruction. A great opportunity
lay open before the Emperor: he could have been the saviour of
Europe and could have assumed the feudal suzerainty over
Hungary which he was offered—if only his hands had been free.

He could in fact do nothing beyond organising the defence of Germany under his son Conrad from a distance by a series of commands, entreaties and appeals for help. The pope, however, preferred to work against everything Frederick tried to do, and all attempts to bring them together foundered upon his invincible obstinacy. In spite of all this, the Mongol threat spared the Empire when the strength of the Austrian and Bohemian defences and their own immediate enjoyment of the Hungarian spoils checked their triumphant advance, and above all when a succession dispute broke out in central Asia at the end of 1241 on the death of the Great Khan Ogodai. Frederick now shut the pope up in Rome again, and found growing support among the citizens and even in the college of cardinals; Gregory seemed at the end of his tether. The situation was like that of 1084 or 1167; if Frederick had captured Rome he would perhaps have deposed Gregory. But the old pope died in the middle of August 1241, profoundly shaken by the events of the last few years, the victim of the convictions he had maintained with so much grandeur and determination. But just because Frederick had hitherto concentrated his attack so exclusively on the person of his enemy, he had now evidently to await the election of a new pope, from whom alone he could expect peace and the lifting of his excommunication.

The two-year vacancy which now began proved the most dramatic and painful in the whole of papal history. The necessary two-thirds majority could for a long time not be secured, in spite of the terrible privations, sickness and ill-treatment suffered by the cardinals, who were shut up in the filthy ruins of the Septizonium[1] by Frederick's enemy, the senator Matteo Orsini. When at last the peace party gained the upper hand, Celestine IV, whom they chose, was already dying. On his death, the remaining cardinals dispersed, to avoid having to undergo the same miseries a second time. Tedious negotiations with the Emperor over the release of the cardinals captured off Elba, which might even have led to an agreement about who should be elected, occupied many months until finally the Genoese Sinibald Fieschi was elected pope on 25 June 1243 and took the name of Innocent IV. Frederick, who thought Innocent his friend because he belonged to a Ghibelline family, welcomed the election as an augury of peace, and ordered thanksgiving services to be held throughout Sicily. He was never more cruelly deceived.

[1] Septimius Severus's building on the Palatine.

The very name 'Innocent' should have opened his eyes to the
intentions of the new pope, who had clearly been careful to disguise
his hostility of late—for Innocent was consciously and resolutely
determined from the beginning to enforce with all the power at his
command every claim to sovereignty made by his great predecessors, the theory behind whose work he explained, justified
and extended in his commentary on the Decretals. Admittedly, he
showed none of the fiery passion and violence of Gregory IX,
but—like Urban II long ago in contrast to Gregory VII—this
made him an even more dangerous political opponent. His
Genoese origin showed itself plainly in his supple and urbane
manners, in his crafty and quite unscrupulous diplomacy, in his
combination of caution and daring, in his adaptability to every
change of circumstance, in his quick recognition and ruthless
exploitation of every advantage, and in the absolutely realistic
way in which he faced events and managed men. Inwardness of
religious feeling, forgetfulness of self in mystical depths and the
scaling of moral heights were all foreign to him. His ice-cold
brain took only the tangible values of this world into account, but
he was masterly in his handling of them; in this respect he was
unquestionably superior to his opponent, the Emperor, the wealth
and variety of whose other talents he could not begin to approach.
With calm and statesmanlike deliberation he set before himself, as
his single object in life, the destruction of the Hohenstaufen
Empire. Consciously neglecting all the Church's other tasks,
disregarding every obstacle that canon law might present, and
sacrificing all sense of justice and finer moral feeling, he encashed
all the Church's assets for their political, military and financial
value. This unparalleled concentration of effort was rewarded by
the avoidance of defeat as long as Frederick lived, and by victory
after his death. But there was another side to the medal: the
ecclesiastical organism lost sight of the purpose for which it
existed; its religious and moral life wasted away, and at the height
of its secular power it was infected with the seeds of decay within.

Concern for Christendom's general need of peace as well as for
the agreements which had been made before his election compelled
Innocent at first to accept the Emperor's offer to negotiate.
Frederick kept the negotiations going, although he must have been
deeply hurt in September 1243 by the desertion of the imperial
city of Viterbo, which cardinal Rainer (the leader of the war-party

in the curia) contrived with the pope's knowledge while they were going on; he still believed that the undertakings made to him had been honourably intended, and hoped that the peace-party would secure a majority among the cardinals. So he broke off the siege of Viterbo soon after beginning it and would not let Rainer's gross treachery turn him against the imperial sympathisers there. Things actually reached the point where, after difficult negotiations and humiliating concessions on his part, the Emperor could agree to a peace-settlement on Maundy Thursday 1244; Innocent could again describe Frederick, the excommunicate, as 'devoted son of the Church and orthodox prince' in one of his sermons. All this was only possible because the trickiest point—the settlement of Lombard affairs, upon which no agreement had been reached— was passed over and reserved for later discussion. Upon this very question, which had already been the decisive element in the struggle under Gregory IX, the hoped-for agreement was now once again to founder at the last minute. Whereas Frederick carelessly took no trouble to conceal the fact that he intended to crush the rebels at once, they tried to get a provision that their differences with the Emperor should be judged by the pope alone written into the treaty itself. This demand was unacceptable to Frederick; when Innocent began to make corresponding alterations in the as yet incomplete draft of the peace-treaty, Frederick rejected them. Next, the papal party did everything they could to put Frederick in the wrong in the eyes of the world. Since Innocent could not justify his refusal of absolution solely on the ground that there was a difference of opinion over Lombard affairs, he disguised the real facts behind the charge that Frederick had broken his oath and had disregarded treaties by refusing the invitation to evacuate the papal states before receiving absolution. At the same time Innocent deceitfully held out the prospect of a personal meeting until his Genoese relations enabled him to flee from Rome at the end of June 1244. As soon as he was back in his native city, he boasted with the psalmist 'Our soul is escaped as a bird out of the snare of the fowlers; the snare is broken, and we are escaped'. But he did not feel safe until he reached Lyons, still nominally imperial territory but in fact almost independent and even inclining towards France. There, where no interference like that in Rome a few years earlier need be feared, he summoned a General Council to meet on 24 June 1245 and pronounce the sentence of God himself upon Frederick.

If until this moment the pope had sought peace in real earnest —which is by no means certain: indeed in view of his clear insight into the irreconcilability of their opposed positions it is very improbable—from now on he became unalterably determined to destroy Frederick and the whole house of Hohenstaufen. His supporters were to have only one further moment of serious hesitation—when the evil tidings came of the fall of Jerusalem in 1244 and of the other disasters to the Latin Christians in the east. Frederick grasped this opportunity to propose a three-year crusade under his personal leadership in return for peace, offered to restore all Church possessions under the strongest possible guarantees and apparently even took another step towards the settlement of the Lombard question, all of which forced Innocent to take into account the pressure of the peace party among the cardinals and the intervention of the French king. Thus on 6 May 1245, he once again, though doubtless without serious intent, let it be understood that Frederick's absolution was still a possibility. But the war-party now began a fierce counter-attack. Cardinal Rainer, who had been left behind in the neighbourhood of Rome to protect the Patrimony, sent violent but very persuasive propaganda to Lyons. When Frederick unwisely indulged his hatred for Viterbo by allowing his troops to raid the papal states, Rainer stoked the fires of discord by representing this as a serious breach of the peace and in the severest terms demanded the deposition of the Emperor. It was perhaps this which provided the excuse for another change in the curia's attitude. In any case, all hesitation was at an end by the time the council opened, but the Emperor had not been allowed to realise it.

In spite of the relatively small number of those attending (the Latin nations predominated), the Council of Lyons is unquestionably to be numbered among the General Councils. The skilful and impressive defence of Frederick by his representative, the justiciar Thaddeus of Suessa, was rewarded by the pope's reluctant grant, at the second session, of a short adjournment so that the Emperor could appear in person or send new plenary powers. But all was in vain against the curia's fixed intention of destroying him. Without waiting for a new envoy from the Emperor, Innocent surprised the council at its third session on 17 July 1245 by solemnly proclaiming the sentence of deposition which he had secretly prepared. A tendentious account of the peace-negotiations of the last few years was followed by a long list of Frederick's crimes (which, however, made no mention of the Lombard question, the chief matter in dispute) and finally by his deposition and anathematisation.[1] Thaddeus, who had to no purpose declared that any condemnation of his master was null and void, and had appealed to a new pope and a new Council, cried amid his tears 'This is a day of wrath, of misery and sorrow', but the majority of the Council raised no objection to the procedure.

Frederick, to whom the pope had so recently held out the prospect of absolution, seems to have been completely surprised by this sudden condemnation. The story is well known that on receiving the news from Lyons he sent for his treasure-chest, set a crown on his head and asked the bystanders to judge whether he had really lost it already. He realised at last that he had no choice but to fight to the death, and proclaimed his realisation with the words 'I have been the anvil long enough, now I will be the hammer'.

The immediate consequence of Frederick's deposition at Lyons was to involve Germany in the quarrel to an extent that was quite new. In spite of the efforts of the papal commissioner Albert Beham, archdeacon of Passau, the curia's propaganda could so far show only a few successes in the south-east; content with the privileges the Emperor had given them, the vast majority of both the ecclesiastical and the secular princes withstood every inducement. Beham had not even been able to prevent the princes from trying to secure peace through mediation in 1240, but in 1241 he had at last succeeded in winning over the three Rhenish archbishops, who from then on (mainly for reasons of territorial policy) formed the core of the anti-imperial opposition. On the other hand, a reversal of the previous situation gave the Hohenstaufen cause a strong hold in the south-east of the Empire, where King Wenzel of Bohemia and still more duke Otto II of Bavaria (to whose daughter Elizabeth the young Conrad IV was betrothed in 1243) provided invaluable support. On the whole the situation had not changed seriously to the Emperor's disadvantage until Innocent IV intervened here too after the Council of Lyons, and with far more effective weapons than his predecessor. He sent a special legate and kept him

---

[1] Tierney 144. Cf. 147 for the encyclical *Eger cui levia*, which justifies the deposition by explaining the grounds of papal authority.

plentifully supplied with money, he ensured that the ecclesiastical censures on Frederick and the threats against his partisans were proclaimed everywhere, he put the possessions of all his chief enemies under an interdict and by secret decree provided for all crusading vows to be converted into promises to wage war against the Hohenstaufen. Above all, he managed gradually and with few exceptions completely to shake the loyalty which, notwithstanding all his conflicts with the papacy, the majority of the bishops had shown towards the Emperor since his great territorial concessions. He did this by totally disregarding all religious, moral and canon-law obstacles which stood in his way—by granting out Church property, issuing pardons and dispensations for political reasons, giving benefices to papal creatures on a scale which often exceeded the number available, dealing in indulgences and simoniacal payments, by threats and punishments, excommunication and interdict, suspension and deposition and lastly in 1246 by the drastic step of suspending the cathedral chapters' right of election and reserving to the pope alone the right of appointment to ecclesiastical office. The backbone of the German Church was finally broken by all these measures.

On the pope's orders, the Rhenish archbishops now set up an anti-king in May 1246, after having for some time vainly hawked the crown round Germany, Denmark and France. The landgrave Henry Raspe, filled with ambition and not insensitive to religious influence, after long hesitation yielded to the persuasion of the curia, although he knew that he scarcely possessed the qualities required in a ruler on the grand scale. His royal seal showed the heads of St Peter and St Paul on the reverse side, exactly like a papal bull, and this was a symbol of his behaviour in regarding himself as the champion and tool of the papacy, in following the directions of the energetic legate Philip of Ferrara, and of his popular reputation as the 'parsons' king'. When King Conrad moved towards Frankfurt against him, papal gold enabled Henry to secure the defection of several lesser Swabian lords who thought they saw their own future advantage in the collapse of Hohenstaufen territorial power; but this was no great triumph. His supporters were few in number, for most of the princes held aloof and did not take sides in the struggle. A great opportunity again presented itself to Frederick in the extreme south-east at this same time, however. The Emperor had not lost sight of the duchy of

Austria, in spite of his earlier failure and of his Italian preoccupa-
tions. He had picked out Gertrude, the niece and heiress of the
last Babenberger, as his fourth wife, and he dangled a crown in
front of the duke's eyes as the reward for his consent. Everything
was settled at a meeting of the princes which Frederick held at
Verona in June 1245, while the Council of Lyons was sitting; but
then slanderous whisperings in ecclesiastical circles persuaded
Gertrude to refuse, and the whole plan collapsed. Duke Frederick
the Quarrelsome now died unexpectedly young and childless.
The Emperor acted at once; he annexed the duchy as an escheated
fief of the Empire, but instead of re-granting it after a year and a
day put it in the permanent charge of captains-general—thereby
most significantly transferring the essentials of his Italian system
of government to Germany.

Thus the whole south, apart from his slender following in
Swabia, was closed to Henry Raspe: for the financially powerful
imperial cities remained faithful to the Emperor, correctly recognising that their own predominant interest in peaceful trade and
free communications required a strong and unified central power.
There were even anti-papal currents among the population at
large. Since the struggle could now no longer be simply about the
person of the pope, after the Council of Lyons Frederick had gone
back to the ideas of Arnold of Brescia and the Waldensians by
contrasting the apostolic simplicity of primitive Christianity with
the pride, luxury and secularism of the papal Church, and
demanded that it return to its former ideals.[1] Demands like these
found echoes among the French nobility and the English clergy
which were highly inconvenient to the curia, while in Germany a
few agitators were bold enough to denounce the pope as Antichrist
and to hail the Emperor as the Heaven-sent reformer of the
Church. A mass-movement against the papacy was still quite
unthinkable, however, and Frederick's call for reform was not an
end in itself but one means among many others.

The papal cause suffered a particularly damaging blow with the
sudden death of the anti-king in February 1247, for not only did
Thuringia thereby come into the Hohenstaufen sphere of influence
but it became very difficult to find another papal candidate for
the throne. Count William of Holland eventually accepted the
position. Like Henry Raspe he was elected on papal orders (in

[1] Tierney 145–6.

October 1247) and almost exclusively by the ecclesiastical princes of the Rhineland. He was a brave and chivalrous young man, but not a prince of the Empire; he disappointed the hopes of the curia and had practically no authority outside the lower Rhineland. Neither of the anti-kings, in fact, had anything like the stature of archbishop Siegfried III of Mainz, for instance, on whose well-known monument they are represented as dwarfs receiving the crown at his hands. This was the main reason why the desperate exertions of the curia were unable, as long as Frederick lived, to shake Hohenstaufen authority north of the Alps.

These events in Germany had only a secondary importance however, beside the great struggle—growing daily more savage and more lurid—in the Italian theatre of war, where the personality of the Emperor was alone enough to hold all Europe spellbound. Small wonder if an attempt at the enemy's total destruction by means verging on the diabolical awakened a boundless fury on the other side, or if all finer feelings were forgotten in the feverish drive for total victory. Ezzelino da Romano, who on the Emperor's behalf extended his own tyrannical rule from Verona throughout the March of Treviso by the most dreadful crimes, was the most typical figure of this phase of the struggle. The example he gave of unlimited self-aggrandisement and of power founded upon wickedness was to be copied only too frequently by the tyrants of the Italian Renaissance. During these years he was only the most terrifying figure among many, and there were even men like him among those who led the papal troops—cardinal Rainer of Viterbo, for instance, or the legates Philip of Ferrara and Gregory of Montelongo.

To begin with there was not the slightest sign of a lessening of Frederick's power because the pope had deposed him. Above all, the kingdom of Sicily seemed in its strict seclusion proof against the pope's sapping and mining, until the great conspiracy of the spring of 1246 revealed how treacherous the ground was here too. The plot, which had wide ramifications, was headed by the pope's Parmesan brother-in-law Bernardo Orlando di Rossi, and its existence was known to Innocent himself; the intention was to make a clean sweep. A number of Frederick's senior and most trusted officials in Sicily and Italy, whose loyalty had been shaken by curial promises and by the dreadful course events had taken, were implicated in the plot. The murder of the Emperor (who was then at Grosseto in Tuscany) by treacherous members of his staff was to give the whole peninsula the signal to throw off the Hohenstaufen yoke. Enzio and Ezzelino, Frederick's most dreaded supporters, were also to be stabbed to death at a feast. Chance led to the premature discovery of the plot. The intending murderers fled from Grosseto to Rome; the papal army under cardinal Rainer which, according to the master-plan, was to attack Sicily, was beaten back from the frontier; and the rising in Sicily which other plotters started, on the false news of Frederick's death, was bloodily suppressed by Frederick himself. Although all this showed very clearly how much the ground quaked beneath his feet, and although it was bound to poison his already suspicious mind still more, this quick victory still represented another success, and it was followed by the recapture of Viterbo in May 1247 and by useful defections to the imperial side in western Lombardy.

After taking new security measures in the spring of 1247, Frederick felt his position in Italy and Sicily strong enough to risk an expedition to Germany. The planned march over the Brenner was cancelled on the news of Henry Raspe's sudden death, and Frederick led his troops through the western Alps towards Lyons to confront the pope in person. He had already gained control of the foothills and of the approaches right up to the city gates through his dynastic connections with the local nobility, notably the count of Savoy, and had even enlisted one or two French magnates in his service. According to an admittedly unreliable source, Frederick now even went as far as offering to renounce the imperial crown in favour of his son Conrad in order to ensure the succession, proposing to restrict himself to the Orient. Altogether it was a situation which caused the pope no little embarrassment.

But King Louis of France, on whose hitherto always carefully preserved neutrality Frederick still thought he could rely, was unwilling to allow a direct attack on the curia. He announced that he was ready to come to Innocent's aid at the head of an army. Further, a part of Frederick's position in Italy had already been undermined, and the explosion came at exactly the right moment for his enemies. Since Bologna was hostile to him, the La Cisa pass, which was protected by the city of Parma, represented his only line of communication with his rear south of the Apennines. In consequence of a bold stroke by Orlando di Rossi, in June 1247, Parma fell into the hands of the exiled papal party, who promptly collected a substantial body of Lombard troops from the surrounding country-side and prepared to defend themselves. This forced the Emperor to halt his march on Lyons. With the assistance of Enzio and Ezzelino, he beleaguered the city with a considerable army, and the siege became a test of strength for the outcome of which the world waited breathlessly. After several months the defenders seemed on the point of being starved out, when a bad piece of carelessness by the Emperor's troops turned hard-won victory into utter defeat. While Frederick was away hunting for a short time in February 1248, a sally by the garrison took by surprise the poorly-guarded wooden siege-works (they had been named Vittoria in over-confident anticipation of victory) and burned it down, scattered the army with heavy loss, killed Thaddeus of Suessa and captured the crown and the imperial seal. Frederick himself escaped only with difficulty to Cremona, whence with amazing resilience he advanced again only three days later with hastily-collected troops. Although he was able to continue the encirclement of Parma at a greater distance and to seize the crossing of the Apennines, the garrison of Parma had won themselves room to breathe and to manoeuvre, and the most serious consequence of their coup was the moral impression it created. This was felt at once in the Romagna, which was as good as completely lost to the Emperor after the defection of Ravenna in May 1248, and it became increasingly difficult for Frederick to maintain his position in central Italy. Indirect consequences could be traced all over Europe, and they can be said to have lasted until the present time. Recent accounts have continued to put forward the view that this defeat in front of Parma was the decisive turning-point in Frederick's career, and that after it he was a broken and defeated man, for whom nothing could now go right.

This impression is very much bound up with the fearful personal blows which fate dealt the Emperor during his last years, and which cast their shadow over the end of his reign. At the beginning of 1248, just as he had begun to feel that he could resume his march on Lyons, an attempt to murder him by poisoning his drink was made by his court doctor, who had been bribed by the enemy while he was in their hands; the attempt failed at the last minute, and in a manifesto addressed to princes and peoples Frederick held the pope personally responsible for it. Still more shocking was the almost simultaneous discovery of the serious embezzlement of which his most trusted minister had made himself guilty. Peter della Vinea had risen to the highest office from middle-class origins through his outstanding legal skill and remarkable gifts of style and oratory, trained in the schools of his native Capua. Prominently occupied as chief justiciar for many years in administering justice and making law in Sicily, concerned in all the most important diplomatic missions and in *de facto* joint control of the chancery with Thaddeus of Suessa, Peter had been appointed sole head of the chancery in 1247 with the title of imperial protonotary, while as logothete he was the Emperor's sole mouthpiece. Since as adviser he enjoyed Frederick's complete trust and in truth 'held the keys to his heart'[1]—because he alone decided which letters and which petitions should reach the Emperor and which should be dealt with summarily—he was rightly regarded as the most powerful man in the state after his master. His strength of moral purpose was plainly not proof in the long run against the temptations of his responsible office; it came to light that he had used his position to enrich himself to an unprecedented degree, and had done this at a time when the imperial treasury, well-nigh emptied by paying the troops, could only be replenished by forced loans and by raising tax-assessments to an almost intolerable level. It was the most terrible disillusionment of Frederick's life. At the same time the fall of this powerful man (he cheated the torturers by suicide in prison at San Miniato) did serious moral harm to the Hohenstaufen cause. The affair attracted a tremendous amount of attention at the time, and since the reasons for Peter's disgrace were not made public there was plenty of room for the wildest rumours. Peter can certainly be cleared of the charge that he had treasonable correspondence with the papacy, a charge which was bound to be suggested by the fact that his fall coincided with the poisoning attempt. On the other hand it is impossible to accept Dante's kindly assertion[2] that he was innocent, and there is in fact not the slightest reason to doubt that Frederick's condemnation was justified.

Frederick lost his most capable general, King Enzio, only a

---

[1] Dante, *Inferno* xiii. 58.
[2] *Inferno* xiii. 74–5.

V

few months after his ablest minister. Enzio was the offspring of
one of the Emperor's German liaisons; blonde, good-looking and
vigorous, he was the most gifted of all Frederick's sons, and the
most like his father in combining strength of will with genuine
intellectual interests. Often foolhardy in battle, he fell into the
hands of the Bolognese in May 1249 during an unimportant
skirmish at Fossalta near Modena. He was well treated, but
neither the threats nor the promises of the Emperor could procure
his release. He suffered the worst fate of all: he spent long years
of inactivity in prison, bewailing the fall of his house. He died
only in 1272.

The effect of all these blows on the temperament of Frederick,
as his loneliness and isolation grew, is certainly not to be underestimated; but in the last resort they were only misfortunes which,
although they might affect the political or military situation in one
way or another, could not decide it in the long run. Nothing
would be farther from the truth than to speak of a gradual decline
in the Emperor's fortunes or to assume that, broken in mind and
body, Frederick himself despaired of victory. He had undoubtedly
suffered serious defections among his Italian supporters, but his
position was improving again in 1250.

The kingdom of Sicily was still the strong and undisturbed
foundation of his power. It had just provided ample resources for
new military preparations. An attack which the pope tried to
launch from central Italy under the cardinal legate Peter Capoccio
had been easily beaten off during the summer of 1249, and most
of the papal conquests in the March of Ancona were reoccupied
twelve months later. It was becoming increasingly difficult to
maintain imperial sovereignty in Tuscany, however: embittered by
taxation and the demands of war, the population of Florence rose
in revolt and set up an independent and non-partisan government
in September 1250, but here again new successes turned the tide
in the Emperor's favour. The Romagna had returned to her
allegiance on the recapture of Ravenna in October 1249. In
Lombardy Frederick's vicar-general, the brutal margrave Hubert
Pallavicini, took in August 1250 a bloodthirsty revenge on Parma
for the defeat at Vittoria and organised forces round Cremona and
the recently recaptured Piacenza which presented a powerful
threat to Milan. A notable victory was gained at sea over the
Genoese, and internal dissensions threatened the Lombard

League. After further victories in Piedmont, nothing more seemed to stand in the way of an advance on Lyons. The pope's rear was no longer protected by France. Louis IX, who had had bitter experience on crusade of the pope's failure to support him, and who had just ransomed himself and his army out of the hands of the Egyptians in April 1250, called loudly from the east for the conclusion of peace with the Emperor, who alone could offer him effective assistance; if peace were not made, he would no longer tolerate the pope's presence in Lyons. Innocent busied himself with inquiries about a refuge among the English in Bordeaux, but found little response; he would have yielded nothing yet, but he had to expect increasingly strong pressure upon him to make peace.

In spite of occasional bouts of illness, Frederick himself was still so full of energy that he was even on the point of contracting a fourth marriage with the daughter of duke Albert of Saxony in order to secure his dynasty. When all the Italian rebels were finally crushed, he intended to move to the north; his last letters to the Greek emperor John Vatazes breathe confidence in victory. An attack of dysentery, carelessly treated, struck him down suddenly at Fiorentino in Apulia on 13 December 1250; he was not quite fifty-six years old. His will provided for his son Conrad IV to succeed to all his territories, and for Conrad's half-brother Manfred to be vicegerent in Italy and Sicily during any absence. He called for a just settlement of the relations of Empire and papacy and, clothed in a Cistercian habit, received absolution and the last rites from his old and trusted friend archbishop Berard of Palermo. His body was laid to rest beside his parents in Palermo cathedral.

Frederick himself died undefeated, but his death brought ruin to the Hohenstaufen cause; for he had no successor worthy of him, and death and disunion played havoc with his dynasty. In spite of these extraordinarily unfavourable conditions the struggle lasted for another eighteen years, and the curia only gained the day by bringing in the French—'this broken reed, whereon if a man lean it will go into his hand and pierce it'—and this speaks volumes for the strong position in which, despite everything, Frederick still left his work when he died.

Germany has little reason, from the nationalist point of view, to wish that he had been victorious: for since Germany offered far

less favourable ground than Italy for the establishment of centralised rule by officials, she would almost certainly have sunk to the
position of a mere appendage of the Empire. But a deep longing
for vanished imperial glories remained in the hearts of thousands
and was magnified by the miseries of later years. It left its mark
in German legend, in which the person of Frederick II became
the focus for a mixture of mythology, national aspiration and
apocalyptic prophecy, all of which was localised on the Kyffhäuser
in Thuringia, not least because the last hopes of the Ghibellines
later rested on the son of the imperial princess Margaret, Frederick
the Bold of the House of Wettin.[1]

But memories of the struggle with the Church were long in
Germany, and it was no less a figure than Ranke who ventured to
assert in his *History of the World* that 'the injustice of the victorious
papacy's conduct was the prime reason for the later rift in the
Church, so far as this sprang from popular feeling and not from
theology alone'. 'What Luther bewails in the opening of his
address to the Christian nobility of Germany', he continues,
'—the fact that the beloved princes Frederick I and II and many
another German Emperor were so lamentably trodden under foot
and oppressed by the popes—the memory of this was preserved all
through the dying medieval centuries, particularly in the cities,
which at the last for just this reason championed the Hohenstaufen
cause as it went down to defeat.'

---

[1] Frederick the Bold, 1257–1323, son of Frederick II's daughter Margaret
and Albert of Thuringia and Meissen. Gregory X forbade his election to the
vacant imperial throne in 1273.

Damietta 256, 257
De Consideratione 147
Deliberatio of Innocent III 240
Denmark: demands of Gregory VII 76–7; dependence on Henry the Lion 198; relations with Empire 206, 241, 259
Dôle, synod of 181
Dominic, Saint 249, 279
Donation of Constantine 76
Dualism 16

Edessa 143, 146
Eger 158, 247
Ekbert of Meissen 95
Elizabeth of Thuringia 279
Engelbert, archbishop of Cologne 258–9, 260
England 237; lay investiture prohibited in 76
Enzio, king of Sardinia 285–6, 288, 302, 304
Ernst II of Swabia 38
Eskil of Lund, archbishop 167–8
Estonia 248
Eugenius III, pope 142, 143, 148, 149, 151, 162
Ezzelino da Romano 300, 302

Forchheim 86
France: popes in 114, 128–9, 180–3, 295–8, 301–2; synods in 99, 111, 179, 181
Francis of Assisi, Saint 249, 262, 278
Frangipani 114, 128
Frederick I, Barbarossa 12–19, chapters 10–13, *passim*; territorial policy 10, 156–9, 179–80, 188–9, 197, 209–11; regard for law 154–5, 159, 172–3; Italian expeditions 162–4, 169–73, 179–84, 190–3, 212; diplomacy 156, 183, 189, 191, 195, 210–1, 215–6; landpeace 159; relations with bishops 159–61, 168, 177–8, 215; treaty of Constance 162; Besançon 167–8; Roncaglia 172–6; papal schism 177–81, 188, 194, 202; relations with Henry the Lion 202–4, 206, 210; revival of culture under 206–7; third crusade 216–8

Frederick II, Emperor 21–32, chapters 16–18 *passim*; religion 24–5, 269–70, 280; as law-maker 25, 257–8, 268, 272, 276; Landpeace of Mainz 28–9, 281; elected king 227; ward of Innocent III 236, 240, 252; end of minority 242; Golden Bull of Eger 247; alliance with France 247; Lombard League 261–2, 283–5; crusade 254, 256–7, 261–2, 264–5; conflict with Gregory IX 264, 266–7, 285–6, 290–1, 293; crowned in Jerusalem 265; treaty of Ceprano 266–7, 271, 273; and culture 269–71; financial system 273–4; Reichstag of Ravenna 274; relations with Henry (VII) 278, 280–1, 283; Parma 302
Frederick of Büren, duke of Swabia 87, 103
Frederick of Upper Lorraine (pope Stephen IX) 52, 60
Frederick II Hohenstaufen, duke of Swabia, brother of Conrad III 120, 123, 127, 133
Frederick the Quarrelsome, duke of Austria 283, 299
Frederick of Rotenburg, duke of Swabia, son of Conrad III 189
Frederick of Swabia, eldest son of Frederick I, duke 189, 216, 219
Fulda 53

Gebhard of Eichstätt (pope Victor II) 53–4
Gelasius II, pope 114
Gelnhausen 18, 203–4, 215
Genghis Khan 292
Genoa 258
Gerhoh of Reichersberg 9n2, 127, 161, 183
German eastward expansion 133–5, 145, 151; under Henry the Lion 198–9; decline of 206
German towns *see* Towns
Gertrude, wife of Henry the Proud 123; secondly of Henry Jasomirgott 140
Gesta Friderici 172–3, 174, 176
Gisela, queen 34, 37
Godfrey de Bouillon, duke of Lower Lorraine 100

Godfrey of Lorraine, duke, opposed
Henry III 57–8, 64–6; married
Beatrix of Tuscany 58, 60, 62, 66,
81
Golden Bull of Eger 247
Goslar 55–6, 193.
Gratian, *decretum* of 72–3, 142
'Great Alleluia' 279
'Great Design' of Barbarossa 13
Gregory VI, pope 50
Gregory VII pope, Saint: as Hilde-
brand, chaplain, archdeacon 50,
52, 62; influence on papal policies
62–4, 71, 73–4; confronted Henry
IV 3, 4, 9, 79, 81–3, 88, 91;
character 74, 178; aims 74–7,
118; *Dictatus Papae* 77; recog-
nised Rudolf 88; alliance with
Roger Guiscard 91; death 92;
Gregory VIII, pope 215
Gregory IX, pope, Hugo (Ugolino) of
Ostia 262, 295; and Frederick II
264, 266–7, 285–6, 290–1, 293
Guiscard *see* Robert, Roger Guis-
card of Socily
Guyot de Provins, troubadour 206

Hadrian IV, pope 12, 13, 163, 176;
alliance with emperor Manuel
164; Besançon 10, 167–9
Halinard of Lyons, monk 50
Halle 21, 240
Harz 7, 70
Harzburg 71, 72, 248
Hattin, battle of 217
Heerschild 160–1, 204
Heidelberg 158
Heinrich von Veldeke, poet 206
Henry II, Emperor 1, 33, 40; and
reform 49; recognised Saxon rights
70
Henry III, Emperor 2–3, 7, Chapter
2 *passim*
Henry IV, Emperor 3–10, 12; Chapters 3–6, *passim*; territorial policy
70, 86–7, 97; Saxon risings against
70, 72, 82–3, 86–7, 90, 95, 103–4;
conflict with Gregory VII 68–93;
supported by towns 71–2, 92;
relations with bishops 73, 77–8,
80, 84, 89, 96; Canossa 83–6;
conflict with Urban II 94–7;
Peace of God 94, 101; conflict

with son Conrad (IV) 97–8; conflict with son Henry V 103–6
Henry V, Emperor 9–10, Chapter 7
passim; conflict with Henry IV
102–6; betrothal to Matilda of
England 108; conflict with Paschal II 108–10; territorial policies
111–3; Concordat of Worms 116
Henry VI, Emperor 19–21, Chapter
14, *passim*; king and co-regent
189, 206, 212–3; married Constance
of Sicily 210, 212–3; territorial
policies 213, 214, 221–3, 224;
plan for hereditary Empire 225–8;
Henry (VII) king of Germany 23,
225–6, of Sicily 246, 254, of
Romans 258; taken to Germany
254–5; conflict with Lombard
League 261–2, 280, 283; conflict
with princes 20, 275–6, 278; relations with towns 275–8; conflict
with Frederick II 278, 280–1, 283
Henry I, king of England 108
Henry II, king of England 155, 273;
relations with Church 181–3, 190,
242; relations with Henry the Lion
183, 201, 205
Henry of Champagne, count 180
Henry Jasomirgott, duke of Bavaria
140, 156; duke of Austria 157
Henry of Kalden, *Reichsmarschall*
225, 229
Henry the Lion, duke of Saxony and
Bavaria 135, 140; relations with
Frederick I 18–9, 169, 182, 189,
192–3, 202–5, 210, 216, 222;
territorial claims 140, 151, 157,
198–200; landpeace 144; relations
with Henry II of England 183,
201, 205; policy and economics
198–202; fall 203–5, 207, 216, 237;
conflict with Henry VI 221; death
224
Henry of Mainz, archbishop 144,
152
Henry the Proud, duke of Bavaria
123, 156; Sicilian territories 133,
135, 137; relations with Innocent
II 136; conflict with Conrad III
138–9; death 140
Henry Raspe, antiking 298–9
Hereditary Empire, plan for 19–20,
225–8, 237

Heresy 249, 256, 279, 280
Hermann of Metz, bishop 88
Hermann of Salm, anti-king 90, 95
Hermann of Salza, Teutonic order 260, 286
Hermann of Thuringia, landgrave 239
Hildebrand *see* Gregory VII
Hildegart of Bingen, visionary 139
Hirsau 87
Hohenstaufen: 'idea of Empire' 16, 154; estates 87, 282; feud with Welfs 133, 139–40, 152, 237
Holstein 198
Honorius II, pope 116, 124, 130
Honorius III, pope 254, 256, 262
Hugh Candidus 52, 80
Hugh of Cluny, abbot 84, 105
Humbert, cardinal 61
Humbert of Moyenmoutier 52–3
Hungary 113, 158; lay investiture prohibited in 76

Innocent II, pope 10, 128, 135, 148; exile from Rome 128–9, 133; refused by investiture 131, 132; crowned Lothar 31–2; supported by Bernard of Clairvaux 128; campaign against Roger II 136, 141
Innocent III, pope 20–3, 178, 256; and German succession 232–50, 254; character 232–3; policies 233–5, 263, 290; guardian of Frederick II 236; relations with Otto IV 239–40, 242–5; *Deliberatio* 240; relations with Philip of Swabia 242–3
Innocent IV, pope 293; character 294; policies 294; Council of Lyons 295–8; set up anti-kings 298–300
Inquisition 279–80
Irene, Byzantine princess 229, 238
Isaac Angelus, Byzantine emperor 217–8, 229
Isabella of Brienne, Empress 261, 264
Ivo of Chartres 115

Jaffa, treaty of 264–5
Jerusalem, fall of 217, 296; ceded to Frederick II 264–5

John XIX, pope 42
John, king of England 223, 241, 242
John of Salisbury 179

Kaiserswerth, coup d'état of 64–5, 70
Knights of the Sword 260
Kyffhaüser, legend of Frederick II at 306

Landpeace 8–10, 101, 133, 144, 159, 280; of Mainz 28–9, 281
Lateran Councils: first 117; second 142; third 196, 210; fourth 249
Lay investiture, prohibition of 62, 74, 76, 78, 82, 89, 103, 106, 108, 110–1, 113, 116, 131–2, 160, 177–8
Legnano, battle of 193, 195, 284
Leihezwang 18, 21, 30, 204, 225
Leo IX, pope 3, 51–4
Leopold of Austria, duke 223
Leopold IV of Austria, margrave 139, 140
Liège 105–6, 222
Liegnitz, battle of 292
Liemar of Bremen, archbishop 78
Lisbon, second crusade at 145
Livonia, conversion of 248
Lodi 97
Lombard League 26, 190, 191, 235; united with League of Verona 187; relations with Frederick I 195, 197; peace of Constance 207–8, 213, 216; revived 261–2, 274, 280; relations with Frederick II 26–7, 32, 274, 283–4, 302
Lombard towns 41, 43, 97; split between 175–6
Lorraine 57–8
Lothar III of Supplinburg, duke of Saxony, Emperor 10; Chapter 8, *passim*; conflict with Henry V 112–3, 120; attitude to church 125, 129; territorial policy 10, 127–8; lay investiture 131; landpeace 133; eastern expansion 133–5;
Lotharingian reform movement 49, 51
Louis VII, king of France 140, 180–3; second crusade 143, 146

Louis IX, king of France 301, 305
Lübeck, founded 151, 198; freedom 205–6; raised to imperial city 259
Lucera 258
Lucius III, pope 209–12
Lukmanier pass 193
Lüneburg 205
Lyons, Council of 295–8; Frederick II expedition to 301, 302

Magdeburg 134, 203
Magnus of Saxony 70–1
Mainz: Landpeace of 28–9, 281; council of 89; Reichstag of 101, 104–5; Adalbert archbishop of 108, 113; Henry archbishop of 144; Whitsuntide feast at (1184) 206
Manfred, vice-regent to Conrad IV 305
Mantua 84, 97; synod of 65, 73
Manuel, Byzantine emperor 145–6; conflict with Frederick I 162, 182; captured at Ancona 184
Markward of Anweiler 20n, 225, 236
Matilda of England: betrothal and marriage to Henry V 108, 113; married Geoffrey of Anjou 119–20
Matilda, countess of Tuscany 80; imprisoned by Henry III 58–9; succoured Gregory VII at Canossa 83–4; settled estates on Roman church 91, 113; marriage to Welf 96, dissolved 100
Matildine lands 19–20n, 91, 113, 128, 132–3, 140–1, 157, 189, 195–6, 209–10, 213, 235, 243–4
Mâze 153, 155
Mecklenburg 198
Meissen, Mark of 21, 70, 134, 200, 158
Melfi, constitutions of 272
Merseburg, Reichstag of 135
Messina, Assizes of 257–8
Milan: conflict with Emperor 44–5, 162, 171–2, 175, 178–9, 182, 194, 284–5, 304; conflict with Church 64, 73; archbishop Wido of 64; joined Lombard League 97, 186–7, 261–2; rivalry with Cremona 190; alliance with Frederick I 212–3;
Ministeriales 6–9, 20–1; in Austria and Styria 30; choice by Conrad

II 39; rise and increasing influence of 55, 70, 106–7, 120–1, 158; rebellion by 103; under Frederick I 158, 174, 213; under Henry VI 225, 230, 236; under Otto IV 243, 244; under Henry (VII) 275, 278, 280
Minnesang 206
'Monarchia Sicula' 99
Mongols 292–3
Montebello, treaty of 191, 192, 105
Monte Cassino 136

Naples, university of 258
Neuss 240–1
Nibelungenlied 207
Nicholas II, pope 60–64
Norbert of Xanten, Saint, archbishop of Magdeburg 127, 129, 132, 134
Normans: supported pope 62, 63, 110; captured Palermo 66; under Roger II 130; bureaucracy and economy of 130; territorial gains 131; union with Empire 210–1, 258
Nuremberg 7, 127, 158

Oppenheim 82
Orlando de Rossi 300–1
Otto I, the Great 1, 33
Otto III, Emperor 1
Otto IV, Emperor: at court of Richard I of England 237–8; character 238–9; crowned 239; relations with Innocent III 240–1, 243, 244; attack on Sicily 245, 252–3; defeated at Bouvines 247–8
Otto of Bamberg, bishop 134
Otto of Bavaria, duke 297
Otto of Freising, chronicler 124, 143; on second crusade 144–6; *Gesta Friderici* 161–2, 174
Otto of Nordheim, of Bavaria 64, 70, 71, 82, 90
Otto of Wittelsbach, duke of Bavaria: supported Frederick I 164, 171, 177; given duchy 204; murdered Philip of Swabia 243

Paderborn 203
Palatinate 158, 224
Papal states 184–5, 188, 195, 211, 215–6, 227, 235, 247, 263–4;

occupied by Emperor 214, 243, 287, 295–6
Parma, siege of 302, 304
Paschal II, pope 99, 101, 108–14
Paschal III, antipope 181, 183, 185
Pataria, Patarini 63, 64, 78, 97, 148
Pavia 186, 187, 193; synod of 50; General Council of 178
Peace of God 44, 101
Peace movement 8, 10 *see also* Landpeace
Pelagius, papal legate 256
Peter Abelard 148
Peter Damiani, cardinal 61, 62n, 63, 73, 74
Peter della Vinea 272, 288, 303
Philip Augustus, king of France 216, 223, 247
Philip of Cologne, archbishop, duke of Westphalia 214–6
Philip of Swabia, duke of Tuscany: administrator of Matildine lands 20–2, 238; marriage 229; excommunicated 238, 241; Declaration of Speyer 240; Halle protest 240; agreement with Innocent III 242; murdered 243
Piacenza 97; council of 98–9
Piedmont 174–5, 179, 200
Pierleoni family, pope Gregory VI 50; Peter, pope Anacletus II 128; Jordan, *patricius* 142
Pilgrim, archbishop of Cologne 33–4
Pisa 258
Podestàs 174
Poland 39, 76, 113, 158
Pomerania 206, 215
Poppo of Stablo, abbot 36
Praxedis, second wife of Henry IV 98
Premonstratensian Order 126–7
Prester John 292
Prussia, Teutonic Order in 260
Pseudo-Isidore 75; decretals 52, 57, 142

Rainald of Dassel, chancellor, archbishop of Cologne, influence on Imperial policy of Frederick I 166–87, 290; at Besançon 168; diplomacy 176–7, 183
Rainald of Spoleto, duke, viceregent in Sicily 265–6

Rainier, cardinal 294–5, 296, 301
Rainulf of Alife, duke of Apulia 136, 141
Rainulf of Aversa 45
Ravenna, Reichstag of 274
Regensburg 127, 203
Reichenhall 200
Reims, Council of 52, 152
Richard I, king of England: conflict with Emperor 221–3, 235; imprisoned 223; supported Otto IV 237; death 239
Richard of Aversa, prince of Capua 63
Richenza, wife of Lothar of Supplinburg 125
'Right of devolution' 69, 160
Robert Guiscard, duke of Apulia 63, 77, 129
Roger I Guiscard of Sicily, duke: alliance with pope 91, 92, 97; territorial gains 99, 129
Roger II Guiscard of Sicily, king: alliance with pope 129–31; territorial gains 129–31, 141; conflict with Emperor 133, 135–6, 150–1, 251, 269, 273; conflict with Manuel 145, 150; death 163; character 268
Roland, cardinal 163, 168
Romagna 209, 213, 235; conflict with Frederick I 180, 188; relations with Frederick II 302, 304
Roman Law 14–5, 162–3, 154–5, 172–3, 237, 268
Romans, Rome: supported by pope 51, 91, 141–2; unrest in city of 77, 85, 185; besieged 91–2; sacked 92; supported Emperor 92, 149–50, 185, 188, 246; rebelled against pope 110, 113–4, 147–8, 162, 275, 278, 292; epidemic in 185; papal sovereignty in 235; synod of 292
Roncaglia 14, 15, 17; Reichstag of 172–3, 175–6, 208; decrees abandoned 191, 197, 288
Rudolf III, king of Burgundy 40
Rudolf of Rheinfelden, Burgundian antiking and king 60, 86–8; death 90
Russia, lay investiture prohibited in 76

Ruthard of Mainz, archbishop 103

Saint Gotthard pass 30n4, 282
Saint Jean-de-Losne 180–1
Saladin 217
Salzburg 183, 190
San Germano, treaty of, 261, 264, 266
Saxony, duchy of *see also* German
eastward expansion, Lothar III,
Henry the Lion 72, 81–2, 95, 134,
139–40; dismemberment of 203
Sighard of Burghausen 103
Silesia 158
Simony 52, 61, 63, 74, 77–9
Slav lands, conversion of 127
Spain, lay investiture prohibited in
76
Speyer 83, 144, 202, 240; cathedral
of 36, 106, 111; privileges of
112; Declaration of (1199) 240;
(1209) 243
Spoleto, duchy of 54, 188, 213, 235,
243, 287
'Statute in favour of the Princes'
27–8, 276
Stephen IX, pope 60, 62
Styria 30, 47, 204, 282
Suger of Saint Denis, abbot 140, 150
Suidger of Bamberg, bishop (pope
Clement II) 51
Sutri 163–4, 168; synod of 50
Switzerland 253
Sylvester III, antipope 50
Synods: Augsburg 65; Clermont-
Ferrand 99; Constance 98; Dôle
181; Mantua 65, 73; Pavia 50;
Piacenza 99; Rome 50, 62, 78,
81, 88, 92, 292; Sutri 50; Toulouse
179; Vienne 111; Worms 80

Tancred, king of Sicily 221–4, 226
Teutonic Order 228–9, 260, 274
Thaddeus of Suessa, justiciar 288,
296–7, 302–3
Thomas Becket of Canterbury, arch-
bishop 177, 182, 190
Thuringia 70, 158; landgrave of
200, 241
Tortona 162, 187, 195
Toulouse, synod of 179
Towns: rise of 8, 11, 16–7, 121,
272–3, 275–6; Lombard 26, 32,
German 27–8; South Italian

141–2; relations with Emperors
Conrad II 38, 40, 42; Henry III
55; Henry IV 71, 106–7; Fred-
erick I 162; Henry VI 225;
Frederick II 27–8, 253, 288;
Henry (VII) 277
Trent, bishopric of 288
Treviso, March of 213, 300
Tribur 82, 83; Diet of 66
Trier, archdiocese of 210, 214, 215
Trifels, Richard I prisoner at 223
Truce of God (*treuga Dei*) 2, 48
Tuscany 113, 180, 185, 213, 235,
287, 304
Tusculum 185, 222; counts of 51

Urban II, pope 11, 94–9; Council
of Piacenza 98–9; first crusade
99; Sicilian church 131
Urban III, archbishop of Milan, pope
212; conflict with Frederick I
213–5

Valvassores 2, 43, 44
Venice 182, 190; peace of 196, 197,
208, 210
Verona 98, 210, 300; League of
182, 186, 187
Vézelay 143
Victor II, pope 54, 59–60
Victor III, pope 94
Victor IV, pope 177–81
Vienna 283
Vienne, synod of 111
Viterbo, conflict with Frederick II
271, 287, 294–6, 301
Vittoria siegeworks at Parma 302
Vogtland 20, 158

Waimar of Salerno 45
Waldemar II, king of Denmark 259
Waldenses, heretics 249
Walther von der Vogelweide, poet
207, 237–8, 246–7, 260
Warmann of Constance, bishop 41
Wazo of Liège, bishop 49–50
Welf III of Carinthia, duke 59
Welf IV, duke of Bavaria 70–1;
conflict with Henry IV 87, 95, 97,
100
Welf V son of Welf IV 96, 97, 100
Welf VI, duke: conflict with Conrad
IV 140, 144, 150; given Matildine

lands 157; ceded lands to Frederick I 188–9, 202
Welfesholze, battle of 113
Wenzel of Bohemia 297
Westphalia, duchy of 203, 214
Wibold of Stablo 150
Wibert of Ravenna, archbishop (Clement III, antipope) 89–92, 99
Wichmann of Magdeburg, archbishop 160, 196
Wido, archbishop of Milan 63
William I of Sicily, king 163, 164
William II of Sicily, king 184, 211, 221

William III of Sicily, king 224
William, abbot of Hirsau 87
William of Holland, count 299–300
Wipo, historian 2, 33
Wolfram von Eschenbach, poet 207
Worms: supported Henry IV 71, 72, 82; Synod of 80, 81; privileges 112; concordat of 116–7
Würzburg 203, 205; Reichstag at 183, 226

Zenki, Imadeddin, ruler of Mosul 143, 146